THE GUARDIANSHIP BOOK

THE GUARDIANSHIP BOOK

How to Become a Child's Guardian in California

by Lisa Goldoftas & Attorney David Brown

NOLO PRESS • 950 PARKER ST. • BERKELEY, CA 94710

YOUR RESPONSIBILITY WHEN USING A SELF-HELP LAW BOOK

We've done our best to give you useful and accurate information in this book. But laws and procedures change frequently and are subject to differing interpretations. If you want legal advice backed by a guarantee, see a lawyer. If you use this book, it's your responsibility to make sure that the facts and general advice contained in it are applicable to your situation.

KEEPING UP TO DATE

To keep its books up to date, Nolo Press issues new printings and new editions periodically. New printings reflect minor legal changes and technical corrections. New editions contain major legal changes, major text additions or major reorganizations. To find out if a later printing or edition of any Nolo book is available, call Nolo Press at (510) 549-1976 or check the catalog in the *Nolo News*, our quarterly newspaper.

To stay current, follow the "Update" service in the *Nolo News*. You can get the paper free by sending us the registration card in the back of the book. In another effort to help you use Nolo's latest materials, we offer a 25% discount off the purchase of any new Nolo book if you turn in any earlier printing or edition. (See the "Recycle Offer" in the back of the book.)

This book was last revised in **January 1993.**

FIRST EDITION	June 1989
Second Printing	January 1993
ILLUSTRATIONS	Mari Stein
BOOK DESIGN	Jackie Clark
	Terri Hearsh
	Amy Ihara
INDEX	Sayre Van Young
PRINTING	Delta Lithograph

Brown, David Wayne
   The guardianship book : how to become a child's guardian in California / by David Brown & Lisa Goldoftas ; illustrations by Mari Stein. — 1st ed.
      p.   cm.
   Includes index.
   ISBN 0-87337-098-8 : $19.95
   1. Guardian and ward—California—Popular works.   I. Goldoftas, Lisa   II. Title.
KFC134.Z9B76   1989
346.79401'8—dc20
[347.940618]
                                                                89-8579
                                                                   CIP

Copyright © 1989 by Lisa Goldoftas and David Brown
All Rights Reserved

DEDICATIONS

To my two outstanding editors, Barbara and Jake, for helping me with this book; and to Hooman and Nina, for helping me in every way.

—LSG

To my wonderful wife Nancy, my daughter Laura and my stepson Sean Lerch. Also, to my publisher, Jake "Job" Warner, for his patience.

—DWB

RECYCLE YOUR OUT-OF-DATE BOOKS AND GET 25% OFF YOUR NEXT PURCHASE

Using an old edition can be dangerous if information in it is wrong. Unfortunately, laws and legal procedures change often. Generally speaking, any book more than two years old is of questionable value. Books more than four or five years old are a menace.

To help you keep up-to-date, we extend this offer:

If you cut out and deliver to us the title portion of the cover of any old Nolo book, we'll give you a 25% discount off the retail price of any new Nolo book. For example, if you have a copy of *Tenants' Rights,* 4th edition, and want to trade it for the latest *California Marriage and Divorce Law,* send us the *Tenants' Rights* cover and a check for the current price of *California Marriage and Divorce,* less a 25% discount.

Information on current prices and editions is listed in the back of this book and in the catalog in the *Nolo News* (see offer at the back of this book).

This offer is to individuals only.

OUT-OF-DATE = DANGEROUS

ACKNOWLEDGEMENTS

The authors extend their thanks to the many people who helped make this book possible:

Paul Muñiz, Deputy County Counsel, Contra Costa County, for his generous gift of time and expertise.

Attorneys Carolyn M. Farren and John P. Kelley (of Greene, Kelley & Tobriner in San Francisco) for sharing their knowledge and experience.

Attorney Virginia Palmer (of Fitzgerald, Abbott & Beardsley in Oakland), for her insightful overview of the guardianship process.

Attorney Gary L. Motsenbocker (of Cone & Motsenbocker in Fresno) and John Boley, Santa Clara County Probate Court Investigator, for reviewing the manuscript and giving excellent suggestions.

Frank Zagone, for his helpful information and for the many resources he suggested.

Legal Services for Children, Inc., and director Christopher Wu, for providing valuable information.

Paralegal Irene M. Zupko (of Paralegal Assistance Unlimited in Fresno) for her suggestions and practical experience.

The many people whose contributions enriched this book, including attorney Michael Surowiec, attorney Jack McElroy, Solano County Superior Court Investigator Michael E. Schmidt, and principal Carol Howell.

Tony Mancuso, for his expertise in providing converted computer software.

Jackie Clark, Terri Hearsh, Toni Ihara, Amy Ihara and Mari Stein for the book's design and artwork.

And thanks to all the other wonderful folks at Nolo: Janet Bergen, Karen Chambers, Ken Cober, David Cole, Lulu Cornell, Jack Devaney, Leili Eghbal, Steve Elias, Sue Fox, Stephanie Harolde, Ann Heron, Barbara Hodovan Elmore, Monica Kindraka, Christine Leefeldt, Robin Leonard, Susan Mather, John O'Donnell, Mary Randolph, Albin Renauer, Barbara Kate Repa, Renee Rivera, Jennifer Spoerri, Susan Stern, Kate Thill, and Nolo publisher, Ralph (Jake) Warner.

CONTENTS

CHAPTER 1   INTRODUCTION: AN OVERVIEW OF GUARDIANSHIPS

A.	How This Book Can Help You	1/1
B.	What This Book Does Not Cover	1/2
C.	What Is a Guardianship?	1/3
D.	Two Types of Guardianships	1/3
E.	Is a Guardianship Really Necessary?	1/6
F.	Should You Be the Guardian?	1/8
G.	Do You Need an Attorney or Other Legal Professional?	1/10
H.	Special Guardianship Situations	1/11
I.	Using This Book Efficiently	1/12
J.	Answers to Common Questions About Guardianships	1/12

CHAPTER 2   GETTING BY WITHOUT A COURT-ORDERED GUARDIANSHIP

A.	How to Use This Chapter	2/2
B.	Alternatives to Guardianship of a Minor's Person	2/2
C.	Dealing with Agencies and Institutions in Informal "Guardianship" Situations	2/7

CHAPTER 3   GETTING STARTED

A.	Documents and Information You Need	3/1
B.	The Courts	3/2
C.	How to Use the Forms	3/3
D.	General Rules on Completing Forms	3/5
E.	How to File Papers with the Court	3/7
F.	Filing Fees and Court Costs	3/12

CHAPTER 4   NOTIFYING MINOR'S RELATIVES AND OBTAINING THEIR CONSENTS

A.	Overview of How to Notify Relatives	4/2
B.	Guardianship Notification Worksheet	4/2
C.	Try to Find Minor's Unknown or Missing Relatives	4/3
D.	After You've Searched for Missing Relatives	4/8
E.	Consent of Proposed Guardian, Nomination and Waiver of Notice Form	4/12
F.	Discussing the Guardianship with the Minor's Relatives	4/15
G.	Obtain Signatures from Relatives on the Nomination and Waiver of Notice Forms	4/16
H.	Continue Filling in the Worksheet	4/17

CHAPTER 5	**PREPARING FORMS TO FILE FOR A GUARDIANSHIP**	
	A. Petition for Appointment of Guardian of Minor	5/2
	B. Declaration Under Uniform Child Custody Jurisdiction Act	5/16
	C. Notice of Hearing	5/21
	D. (Proposed) Order Dispensing Notice	5/21
	E. (Proposed) Order Appointing Guardian of Minor	5/25
	F. (Proposed) Letters of Guardianship	5/30
	G. Prepare Supplemental Documents if Required	5/30
	H. When You Need a Guardianship Right Away	5/32
CHAPTER 6	**FILING AND SERVING THE GUARDIANSHIP PAPERS**	
	A. Check Your Work	6/1
	B. File Guardianship Documents and Get a Hearing Date	6/1
	C. Local Court Forms May Be Required After You File Your Papers	6/6
	D. What, When and How Papers Are Served	6/7
	E. Use Guardian Notification Worksheet to Determine Who Must Be Served	6/8
	F. Personal Service and Notice and Acknowledgment of Receipt	6/11
	G. Having Documents Served by Mail	6/16
	H. Copy and File Proofs of Service and Possibly Notice of Hearing	6/20
	I. Complete the Guardianship Notification Worksheet	6/21
CHAPTER 7	**TEMPORARY GUARDIANSHIPS OF A MINOR'S PERSON**	
	A. When to Seek a Temporary Guardianship	7/1
	B. Overview of the Temporary Guardianship Process	7/2
	C. Call the Court	7/3
	D. Complete the Regular Guardianship Documents	7/4
	E. Complete Temporary Guardianship Documents	7/4
	F. Filing Documents, Serving Papers, Obtaining Letters of Temporary Guardianship	7/14
	G. How to Extend the Temporary Guardianship	7/15
CHAPTER 8	**THE GUARDIANSHIP INVESTIGATION**	
	A. Each Court Has Its Own Policies for Investigations	8/1
	B. Investigation Procedure	8/2
	C. Tips on Dealing with the Investigator	8/3
	D. The Investigator's Report	8/3
	E. Fees for the Investigation	8/4
	F. If the Investigator Recommends Against Granting Guardianship	8/4
	G. If the Investigator Recommends Granting Temporary Guardianship	8/4

CHAPTER 9	**THE HEARING: PREPARING, ATTENDING AND WHAT TO DO AFTERWARDS**	
	A. Getting Ready for the Hearing	9/1
	B. Make Sure Your Hearing is on the Court Calendar	9/3
	C. The Day of the Hearing	9/3
	D. Attend the Hearing	9/4
	E. Getting the Letters of Guardianship Issued by the Clerk	9/7
CHAPTER 10	**GUARDIANSHIP OF A MINOR'S ESTATE**	
	A. How to Use This Chapter	10/1
	B. Completing Estate Items in the Petition for Appointment of Guardian of Minor Form	10/2
	C. After the Guardianship Hearing	10/5
	D. Obtain Help from a Legal Professional to Meet Court Reporting Requirements	10/6
	E. Using Funds from the Estate for Support of the Minor	10/9
	F. Ongoing Responsibilities for the Guardian of a Minor's Estate	10/10
CHAPTER 11	**NOW THAT YOU'RE A GUARDIAN: RIGHTS AND RESPONSIBILITIES**	
	A. What to Do with Letters of Guardianship	11/1
	B. Responsibilities of Guardians of a Minor's Estate	11/1
	C. Responsibilities of Guardians of a Minor's Person	11/1
	D. Responsibilities to the Court	11/3
	E. Transferring the Guardianship to Another California Court	11/5
	F. Reimbursements and Compensation of the Guardian	11/12
	G. If the Guardianship Is Contested After You are Appointed	11/13
CHAPTER 12	**ENDING THE GUARDIANSHIP**	
	A. Termination of the Guardianship	12/2
	B. Resignation of the Guardian	12/8
	C. Contested Situations: Removal or Suspension of the Guardian	12/9
CHAPTER 13	**LAWYERS AND LEGAL RESEARCH**	
	A. Finding Free Legal Help	13/1
	B. What an Independent Paralegal Can Do	13/2
	C. Finding and Hiring a Lawyer	13/2
	D. Doing Your Own Legal Research	13/5

APPENDICES

- A. Glossary of Guardianship Vocabulary
- B. How to Obtain Birth, Death and Marriage Certificates
- C. Forms for Temporary "Guardianship" Situations
- D. Forms for Obtaining a Court-Ordered Guardianship

CHAPTER 1

INTRODUCTION: AN OVERVIEW OF GUARDIANSHIPS

A.	How This Book Can Help You	1/1
B.	What This Book Does Not Cover	1/2
C.	What Is a Guardianship?	1/3
D.	Two Types of Guardianships	1/3
E.	Is a Guardianship Really Necessary?	1/6
F.	Should You Be the Guardian?	1/8
G.	Do You Need an Attorney or Other Legal Professional?	1/10
H.	Special Guardianship Situations	1/11
I.	Using This Book Efficiently	1/12
J.	Answers to Common Questions About Guardianships	1/12

A LEGAL GUARDIANSHIP IS RECOGNITION by a court that an adult is responsible for taking care of a minor (person under age 18). The adult may be taking care of the minor's physical needs, managing the minor's assets, or handling both.

A. How This Book Can Help You

THIS BOOK GIVES HELPFUL INFORMATION about legal guardianships of minors in California. We provide the forms and instructions you'll need to obtain a guardianship without a lawyer's help. We also alert you to some situations where a lawyer's help is recommended, and give you tips on finding and dealing with lawyers.

The Guardianship Book is specifically directed to the adult who is planning to be the guardian of a minor. However, if you are a minor's parent, or an adult friend or relative who wants to designate someone else as the minor's legal guardian, you can easily modify the instructions in this book to fit your situation.[1]

If you're wondering whether to seek a legal guardianship, this book can help you decide. In some situations where an adult cares for a minor, a legal guardianship may not be desirable or practical, or there may be easier ways to handle the situation. For example, where a stepparent is taking care of a minor, adoption or a legal guardianship might not be necessary or practical, but some documentation is still advisable. We discuss alternatives to a legal guardianship, and provide you with forms you'll need and instructions for completing them. We give you practical information on dealing with schools, medical facilities, insurance companies, Social Security and U.S. passport offices.

In addition, we discuss the legal responsibilities of a guardian and give a number of considerations to help you figure out whether you want to accept these responsibilities and duties.

No matter why you are seeking a guardianship, the actual process of getting one is not difficult. A legal guardianship will require that the proposed guardian and minor make at least one appearance in

---

[1] If you are a minor who is at least 12 years old, you also can petition to have a guardian appointed for you. Minors may also want to contact an organization that gives information, referrals and legal assistance to children—confidentially and generally free of charge. See Chapter 13, Section A3.

court. In most situations, this is entirely routine and you will have no difficulty as long as you follow the detailed instructions in this book. The only other equipment you'll need is patience—for completing the required forms and dealing with the legal bureaucracy.

LEGAL CITATIONS

Throughout the book you will encounter references to California law, called legal "citations." If you are interested in doing legal research, you can look up these citations. (Legal research is discussed in more detail in Chapter 13, Section D.)

Abbreviation	Legal Reference
CC	Civil Code
CCP	Code of Civil Procedure
CRC	California Rules of Court
EC	Education Code
PC	Probate Code
W&I	Welfare & Institutions Code
USC	United States Code

B. What This Book Does Not Cover

WHILE THIS BOOK PROVIDES ALL the help most people will need to obtain a legal guardianship, it does not cover every possible situation. You should consult a lawyer:

- If anyone objects to (contests) the guardianship, or if anyone tries to have you removed after you are named guardian. These are unusual occurrences, but sometimes they do happen.
- If you are seeking a guardianship to manage substantial assets inherited by a minor—usually $5,000 or more. Although we provide all the information and forms to obtain the guardianship, we do not give step-by-step instructions on how to manage the minor's assets, arrange to have the estate appraised, prepare and file a required Inventory and Appraisement, or prepare and file periodic accountings with the court in future years. Normally the help of a legal professional and perhaps an accountant is in order here, and can be paid for out of the minor's estate. Or you may be able to handle the estate yourself using another self-help resource, such as Nolo's *The Conservatorship Book*, by Lisa Goldoftas and Carolyn Farren. (See Chapter 10.)
- If you want to become guardian of a minor who lives in California, but you live in another state.
- If there are any unresolved legal proceedings affecting the minor. This includes adoption, divorce, custody, juvenile charges against the minor, or other proceedings that have not been finally settled by a court.
- If you want to become guardian of a minor who is physically or emotionally disabled, such as a minor on leave from the California Department of Mental Health or the State Department of Developmental Services. An attorney's help is advisable, since the minor can be protected additionally by such means as establishing a "special needs trust."
- If you want to become guardian of a minor who is "gravely disabled" because of a mental disorder or chronic alcoholism. By law, a special type of mental health conservatorship must be established.
- If the minor is a Native American (American Indian). Because courts must enforce federal law in this area, you will need the help of an attorney.

C. What Is a Guardianship?

CALIFORNIA LAW REQUIRES that in almost all situations, minors must have an adult who is responsible for them.[2] This makes sense. After all, you can't expect a six-year-old to register himself in school, open a checking account, pay his own bills, and apply for Social Security benefits or public assistance.

A court-ordered guardianship is simply legal recognition that an adult has responsibility for taking care of the physical needs of a minor, or for handling the minor's assets. Some people think a guardianship can also be established informally if a parent and some other adult sign an agreement that states that the other adult has authority to care for the minor. Others believe that if you are named in a deceased parent's will as guardian, you automatically become the minor's legal guardian. Neither assumption is true. In California, you can become a minor's legal guardian only if you file legal documents with a court, appear in a court hearing, and are then appointed guardian by a judge.

When you are appointed guardian of a minor, you must serve as guardian until you're legally released by the court from your duties. This could be when the minor reaches age 18, or earlier if the court ends the guardianship or your role as guardian—for example, if it is determined that you are no longer an appropriate guardian. (See Chapter 12 for information on when and how guardianships are ended.)

While at first the biggest burden of becoming a guardian may seem that it means entering into a long-term relationship with a California court, in reality you typically have little contact with the court after you obtain the guardianship. If you are guardian of a minor's estate (handling the minor's assets), the court requires that you have the minor's assets appraised and file a document listing details of what the minor owns, as well as periodically file detailed financial statements. But if you are just going to be guardian of the minor's person (having physical custody of the minor but not managing substantial property she owns) you probably will not have any contact with the court after you are appointed guardian.

D. Two Types of Guardianships

IN CALIFORNIA THERE ARE TWO TYPES of legal guardianships for minors: guardianship of the person and guardianship of the estate (property such as money, stocks, real estate). An adult can be named guardian of a minor's person, estate, or both. The general term "guardianship" is commonly used to cover both types.

1. Guardianship of a Minor's Person

A guardian of the minor's person has legal custody of the minor and is responsible for taking care of her well-being. The guardian would provide food, shelter and health care and take charge of the minor's educational and religious development. In most instances, the minor is or will be living with the proposed guardian, who must have an established permanent residence for the minor in California. However, a guardianship is not affected if the minor attends a boarding school or camp for a substantial part of the year—and while doing so doesn't live in the home. Before permanently moving the minor out of California, a legal guardian first must obtain a court order (PC §2352).[3] Generally the guardian has the same right as the parent to consent to or require medical treatment for the minor.

Important: A guardian of the minor's person usually may handle relatively small financial matters on behalf of the minor—for example, income of no more than $300 per month, plus public assistance benefits—without having to also become guardian of the minor's estate. The guardian of a minor's person

---

[2] A guardianship is not necessary for an "emancipated minor." In California, this is someone under 18 who has achieved legal adult status by marriage, military service, or by court order (CC §62). A guardian cannot be appointed for a minor's person if the minor is married or has been divorced, although a guardian could be appointed for such a minor's estate. If a minor's marriage has been annulled, a guardian could be appointed for his person, estate or both. See Section D in this chapter for more information on the difference between guardianship of a person and an estate.

[3] We do not cover the procedure in this book. You must either do your own research or see an attorney to obtain a court order before moving the minor out of California. (See Chapter 13.)

can receive benefits for which the minor qualifies, for example, welfare or Social Security, unless the agency dispensing benefits specifically requires a guardianship of the minor's estate.

2. Guardianship of a Minor's Estate

A guardianship of the minor's estate is necessary if the minor has substantial assets, such as through an inheritance.[4] If you are going to be handling relatively complicated or extensive financial matters for a minor, you will probably need to become the guardian of the minor's estate. A guardianship of a minor's estate may be needed if:

- The minor has, or is going to receive, through a gift or inheritance, assets worth over $5,000.[5]
- The minor is the named beneficiary of insurance money or other assets, and estate planning measures were not taken.
- The minor is entitled to receive financial benefits, and the agency dispensing benefits specifically requires guardianship of the minor's estate.
- You were named guardian of the minor's estate in a will, and the person who wrote the will dies.
- A court determines that a guardianship of the minor's estate is necessary.[6]

As previously noted, if the minor is living with you and you plan to apply for welfare or other public assistance benefits, you will only need to obtain guardianship of the minor's person unless the agency requires otherwise.

A guardian of the minor's estate is required by law to use the estate money and other assets to provide "comfortable and suitable support, maintenance, and education" for the minor and "those legally entitled to support, maintenance, or education" from the minor (PC §2420). The guardian must at all times preserve the assets of the estate for the minor (PC §2401). To be blunt, this really means that the court wants to ensure that the guardian handles the minor's assets wisely, and doesn't steal any money.

This book instructs you on how to become the guardian of a minor's estate. However, once you are appointed guardian of a minor's estate, you may need to have the minor's property appraised by a probate referee. You will need to file a document with the court itemizing the estate's property and appraisal values, file periodic detailed accountings with the court, and possibly attend several court hearings. You will need to hire a legal professional if you become the guardian of a minor's estate, as the details are beyond the scope of this book. (See Chapter 10 for more information about the procedures and responsibilities required for guardianship of a minor's estate. Also see Chapter 13 for information about finding and dealing with lawyers.)

3. Choosing the Type of Guardianship You Need

Depending on your situation, you may need a guardianship of the minor's person, estate or both. To help you determine which, refer to the accompanying box, and consider the following examples.

Example 1: Donnie, who is 17 years old and on the basketball team at school, lives with her aunt while her parents are on a one-year sabbatical in another country. The school district allows Donnie to enroll without a guardianship after Donnie's mother and aunt sign school authorization forms. However, the school also requires a legal guardianship, so Donnie's aunt promptly obtains a guardianship of the person, and then has authority to sign required release forms for Donnie when she travels with the basketball team. Once Donnie turns 18, the guardianship will no longer be in effect.

---

[4] This is generally true even if you are the minor's parent. However, a minor's parent may hold her child's property without obtaining a guardianship of the estate if the minor's property is worth less than $5,000 (PC §§3400-3402), or if the Uniform Transfers to Minors Act is used.

[5] There are ways to avoid this type of situation, such as by using the Uniform Transfers to Minors Act (UTMA). With minimal documentation, under the UTMA an adult generally can receive assets on behalf of a minor without court approval (PC §3900-3925). See Section E2a of this chapter.

[6] This is likely in legal actions where compromise settlements or claims are made on behalf of a minor. A judge generally determines how the settlement award will be distributed when the compromise settlement or claim is made, and whether a legal guardianship is required.

SEEKING GUARDIANSHIP OF A MINOR'S PERSON, ESTATE, OR BOTH

You will need a guardianship of the minor's person if:

- The minor is or will be living with you for an extended time period;
- You will be receiving benefits on behalf of the minor, and the agency giving the benefits requires guardianship of the minor's person, but does not require you to be guardian of the estate;
- School administrators require a legal guardianship for a minor to be enrolled in school or participate in school activities;
- Your health insurance plan requires a legal guardianship before it will cover the minor; or
- You were named guardian of a minor's person in a deceased person's will, and you intend to have the minor live with you or to care for her needs.

You will need a guardianship of the minor's estate if:

- You were named guardian of a minor's estate in a deceased person's will, there were significant assets left to the minor, and you intend to administer those assets for the minor;
- You are the person responsible for managing a minor's business affairs, and will receive insurance benefits or an inheritance on behalf of the minor (if the agency or company giving the benefits requires guardianship of the minor's estate);
- The minor is entitled to receive benefits, and the agency giving them requires guardianship of the minor's estate;
- The minor is entitled to receive property for which title is required (such as real estate or a vehicle); or
- You will be managing major assets or property for a minor.

You will need a guardianship of both the minor's person and estate if:

- You were named guardian of a minor's person and estate in a deceased person's will, substantial assets were left to the minor, and you are willing to accept the responsibility of being a guardian; or
- Any of the circumstances listed above require a guardianship of the person *and* any of the above requirements also require a guardianship of the estate.

Example 2: When Fred is five years old, his mother is unable to take care of him because of personal problems, and Fred's father is dead. Fred's Aunt Ethel wants to take care of him but she is financially strapped. Aunt Ethel applies for welfare, but is told that in her county she must become Fred's legal guardian before benefits will be paid. As the welfare agency in her county does not require guardianship of the estate, Aunt Ethel obtains a guardianship of Fred's person, which enables her to receive Fred's benefits. The county requires that she keep records of how money is spent on Fred's behalf, but the record-keeping requirement is minimal.

Example 3: Jaime is 15 when his mother, Ellen, decides to go into the military. She discovers that they will not accept her if she has custody of her son. Jaime's father is in jail, and has never supported or visited his son. Ellen asks her parents to take care of Jaime while she is in the service, which will probably be at least three years. To deal with the military's "no custody" rule and because it's a good idea anyway, she asks her parents to become Jaime's legal guardians. They obtain guardianship of Jaime's person.

Example 4: Alice is four years old when her father dies, leaving her as the beneficiary of his insurance benefits. The insurance company refuses to turn the benefits over to her mother, with whom Alice continues to live, since the minor, not the mother, was named as the beneficiary. Alice's mother obtains a guardianship of her daughter's estate only, since as a parent she is already legally responsible for Alice's physical well-being.[7]

Example 5: Bob's parents both die suddenly when he is eight, leaving a request in their will that Bob's maternal grandparents be appointed guardians of both his person and estate. They also leave Bob all their property that includes equity in a house, securities, a car and other personal property. The grandparents obtain guardianship of both Bob's person and estate so they can manage his finances and have legal custody of him. It also enables them to add Bob to their health insurance policy, and avoid hassles when they travel

---

[7] This problem could have been avoided if Alice's father had filled out the insurance policy differently or if Alice's parents had prepared proper estate planning documents before his death. See Section E2a of this chapter.

out of the country. (See a discussion of traveling with a minor in Chapter 2, Section C7.)

E. Is a Guardianship Really Necessary?

BEFORE YOU JUMP TO THE CONCLUSION that a guardianship is a must for your situation, read this section carefully. There are a number of circumstances that typically cause an adult to begin the process of obtaining a guardianship. Many times, guardianships are necessary, but in other situations, alternative documentation will suffice.

1. Do You Need a Guardianship of a Minor's Person?

It is common for a representative of a school district, hospital or some other "official" to insist that a guardianship of a minor's person is needed. However, it's quite possible that signed authorization from the minor's parents will do just fine. If someone says you must obtain a guardianship of a minor's person, consider these three rules:

Rule 1. If the minor will be in danger unless you get a legal guardianship, take immediate action to protect the minor. For example, a parent who previously neglected her child might threaten to remove that child from your care and put the child in a dangerous situation.[8]

Rule 2. If you plan to take care of a minor for an extended (perhaps indefinite) time, it makes good sense to get a guardianship of the minor's person—even if you are not absolutely required to do so. The time and inconvenience it takes to get the guardianship will be well worth it. For example, legal guardianships can help avoid hassles with school officials or agencies.

Rule 3. If you were named guardian of a minor's person in his deceased parent's will, the minor has no surviving parent and you plan to take care of him, you will need to obtain a formal legal guardianship.

You probably won't need a guardianship of the minor's person if:
- You only plan to take care of a minor for a short time—up to three months.
- You live in a community where you are well known and there is general support for informal solutions to problems, instead of official court-ordered resolutions.
- You don't anticipate having contact with agencies and institutions on behalf of the minor. For example, you might temporarily be caring for a minor who is already enrolled in school, has a doctor, is covered by medical insurance, and whose parents are sending money to support their child.

If your situation is similar to any of the situations listed just above, we suggest you read Chapter 2 carefully before proceeding with a legal guardianship. Chapter 2 discusses alternatives to getting a legal guardianship of a minor's person.

2. Do You Need a Guardianship of a Minor's Estate?

A guardianship of a minor's estate involves a lot of extra work for the guardian, such as having property appraised, maintaining financial records and preparing periodic accountings for the court. Unfortunately, if a guardianship of a minor's estate is required—for example, by an insurance company, court or by a deceased person's will—there probably isn't a way around it.

Just to make sure that you really need a guardianship of a minor's estate, consider these rules:

Rule 1. A parent can receive money or property on behalf of his child as long as the child's assets will not exceed $5,000.[9]

---

[8] If you aren't sure whether the minor would be in danger if you don't get a legal guardianship, you can call a local agency for more information and possible intervention. Check the phone book under your county's agencies for "Children's Emergency Services," "Children's Protective Services," "Social Services," or a similar heading. This book does not cover situations in which a minor is in danger of abuse, neglect, or other harm, which would require immediate action.

[9] To receive the assets, the parent must sign a document swearing that the minor's total estate does not exceed $5,000—including the money or property that is to be received. Once the parent provides this document to the

Rule 2. An adult can transfer money or property to a minor without court approval, using the Uniform Transfer to Minors Act as long as the value of the minor's property is less than $10,000 (PC §§3900-3925).[10]

Rule 3. If the minor is in the position of acquiring substantial assets not covered in Rule 1 or Rule 2 above, you will need a legal guardianship of the minor's estate.[11] Note that "substantial assets" here does not include public assistance benefits or other relatively small sums of money—in these instances only a guardianship of a minor's person is required. (See Section E1 above and Chapter 10.)

a. Using Estate Planning to Avoid Guardianship of a Minor's Estate

In American culture, death is a difficult topic. Many people shut down when the subject of death is raised, preferring the head-in-the-sand technique of avoidance to facing the reality of their own or others' mortality. We bring up the subject because many times, guardianships of a minor's estate could be avoided or simplified with just a little bit of advance planning. "Estate planning" is the term for designating to whom and how property is to be transferred before and after death. Estate planning covers many methods of dealing with assets, including wills, trusts and gifts. Estate planning helps eliminate the guesswork in distributing property, allows things to be much simpler and less stressful for the survivors, and may also allow for huge savings in taxes and various legal costs. There is a variety of estate planning devices that allow an adult to leave assets to minors with little or no use of the probate courts.[12]

b. When a Minor's Parents Need Guardianship of Their Own Child's Estate

It may seem strange that parents might need to obtain a guardianship of their own child's estate, even if their child lives with them. This situation usually arises when a minor inherits money or other property, and there was inadequate—or no—estate planning. Unfortunately, in these instances, the parents generally don't have any alternative to going to court to obtain a legal guardianship of their child's estate.

Example 1: Karen White and Jeff Black are not married, and they live together with their three young children. Karen dies suddenly, leaving the proceeds of her life insurance policy and all of her assets—which are substantial—to their three children. Jeff has not worked for many years, since he has been staying home taking care of the children, and he has very few assets of his own. Jeff goes to court and becomes guardian of his children's estates, so that he may manage the life insurance proceeds and assets for them. He does not need to obtain guardianship of their persons, since he is a parent and they already live with him.

Jeff needs some job training to go back to work, but he wants to spend a few months at home before starting the training, as the children are terribly upset about the death of their mother and need him around. With the help of a lawyer, Jeff makes a motion asking for use of the estate for the support of his children. The judge allows Jeff to use funds from his children's estates to fully support his three children for six months, when he plans to return to the work force. After the six months, Jeff will continue to manage the assets of his children's estates, but he will financially support his children.

---

person delivering the money or property, it can be released to be held in trust until the minor reaches age 18 (PC §3401). We do not tell you how to handle this procedure in this book. See Section E2a of this chapter.

[10]A simple document can be prepared and signed to transfer the property. We do not cover that procedure in this book. See Section E2a of this chapter.

[11]If the minor's assets consist solely of money, and the amount does not exceed $20,000, the court has discretion to terminate the guardianship of an estate with specific conditions about how the money is to be held, such as a blocked account (PC §3412).

[12]You can obtain valuable information and step-by-step instructions on estate planning in *Plan Your Estate: Wills, Probate Avoidance, Trusts & Taxes* by Denis Clifford (Nolo Press). *The Simple Will Book* by Denis Clifford (Nolo Press) and, for those with access to a personal computer, *WillMaker* (Nolo Press/Legisoft) provides software and a manual to take you through the steps of making your own will. All three Nolo resources also give guidance and information on minors and guardians.

Example 2: The Stones live next door to an elderly widower who is extremely fond of their small daughter. When the widower dies, he leaves his house to five-year-old Alice Stone. Alice's parents, Jill and Mike, go to court and obtain guardianship of their daughter's estate so that the asset can be transferred to Alice (via the guardianship of Alice's estate). Both Jill and Mike work full-time and have no problem supporting their daughter. They plan to sell the house Alice inherited and invest the money for Alice's use when she reaches age 18. If Jill and Mike were to make a motion in court asking to use the money for the support of their child, this request would not be granted since they are able to support her financially.

F. Should You Be the Guardian?

AS YOU'VE LEARNED, a guardianship is an ongoing responsibility that can last until the minor reaches age 18.[13] You should thoroughly consider the possible difficulties of being a guardian before you decide to become one. The guardian's duties and responsibilities are covered in more detail in Chapter 11.

As guardian of a minor's person, you basically assume the role of the minor's parent. This is a responsibility that is never easy—even in the best of times. Often the guardian will be stepping into a family situation that is already laden with problems—perhaps taking on a child who is difficult to handle. While being a guardian can be rewarding, it can be a real source of stress. It can also be a time-consuming job.

As guardian of a minor's estate, you must commit yourself to the time and planning necessary to wisely handle the minor's assets. You must have a non-cash estate appraised by a probate referee, file documents with the court itemizing the estate and its appraised value and periodically complete financial accountings for the court. You must also go to court to get permission for any but the most conservative financial transactions. (See Chapter 10 for more details on guardianship of a minor's estate.)

1. Do You Want to Be the Guardian?

An obvious but extremely important question to ask yourself before you take any steps to establish a guardianship is: Do you want to be the guardian?

Of course, your feelings about your potential role as a guardian relate to the circumstances. In a real emergency where everyone involved agrees, such as when a close relative dies or can't take care of her children, it may be easy to agree to be a guardian. On the other hand, if there are ill feelings between family members or the minor has not been cared for properly (perhaps abandoned or abused) and is hostile, uncommunicative or emotionally disturbed, you may sensibly want to think twice before going ahead. Obviously you will want to do some additional soul-searching if someone else (perhaps even a natural parent) seems determined to go to court to challenge your petition to be named guardian.

It is sensible to consider your options carefully before going through with the guardianship procedure. After honestly answering the questions in the accompanying box, you may realistically have second thoughts.

---

[13]The guardianship can be terminated for a variety of reasons including death of the minor, marriage of the minor (guardianship of the person terminates), when the minor's estate is exhausted (guardianship of the estate terminates with court approval after appropriate documents are filed), adoption of the minor, and where it's not in the minor's best interests. See Chapter 12 for more information on when and how guardianships are ended.

DECIDING WHETHER YOU WANT TO BE A GUARDIAN

• Do you want the ongoing responsibilities of a legal guardianship—including potential liability for the minor's actions? Chapter 11 gives a thorough explanation of these responsibilities. If you don't want these obligations, look into some of the alternatives to guardianships. (Informal alternatives to guardianship of a minor's person are discussed in Chapter 2).

• For guardianships of the estate, are you willing to continuously manage the minor's assets, provide the court with a required inventory and periodic accountings, and return to court if you need permission to handle certain financial matters? (See Chapter 10 for a discussion of the ongoing responsibilities of a guardianship of a minor's estate.)

• What kind of personal relationship do you have with the minor? Given the nature of this relationship, do you want to act as the legal parent of the minor for the duration of the guardianship?

• Would the guardianship adversely affect you or your family because of your own children, health situation, job, age, or other factors?

• Can you handle the work involved? Do you have the time and energy to take care of the minor or his assets?

• What is the financial situation? If the child will receive income from Social Security, welfare, a parent or the estate of a deceased parent, is this adequate to allow you to provide a decent level of support? If not, are you willing and able to spend some of your own money on the minor?

• Do you anticipate problems with the minor's relatives—including a parent who "abandoned" a minor, and who might suddenly reappear and contest the guardianship? This is rare, but it can happen. If you expect objections, be aware that issues concerning your background could be used in an attempt to disqualify you from obtaining a guardianship, or later may even be used to have you removed as guardian.

• What kind of relationship do you have with the minor's parents? Are they likely to support the guardianship, or will they probably be hostile, antagonistic and interfering?

2. Are You an Appropriate Choice for Guardian of a Minor's Person?

There are no hard and fast rules on who is appropriate to be a guardian. It is up to the discretion of the court (a judge or court commissioner) who will weigh many factors in making a decision. While there is an order of preference for appointing a guardian of a minor's person (see the box on the following page), this system is very flexible, especially if neither parent is responsible for caring for the minor—a common situation where a guardianship is needed. Usually, the debate of preferring one guardianship candidate over another never arises, as there is usually only one person willing and able to assume the role.

The most important consideration in naming a guardian is the "best interests of the child." A judge will consider the love and emotional ties between you and the minor and your basic ability to "parent" the minor. The judge will also look at practical considerations such as your health and ability to provide the minor with food, shelter, clothing and medical care. Any established school, community and religious ties also will be considered. If you have already taken care of the child for some time, this should be a positive factor in deciding whether it makes sense for this relationship to continue. Finally, the judge might consider your ability and desire to foster healthy communication and contact between the minor and his parent, if that is relevant.

A judge typically will consider the minor's wishes (especially for older children), the parents' and other close relatives' wishes (if they are expressed), the proposed guardian's ability and desire to take care of the child, whether the child will be harmed if a guardianship isn't granted and possibly other alternatives to a guardianship such as foster care placement through the county. While many judges will try to keep families together as much as possible by appointing one guardian for all brothers and sisters, this is not required by law.

> **ORDER OF PREFERENCE FOR APPOINTING GUARDIAN OF THE PERSON**
>
> Judges have some flexibility in choosing who to appoint as guardian. There are, however, some guidelines provided by law (CC §4600). The law recognizes that other factors enter into every decision, but gives custody preference:
>
> **#1**: To one or both parents (either sole or joint custody);
>
> **#2**: To the person with whom the minor has been living in a wholesome and stable environment;
>
> **#3**: To any person determined suitable and able to provide adequate and proper care and guidance for the minor (PC §1514).

3. Are You an Appropriate Choice for Guardian of a Minor's Estate?

In deciding whether to appoint you guardian of a minor's estate, a judge should consider your ability to manage and preserve the estate's assets, as well as your concern and interest for the minor. A judge may consider your own financial situation and your ability to manage or hire people to handle relatively large sums of money. (See Chapter 10 for more details on the ongoing responsibilities of guardianship of a minor's estate.)

4. Are There Reasons Why You Shouldn't Be Named Guardian?

When a judge decides whether to grant a guardianship, she makes the decision on the basis of what will best meet the minor's needs. This is sensible; the judge must focus on what is best for the child, not what's best for you. Obviously, however, your lifestyle and your background may well influence a decision about what is best for the minor. The proposed guardian and minor often are routinely interviewed by a court investigator who gives the judge a recommendation about whether to grant the guardianship. In some counties, the proposed guardian must be fingerprinted, and a check into her criminal record is made. In addition, a routine screening of whether the proposed guardian of a minor's person has ever been reported for child abuse or neglect is always made. Understand that investigations of proposed guardians are not scary,

and this book contains guidelines about how to deal with them in Chapter 8.

There are several obvious reasons why you might not be appointed guardian, or why you later could be removed as guardian. Bear in mind that conduct that falls in one or more of these categories won't automatically disqualify you—it's up to the judge's discretion. But a court might consider you to be an improper guardian:

- If you have been charged with neglecting or abusing a minor. This would make you an inappropriate choice for guardianship of a minor's person.
- If you have been convicted of a felony. This could prevent you from being named guardian, or it could be grounds for removal (PC §2650). If you have had other run-ins with the law, your appropriateness as a guardian would probably depend on the crime, how long ago it was committed and what your lifestyle is like now.
- For guardianships of a minor's estate, if information about your finances or ability to manage money (such as bankruptcy or financial problems) indicates that you would be an inappropriate choice.
- If there is any well-known undesirable information about your personal life. For example, alcohol, drug, or gambling problems could influence the judge's decision.

If you are in any of these situations, you may be better off not petitioning to be the minor's guardian, especially if anyone is likely to challenge your qualifications in court. However, if the minor is in a needy situation where there is no one to provide proper care, you still might opt to petition for the guardianship.

G. Do You Need an Attorney or Other Legal Professional?

AFTER READING THIS CHAPTER, you will probably decide to start guardianship proceedings yourself without a lawyer, as long as you expect it to be uncontested. Certainly if the minor's parents can't care for their child, you have the approval of the minor's close relatives, and are the natural person to take over, there's normally no reason why you can't do the whole job on your own. If you need some help with the forms, you might find an independent paralegal to assist you for a much lower fee than an attorney would charge. You can save the money you would have spent for a lawyer for the immediate needs of the child. (See Chapter 13, Section B for information on independent paralegals.)

What if you're not sure whether you'll have the support of the minor's relatives, or the natural parents are not completely out of the picture and might contest the guardianship? You may still sensibly choose to start the process of obtaining a guardianship on your own. If you run into problems later, you can involve a lawyer then.

If you clearly anticipate problems from the start, such as relatives contesting the guardianship or a parent who you think is unfit insisting on trying to keep or get custody, you will probably want to consult a lawyer first. Then, if someone takes legal action that requires an immediate response, you will not need to hunt for a lawyer in the midst of a crisis. Even if you do use an attorney for the entire process (maybe you decide that the situation is too touchy attempt alone), this book will help you understand the guardianship procedure and help you make sure that the attorney is doing the job right.

If you are seeking guardianship of a minor's estate or person and estate, you may need the help of a legal professional after you are appointed guardian. (Chapter 13 contains information and tips on how to find and hire attorneys and other legal professionals.)

H. Special Guardianship Situations

ADDITIONAL LEGAL AND PRACTICAL CONCERNS about the guardianship decision may be caused by your particular circumstances.

1. Special Concerns of Stepparents and Co-Parents

If both of the minor's parents are living, it may not make sense for you to file for a legal guardianship. Even if you are living with and parenting the minor as a stepparent[14] or co-parent (lesbian, gay, or partner of one of the minor's parents but are not related to the minor),[15] filing guardianship papers may well precipitate a custody battle from the other parent. You may wisely decide not to put everyone involved through such a court battle, unless it would be detrimental to the minor for the other parent to have legal custody.

However, adults who have played the role of natural parents for years suddenly may find themselves with no legal authority to seek medical care or to enroll the child they are raising in school. If you are in such a situation, it is extremely important that you obtain signed documentation from your spouse. There is a Guardianship Authorization form provided in Chapter 2 for this purpose.

2. If the Minor Is a Dependent of the Court

If you are a foster parent[16] or other adult seeking a guardianship where the minor is a dependent child of the court,[17] the local social services agency and county counsel should handle the guardianship for you. There is a simplified procedure for appointing guardians for

---

[14] Stepparents who are considering adopting a child may be able to do it themselves using *How to Adopt Your Stepchild in California* by Frank Zagone and Mary Randolph (Nolo Press).

[15] For lesbian and gay couples, a source of important information is *A Legal Guide for Lesbian and Gay Couples* by Hayden Curry and Denis Clifford (Nolo Press). For unmarried couples, a source of important information is *The Living Together Kit*, by Toni Ihara and Ralph Warner (Nolo Press).

[16] Foster parents are adults who take minors into their home after the minors have been removed from their biological parents' home by a court. Foster parents are specially licensed to serve in this capacity.

[17] A minor would be a dependent of the court if she was involuntarily removed from her natural parents' home. Usually the child would be placed in a foster home temporarily.

minors who were adjudged dependents of the Juvenile Court on or after January 1, 1989 (W&I 366.25, 366.26).

If for some reason you want to expedite the process by preparing guardianship documents yourself for a minor adjudged a dependent of the court prior to January 1, 1989, this book can be of great help. The procedures described here for use in the Probate Division of the Superior Court are almost identical to the ones followed in Juvenile Court. But before you take any steps to obtain a guardianship, you will need to check with your local social services agency or county counsel who is handling the case to find out whether you can prepare the papers yourself. If a case has already been opened in Juvenile Court, find out whether it requires the same documentation and follows the same procedures as the Probate Division of the Superior Court.

I. Using This Book Efficiently

HERE'S HOW TO USE THIS BOOK to best meet your needs.

- If you want to avoid going to court for a guardianship of a minor's person, turn to Chapter 2. There you'll find informal alternatives to a legal court-ordered guardianship and suggestions for how to use these informal guardianship authorization documents.
- If you will be seeking benefits for the minor, or if you will be dealing with agencies and institutions (such as schools, medical facilities, insurers), read Chapter 2, Section C. The information is useful for those who are not seeking a legal guardianship, and may also be helpful for those who obtain a legal guardianship.
- If you have decided to obtain a legal guardianship, read Chapter 3 for an overview of how to prepare and file your papers with a California court. Then read and follow the instructions in Chapters 4, 5 and 6. If you will be seeking guardianship of a minor's estate, you also will be directed to Chapter 10 to help you understand and prepare papers needed to initiate a guardianship of a minor's estate.
- If you need a legal guardianship of a minor's person right away, read and follow the instructions in Chapter 7 in addition to following the instructions for a regular guardianship (Chapters 4, 5 and 6).
- After filing and having your guardianship papers served, read Chapter 8, which gives valuable information about a court investigation that may take place. Then, before the court-appointed hearing date, read Chapter 9 and talk to the minor about the hearing.
- Once you've become a guardian, Chapter 11 gives you an overview of your responsibilities and liabilities. Guardians of the estate also need to read Chapter 10.
- If a guardianship is no longer needed, you'll find information about how to end it in Chapter 12.
- If you think you need an attorney, you'll find helpful information on how to find a lawyer or paralegal, and on how to do some of your own legal research in Chapter 13.

1. The Vocabulary of Guardianships

We have done our best to define terms used in the book. Appendix A, at the back of this book, provides a glossary of terms you are likely to come across in the guardianship process.

2. Guardianship Forms

Appendices C and D, at the back of this book, contain the forms you'll need to obtain a legal guardianship, or to handle alternatives to a legal guardianship. The entire book explains the step-by-step details of how to fill out and use all of the forms.

J. Answers to Common Questions About Guardianships

Q: What is the difference between an adoption and a guardianship?

A: An adoption permanently changes the adult-child relationship. For all purposes, the adopting adult legally becomes the parent of the child. The natural parent (if living) loses all parental rights and obligations to his child, including the obligation to pay child support. While a guardianship establishes a legal relationship between an adult and a child that a court oversees, it does not sever the legal relationship between the natural parent and the child. For example, the natural parent is still legally required to support the child and if the natural parent dies without a will, the child inherits some of his property. Also, the scope of a guardianship could be limited. For example, a guardian of a minor's estate could be responsible solely for taking care of a minor's finances, but not have physical custody.

Q: Can I get a guardianship for an adult who can't take care of herself?

A: No. In California, a guardianship only allows you to legally care for a minor (someone under the age of 18). However, a "conservatorship" allows an adult to legally care for another adult who is unable to care for himself. Many people confuse guardianships and conservatorships. The source of some of that confusion is that until 1981, it was possible to get a guardianship of an adult who could not take care of himself. The legal procedures for taking care of an adult now include a conservatorship and a durable power of attorney. These procedures are not covered in this book.

Q: I don't think my sister is a good parent, so can I become her child's guardian?

A: Maybe. The court won't simply grant a guardianship because you don't approve of your sister's parenting. Usually a parent must either voluntarily consent to a guardianship, abandon a child, or it must be determined that it would be detrimental to a child to give the parents custody. It is much more difficult to get a guardianship if the parent objects. If the child is not being being abused or neglected, and your sister is still taking care of the child, your best bet is probably first to try to work it out voluntarily within the family. But if the child is in danger because of abuse or neglect, you can notify a local social services agency, which can intervene. To do this, check in the phone book under your county's agencies for "Children's Emergency Services," "Abuse" or "Children's Protective Services" or a similar heading. The situation will be investigated and the agency will intervene if necessary. Depending on the results, you may choose to file for a guardianship. The court's choice of guardian will be based on the best interests of the child. If there is a conflict of the parents' and child's interests, the child's interests are to be protected.

Q: Could I become a minor's guardian without letting anyone know about it?

A: Probably not. The parents and close relatives of the minor are legally entitled to be notified. A judge is unlikely to waive any of these notice requirements unless there is an extremely good reason, such as where a relative cannot be located. The parents and close relatives of the minor must almost always be notified about the guardianship hearing beforehand.

Q: My daughter is dead, and I don't know where her ex-husband is. Her two preschool-age children live with me. Do I need to get a guardianship?

A: Yes. You'll have those children around for a long time, so you'll need to obtain guardianships of their persons. Also, if they have substantial assets, you'll need to get guardianships of their estates as well.

Q: I don't want my ex-husband to have custody of our small child in case something happens to me, because he is unreliable and dangerous. Can I name someone else, such as my mother, or the man I live with, as my daughter's guardian?

A: Yes, you can execute a will naming someone other than your husband as guardian of your child when you die, but that is not guaranteed to have any legal effect. Several Nolo Press books give you instructions for preparing a will of this sort, or making other estate planning arrangements. However, if the living natural father of your daughter has objections to the guardianship, it's unlikely that a judge will approve it unless the natural father has abandoned the child (failed to support and visit for an extended period) or giving custody to the natural father would be detrimental to the child. A finding of detriment to the child usually occurs only if the other parent is unable to care properly for the child, or is abusive or violent. If you wish, you can use your will, or an accompanying letter to state the reasons why it would be detrimental to the child to give the other parent legal custody and why the person you nominate as guardian is the best choice to care for the child.

Q: What happens if two people want guardianship of the same child?

A: Usually courts follow a system of preference when selecting a guardian for custody of a minor. First, they usually give custody to both or one natural parent. Next, they usually choose the person with whom the child has been living in a wholesome and stable environment. Next, they should choose any person deemed suitable and able to provide adequate and proper care and guidance to the minor. The final decision would be up to a judge. If you are competing with someone else for guardianship of the minor, consult a lawyer.

Q: Can I stop guardianship proceedings once I start them?

A: Yes. Until you are appointed guardian by the court, you can discontinue the process if you decide not to become a guardian or if circumstances change and the guardianship is not needed. There are step-by-step instructions for this in Chapter 3, Section E5.

Q: How permanent is a guardianship? Can I change my mind after I've been appointed?

A: If you become unable or unwilling to take care of the minor, the court may allow you to resign from the guardianship, if it is in the best interests of the minor. However, to protect the minor, it is possible that a judge could decide not to allow you to resign as guardian or, more likely, prolong your role as guardian until someone else can be found to take over.

Q: What happens if I am named as a guardian in a will?

A: If a parent names you as guardian of her child, nothing happens unless she dies before the child is 18, and the other natural parent is not living or cannot be found, or is unable or unwilling to take care of the child. If both parents die while the children are minors, you should start the formal guardianship proceedings described in this book. It is likely, though not absolutely certain, that a judge would grant the guardianship to you if you were named in someone's will.

Q: Can I be held liable as guardian if the minor does something wrong?

A: Possibly. Like a parent, a guardian of a minor's person can be liable for money damages up to happen, the minor must willfully do something wrong and cause damage. But neither a minor nor a guardian is liable for damages caused by the minor's carelessness, unless the guardian is also careless (negligent). This is discussed more thoroughly in Chapcertain limits established by California law. For this to ter 11.

Q: What if I need a guardianship right away, or only need it for a limited time?

A: While the regular guardianship is pending, you may file for a temporary guardianship. More information about the scope of temporary guardianships and instructions for temporary guardianships of a minor's person are provided in Chapter 7.

Q: If I am named guardianship of a minor's estate, can I hire an attorney and accountant to help me manage the minor's estate?

A: Yes. And with court permission, the payments for these professionals may be taken out of the estate's assets.

Q: As guardian of a minor's estate, may I take money from the estate for my own use?

A: Absolutely not. Your money and the estate's money must always be kept separate. There is an overview of the requirements of guardianship of a minor's estate in Chapter 10. If you believe you should be compensated for time you spent on the guardianship, you could petition the court to allow you to be paid. Without such an order, you cannot take the money for yourself. (See Chapter 10, Section F6 and Chapter 11, Section F.)

Q: If I become guardian of a minor's estate, may I use money from the estate to support the minor?

A: It depends on your situation. California law says that parents must support their own children. What this means is that if you are a parent and also guardian of your child's estate, you cannot automatically use the estate's money to support your child. On the other hand, if you're not the minor's parent, money from the estate may be used to take care of the minor. Generally this would mean that you'd be guardian of the minor's person and estate. Regardless of the situation, you would need special written permission from the court to use funds from the estate to support the minor.

CHAPTER 2

GETTING BY WITHOUT A COURT-ORDERED GUARDIANSHIP

A.	How to Use This Chapter	2/2
B.	Alternatives to Guardianship of a Minor's Person	2/2
C.	Dealing with Agencies and Institutions in Informal "Guardianship" Situations	2/7

YOU ARE PROBABLY READING this chapter because you want to explore the possibility of caring for a minor without getting a formal legal guardianship. Most likely, you either already have or anticipate having a minor live with you. An agency or institution may have informed you that you must get a legal guardianship, but perhaps you still wonder if there isn't a simpler alternative. There often are easy, reasonably efficient ways to take responsibility for a minor without bringing the court system into play.

This chapter covers alternatives to guardianship of a minor's person, but not alternatives to guardianship of a minor's estate. This is because when guardianship of a minor's estate is needed (such as to disburse insurance proceeds, or to manage a minor's inheritance), there generally is no informal alternative.

At the risk of oversimplifying, you can sensibly avoid going through the formal court process of getting a legal guardianship of a minor's person if:

1. You have concluded after reading Chapter 1 and this chapter that the minor will not suffer negative consequences if you don't get a legal guardianship.

2. You will be taking care of a minor for a short time (three months or less), or you are a stepparent or co-parent (lesbian, gay or partner of one of the minor's parents but are not related to the minor) and are not in a position to get a guardianship (usually because the other parent would contest the guardianship, and is a suitable parent); and

3. You are willing to deal with the possible inconvenience and potential problems of "sliding by" using less formal substitute procedures.

Several examples illustrate when alternatives to a legal guardianship might be appropriate.

Example 1: Katrina stays with her uncle for about a month each year, when her parents' work takes them out of the country. There is no need for a legal guardianship, since Katrina lives with her uncle for relatively short periods of time. Katrina's parents and uncle can use the informal Guardianship Authorization form set out in Section B1 to cover any situation that might need parental consent while the parents are out of town. Of course, if authorization is needed for a situation that the uncle isn't sure about, he can probably contact Katrina's parents by telephone to ask their advice.

Example 2: Fourteen year-old Alex has been living with his natural mother and stepfather for several years. His father lives in another state and sees Alex in the summers. Alex's mother frequently goes on business trips, leaving Alex in his stepfather's care. They are concerned that a school or medical situation will arise that requires a parent's consent when neither of Alex's natural parents will be around. Alex's stepfather uses the Guardianship Authorization form found in Section B1 for situations that might require parental consent.

Example 3: Cindy's grandparents are taking care of her because her mother is unstable, moves constantly and has problems with substance abuse. Cindy's grandparents believe that unless they have legal custody of Cindy, the mother is likely to show up at any time and take Cindy away. They can't live with this possibility, so they gently but firmly insist on a legal court guardianship. After thinking about it,

Cindy's mother agrees that a legal guardianship would be better for Cindy. Cindy doesn't have any assets, so her grandparents obtain a guardianship of her person using the instructions in this book.

> PERSONAL REASONS FOR AVOIDING FORMAL GUARDIANSHIPS
>
> An adult who has care and physical custody of a minor may also have strong personal reasons not to become a legal guardian of the minor's person:
>
> • Dynamics between family members may be such that filing for a guardianship immediately might precipitate a fight for full legal custody. This would be especially likely where a stepparent and one natural parent care for a minor.
>
> • You expect that the minor's parents probably will not consent to a legal guardianship, and will immediately try to remove their child from your custody if you start the process.
>
> • You don't want your personal life scrutinized in court or by a court-appointed investigator. (See Chapter 8 for more information about court investigations of proposed guardians.)
>
> You can always choose whether to apply for a guardianship. However, if you decide not to, and a guardianship turns out to be required by a public agency, you eventually could be faced with the choice of either obtaining one or giving up physical custody of the minor.

A. How to Use This Chapter

EVERYONE SHOULD READ SECTION B, which contains a Guardianship Authorization form to be used as an agreement between you and the minor's parents. Complete the Guardianship Authorization form and obtain the parents' signatures. This form can be used whether you will be taking care of a minor for a limited time (a few weeks or months while the parents are out of the area) or for an extended time (and you want to avoid getting a guardianship if at all possible).

If you will have contact with agencies or institutions and do not plan to obtain a legal guardianship of a minor's person, read Section C. This section gives you helpful information and tips for dealing with agencies and institutions without being a minor's legal guardian, and alerts you to situations where a legal guardianship may be mandatory.

B. Alternatives to Guardianship of a Minor's Person

THROUGHOUT THIS CHAPTER we refer to informal custody arrangements as informal "guardianship" situations, but the use of the term "guardianship" is not technically correct. A legal guardianship can only be obtained through a court proceeding. But we use the word here to describe non-court procedures simply because if the term "guardianship" is used in parental consent forms and other non-court documents, they are more likely to be accepted by agencies and organizations that do not insist on a formal, court-approved guardianship. Remember that these are not true guardianship papers, and that if an agency or institution does insist on a formal guardianship, you'll probably need to get one.

The time lapse between filing for a guardianship and getting court authorization usually is a minimum of six to eight weeks if everything goes smoothly. If you will be taking care of a minor for three months or less, a formal guardianship proceeding may not be desirable.[1] To get a legal guardianship, you must prepare and file documents, notify relatives, and appear in court.

Although taking care of a minor for a short time will not usually present you with any problems at all, you sometimes need to prove that a minor's parents have given you authority to take care of their child. Situations requiring this proof range from authorizing medical treatment to authorizing a school field trip to the zoo. If you are told that you must have a legal guardianship and instead you provide a notarized statement such as the Guardianship Authorization form set out below, the requesting agency or institution often will be satisfied. These agencies simply want reasonable proof that you are authorized to make decisions in place of the minor's parent.

Bear in mind that the Guardianship Authorization form should never be used to attempt to resolve custody issues. If your situation involves a custody problem, you should consult an attorney. (See Chapter

---

[1] If you need a guardianship right away, you can petition for a temporary guardianship, which usually takes about five days from the time papers are filed with the court. This procedure is discussed in Chapter 7.

13.) The Guardianship Authorization form may be used when:

- Both parents—or the single parent having sole custody without the other parent having visitation rights—agree to the arrangement; or
- A stepparent or unrelated co-parent is not in a position of being able to obtain a guardianship, but wants some documentation giving him authorization to make decisions for the minor in case of an urgent situation.

1. Guardianship Authorization Form

Appendix C contains a blank Guardianship Authorization form that gives consent for a non-parent to care for a minor. Use this form only as a temporary measure or if you are a stepparent or unrelated co-parent without other documentation giving you authority to make decisions for the minor. The Guardianship Authorization form will not be accepted by all institutions or for all purposes. Still, it is advisable to have some document signed by a parent if an urgent situation involving the minor arises and a parent can't be reached.

You might use this form with schools, medical facilities and other agencies or institutions that require some documentation (but not necessarily a formal guardianship) showing that the parent has left his child under your care and supervision. However, if you know in advance that you will need to deal with a particular agency, you will also be wise to find out its requirements first. An agency may have its own informal "guardianship" form, or may insist that you go to court and obtain a formal guardianship.

The Guardianship Authorization form should be signed by you and if possible, by both parents or the parent who has legal custody of the child.[2] It is important that you and the minor's parents sign this form in the presence of a notary public. Obviously, if you know that the parents will be leaving the area, it would be best to have the form signed beforehand. If the parents have already left, mail the form to them so they can have their section of the form notarized wherever they are.

Single Parent Note: If the minor has only one parent, that parent can sign the Guardianship Authorization form alone. But if there is another living natural parent—for example, an ex-husband or lover—the Guardianship Authorization form will probably not be sufficient if that other parent wants to claim physical custody of the minor. The Guardianship Authorization form is not intended to be used to resolve custody issues. If your situation involves a custody problem, consult an attorney. (See Chapter 13.)

a. How to Complete the Guardianship Authorization Form

If you will be taking care of more than one minor, complete a separate form for each minor. Here is how to fill out the Guardianship Authorization form.

Information About Minor: Fill in the minor's name, birthdate, age and year in school (if applicable).

Information About Parents: Fill in the names of whichever of the minor's mother and father will be signing the form. If you can get signatures from both parents, fill in the information requested for both parents. If you can only get a signature from one parent, only fill in information about that parent. Fill in the addresses and telephone numbers of each parent who will be signing the form. If the parents will be out of the area, fill in the address and phone numbers where they can most likely be reached.

Information About Proposed Guardian: It's usually preferable to have only one person take on this responsibility, to avoid conflicts between the two caretakers. Fill in your own name, address and phone number. Also fill in your relationship to the minor.

---

[2] If you are a stepparent or unrelated co-parent who wants some documentation from a spouse giving you authorization to make decisions about her children, you might only seek the signature of your partner.

GUARDIANSHIP AUTHORIZATION

MINOR
Name: Jennifer Catherine Jones

Birthdate: 11/18/86   Age: 5   Year in School: Kindergarten

MOTHER
Name: Betsy Jones

Street Address: 100 Any Street

City: Any City   State: CA   Zip Code: 99999

Home Phone: 999/555-1212   Work Phone: 888/555-1212

FATHER
Name: Aaron Jones

Street Address: 100 Any Street

City: Any City   State: CA   Zip Code: 99999

Home Phone: 999/555-1212   Work Phone: 777/555-1212

PROPOSED GUARDIAN
Name: Tom Parks

Street Address: 500 Any Street

City: Any City   State: CA   Zip Code: 99999

Home Phone: 666/555-1212   Work Phone: 555/555-1212

Relationship to Minor: Maternal uncle

In case of emergency, if proposed guardian cannot be reached, please contact: Jean Parks

12 Any Street, Any City, CA 99999   Phone: 444/555-1212

Authorization & Consent of Parent(s)

1. I affirm that the minor indicated above is my child and that I have legal custody of her/him. I give my full authorization and consent for my child to live with the proposed guardian, or for the proposed guardian to set a place of residence for my child.

2. I give the proposed guardian permission to act in my place and make decisions pertaining to my child's educational and religious activities including but not limited to enrollment, permission to participate in activities and consent for medical treatment at school.

3. I give the proposed guardian permission to authorize medical and dental care for my child, including but not limited to medical examinations, X-rays, tests, anesthetic, surgical operations, hospital care or other treatments that in the proposed guardian's sole opinion are needed or useful for my child. Such medical treatment shall only be provided upon the advice of and supervision by a physician, surgeon or dentist or other medical practitioner licensed to practice in the United States.

4. I give the proposed guardian permission to apply for benefits on my child's behalf including but not limited to Social Security, public assistance, health insurance, and Veterans' Administration benefits.

5. I give the proposed guardian permission to apply and obtain for my child any or all of the following: Social Security number, Social Security card, and U.S. passport.

6. This authorization shall cover the period from _____12/2_____, 19_92_ to __1/30_____, 19_93_.

7. During the period when the proposed guardian cares for my child, the costs of my child's upkeep, living expenses, medical and dental expenses shall be paid as follows: _____
_____

I declare under penalty of perjury under the laws of the State of California that the foregoing is true and correct.

Mother's Signature: _____ Date: _____, 19_____

Father's Signature: _____ Date: _____, 19_____

Notarization

State of California
County of _____ } ss.

On this this _____ day of _____, 19____, before me, a notary public of the State of California, personally appeared
_____, personally known to me (or proved to me on the basis of satisfactory evidence) to be the person(s) whose name(s) is/are subscribed to this instrument, and acknowledged that she/he/they executed it.

Notary Public: _____ [Seal]

Consent of Proposed Guardian

I solemnly affirm that I will assume full responsibility for the minor who will live with me during the period designated above. I agree to make necessary decisions and to provide consent for the minor as set forth in the above Authorization & Consent by Parent(s). I also agree to the terms of the costs of the minor's upkeep, living expenses, medical and/or dental expenses set forth in the above Authorization & Consent of Parent(s).

I declare under penalty of perjury under the laws of the State of California that the foregoing is true and correct.

Proposed Guardian's Signature : _____ Date: _____, 19_____

Notarization

State of California
County of _____ } ss.

On this this _____ day of _____, 19____, before me, a notary public of the State of California, personally appeared _____, personally known to me (or proved to me on the basis of satisfactory evidence) to be the person whose name is subscribed to this instrument, and acknowledged that she/he executed it.

Notary Public: _____ [Seal]

Emergency Contact: Fill in the name of a person who can be contacted in case of an emergency if you cannot be reached. This might be a friend, relative, or neighbor who lives nearby. If possible, it's best to give the name of someone who has a car or ready access to transportation.

Items 1 through 5: Leave these items blank, but make sure you read what they say.

Item 6: Fill in the period of time during which the informal guardianship arrangement will be valid. For example, if the parents will be overseas from September 4, 1990 through November 18, 1990, you would fill in those dates.

Item 7: By law, parents are required to support their children, regardless of where the children are living (CC §§196, 242, 244). But in the real world, people sometimes make other arrangements. Maybe you are helping out your son, who is going through a difficult emotional and financial time, and you are willing and able to pay expenses of his minor child's upkeep. But on the other hand, maybe you can't afford to take on the financial responsibility. The blank space in this item is the place for you to clearly and simply state how costs of taking care of the minor will be paid. If, for example, you are willing to pay the expenses of taking care of the minor during the informal "guardianship," you might fill in: "The proposed guardian will pay all costs of the minor's upkeep, medical, dental and living expenses." If a parent will give you money to take care of her child, you might fill in: "The minor's mother will pay all costs of the minor's upkeep, living expenses, medical and dental expenses." If you agree to provide food and cover school expenses for the minor, but her parents promise to pay for medical and dental expenses, you might fill in: "The proposed guardian will pay all costs of the minor's upkeep, living expenses, and school expenses. The minor's parents will pay all medical and dental expenses."

You have now completed the form. Do not sign it yet, or have the parents sign it. It should be signed by both you and the parents in front of a notary public. We tell you how to do that next, in Section B1b.

b. Copy, Sign and Notarize the Guardianship Authorization Form

You're now ready to make several copies of the Guardianship Authorization form. We suggest you make at least four copies of the completed but still unsigned form for each minor. That way you will be able to provide an original form for each agency or institution that requires one.

Next, you will need to locate a notary public. It is important to have this document notarized because the notary's signature and seal confirm that the signatures are legitimate. Banks and real estate offices are good places to find notaries, or you can look in the Yellow Pages of the phone book under "Notary Public" or a similar heading. Notaries may charge around $5 per signature. But if you look around, you may be able to find a notary for free, or for a very low price. For example, a local bank may offer notary services free as a service to its customers.

Naturally, if you have to pay a lot for the notary (it might cost around $15 per document if two parents and you are signing) you may opt to obtain fewer original notarized Guardianship Authorization forms. Make sure you get at least one notarized copy, and preferably two. Don't hesitate to call around and see if you can't find some notary who will help you out for less money.

If possible, go to the notary public along with the parents who will be signing the Guardianship Authorization form. The notary will have each of you produce some kind of identification (such as a driver's license or passport), and watch each of you sign the document. The notary will then fill out the "Notarization" parts of the form, and imprint it with an official notary seal. You will need to sign your name in the notary's book, stating that you signed the document in front of the notary.

If you can't go to a notary with the parents—for example, one of them lives in another state—each form will have to be notarized twice. Send the parents several unsigned copies of the document to sign and have notarized. Then go to a notary yourself along with the Guardianship Authorization forms that the parents signed and had notarized. There you should sign and have your portion of the document notarized.

c. What to Do with the Completed Guardianship Authorization Form

Now that you have an informal "guardianship" document, you can provide a copy of it to agencies and institutions that require some proof of your authority to care for a minor. Make sure you keep one original of the Guardianship Authorization document in a safe, convenient place. When an agency asks for the document, be sure you hand over a copy or one of several originals. Don't give away your only signed and notarized original.

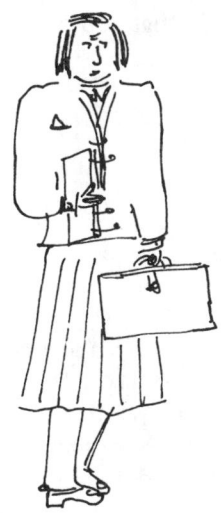

C. Dealing with Agencies and Institutions in Informal "Guardianship" Situations

IF YOU CARE FOR A MINOR who isn't your child, agencies and institutions may give you some unexpected hassles. Agencies—especially those that are distributing benefits—are often cautious when dealing with an adult who claims to be taking care of a minor. They generally want to make sure the benefits will be going to an adult to help out the minor.

Unfortunately, in informal "guardianship" situations, it can be very confusing to deal with agencies and institutions that require proof of your authority to act on behalf of a minor. Policies vary so greatly that there are no rules to help you through all situations. The policy of one school district or hospital might be quite different from that of a similar agency a few miles away. And unfortunately, even the requirements of a given agency can sometimes depend more on the opinions of the person with whom you're dealing than with any well-thought agency policy.

In general, most agencies are more willing to accept informal "guardianship" authorization as proof if a relative, rather than an unrelated adult, is taking care of a minor. If you are a close relative (grandparent, uncle or aunt, sister or brother), you might not be asked to provide any documentation showing that you are acting as the minor's guardian. However, if you are not a close relative or you move to a new area where you and the minor aren't known and you need agency support, you will likely be asked to produce documentation showing authorization from a parent or even a court.

If you do not plan to get a legal guardianship, here are some rules for dealing with agencies and institutions:

- Find out the agency's policies for written authorization before you deal with them about your specific situation. If you call for information, you don't have to give your name, and you should be able to get valuable information. For example, an agency may have preprinted authorization forms it prefers you to use. Or it may be more willing to accept an informal "guardianship" arrangement if a natural parent contacts someone there first.

- Be as cooperative as possible, but don't volunteer more information about your custody situation than you are asked. Often you will be able to simply sign the agency's forms, and no one will ask any questions.

- If possible, get a signed and notarized copy of the Guardianship Authorization form following the instructions in Section B of this chapter. Carry this with you when you go to the agency in person. Then, if written authorization is required, you can provide it on the spot.

- If an agency uses its own preprinted authorization forms, obtain copies and, if possible, have the minor's natural parents complete and sign them. You may need to meet with a representative of the agency to get the forms, and return later once you've obtained the parents' signatures.

- Don't be intimidated by bureaucracy. One agency employee may insist that only a formal guardianship will be accepted, but as noted, others may be lenient—especially if you produce a legal-looking document such as the Guardianship Authorization form. If you meet resistance, keep trying. Ask to see another agent, or a supervisor if need be. You might even be better off coming back another day rather than trying to cope with one obstinate person.

- If you will receive money or benefits on behalf of the minor from an agency requiring periodic accountings to show how the money has been spent, you must comply with that requirement. For example, the Veterans' Administration is almost certain to require these accountings. Social Security and other agencies may also require them.

Here we provide information on the typical policies of a variety of agencies and institutions, and wherever possible, give you the inside scoop on how to approach them. You should be able to get most of them to accept the informal short-term Guardianship Authorization form without hassle.

1. Schools

There is no statewide law that specifically addresses guardianship issues, so schools set their own policies. As a result, California school districts vary widely in their policies on guardianships of minors. Depending on the school district's historical problems, as well as overall community attitudes, you may or may not have difficulties enrolling a minor in school without a formal, court-approved guardianship. Depending on the school district, you may be required to do one or none of the following:

- Simply say that you are legally responsible for the minor, and comply with the district's general procedures, such as filling out a registration application and providing medical immunization information about the minor.
- Provide a signed letter from the minor's parent giving the minor permission to live with you, and acknowledging your responsibility to take care of the minor during the school year.
- Sign a document authorizing you to enroll the minor in school and have the minor's parents sign an authorization document. This might be the Guardianship Authorization form in this chapter or a different form the school district supplies. Generally these documents must be notarized.
- Obtain a formal court guardianship using the instructions in this book, and provide documentation to the school system.

Many school districts prefer a formal court-ordered guardianship of the minor's person when a non-parent cares for a minor, but will also accept a signed (and preferably notarized) statement, especially if the parent is only absent temporarily. The Guardianship Authorization form in Section B of this chapter should suffice in such situations. Some school districts have their own authorization forms that you would need to complete.

STRICT ENROLLMENT POLICIES OF SOME SCHOOL DISTRICTS

School districts in some of California's larger cities tend to have more rigid enrollment policies than other districts in the state. In addition, enrollment policies tend to be much stricter in school districts that have a history of non-district residents trying to enroll children there. This is common when a crowded, poorly-funded school district is geographically close to a school district with more extensive curricula and better-funded facilities. Parents who live outside of the district often try to sneak their kids into the better school district by providing a mailing address of a relative or friend within the school district.

If you live in one of these districts, chances are that you'll be faced with stringent enrollment requirements. These may include providing a lease or utility bill to prove that you live in the district, a copy of the minor's birth certificate and possibly a copy of your own birth certificate showing that you're related to the minor. Since it may not be too difficult to come up with these documents, some school districts will not register a minor in school if the parents live out of the district—even if the child genuinely lives with relatives in the district, unless a formal, court-ordered guardianship is in force. However, some school districts make exceptions for hardship situations when a minor must be placed with close relatives because one or both of the parents' jobs require extensive travel out of the area.

2. Medical and Dental Care

The need to have some adult available to consent to a minor's medical treatment may seem at first like one of the most important reasons to get a guardianship. Perhaps you have visions of a child being hit by a car and no doctor being willing to treat her. Fortunately, this is not a realistic worry, as consent by an adult is not required to treat a minor in an emergency.

A formal legal guardianship is advisable if you anticipate that the minor will need ongoing health care for serious medical problems. For example, a guardianship would be in order if the minor has a chronic illness that requires periodic hospitalization, surgery, prescription drugs or other treatments.

In general, a legal guardian has the same right as the parent to consent to and require medical treatment for the minor. But a legal guardian is not automatically entitled to authorize all of the minor's medical, dental and mental health treatment. Here are are some exceptions:

- Non-emergency surgical procedures generally require the consent of a minor age 14 or older, as well as that of the guardian.
- A guardian cannot involuntarily place a minor in a mental health treatment facility unless the minor is a danger to himself or others, or is gravely disabled (PC §2356(a), W&I §5150).
- A guardian cannot authorize a minor to be treated with experimental drugs, to be given convulsive treatment, or to be sterilized.

a. Medical Emergencies (Hospitals)

As mentioned, treating a minor in a medical emergency does not require authorization by a parent or guardian. If a minor is taken to a hospital in an emergency, the doctor who's providing care can sign a document authorizing emergency medical treatment (sometimes called a "treating permit"). Assessing the emergency and the treatment needed is up to the doctor. The doctor's willingness to sign a treating permit would probably depend on the severity of the situation and the medical procedure required.[3]

b. Routine Medical and Dental Care

Some physicians, dentists and hospitals will allow a grandparent, or possibly another close relative, to give consent for a medical procedure for a minor. Others require a parent's consent either over the phone or in writing, such as the notarized Guardianship Authorization form set out in Section B above or the medical provider's own release form.

It's also possible that a formal court guardianship could be required before a particular medical professional will treat the minor. Whether a legal guardianship will be required often depends partly on the needed medical treatment. The more serious the medical problem—short of an acute medical emergency—and the more time there is before action must be taken, the more likely you are to deal with the question of a formal guardianship.

c. Medical and Dental Insurance Coverage

You and your family may be covered by health insurance, perhaps under an insurance policy at a job. If so, you will probably want to include coverage for any minor for whom you are caring. Some insurance companies are strict about requiring papers showing a court-appointed guardianship before they will extend coverage to minors who live with you. Others will accept alternative documentation, usually if you suggest it. If your insurance company requires a court-ordered legal guardianship, you will either need to comply with the company's rules, or seek coverage with a different health insurance carrier.

Before you obtain a legal guardianship, check with your insurance carrier to find out:

- Whether the minor will be eligible for coverage if you obtain a guardianship[4] and, if so, whether a

---

[3] As you probably guessed, the doctor's willingness or reluctance to treat a minor without a parent's or legal guardian's consent may depend at least in part on available coverage for malpractice. For example, if surgery for a minor isn't required immediately but is desirable within a few months, a doctor might require a legal guardianship before proceeding with the operation.

[4] Get a firm commitment from the insurance company that the minor will be covered by your insurance if this is the only reason you are seeking a formal guardianship. You might want to get a written statement from the insurance agent, or check the policy regarding coverage in guardianship situations.

formal, court-ordered guardianship is required for the minor to be covered; or
- Whether the insurance carrier will accept alternate documentation to a court-ordered guardianship for children who live with you. This might be a signed letter from the minor's parent, a document such as the Guardianship Authorization form, or some other document the insurance company provides.

3. Public Assistance

Depending on your income, you and the minor may be eligible for a variety of public assistance benefits. This might include Medi-Cal, Aid to Families with Dependent Children (AFDC) for relatives of a minor, or Boarding Home & Institution (BHI)—also called Foster Care payments in some counties—for people caring for an unrelated minor. Public assistance funding comes from three sources: the federal government, the state of California, and from each county.

You are likely to qualify for public assistance without a legal guardianship if you are a close relative of the minor. How closely you must be related (grandmother, uncle, etc.) depends on the policies of the county in which you live. Section B above sets out a Guardianship Authorization form that will work instead of a legal guardianship in some counties. But others may require a formal guardianship.

If you are not related to the child you are caring for, you will probably need a guardianship. Also, if you already have a legal guardianship and you move to a different county, the new county could require you, as a condition of receiving benefits, to have the case transferred to the court in that county. (See Chapter 11, Section E.)

Note: To handle the small amounts of money involved in public assistance programs, remember that unless the agency specifies otherwise, you only need to get a guardianship of the minor's person, not of the estate. You will need to follow the accounting or investigation requirements of the public assistance programs.

CHECKLIST FOR APPLYING FOR WELFARE

Here is an overview of the documentation you'll need when applying for public assistance. Check with your local welfare agency for exact requirements in your county.

- Birth certificate of minor;
- Minor's Social Security card;
- Birth certificate of minor's mother;
- Your birth certificate; and
- Your photo ID.

Note: If you need to obtain copies of birth certificates, see Appendix B.

---

a. Aid to Families with Dependent Children (AFDC)

AFDC is a program that provides money to help low-income families with children. If you are a grandparent taking care of your grandchild, you probably can qualify for AFDC without obtaining a guardianship, if you meet the program's income and need requirements. Some welfare departments will allow other close relatives (brother, sister, uncle, aunt) to obtain AFDC without a guardianship. Others require an aunt or even a sister of a minor to get a formal court guardianship first.

b. Boarding Home and Institution (BHI) or Foster Care

BHI, called Foster Care in some counties, is similar to AFDC, but it is available to adults with minors living with them who either aren't related or aren't closely related. These payments are only made when there is a formal court guardianship. BHI is also available to licensed foster homes, which would qualify for this type of assistance when they obtain licensing. These benefits tend to be slightly higher than AFDC, and include a back-to-school clothing allowance.

c. Medi-Cal

Medi-Cal is a program that provides certain low-income people with free or shared costs of medical and some dental care, depending on need. This assistance is available to people who are under age 21, blind, pregnant, or permanently disabled. The minor may be eligible for Medi-Cal depending on income level. To obtain Medi-Cal for a minor living with you, you must be related to the minor (usually grandparent, aunt or uncle, sister or brother, or possibly first cousin), or you must have a legal guardianship. Check with your local welfare office.

d. Custody Problems after Applying for Public Assistance

When a relative applies for public assistance to take care of a child, the family situation is reviewed by the welfare agency and an effort made to collect support from the natural parents. Occasionally this prompts a natural parent who has been out of the picture for some time to show up and demand physical custody of the child. Where the natural parent is stable and able to care for the child, the appearance may be for the best. Often it isn't, if the motive of the parent demanding custody is to avoid paying child support.

Example: Alfred's grandmother has been taking care of him for several years, since her daughter is unable to do so. She does not know the whereabouts of Alfred's father, who abandoned Alfred when he was a baby. After she applies for AFDC benefits and supplies the welfare department with the father's Social Security number, he is located and suddenly appears. He says he would rather take Alfred than make the support payments to the District Attorney's office that located him. Alfred's grandmother wants to keep the child, and doesn't trust the father's motives. She decides to petition for a legal guardianship, and with the help of a lawyer, to fight the father's right to have custody of Alfred. She plans to base her case on the fact that Alfred's father has abandoned him, that Alfred's needs will be better served by continuing to live with her as the person who has cared for him since birth and to whom he is very close. (In a contested case such as this, a lawyer's help would be needed. Information on obtaining and working with lawyers is in Chapter 13.)

4. Subsidized (Section 8) Housing

Section 8 Housing is a housing program for low-income people subsidized by the government.[5] Eligibility requirements for Section 8 Housing vary from place to place, since the funding for the housing comes from each city or county. The number of bedrooms for which you qualify might increase if you are taking care of a minor. For example, in some cities there must be a separate bedroom for boys and girls, so if you take in your nephew and already have a daughter and no extra bedroom, in those cities you should qualify for another bedroom.

Since the policies for Section 8 Housing vary depending on the location, you will need to call the local Housing Authority for information on what documentation is required. Usually some proof of your authority to care for a minor will be sufficient, and you will not need a formal guardianship. In some counties, the only documentation you will need is proof that you are receiving AFDC on behalf of a minor who is living with you. If you are not receiving AFDC, in many counties the Guardianship Authorization form in this chapter should be sufficient proof to qualify you for benefits. However, if the minor's parent is not available to sign such a form, some offices will accept a notarized statement from you instead. Following is an example that you can modify to fit your situation and the requirements of your local Housing Authority office.

5. Social Security

Social Security is made up of three different but related benefit programs for retired or disabled people and their dependents or survivors. Social Security benefits are not distributed entirely by need, but are paid to the retired or disabled worker or dependent family largely based on the average wages earned on jobs covered by Social Security.

You will likely deal with Social Security if either:
- You need a Social Security number or card for the minor; or

---

[5]The program is called "Section 8" because it refers to subsidized housing covered in Section 8 of the Federal United States Housing Act (42 USC §1437f).

SAMPLE NOTARIZED STATEMENT REGARDING PHYSICAL
CUSTODY OF ELIZABETH JONES (FOR SECTION 8 HOUSING)

I, Lily Jones Kerr, declare that I am Elizabeth Jones' aunt (her father's sister), that I have had physical custody of Elizabeth Jones since July 3, 1990, and that Elizabeth Jones lives with me at 9 Wild Way, Calcity, California 99999. Elizabeth Jones was born on April 12, 1985.

I declare under penalty of perjury under the laws of the State of California that the foregoing is true and correct.

_____ Date: _____
(Signature) Lily Jones Kerr

NOTARIZATION

State of California   )
County of _____)

On this this _____ day of _____, 19_____, before me, a notary public of the State of California, personally appeared _____, personally known to me (or proved to me on the basis of satisfactory evidence) to be the person whose name is subscribed to this instrument, and acknowledged that she/he executed it.

Notary Public: _____

[Seal]

- The minor is eligible for Social Security benefits, usually because a covered parent is deceased or disabled.

a. Social Security Number or Card

The policies of Social Security offices vary slightly. In most circumstances, you may not need a legal guardianship to apply for a Social Security number for a minor who is not your child. The application for a Social Security number has a signature line for either the parent or other specified adult. When you sign the application, indicate your relationship with the minor, such as "uncle, aunt, grandmother." If you have any trouble obtaining a Social Security number or card for the minor, a signed copy of the Guardianship Authorization form probably will be sufficient documentation for your local Social Security office. (Note that in Item 5 of the Guardianship Authorization form, the parents specifically authorize you to apply for a Social Security number or card on behalf of their child.)

It should be no problem to obtain a duplicate card once the minor has been assigned a Social Security number. Minors over the age of 12 should be able to apply for a duplicate Social Security card on their own.

b. Social Security Benefits

If the minor is entitled to benefits from the Social Security Administration (such as death or disability benefits) and already has a Social Security number, you may not need a legal guardianship. The Social Security Administration (SSA) does not require a guardianship for an adult to receive benefits on behalf of a minor. The person who receives benefits for someone else is the "representative payee," according to bureaucratic jargon.

To become a representative payee, you must contact the SSA and complete an application form. The application, which is about four pages long, asks a variety of questions about you and the minor, such as whether you are the legal guardian (although it isn't required that you be), whether the minor is living with you, and the names and locations of the minor's relatives. Once you complete the application, the SSA will process it and determine if you are eligible to become the representative payee.

If a minor who is eligible for benefits lives with you, a legal guardianship will not be required by the SSA. However, if the SSA is apprehensive about turning benefits over to you, obtaining a legal guardianship of the minor's estate may help convince it, since you would be required to account to the court as to how you spend the money.

6. Veterans' Administration Benefits

A minor who is a child of a veteran (whether living or deceased) may be eligible for money benefits through the Veterans' Administration (VA). The type and amount of these benefits depend on the veteran's history of service, and whether he served in a war or during peacetime. Legal guardianships are not required by the VA, and in fact the existence of a legal guardianship does not automatically qualify a guardian to receive benefits on behalf of a minor. The VA's term for the person who receives benefits on someone else's behalf is "fiduciary." To become a fiduciary, you must complete forms that the VA provides. The VA will arrange a personal interview, check into your references, and possibly require periodic accountings. To start the process, contact the VA to find out whether the minor qualifies for benefits, and if so, how to proceed.

7. Traveling With a Minor Outside the U.S.

Traveling outside the U.S. with a minor who is not your child could be a problem if you don't have documentation showing your legal relationship. Immigration officials could detain you either when entering or leaving the country. And if the unexpected arises—such as a medical emergency or a problem with customs—the last thing you'll want to do is explain the relationship between you and a minor who is not your child. Here we provide valuable information and forms to minimize potential hassles.

It's best to have the minor's parents sign a Guardianship Authorization form (see Section B above), and take an original signed and notarized copy of this document with you on your trip. That way, if any problems arise, such as authorization for medical treatment, you will be prepared.

It may also be necessary to have a signed, and preferably notarized, letter from the minor's parents stating that they know about and approve of your specific travel plans. (Section C7b below discusses how to do this.)

TRAVEL FOR NON-CITIZENS OF THE UNITED STATES

In this section we assume that you and the minor who is not your child both are citizens of the United States. If you or the minor are not U.S. citizens, check with the U.S. immigration office or consult with an immigration attorney before attempting to leave the country. (See Chapter 13 on how to find and deal with an attorney.)

---

a. U.S. Passports

Most countries outside of the United States (except Canada and Mexico) require passports for everyone traveling there from the U.S., including all minors. Passport applications are available at U.S. Passport offices, some courts and authorized post offices. A minor under 13 years of age must appear in person when applying for a passport.

If you aren't the minor's legal guardian, you will probably need to carry a notarized statement from a parent stating that you are authorized to obtain a passport for the minor when traveling to a foreign country with him. The Guardianship Authorization form provided in Section B above should be sufficient documentation for your local passport office. (Note that Item 5 of the form specifically authorizes you to apply for a passport on behalf of the minor.)

b. Letter Authorizing Minor to Travel Outside U.S.

If you will be taking a minor who is not your child outside of the United States (see special information on travel to Canada and Mexico below), it is a good idea to obtain a signed, notarized letter from the minor's parents authorizing you to travel outside of the country with the minor. It is not uncommon for children to be kidnapped either by a parent or other adult, so a number of countries (and airlines, trying to be sure you won't be sent back) are strict when dealing with non-parent adults traveling with minors.

The letter should be as specific as possible about information such as dates of travel, places you will be visiting and where you will be staying. We emphasize that such a letter should be signed by the minor's parents and notarized. (See Section B1b of this chapter for information on having documents notarized.) A sample is provided on the next page.

c. Travel to Canada

The sample letter should suffice for travel to Canada. In addition you will need proof of the minor's U.S. citizenship (a birth certificate or passport). Contact the Canadian Consulate before your trip if you have questions or need more information.

d. Travel to Mexico

The sample letter should suffice for travel to Mexico. In addition, you will need proof of the minor's U.S. citizenship, such as a birth certificate or passport. You will need to get signed permission from *both* living parents (if at all possible) to take a minor who is not your child into Mexico.[6] If one or both parents are dead, it would be advisable to take along a copy of the parent's death certificate. (If you need to obtain a copy, you can follow the instructions for getting one in Appendix B.) If you have questions or need more information, contact the Mexican Consulate before your trip. Finally, if you anticipate any problems, contact the Mexican Consulate and obtain a tourist card before your trip, rather than trying to do so at the border.

8. Insurance Coverage

A minor who lives with you and is old enough to drive should be added to your automobile insurance coverage. A legal guardianship should not be necessary. Most automobile policies routinely will add non-relatives if you're willing to pay the premium. Since policies differ, check with your insurance agent for information on how to do this.

If you want other types of insurance coverage for the minor (life, accident, property), you should also check with your insurance agent for details. (Information on medical and dental insurance coverage is given in Section C2 of this chapter.)

---

[6]Even if a child lives with both parents, Mexico requires a signed permission letter from the other parent if only one parent is taking the child across the border. California's laws are less stringent. To return to California from Mexico, a minor must be accompanied by a parent or legal guardian, or have written consent to come into California from the parent, or have a passport (CC §1500).

SAMPLE

[Date]

To Whom It Concerns:

This letter concerns my child, [state child's name], a United States citizen and a minor born on [state date of minor's birth]. I affirm that I have legal custody of my child, and that there are no pending custody proceedings that involve him/her. I give my full authorization and consent for my child to travel out of the United States with [state name of person with whom minor will be traveling], who is [state relationship to minor] of my child.

The travel plans I approve, with modifications as [again state name of person with whom minor will be traveling] may deem necessary are:

Dates of Travel: From [starting date] to [ending date].

Anticipated Dates and Places of Travel: [State specific countries, cities, towns, and places where the minor and adult will be staying, as well as the anticipated dates]

Date(s) of Travel　　　　　　　　Places of Travel/Places Staying
[Fill in dates and places of travel] _____
_____
_____
_____
_____

Purpose of Travel: [State whether it is vacation, tourism, to visit relatives, to accompany adult on a business trip, or any other reason.]

I declare under penalty of perjury under the laws of the State of California that the foregoing is true and correct.

Mother's Signature: _____ Date: _____
Print Name: _____

Father's Signature: _____ Date: _____
Print Name: _____

NOTARIZATION

State of California　　　　　　　　)
County of _____　　)

On this this _____ day of _____, 19_____, before me, a notary public of the State of California, personally appeared _____, personally known to me (or proved to me on the basis of satisfactory evidence) to be the person(s) whose name(s) is/are subscribed to this instrument, and acknowledged that she/he/they executed it.

Notary Public: _____

[Seal]

CHAPTER 3

GETTING STARTED

A.	Documents and Information You Need	3/1
B.	The Courts	3/2
C.	How to Use the Forms	3/3
D.	General Rules on Completing Forms	3/5
E.	How to File Papers with the Court	3/7
F.	Filing Fees and Court Costs	3/12

A. Documents and Information You Need

BEFORE YOU START FILLING in the forms for a legal guardianship, collect the following information and documents:

SUMMARY OF DOCUMENTS AND INFORMATION TO COLLECT

- Names and addresses of all of these living relatives of the minor:

    Parents;

    Grandparents (parents of both the minor's mother and father);

    Sisters and brothers (if they are under 18 and have one different parent from the minor, you need the name and address of that parent as well);

    Spouse (this is unlikely, and if the spouse is married or divorced you may only petition for guardianship of the estate);

    Children (this is unlikely, but if the minor has any children you will need their names and addresses);

    Any legal guardian of the minor, or anyone who has been nominated as legal guardian;[1] and

    The adult with whom the minor is living (other than you or anyone else in this list).

- Copies of death certificates of the minor's parents if either of them has died. If you don't have copies of the death certificates, you can obtain them by writing to the vital records office of the state where the parent died. There is a list of these addresses in Appendix B in the back of this book.

- If the guardianship is being obtained because you were named guardian in the will of someone who died, a copy of the will.[2] If a probate has been opened, get copies of all court-filed documents.

- Copies of any documents relating to property the minor owns or is subject to inherit once a guardianship has been obtained (such as bank accounts, life insurance policies, real estate, vehicles).

- Copies of court documents involving the minor. This includes any marriage dissolution, pending custody, adoption, or juvenile court proceedings that affect the minor (for example, copies of the minor's parents' divorce papers, copies of any court papers that anyone has filed to adopt the minor, even if the adoption was not completed).

- The birth certificate of the minor for whom you are seeking a guardianship is needed if you are claiming that the natural father is unknown. It is a good idea to have a copy of the minor's birth certificate, anyhow. You can obtain copies of the minor's birth certificate by calling or writing to the vital records office of the state where the minor was born. (These addresses are listed in Appendix B in the back of this book.)

---

[1] If someone other than you is legal guardian of the minor and that person is not in favor of you being guardian, or if someone other than you already has been nominated legal guardian, the guardianship probably will be contested. If this is your situation, consult a lawyer. (See Chapter 13.)

[2] The law requires anyone holding an original will of someone who died to deposit it with the county clerk in the county in which the deceased person lived. If this has been done, you can get a certified copy from the court for a small fee.

By the time you've finished your guardianship, you will have accumulated a good many papers and file-endorsed copies of court documents. Make sure that you establish a system to keep all of these documents in a safe place. There are few things more frustrating than losing an important document and having to replace it. File folders or large manila envelopes are particularly helpful for getting and keeping your guardianship case organized. Even better is a cardboard accordion file with a top flap that can be tied securely. You might want to keep several file folders in the accordion file that are separated by category (such as court guardianship papers, birth certificates, other legal proceedings affecting minor, searching for missing relatives, correspondence). Then, when you start a new procedure (such as searching for missing relatives), you can open a new file folder with a new label.

B. The Courts

AS YOU PROBABLY KNOW, in the United States legal system, different types of courts handle different types of legal matters. In California, guardianships are handled in the Probate Division of the Superior Court.[3] All California probate courts follow the same basic procedures for guardianships. In addition, courts in different counties (especially those with large populations) commonly have several special procedural rules of their own. Many counties have these court rules printed in small pamphlets called Probate Policy Manuals or Memoranda. You can check with the probate court clerk where you are filing your papers to obtain a copy. If you cannot get a Probate Policy Manual through the court, you can find it at the county law library. (See Chapter 13, Section D3 for more information on Probate Policy Manuals and legal research.) Whenever possible in this book, we refer to individual county's rules, but we cannot possibly identify every one used in all counties.

1. Where to File the Guardianship

You usually will file your guardianship in the county where the minor lives.[4] If the guardianship is only for the estate of the minor, the guardianship petition may be filed in any county in California where the minor has property.[5]

In many counties, the courthouse you deal with will be located in the "county seat," often the largest city in the county. Several of the bigger counties have branch courts in cities other than the county seat. For example, the Santa Clara County Superior Court has a North County branch in Palo Alto, in addition to the main court in San Jose. Los Angeles County has a main branch in Los Angeles, and in addition twelve district branches. If there is a branch court close to where the minor lives, local court rules probably will require you to file your guardianship there. To find the Superior Court in your county, check the telephone directory in the county government listings section. If you find several listings for the Superior Court, which is likely in larger counties, the one you want is the Probate Division of the Superior Court.

---

[3]Where a minor is a dependent of a juvenile court, a guardianship proceeding is handled in juvenile court.

[4]The minor may live in this county as a resident of California (PC §2201), or temporarily as a nonresident (PC §2202).

[5]"Property" includes real estate as well as personal property such as vehicles, jewelry, bank accounts and other assets. If guardianship proceedings are started in one county, they later may be transferred to a different county. For example, a case might be transferred if it would be more convenient for you to have it in a different court or if you move. (See Chapter 11, Section E for instructions on transferring cases.)

2. Many Courts Have Special Clerks to Answer Procedural Questions

In most of the larger courts, special court clerks give information about guardianship procedures. These clerks are well-versed in the court's specific rules and in guardianship law. The clerks cannot give legal advice, but they will answer questions about the court's procedural requirements. Many courts have designated times of the day when you may call these clerks.

3. Obtain Information from the Court Clerk

Using the checklist on this page, phone the probate court and ask the filing clerk for some basic information you'll need to complete your guardianship forms.

C. How to Use the Forms

HERE ARE SOME GENERAL TIPS on how to use the forms provided in this book. If you follow these suggestions, you can save yourself a lot of time and trouble.

Tips for Using the Forms in This Book

- Before you fill out any of the tear-out forms provided in the Appendices at the back of this book, make several photocopies of each. This will save you many worried moments if you make a mistake or misplace a form. Also, note that many forms have printing on both sides. If the form is two-sided, make sure you copy both sides. You can either make a two-sided copy, or simply staple the pages together before filing the form with the court.
- All forms should be completed carefully and neatly, preferably using a typewriter. It is best to use the larger type size (called "pica" or "10-pitch" type). Some courts may refuse to accept forms with smaller type (called "elite" or "12-pitch" type). If you do not have access to a typewriter, there are typing and paralegal services which can prepare forms for you at a reasonable cost. (See Chapter 13, Section B.) Depending on the court's policies, handwritten forms may be accepted if you print clearly and neatly, generally in black ink. If you want to submit handwritten forms, call the court beforehand to make sure they'll be accepted.
- Carefully follow the instructions in this book for completing the forms. Also look at any samples provided to make sure you fill in the forms correctly.
- Whenever you send a completed form to the court, always keep copies for yourself. When you file papers with the court clerk, take along an extra copy for the clerk to stamp and return to you. Documents can be lost in the mail, misplaced by a clerk, or otherwise sent off into the twilight zone.

CHECKLIST OF INFORMATION TO OBTAIN FROM COURT CLERK

- ☐ The proper branch of the court for filing your guardianship papers. You'll need to tell the clerk in what city or town the minor lives.
- ☐ Mailing address of the court.
- ☐ Street address of the court—if it is different from the mailing address.
- ☐ Fee for filing a petition for a guardianship. (If you cannot afford the fees, you may be able to get them waived. See Section F in this chapter.)
- ☐ Whether there are any special forms or procedures the court requires for guardianships. You may get a roundabout or unhelpful answer from the clerk—such as to check the Probate Policy Manual or local rules of court—but it's worth asking.
- ☐ Whether the court requires an investigation. This is generally required only when you are seeking guardianship of a minor's person. Who investigates the guardianship will depend on whether you are a blood relative of the minor. Tell the clerk your relationship to the minor, and ask for the name, title, address and phone number of the investigator. (The investigation is routine, and not a scary process. Chapter 8 tells you all about it.)

1. Judicial Council Forms

Most of the forms you'll use are called "Judicial Council forms." These are standard forms that were designed and approved by a group of experts called the California Judicial Council. The Judicial Council forms are used in all California courts. Each of these forms has a title in bold print at the bottom of the page, and information in the lower left-hand corner that will help you identify the form and determine whether it is up-to-date. The number in the lower left-hand corner is the Judicial Council's own identification number. In the sample shown below, the Notice of Hearing citation number is "GC-020(81)."[6]

Near the citation number is the date the form was last revised. The forms were current when this book was published. However, Judicial Council forms are subject to change approximately once a year, although many of them stay current for years. To be safe, if you use this book more than one year after it was last printed (see the printing history at the beginning of the book), call the court clerk and find out if the forms are still current. The clerk will need to know the name and number of the forms.

If the form you need to use is outdated, or if you accidentally used your original form, new Judicial Council forms are available from the clerk of the Superior Court either free or for a small fee. Or you can visit a law library where there are several sources for obtaining Judicial Council forms to photocopy. (There is a list of these sources in Chapter 13, Section D4.)

2. Local Court Forms

Some courts have their own forms which must be used in addition to the forms in this book. Wherever possible, these forms are mentioned. Later on in the book, we discuss when and how to check with the court clerk to see if additional local court forms are required.

3. Forms to Fill the Gaps

In some instances, a form is desirable but the Judicial Council does not provide one. We have provided forms which are specially designed to fill this gap. These forms are designated "NP" in the lower left-hand corner.

Form Approved by the
Judicial Council of California
Revised Effective January 1, 1981
GC-020(81)

**NOTICE OF HEARING
GUARDIANSHIP OR CONSERVATORSHIP**

SAMPLE BOTTOM OF JUDICIAL COUNCIL FORM

---

[6]Some forms also have citations to California law. For instance, the Declaration Under Uniform Child Custody Jurisdiction Act has a citation in the lower right-hand corner which reads "Civil Code, §5158, Probate Code, §§1510(f), 1512," meaning that the form was designed according to those referenced statutes.

```
┌─────────────────────────────────────────────────────────────────┬──────────────────────┐
│ ATTORNEY OR PARTY WITHOUT ATTORNEY (Name and Address):  TELEPHONE NO.: │ FOR COURT USE ONLY   │
│   ALICE JANE SMITH                    (209)555-1212             │                      │
│   100 Any Street                                                │                      │
│   Fresno, CA 93717                                              │                      │
│ ATTORNEY FOR (Name):  In Pro Per                                │                      │
│ SUPERIOR COURT OF CALIFORNIA, COUNTY OF  FRESNO                 │                      │
│   STREET ADDRESS:  1100 Van Ness Avenue                         │                      │
│   MAILING ADDRESS: P.O. Box 1628                                │                      │
│   CITY AND ZIP CODE: Fresno, CA 93717                           │                      │
│   BRANCH NAME:                                                  │                      │
│ GUARDIANSHIP OF (NAME):                                         │                      │
│                                                                 │                      │
│      MARK DONALD JONES                                          │                      │
│                                                        MINOR    │                      │
├─────────────────────────────────────────────────────────────────┤ CASE NUMBER:         │
│ PETITION FOR APPOINTMENT OF GUARDIAN OF  [X] MINOR  [ ] MINORS  │    12345             │
│                           [X] Person  [ ] Estate                │                      │
└─────────────────────────────────────────────────────────────────┴──────────────────────┘
```

SAMPLE CAPTION

D. General Rules on Completing Forms

AS YOU FILL IN the guardianship forms, you'll find they follow a standardized, check-the-boxes, fill-in-the-blanks format. With just a little experience, you'll quickly get comfortable with it. Throughout the book, there is specific information about each item on every form. To help you become familiar with the general forms, here is an overview.

1. The Caption

Most forms have a heading of several boxes with blank spaces, which is referred to as a "caption." The caption is filled out the same way on almost every form. Here is how to do it.

Attorney or Party Without Attorney: You are a "Party Without Attorney." In capital letters, fill in your full first, middle and last names, followed by your telephone number and mailing address.

Attorney for (Name)—In Pro Per: Here the court is asking for the name of the person you are representing. Fill in the words "In Pro Per." This means that you are representing yourself in the proceeding.

Superior Court of California, County of _____: In capital letters, fill in the county in which you are filing the guardianship.

Court Address: Fill in the court's street address, mailing address, and city and zip code. Also fill in the branch name, if there is one. You will get all of this information from the court clerk.

Guardianship of (Name): In capital letters, fill in the full first, middle and last names of the minor or minors. Make sure that the names are complete and correctly spelled. Do not use nicknames.

Depending on the form, this part of the caption may vary a little bit. You will need to check any boxes that apply.

Minor: Check this box if the guardianship is for only one minor.

Minors: Check this box if the guardianship is for more than one minor. The minors must be full or half-sisters or brothers.

Person: Check this box if the guardianship is for the minor's person. (See Chapter 1, Sections D and E.)

Estate: Check this box if the guardianship is for the minor's estate. (See Chapter 1, Sections D and E.)

Case Number: When you file your first court papers, leave this space blank, since you don't have a case number yet. You will be assigned a case number which will be stamped or written in on the initial guardianship papers you file with the court. From that time on, always fill in that case number here. Copy this number carefully from your filed papers.

2. Declarations (Oaths)

In some of these forms you will need to sign what is called a Declaration Under Penalty of Perjury.

This declaration has the same effect as an oath or sworn statement, which means that you could be prosecuted under California law if you lie in it. The word "executed" means signed. To complete the declaration, fill in the date and the city and state (which should be in California)[7] where you signed the document. Then type or print your name and sign the declaration.

Appendix D has a blank Declaration form, if at any time you need to submit an additional Declaration either by itself or attached to another form.

3. Attachment (Additional) Pages

If you ever need more room to complete any item on any form, you can use a blank piece of typing paper, lined legal paper (this book contains a blank sheet in Appendix D), or a copy of the Additional Page Judicial Council form in Appendix D. If you use lined legal paper or the Additional Page Judicial Council form, make several blank copies of the form before you use it. Save the original form in case you need to add continuation pages later on. Samples of completed attachments for several items of the Petition for Appointment of Guardian of Minor are contained in Chapter 5, Section A.

To complete attachment pages, at the top of each page, in capital letters fill in the title of the guardianship with the full name of the minor and the case number, once it has been assigned.

Next, indicate what form and item you are continuing, call that continuation page an "ATTACHMENT," and indicate the item number on the form from which you continued. For example, a continuation sheet expanding on the information you supplied in paragraph 8 of the Petition for Appointment of Guardian of Minor would be called "ATTACHMENT 8 TO PETITION FOR APPOINTMENT OF GUARDIAN OF MINOR." Use a new attachment page for each new item number you continue.

At the bottom right-hand corner of the form, number the pages you're adding to the form. Show which page each one is out of the total, such as Page "1 of 1" or "2 of 4." Obviously, you will need to number these pages after you finish the document, when you know how many total pages you are attaching.

I declare under penalty of perjury under the laws of the State of California that the foregoing is true and correct.

Date:

....
(TYPE OR PRINT NAME)

▶ _____
(SIGNATURE OF DECLARANT)

SAMPLE DECLARATION

---

[7] If you sign a document outside of the state of California, you will either need to have it notarized, or sign a declaration which says that it is signed "under penalty of perjury under the laws of the state of California." Some, but not all, forms already use this language which is valid for declarations signed either inside or outside of California.

4. Special Local Rules on Filing Papers

Certain courts have special local rules that tell how papers must be filed. Some of these rules don't seem logical or even sensible, but if you use a court that has them, you have no choice but to comply.

a. Los Angeles County's Local Rules

You must follow special procedures for preparing and filing papers in Los Angeles County:
- All papers must be two-hole punched at the top of the page.
- Except for preprinted forms, all papers filed in the probate court must have "bluebacks." This is blue paper that identifies the people involved in the legal action, the court and the nature of the document being filed, and is stapled to the backs of the papers. Bluebacks can be obtained from most office supply stores.

E. How to File Papers with the Court

WHAT HAPPENS WHEN YOU TAKE or send your papers to the court might be a mystery to you, especially if you've never gone to court before. Fortunately, it's really quite simple. Each time you deliver a paper to the court, the court clerk will likely record and make it part of the official court record of your case.

1. How Many Copies Do You Need?

The court usually gets the original version of all your completed forms, and some courts, especially branch courts, require one additional copy—you'll need to call the court clerk and check. You should always take or send at least one extra copy of the form to the court to be file-stamped and returned to you for your records. Whether you mail or personally take papers to the court, make sure that you also keep one copy at home in case the papers are lost or misplaced. Depending on the document, you may also need to make more copies so that they can be served on a number of people or agencies. You can make all the copies of completed forms before you file them with the court, and have each copy file-stamped, or you can file your papers with the court and then make copies. It all depends on what's more convenient for you. When in doubt, make extra photocopies. You're better off having too many copies than not having enough.

2. Take or Mail Papers to the Court

You file a document with the court simply by mailing or handing the document across the counter at the court clerk's office. When you file a document, give the county clerk the original and photocopies. The clerk will keep the original, which goes in your guardianship case file, and may also keep one photocopy, depending on the county policy. The clerk will return to you any extra copies. In the upper right-hand corner, the copies will have rubber-stamped information showing the date and often the time that the original was filed, and indicating that the copy is a file-stamped copy. On the next page is a sample of a document that has been filed with the court.

```
ATTORNEY OR PARTY WITHOUT ATTORNEY (NAME AND ADDRESS):    TELEPHONE NO.:     FOR COURT USE ONLY
ALICE JANE SMITH                                          (209) 555-1212
100 Any Street                                                             FILED
Fresno, CA 93717
                                                                           MAY 20 1988
ATTORNEY FOR (NAME):  In Pro Per
SUPERIOR COURT OF CALIFORNIA, COUNTY OF FRESNO                             FRESNO COUNTY CLERK
1100 Van Ness Avenue                                                       By ..................................
P. O. Box 1628                                                                                    DEPUTY
Fresno, California 93717

[X] GUARDIANSHIP  [ ] CONSERVATORSHIP OF THE  [X] PERSON  [ ] ESTATE OF
   (NAME):   MARK DONALD JONES
                                              [X] Minor  [ ] Conservatee   CLK 4040.00 E01-82 R0-00

                      NOTICE OF HEARING                                    CASE NUMBER:
   [X] Guardianship  [ ] Conservatorship  [ ] Limited Conservatorship      12345
```

SAMPLE COURT-FILED DOCUMENT

You may choose to go to the court in person to file your papers, in case you've made a mistake or want more information from the clerk. But if going to the courthouse is inconvenient, you can mail your documents to the court. To do this, send your papers to the court along with a self-addressed, stamped envelope with the correct amount of postage. If you send your papers by mail, remember to keep an extra photocopy at home, in case your papers are lost in the mail. In a letter, ask the clerk to file the original documents and have extra copies stamped and sent back to you. On the next page is a sample letter.

a. Getting a Case Number

When you first file your papers with the court, the clerk assigns you a case number. This will either be written or stamped in the caption part of the form. Once the case number has been assigned, put that number on all court papers you later complete. The case number is the court's system of keeping track of cases, and it will be printed on a file folder in which all your court guardianship papers are kept. If you ever need to get information about your case over the telephone, you usually must tell the clerk your case number so that she can locate your file.

3. Some Papers Are Not Returned Right Away

Some forms you prepare will not be file-stamped and returned to you right away. In this book, these papers are flagged by the word "(proposed)," indicating that you won't get them back from the court until a judge has reviewed and approved their contents. These are:

a. (Proposed) Orders

An order is signed permission by a judge allowing you to do something. For example, after you prepare your proposed Order Appointing Guardian of Minor, it must be signed by a judge to go into effect. Until the judge signs the order, you are not allowed to serve as the minor's legal guardian. In general, after preparing a proposed order, you take or send the original and copies to court. File-stamped copies are returned to you only after the judge signs the original order (which goes into the court's file). In the instructions we give for guardianship cases, orders are signed only after a court appearance.

SAMPLE

June 14, 1990

County Clerk
Superior Court of California
Probate Department
County of San Diego
P.O. Box 128
San Diego, CA 92112-4104

Re: Guardianship of: Kee Wong
    Case No. (Not Assigned Yet)

Dear Clerk:

Enclosed please find:

1) Original and 5 copies of:

   PETITION FOR APPOINTMENT OF GUARDIAN OF MINOR;
   CONSENT OF GUARDIAN, NOMINATION AND WAIVER OF NOTICE; and
   NOTICE OF HEARING (GUARDIANSHIP).

2) Check in the amount of $108.00; and

3) Self-addressed, stamped envelope.

Please return copies to me after you file them. Also please provide me with a guardianship hearing date at least six weeks away from the date of this letter.

Sincerely,

David Wong
1 Main Street
San Diego, CA 92101
Phone: (619) 555-1212

b. (Proposed) Letters of Guardianship

The document notifying the world that you are authorized to act as guardian is called Letters of Guardianship. If you are appointed guardian for a limited time, you will obtain Letters of Temporary Guardianship. This form has a seal on it, meaning it was "issued" by the court. Letters can only be obtained after a judge signs an order appointing you guardian or temporary guardian.

4. Amending Filed Documents

If, after you file the papers for the guardianship, but before you are appointed guardian, you find a serious error or want to change some wording on the documents, you can file an "amended" document to take the place of the incorrect document. Use the same title as the original document, but print or type the word "AMENDED" before the name of the form. If you are using a pre-printed form, print or type the word "AMENDED" both before the form's printed name in the caption and on the bottom of the page. Then complete and file the original and copies of the amended form with the court, and have copies served on all of the people or agencies who were served with notice of the guardianship. You might need to amend a document if:

- The facts or situation stated change substantially after you file the document with the court.
- You discover a serious error on the document after it is filed.
- After filing a Petition for Appointment of Guardian of Minor, you become aware of any proceedings which affect the minor and weren't included in the initial petition. You *must* amend the petition within 10 days of the time you find out about them. This includes adoptions, juvenile court matters, marriage dissolution, custody, or other similar proceedings affecting the minor (PC §1512). This is discussed in more detail in Chapter 6, Section B6.

5. Stopping the Court Procedure

What happens if you have filed your initial guardianship documents, and you change your mind about becoming a guardian, or the situation changes so that a guardianship is no longer needed? As long as you have not yet been appointed guardian, you can stop the process simply by filing a document called a Request for Dismissal with the court clerk.[8] Here is how to do it.

a. Prepare and File a Request for Dismissal

Use the Request for Dismissal form in Appendix D. Make at least one copy of the form, in case you make a mistake or later need to change or amend it.

---

[8] This procedure covers guardianships which have not yet been granted. If you have already been named guardian of a minor, you must get the court's permission to resign as guardian or end the guardianship altogether. (See Chapter 12.) If you don't wish to stop the process, but simply need more time before the hearing on the guardianship petition, you may be able to obtain a new hearing date. (See Chapter 6, Section B5.)

CAPTION: REQUEST FOR DISMISSAL

This caption is slightly different from the usual caption, but it asks for the same basic information. In the first box fill in your name, address, telephone number and the words "In Pro Per," following the general instructions in Section D1 of this chapter.

Just below, in the first blank before the words "COURT OF CALIFORNIA," insert the word "SUPERIOR." After the words "COUNTY OF" insert the county in which your guardianship proceeding is taking place. If your case is in a certain branch of the court, fill in the name of that branch.

After the words "GUARDIANSHIP OF," in capital letters fill in the full first, middle and last names of the minors.

Fill in the case number at the far right. It's easy to miss this. Underneath the case number, where it says "REQUEST FOR DISMISSAL, TYPE OF ACTION" check the last box entitled "Other (Specify)." Then fill in the words "Guardianship of the "person," "estate," or "person and estate"—whichever applies.

Item 1: Check the second box entitled "Without prejudice." This means that if you change your mind, you can re-file another guardianship action.[9]

Item 2: Check the first box entitled "Entire action."

Skip down to the first place where it says "Dated," and fill in the date. After "Attorney(s) for," fill in the words "Petitioner In Pro Per." Type or print your name on the line provided. Finally, sign the form in the space at the right.

You have now completed the Request for Dismissal. You do not need to fill out the rest of the form.

Make at least two copies of the completed document, and take or send the original and one copy to the clerk, using the instructions given earlier in Section E.

Note: If you have already obtained a hearing date for the guardianship, call the court and have the hearing date canceled as soon as possible before it is scheduled to take place. In legal slang, this is called being "taken off calendar." You will probably also need to send a confirming letter to the court stating that you wish to cancel the hearing date.

---

[9] If you decide to re-file, you will need to start all over again by preparing new documents, paying a new filing fee and getting a new case number.

Name, Address and Telephone Number of Attorney(s)

DANIEL ERIC HONG (209) 555-1212
120 Any Street
Madera, CA 93637

Attorney(s) for: In Pro Per

Space Below for Use of Court Clerk Only

SUPERIOR COURT OF CALIFORNIA, COUNTY OF MADERA
(SUPERIOR, MUNICIPAL, or JUSTICE)

(Name of Municipal or Justice Court District or of branch court, if any)

GUARDIANSHIP OF (Name):

JOYCE AMELIA HONG
                              Minor
(Abbreviated Title)

CASE NUMBER 123

REQUEST FOR DISMISSAL
TYPE OF ACTION

☐ Personal Injury Property Damage and Wrongful Death:
  ☐ Motor Vehicle   ☐ Other
☐ Domestic Relations   ☐ Eminent Domain
☒ Other: (Specify) Guardianship of the person

TO THE CLERK: Please dismiss this action as follows: (Check applicable boxes.)
1. ☐ With prejudice   ☒ Without prejudice
2. ☒ Entire action   ☐ Complaint only   ☐ Petition only   ☐ Cross-complaint only
   ☐ Other: (Specify)*

Dated: March 30, 1991

*If dismissal requested is of specified parties only, of specified causes of action only or of specified cross-complaints only, so state and identify the parties, causes of action or cross-complaints to be dismissed.

(signature) Daniel Eric Hong

Attorney(s) for: Petitioner In Pro Per

DANIEL ERIC HONG
(Type or print attorney(s) name(s))

TO THE CLERK: Consent to the above dismissal is hereby given.**

Dated: ....

**When a cross-complaint (or Response (Marriage) seeking affirmative relief) is on file, the attorney(s) for the cross-complainant (respondent) must sign this consent when required by CCP 581(1), (2) or (5).

Attorney(s) for: ....

(Type or print attorney(s) name(s))

(To be completed by clerk)
☐ Dismissal entered as requested on ....
☐ Dismissal entered on .... as to only ....
☐ Dismissal not entered as requested for the following reason(s), and attorney(s) notified on ....

_____, Clerk

Dated: .... By _____, Deputy

Form Adopted by Rule 982 of
The Judicial Council of California
Revised Effective July 1, 1972

REQUEST FOR DISMISSAL

CCP 581, etc.;
Cal. Rules of Court,
Rule 1233

F. Filing Fees and Court Costs

WHEN YOU FIRST FILE your guardianship documents, you will be required to pay a filing fee. The filing fees for guardianships generally run in the neighborhood of $75 to over $130, depending on the county. In addition, if your county requires an investigation, those costs run approximately $100 to $175. A routine investigation is almost always required for non-relatives petitioning to be guardians of a minor's person, and it may be required for relatives of the minor as well, depending on the individual court's policy. (There is more information about investigations in Chapter 8.)

1. Waiving Court Fees and Costs

If you have a very low income, the court may order that you do not have to pay court fees and costs. You don't have to be absolutely destitute, but you really must be unable to pay.[10] To have your fees waived, you need to fill out two forms which give information about your income and expenses. If you are currently receiving public assistance such as AFDC, Food Stamps, County Relief, General Relief, General Assistance, SSI or SSP, you should have no problem qualifying for the fee waiver. You should also qualify for a waiver of court fees and costs if your gross monthly income (your monthly income before taxes or deductions are taken out) is equal to or less than the amounts shown in this chart:[11]

QUALIFYING INCOME FOR WAIVER OF COURT FEES AND COSTS

Number in Family	Monthly Family Income
1	$709.38
2	$957.30
3	$1,205.21
4	$1,453.13
5	$1,701.05
6	$1,948.96
7	$2,196.88
8	$2,444.80
Each additional	$247.92

If you aren't receiving public assistance, you must provide some income information to the court before it will waive court fees and costs. If you get more monthly income than indicated in the chart but can't afford to pay court fees and costs, you will also have to include information about your monthly expenses. A judge will then review your financial situation and decide whether all or part of the expenses will be waived.

If you qualify to have court fees and costs waived, and your financial situation later changes, you must immediately notify the court if you become able to pay them. By law, the court could order you to appear anytime within three years after you file for a fee waiver to answer questions about your ability to pay.

It's easy to apply for a waiver of court fees and costs. You complete two forms:

- Application for Waiver of Court Fees and Costs; and
- Order on Application for Waiver of Court Fees and Costs.

---

[10]If you are petitioning for guardianship of a minor's estate, and have a very low income, you can still apply for a waiver of court fees and costs. Once you are appointed guardian of the minor's estate, you will need to reimburse the court using money from the estate.

[11]These figures were taken from the Judicial Council form entitled "Information Sheet on Waiver of Court Fees and Costs," revised May 22, 1987. The figures were current as of 2/89. Check with the clerk to make sure the form—and the amounts listed—are up to date.

You will make copies of these forms, and file them along with the rest of your guardianship papers. Here are instructions on how to complete the fee waiver forms.

a. Application for Waiver of Court Fees and Costs Form

In this form, you tell why you cannot pay court expenses, and request that they be waived.

> **CAPTION:** APPLICATION FOR WAIVER OF COURT FEES AND COSTS FORM
>
> Fill in the caption following the general instructions in Section D1 of this chapter.
>
> Leave the Case Number blank for now, since it hasn't been assigned yet.

Item 1: Fill in your address and the date you were born.

Item 2: If you are receiving public assistance, check the first box. Then check all of the boxes that tell which kind of public assistance you are receiving.

Item 2a: Check this box if you are receiving SSI or SSP.

Item 2b: Check this box if you are receiving AFDC.

Item 2c: Check this box if you are receiving Food Stamps.

Item 2d: Check this box if you are receiving County Relief, General Relief, or General Assistance.

Important: If you checked Item 2, do not fill out the rest of the form. Simply fill in the date at the bottom of the front page, print or type in your name in the lower left-hand corner, and sign the form on the signature line in the lower right-hand corner.

If you did not check Item 2, you must complete the rest of the form.

Item 3: Check this box if your gross monthly income (the amount you receive before any taxes or deductions are taken out) is less than the amount shown in the chart entitled "Qualifying Income for Waiver of Court Fees and Costs" above.

Important: If you checked Item 3, skip Item 4, and complete only Items 5 and 6 on the back of the form.

Item 4: Skip this Item if you checked Item 3. If you didn't check Item 3, and you believe that you don't make enough money to support yourself and your family, check this box. Remember that you genuinely must be unable—rather than unwilling—to pay court fees and costs. If you checked Item 4, you will need to complete the entire back side of the form.

> **CAPTION:** PAGE TWO OF THE APPLICATION FOR WAIVER OF COURT FEES AND COSTS
>
> After the words "GUARDIANSHIP OF (NAME)," in capital letters fill in the full first, middle and last names of the minor.
>
> Leave the Case Number blank for now, since the number hasn't been assigned yet.

Item 5: Check this box if the amount of your earnings changes a great deal each month, such as if you are self-employed and make a fair amount of money one month but little another month.

Item 6: In this Item you provide information about your monthly income. If you checked Item 5, you will need to use averages for each of the figures required. For example, to get a monthly average of your income for the last year, add up your total earnings for the last 12 months and divide that amount by 12.

Item 6a: Fill in the amount of your gross monthly pay. This is the income you receive each month before any taxes or deductions are taken out.

Items 6b(1)-(4): Fill in the type and amount of each of your payroll deductions in the spaces provided. Then add together all of the amounts you filled in for Items 6b(1)-(4) and fill in the total payroll deduction amount.

Item 6c: Subtract the total payroll deductions amount from your gross monthly pay: Item 6a minus the total of Items 6b(1)-(4). Fill in this amount.

— **THIS FORM MUST BE KEPT CONFIDENTIAL** —

ATTORNEY OR PARTY WITHOUT ATTORNEY (Name and Address):	TELEPHONE NO.:	FOR COURT USE ONLY
MARCIA JUDITH JONES 2001 City Street Oakland, CA 94612	(415)555-1212	
ATTORNEY FOR (Name): In Pro Per		
NAME OF COURT: Alameda Superior Court STREET ADDRESS: 1225 Fallon, Room 105 MAILING ADDRESS: CITY AND ZIP CODE: Oakland, CA 94612 BRANCH NAME: Northern Division		
GUARDIANSHIP OF (Name): MARK ANDREW JONES Minor		
APPLICATION FOR WAIVER OF COURT FEES AND COSTS	CASE NUMBER:	

I request a court order so that I do not have to pay court fees and costs.

1. My address and date of birth are (specify):

   2001 City Street
   Oakland, CA 94612

   Date of Birth: 12/31/52

2. [X] I am receiving financial assistance under one or more of the following programs:
   a. [ ] SSI and SSP: The Supplemental Security Income and State Supplemental Payments Programs
   b. [X] AFDC: The Aid to Families with Dependent Children Program
   c. [X] Food Stamps: The Food Stamps Program
   d. [ ] County Relief, General Relief (G.R.) or General Assistance (G.A.)

[If you checked box 2 above, sign at the bottom of this side and DO NOT fill out the rest of the form.]

3. [ ] My gross monthly income is less than the amount shown on the Information Sheet on Waiver of Court Fees and Costs available from the clerk's office.

[If you checked box 3 above, skip 4, complete 5 and 6 on the back of this form, and sign at the bottom of this side.]

4. [ ] My income is not enough to pay for the common necessaries of life for me and the people in my family I support and also pay court fees and costs. *[If you checked this box you must complete the back of this form.]*

> **WARNING:** You must immediately tell the court if you become able to pay court fees or costs during this action. For the next three (3) years you may be ordered to appear in court and answer questions about your ability to pay court fees or costs.

I declare under penalty of perjury under the laws of the State of California that the foregoing is true and correct.

Date: 6/12/92

MARCIA JUDITH JONES   *Marcia Judith Jones*
. . . .
           (TYPE OR PRINT NAME)   (SIGNATURE)

Form Adopted by the
Judicial Council of California
982(a)(17) (Rev. January 1, 1985)

APPLICATION FOR WAIVER OF COURT FEES AND COSTS
(In Forma Pauperis)

Gov. Code.
§ 68511.3

GUARDIANSHIP OF (Name):	CASE NUMBER:
MARK ANDREW JONES Minor	

FINANCIAL INFORMATION

5. ☐ My pay changes considerably from month to month. *[If you check this box, each of the amounts reported in 6 should be your average for the past 12 months.]*

6. My monthly income:
   a. My gross monthly pay is: .... $_____
   b. My payroll deductions are *(specify purpose and amount)*:
      (1) _____ $ _____
      (2) _____ $ _____
      (3) _____ $ _____
      (4) _____ $ _____
      My TOTAL payroll deduction amount is: $_____
   c. My monthly take-home pay is
      (a. minus b.): .... $_____
   d. Other money I get each month is *(specify source and amount)*:
      (1) _____ $ _____
      (2) _____ $ _____
      The TOTAL amount of other money is: $_____
   e. **MY TOTAL MONTHLY INCOME IS**
      (c. plus d.): .... $_____
   f. The number of people in my family, including me, supported by this money is: _____

7. a. ☐ I am *not* able to pay any of the court fees and costs.
   b. ☐ I am able to pay *only* the following court fees and costs *(specify)*:

8. My monthly expenses are:
   a. Rent or house payment & maintenance $_____
   b. Food and household supplies ...... $_____
   c. Utilities and telephone .... $_____
   d. Clothing .... $_____
   e. Laundry and cleaning .... $_____
   f. Medical and dental payments ...... $_____
   g. Insurance (life, health, accident, etc.) $_____
   h. School, child care .... $_____
   i. Child, spousal support (prior marriage) $_____
   j. Transportation and auto expenses
      (insurance, gas, repair) .... $_____
   k. Installment payments *(specify purpose and amount)*:
      (1) _____ $ _____
      (2) _____ $ _____
      (3) _____ $ _____
      The TOTAL amount of monthly
      installment payments is: .... $_____
   l. Amounts deducted due to wage assignments and earnings withholding orders $_____
   m. Other expenses *(specify)*
      (1) _____ $ _____
      (2) _____ $ _____
      (3) _____ $ _____
      (4) _____ $ _____
      (5) _____ $ _____
      (6) _____ $ _____
      The TOTAL amount of other monthly
      expenses is: .... $_____
   n. **MY TOTAL MONTHLY EXPENSES ARE**
      (add a. through m.): .... $_____

9. I own the following property:
   a. Cash .... $_____
   b. Checking, savings and credit union accounts *(list banks)*:
      (1) _____ $ _____
      (2) _____ $ _____
      (3) _____ $ _____
   c. Cars, other vehicles and boat equity *(list make, year of each)*:
      (1) _____ $ _____
      (2) _____ $ _____
      (3) _____ $ _____
   d. Real estate equity .... $_____
   e. Other personal property — jewelry, furniture, furs, stocks, bonds, etc. *(list separately)*:

   $_____

10. Other facts which support this application are *(describe unusual medical needs, expenses for recent family emergencies, or other unusual expenses to help the judge understand your budget)*. If more space is needed, attach page labeled attachment 10.

WARNING: You must immediately tell the court if you become able to pay court fees or costs during this action. For the next three (3) years you may be ordered to appear in court and answer questions about your ability to pay court fees or costs.

982(a)(17) [Rev. January 1, 1985]   **APPLICATION FOR WAIVER OF COURT FEES AND COSTS**   Page two
(In Forma Pauperis)

Item 6d: Fill in any other amounts of money you get each month, and tell where you get them from (Items 6d(1)-(2)). Then fill in the total amount of additional money you receive each month by adding together the amounts you filled in for Items 6d(1)-(2).

Item 6e: Add together Items 6c and 6d and enter this amount.

Item 6f: Fill in the total number of people in your family you are supporting with the amount of money you have listed in Item 6e. Remember to count yourself as one of them.

Items 7-10: Skip all of these Items (Items 7-10) unless you checked Item 4 on the front of this form.

Item 7: Only check one of the two boxes listed in this item.

Item 7a: Check this box if you believe that you can't pay any of the court fees and costs for the guardianship case. Remember that you must be unable to pay, rather than unwilling to pay.

Item 7b: Check this box if you believe that you can only pay part of the court fees and costs for the guardianship case. Then fill in the amounts that you believe you can pay for court fees and costs.

Items 8a-m: In these Items you tell how much you pay each month in living expenses. Make sure you list all of your expenses.

Item 8n: Fill in the total of all your monthly expenses by adding together all of the amounts you filled in for Items 8a-8m and entering this amount.

Items 9a-e: Fill in the value of any property you own, including money, vehicles, real estate and personal property.

Item 10: Fill in this item if there is any reason why you can't pay court fees and costs. This might include unusual medical expenses, money spent for recent family emergencies, or other unusual expenses. You will need to attach an additional page to the Application for Waiver of Court Fees and Costs to provide this information. Follow the instructions for preparing attachment pages in Section D3 in this chapter, and label the page "Attachment 10 to Application for Waiver of Court Fees and Costs." Then, in your own words, explain why you cannot pay the court fees and costs.

Important: If you have not already dated and signed the form on the first page, make sure you do this now.

b. Order on Application for Waiver of Court Fees and Costs Form

When a judge signs this form, you are given permission for your court fees and costs to be waived.

CAPTION: ORDER ON APPLICATION FOR WAIVER OF COURT FEES AND COSTS FORM

Fill in the caption following the general instructions in Section D1 of this chapter.

Leave the Case Number blank for now, since it hasn't been assigned yet.

After you complete the caption, leave the rest of the front side of the form blank. The court clerk and judge will complete it.

CAPTION: PAGE TWO OF THE ORDER ON APPLICATION FOR WAIVER OF COURT FEES AND COSTS

After the words "GUARDIANSHIP OF (NAME)," in capital letters fill in the full first, middle and last names of the minor.

Leave the Case Number blank for now, since it hasn't been assigned yet.

In the blank area after the clerk's certificate of mailing declaration, fill in your full name and complete mailing address. You have now completed your part of the Order on Application for Waiver of Court Fees and Costs. The clerk will fill out the rest of this form.

Put these two completed forms in a safe, convenient place. When you come to Chapter 6, Section B2a, you will find specific instructions on applying for a fee waiver. For now, you are ready to turn to Chapter 4.

ATTORNEY OR PARTY WITHOUT ATTORNEY (Name and Address)	TELEPHONE NO.	FOR COURT USE ONLY
MARCIA JUDITH JONES 2001 City Street Oakland, CA 94612	(415)555-1212	
ATTORNEY FOR (Name): In Pro Per		
NAME OF COURT, JUDICIAL DISTRICT OR BRANCH COURT, IF ANY: Superior Court of California, County of Alameda Northern Division		
GUARDIANSHIP OF (Name): MARK ANDREW JONES Minor		

ORDER ON APPLICATION FOR WAIVER OF COURT FEES AND COSTS	CASE NUMBER:

1. The application was filed
   a. on (date):
   b. by (name):
2. ☐ **IT IS ORDERED THAT the application is granted and the applicant is permitted to proceed in this action as follows:**
   a. ☐ without payment of any court fees or costs listed in rule 985(i), California Rules of Court.
   b. ☐ without payment of any court fees or costs listed in rule 985(i), California Rules of Court, except the following:
   c. ☐ without payment of the following court fees or costs (specify):

   d. The reasons for denial of any requested waiver are (specify):

   e. ☐ The clerk of the court is directed to mail a copy of this order to the applicant's attorney, if any, or to the applicant if unrepresented.
   f. ☐ All unpaid fees and costs shall be deemed to be taxable costs if applicant is entitled to costs and shall be a lien on any judgment recovered by the applicant and shall be paid to the clerk upon such recovery.
3. ☐ **IT IS ORDERED THAT the application is denied for the following reasons** (specify):

   a. The applicant must pay any fees and costs due in this action within ten days from the date of service of this order or any paper filed by the applicant with the clerk will be of no effect.
   b. The clerk of the court is directed to mail a copy of this order to all parties who have appeared in this action.
4. ☐ **IT IS ORDERED THAT a hearing be held.**
   a. The substantial evidentiary conflict to be resolved by the hearing is (specify):

   b. Applicant should be present at the hearing to be held:

hearing date:	time:	in ☐ Dept.:	☐ Div.:	☐ Rm.:
address of court:				

   c. The clerk of the court is directed to mail a copy of this order to the applicant only.

Dated: _____   _____
(Clerk's certification on page 2)   (Signature of Judge)

Form Adopted by Rule 982
Judicial Council of California
Revised effective July 1, 1981

ORDER ON APPLICATION FOR WAIVER OF COURT FEES AND COSTS (IN FORMA PAUPERIS)

Govt. Code § 68511.3

GUARDIANSHIP OF (Name):	CASE NUMBER:
MARK ANDREW JONES Minor	

ORDER ON APPLICATION FOR WAIVER OF COURT FEES AND COSTS   Page 2

CLERK'S CERTIFICATE OF MAILING

I certify that I am not a party to this cause and that a copy of the foregoing was mailed first class, postage prepaid, in a sealed envelope addressed as shown below, and that the mailing of the foregoing and execution of this certificate occurred at (place): . . . . , California,

on (date): . . . . Clerk, by _____
                                                                                                            (Deputy)

CLERK'S CERTIFICATION

(SEAL)

I certify that the foregoing is a true copy of the original on file in my office.

Dated: . . . . Clerk, by. . . . .
                                                                                                               (Deputy)

MARCIA JUDITH JONES
2001 City Street
Oakland, CA 94612

CHAPTER 4

NOTIFYING MINOR'S RELATIVES AND OBTAINING THEIR CONSENTS

A.	Overview of How to Notify Relatives	4/2
B.	Guardianship Notification Worksheet	4/2
C.	Try to Find Minor's Unknown or Missing Relatives	4/3
D.	After You've Searched for Missing Relatives	4/8
E.	Consent of Proposed Guardian, Nomination and Waiver of Notice Form	4/12
F.	Discussing the Guardianship with the Minor's Relatives	4/15
G.	Obtain Signatures from Relatives on the Nomination and Waiver of Notice Forms	4/16
H.	Continue Filling in the Worksheet	4/17

ALTHOUGH MOST GUARDIANSHIPS are not contested, certain relatives of the minor are entitled by law to know in advance about the guardianship proceeding.[1] Frequently, notification is a formality, because everyone agrees with the guardianship. Formality or not, all those entitled to notice must be given or mailed copies of guardianship documents at least 20 days before the hearing date,[2] unless they sign a document stating that they waive notification. They have a legal right to contest the guardianship in court.

Notifying the required people about the proceeding is one of the most important factors in obtaining a guardianship. It is essential that you read this chapter very carefully and follow the instructions. We cover notification procedures here—before you complete and file the guardianship papers with the court—because, depending on who you have to notify and how hard this may be, the process of obtaining a guardianship will vary. In short, figuring out who to notify and how to notify them will affect what comes later.

By law, close relatives of the minor must be notified about the guardianship proceeding, unless they waive this right. Documents must be given or mailed by a certain procedure called "service of process." (This is covered in detail in Chapter 6.) The minor's parents, the minor—if she is over 12, and anyone who is either the minor's legal guardian or has been nominated as legal guardian must personally be given copies of the guardianship documents. The minor's grandparents, sisters and brothers, spouse, and any adult with whom the minor is living can be sent copies of the guardianship documents by regular U.S. mail.[3]

If any of the relatives entitled to notice are deceased, you will simply list them on a form and indicate that they are deceased. But maybe you don't know or can't locate some of the relatives. For example, maybe the minor's father is not known by name,

---

[1] When we refer to notifying relatives in the rest of this chapter, it also includes anyone who is the minor's legal guardian, has been nominated legal guardian, or has physical custody of the minor (other than you). When more than one adult wants to be guardian, the guardianship probably will be contested. If this is your situation, you should consult a lawyer. (See Chapter 13.)

[2] You will get a hearing date when you file your initial guardianship papers with the court. The hearing date usually is about 45 days after you file your papers. If you need a guardianship sooner, you may file for a temporary guardianship as well. (See Chapter 7.)

[3] You will probably need to have several agencies served in addition to the minor's relatives who are entitled to notice. There are instructions for how to do this later on in the book.

he's not listed on the minor's birth certificate, and you don't know how to find out who or where he is. If you don't know the whereabouts of all those who must be notified, you must go through a special procedure to attempt to locate them. This chapter will give you instructions on how to search for relatives.

A. Overview of How to Notify Relatives

IN THE REST OF THIS CHAPTER, you will find out how to notify the minor's relatives and possibly get their written consents to the guardianship, which means that you won't need to have them served with guardianship papers. If you haven't discussed the guardianship with the minor's relatives yet, that's fine for now. Here is an overview of the steps you will be taking throughout this chapter:

Step 1: In Section B, you will begin to complete the Guardianship Notification Worksheet form. You'll list the names and addresses of relatives who are entitled to notice of the guardianship, and designate whether you need to locate them.

Step 2: If you don't know the names or whereabouts of some relatives, you will try to locate them, using the methods described in Section C. If you know the names and addresses of all relatives, skip Section C.

Step 3: If you can't locate all of the relatives, you will complete a Due Diligence Declaration that states your attempts and what happened, following the instructions in Section D.

Step 4: You will complete the Consent of Proposed Guardian, Nomination and Waiver of Notice form following the instructions in Section E.

Step 5: Read Section F, which discusses bringing up the subject of the possible guardianship with relatives who don't know about it yet and the minor's parents.

Step 6: Obtain signatures of the minor's parents, if they are willing, on both the Nomination of Guardian and the Waiver of Notice and Consent forms.

Step 7: Contact those relatives you think will be willing to sign the Waiver of Notice and Consent form, which states that they know about the guardianship, agree to it and don't need to receive any legal documentation about it. Obtain signatures of relatives who agree to sign the form.

Step 8: Continue filling in the Guardianship Notification Worksheet as instructed in Section H. You are then ready to go on to Chapter 5, where you will find out how to complete the rest of the required forms needed to petition for a guardianship.

B. Guardianship Notification Worksheet

IN APPENDIX D AT THE BACK of this book, you'll find a Guardianship Notification Worksheet. Before you get started, make at least one photocopy of the worksheet. The Guardianship Notification Worksheet is used throughout this book to determine who is required to know about the guardianship, and how best to handle the notification. As you go through this chapter, it may be helpful to look at the completed sample of the worksheet provided here.

You're ready to start filling in the Guardianship Notification Worksheet. But first, understand that you'll be completing more of the worksheet as you go through the chapter. Don't worry about being able to completely fill in or even understand it all at once. By the end of this chapter, you'll have completed most of the worksheet.

1. Begin Filling in the Worksheet

To start with, complete Items 1 and 2 in Part 1 of the Guardianship Notification Worksheet.

Item 1: In the blanks in the first column, fill in the names and addresses of each of the minor's relatives and legal guardians or nominees (other than you). If relatives are unknown or deceased, fill in their names followed by the word "unknown" or "deceased." Here are the people you will list:

- **Minor:** The person for whom you are seeking the guardianship.
- **Minor's mother:** The minor's natural mother (related by blood).[4]
- **Minor's father:** The minor's natural father (related by blood).
- **Minor's maternal grandparents:** The parents of the minor's mother.
- **Minor's paternal grandparents:** The parents of the minor's father.
- **Minor's spouse:** This only applies if you are seeking guardianship of a minor's estate. You cannot seek guardianship of a minor's person if she has married, unless that marriage was annulled.
- **Minor's sisters and brothers:** The brothers and sisters of the minor who have the same two parents as the minor. In addition, if the minor has any half-sisters and half-brothers, include them. If any of the minor's half-sisters or half-brothers are under age 18, also fill in the name and address of the different parent if they're not listed elsewhere on the worksheet. You do not need to list step-sisters or step-brothers who are children by a prior marriage but not blood relatives.
- **Minor's children:** If the minor has any children, list their names and addresses. Also find out and fill in the name and address of the other parent of the minor's children, if it's not listed elsewhere on the worksheet.
- **Anyone presently having legal custody of minor:** It's unlikely, but possible, that the minor already has a legal guardian, or someone other than the minor's parents have legal custody. If so, list his name and address. Remember that this does not include you.
- **Anyone nominated as minor's legal guardian:** It's unlikely, but possible, that someone other than you has also been nominated legal guardian of the minor. If so, list her name and address. Remember that this does not include you.
- **Anyone having physical custody of the minor:** If the minor is living with someone other than you, and that person is not listed elsewhere on this worksheet, list her name and address here.

Item 2: Indicate whether each of the relatives listed must be located. If you know the name and address of a relative, or if a relative is deceased, fill in the word "No," meaning that you don't need to locate her. If you don't know the relative's name or address, fill in the word "Yes," meaning that you'll need to locate her.

For now, leave the rest of the form blank. You'll be using this worksheet several times later on in this book, so keep it in a convenient place.

C. Try to Find Minor's Unknown or Missing Relatives

IF YOU HAVE THE NAMES and addresses of all living relatives listed on the Guardianship Notification Worksheet, you may skip this section. But you may be in the unlucky position of not knowing the names or addresses of all of the minor's relatives who are entitled to notice of the guardianship proceeding. Unfortunately, this means you will need to put in some time and effort trying to track down these relatives.[5]

---

[4] If the minor was adopted, you'll probably need to see a lawyer. (See Chapter 13.)

[5] If you don't need a guardianship immediately (within two months of the time you complete a search for any missing relatives), follow the steps set out in this section. However, if you need a guardianship right away, you may be able to get a temporary guardianship quickly, before your search is complete. (See Chapter 7 for instructions.)

GUARDIANSHIP NOTIFICATION WORKSHEET
PART I. RELATIVES

(1) NAMES AND ADDRESSES OF MINOR'S RELATIVES AND OTHER PEOPLE ENTITLED TO NOTICE	(2) NEED TO LOCATE?	(3) DATE LOCATED	(4) WILL SIGN WAIVER OF NOTICE & CONSENT?	(5) NEED TO HAVE SERVED?	(6) SERVICE TYPE, IF NEED TO HAVE SERVED	(7) DATE SERVED OR ORDER DISPENSING NOTICE	(8) DATE FILED PROOF OF SERVICE
Minor MOLLY DENISE SCHWARTZ 60 W. West Street Oakland, CA 94612	No	—	Cannot sign since under 18	Only if 12 or over, or if minor has a child No	Personal (Chapter 6, Section F)		
Minor's mother ANGELA NATALIE SCHWARTZ 100 N. North Street Byron, CA 94514	No	—	Yes	No	Personal or Notice and Acknowledgment of Receipt (Chapter 6, Section F)		
Minor's father JERRY SCHWARTZ	Yes				Personal or Notice and Acknowledgment of Receipt (Chapter 6, Section F)		
Minor's maternal grandparents (mother's parents) BETTY BROWER NATE BROWER 9 Bright Street Boston, MA 02131	No No	— —	No No	Yes Yes	Mail (Chapter 6, Section G)		
Minor's paternal grandparents (father's parents) PENNY SCHWARTZ, Deceased BRIAN SCHWARTZ	— Yes		— —	— —	Mail (Chapter 6, Section G)		
Minor's spouse—can only petition for guardianship of the estate	—	—	Can sign only if 18 or over	—	Mail, and also serve parents, if under 18 (Chapter 6, Section G)		

GUARDIANSHIP NOTIFICATION WORKSHEET
PART I. RELATIVES (continued)

(1) NAMES AND ADDRESSES OF MINOR'S RELATIVES AND OTHER PEOPLE ENTITLED TO NOTICE	(2) NEED TO LOCATE?	(3) DATE LOCATED	(4) WILL SIGN WAIVER OF NOTICE & CONSENT?	(5) NEED TO HAVE SERVED?	(6) SERVICE TYPE, IF NEED TO HAVE SERVED	(7) DATE SERVED OR ORDER DISPENSING NOTICE	(8) DATE FILED PROOF OF SERVICE
Minor's sisters and brothers (include their ages; if parents not listed elsewhere on worksheet, list their names and addresses)			Can sign only if 18 or over	Only if over 12 (and serve parents if under 18)	Mail, if over 12. Serve parents, if under 18 (Chapter 6, Section G)		
DANA SCHWARTZ (Age 20) 1 E. East Ave. New York, NY 10003	No	—	YES	No			
MICK SCHWARTZ (Age 4) 100 N. North St. Byron, CA 94514	No	—	No	No (serving parents)			
Minor's children (if child's other parent not listed elsewhere on worksheet, list name and address) —	—	—	Cannot sign since under 18	—	Not required, but must serve both of child's parents		
Anyone presently having legal custody of minor (not including you) —	—	—	—	—	Personal or Notice and Acknowledgment of Receipt (Chapter 6, Section F)		
Anyone nominated minor's legal guardian (not including you) —	—	—	—	—	Personal or Notice and Acknowledgment of Receipt (Chapter 6, Section F)		
Anyone who has physical custody of minor (not including you) —	—	—	—	—	Mail (Chapter 6, Section G)		

There is no legal requirement that you notify a person who simply can't be located. You must, however, try with "due diligence" to locate the relative. This means that you must do your very best to find and give that person notice. If, after doing everything reasonably within your power, you still can't locate the relative, Chapter 5 gives you instructions on seeking an order from a judge allowing for that relative not to be served. The judge has the right to decide what is reasonable, however, and may require that you try harder than you already have. There are no hard and fast rules about what an individual judge will require, but in general, courts tend to be very reluctant to dispense with notice to the parents of a minor, and are somewhat more lenient in dispensing with notice to other relatives.

Example 1: You know that the minor's father went to Alaska several years ago, but you don't know where he lives and you don't want to go to the library to look in the telephone book for all fairly populous cities in Alaska to try to locate him. This would not be considered adequate reason not to give notice. However, if you had checked all of the phone books and other resources reasonably available to you (set out in Section C of this chapter) and still couldn't locate the minor's father, a judge probably would determine that you couldn't reasonably be expected to give him notice.

Example 2: You are seeking guardianship of your daughter's child. The child's father has never seen or known his daughter. Your daughter does not know where the father is. She knows only that his name is John Jones, and that he lived with his wife in Los Angeles five years ago. You would prepare documents asking for a judge to waive notice requirements for the minor's father and paternal grandparents. A judge probably would determine that you couldn't reasonably be expected to give the child's father or paternal grandparents notice.

1. How to Locate Relatives

This section gives a summary of some of the most stringent requirements in California for searching for relatives who are required to get notice of a guardianship. Your county may be much more lenient, depending on which relatives cannot be located, and on the attitude of the particular judge. Some judges expect you to spend at least three hours in the search for a relative, particularly a parent. We recommend that you follow all suggestions in this section when attempting to find the minor's parents. To find any other missing relatives, you may also want to follow all the suggestions in this section as well.

When you attempt to locate the missing relative, keep an accurate written record of your activities. Enter the date of each attempt, and a simple explanation of what happened. For example, "On September 1, 1990, I called Directory Assistance in Sacramento, California and requested the telephone numbers and addresses for John Xerox, and there were no listings." If inquiry is made by mail, keep copies of the letter and returned correspondence. If someone else conducts the search for missing relatives for you, have that person keep accurate records of her attempts. Follow up any leads you get.

When checking with friends or employers who may know the missing relative, be discreet. Simply say that you are trying to contact the person, but don't volunteer information about the guardianship or that the person may have something to do with a court proceeding.

a. Check with the Telephone Company

To find the missing relative, begin with the obvious. Check telephone directories and Directory Assistance in cities where the relative has lived recently. Most public libraries carry copies of telephone directories for many cities, including phone books for areas outside of California. Local telephone company offices also may have copies of phone books for many areas.

b. Check with Friends and Relatives

Contact the minor's other relatives to see if they know how to locate the missing relative. They may be able to give you leads such as a former address, telephone number, or the name of someone else who might know how to locate the relative. Remember to be discreet when you contact friends and relatives. Make sure you keep a written record of the dates and results of your inquiries.

c. Check with Former Employers

If you know where the missing relative used to work, contact former employers to find out if they have an address, telephone number, or the name of someone else who might know how to locate the relative. Again, do not volunteer information about why you are trying to find the person. Keep a written record of the dates and results of your inquiries.

d. Check Last Known Address

Talk to the people living at the relative's last known address, if you have one. If the people living there don't know the whereabouts of the missing relative, check with the neighbors on both sides either by letter, phone, or in person.

If the last known address is a mental or penal institution, contact the person in charge of the institution, and ask if you can obtain the relative's current address from the institution's records. Remember to be discreet about why you are trying to find the person. The institution's records may be confidential, but they may forward mail, and you can write to the relative in care of the institution.

If the missing relative has moved and left a forwarding address, you can obtain it from the U.S. Post Office. Simply send a post card or envelope to the last known address with the words "Address Correction Requested" printed next to the old address. The post office will return it to you with the correct address. Or, if you want to send a letter to the missing relative, next to the last known address print the words "Address Correction and Forwarding Requested." The post office will forward the letter and return a postcard to you with the new address and 30¢ postage due. Or you can send a letter along with $1.00 to the post office of the missing relative's old zip code, requesting the forwarding address on file.

e. Check Voter Registration Records

In California, you can find a listing for registered voters that includes their name, address, phone number, birthdate, party affiliation if any, and date of registration. To look at these records, contact the registrar of voters for the county where you believe the relative lives. You may be able to get this information over the phone. If the person has moved within the same county, the registrar may have the new address.

f. Check with the Department of Motor Vehicles

The motor vehicle department in each state has information on registered vehicles and drivers, and may have a current address for the unlocatable relative. For a fee (usually $4 to $10), you may be able to get this current information, although the relative has an opportunity to request that the DMV not give you his address. In any event, it will usually be several weeks before you receive the report. If you believe the relative lives in a state other than California, contact the motor vehicle department in that state to find out how to initiate a search there.

In California, the Department of Motor Vehicles (DMV) checks for an exact match of the name you provide. Thus, if you specify John Smith, and DMV records show Jon Smith, the search may turn up nothing. You may want to submit several requests with variations of the relative's full name (John P. Smith, John Paul Smith, J.P. Smith, J. Paul Smith). However, you must pay for each name search. You can get a copy of a Driver License Registration Information Request form and a schedule of fees by stopping by or calling your local DMV office, or by writing to the DMV, Division of Driver's Licenses, P.O. Box 2590, Sacramento, CA 95812.

g. Military Services

If you think the missing relative is a member of the military, check with the military services (Army, Navy, Air Force, Coast Guard, or Marines). You can do this by writing to the Personnel Records Branch of the military in Washington, D.C., paying a fee (approximately $15), and requesting information as to whether or not they're on active duty in that branch of the military service. Here are the addresses of the military services:

Army
Personnel Records Branch, Personnel Division
Office of the Adjutant General
Department of the Army
Washington 20025, DC

Navy
Chief of Naval Personnel
Attn: Perse-2 and E 0 3
Department of the Navy
Washington 20025, DC

Air Force
Director, Administrative Services
Attn: Military Personnel Records
Service Headquarters
United States Air Force
Washington 20025, DC

Coast Guard
The Commandant
U.S. Coast Guard
Washington 20025, DC

Marines
Data Processing Section - Code D G K
Headquarters
United States Marine Corps
Washington 20025, DC

D. After You've Searched for Missing Relatives

ONCE YOU'VE FOUND THE NAMES and addresses of any missing relatives, fill in the information in Items 1 of the Guardianship Notification Worksheet. Fill in the date each relative was located in Item 3.

If, after carefully following the instructions in Section C of this chapter, you still can't find the names and addresses of all the minor's relatives, you must prepare a document that tells how you searched for the relatives.

1. Due Diligence Declaration (Attachment 14 to Petition for Appointment of Guardian of Minor)

If you have located all of the minor's living relatives listed on the Guardianship Notification Worksheet, you may skip this section and go on to Section E.

However, if any relatives are missing, you must complete a form called a "Due Diligence Declaration," which tells how you searched for the relatives. Before you begin filling in this form, you will need to make some photocopies. A Due Diligence Declaration must be filled out for each missing relative, so for each missing relative, make one photocopy. If anyone other than you helped search, make one photocopy for each relative that person tried to find.

> **CAPTION:** DUE DILIGENCE DECLARATION (ATTACHMENT 14 TO PETITION FOR APPOINTMENT OF GUARDIAN OF MINOR)
>
> Fill in the caption following the general instructions in Chapter 3, Section D1.
> Leave the case number blank, since it hasn't been assigned yet.

After the word "I," fill in either your name or the name of the person who conducted the search.

In the next blank, after the word "I am," fill in the word "petitioner," if you are the person who searched for the relative. If someone else searched for the relative, fill in the words "not a party," which means they are not petitioning to be the minor's guardian.

In the blank following the words "I have made the following attempts to locate," fill in the name of the missing relative.

In the blank following the words "who is related to the minor in this action as," fill in how the missing relative is related to the minor. For example, this might be "maternal uncle," if the relative is a brother of the minor's mother, or "paternal grandmother," if the relative is the mother of the minor's father.

In Items 1 through 8, you will give a detailed description of each attempt made to locate the missing relative. If you need additional space, fill in the words "This item continued on attachment," and complete an attachment following the instructions in Chapter 3, Section D3. If you or the person conducting the search wrote letters to anyone during the course of the search, add the words "copies of correspondence attached" for that item and attach copies.

Item 1: Check this item if the person conducting the search looked in telephone directories. Then list the date each attempt was made, the city of the telephone directory and the results of the search (such as no one was listed under that name, or you called and it was the wrong person).

Item 2: Check this item if the person conducting the search contacted Directory Assistance. Then list the date each attempt was made, the city or area code that was called and the results of the search (such as no one was listed under that name, or you called and it was the wrong person).

Item 3: Check this item if the person conducting the search contacted the missing relative's friends and relatives. Then list the date each attempt was made, the name and relationship to the missing relative of each person who was contacted and the results of the search (such as a friend didn't know the whereabouts of the missing relative, or a sister gave a telephone number for the missing relative that had been disconnected). Be specific and detailed about each attempt.

Item 4: Check this item if the person conducting the search contacted the missing relative's former employers. Then list the date each attempt was made, the name of each former employer who was contacted and the results of the search (such as the former employer had fired the missing relative and didn't know where he'd gone, or the former employer had the forwarding address of a business that went bankrupt two years ago).

Item 5: Check this item if the person conducting the search looked into the missing relative's last known address. Then list the date each attempt was made and the results of the search (such as you went to the house and the missing relative was no longer living there and the tenant didn't know where he had moved, or the post office did not have a forwarding address on file).

Item 6: Check this item if the person conducting the search consulted voter registration records. Then list the date each attempt was made, the county and state of each registry of voters that was contacted and the results of the search (such as the missing relative was not registered to vote, or was no longer at the address listed with the registry of voters).

Item 7: Check this item if the person conducting the search consulted the department of motor vehicles. Then list the date each attempt was made, the state in which the motor vehicles department was contacted and the results of the search (such as the missing relative was not registered with the motor vehicles department, or there was no current address listed).

Item 8: Check this item if the person conducting the search contacted any other source not listed in Items 1 through 7. Then list the date each attempt was made and a detailed description of the results of the search (such as you checked with the army and there was no forwarding address on file, or you checked with the court where the missing relative had filed a divorce and there was not a current address listed in the court's files).

Finally, fill in the date, print the name of the person who conducted the search and either sign the form, or have it signed, depending on whether you or someone else conducted the search.

For now, you can put this form aside. You will come back to it later—in Chapter 5.

GUARDIANSHIP OF (Name): BRIAN TIMOTHY MICHAELS	Case Number:

ATTACHMENT 14
to Petition for Appointment of Guardian of Minor

I, SUSAN STEVENSON, declare that I am the proposed guardian in this guardianship case, that I have made the following attempts to locate FRED MICHAELS, who is related to the minor in this action as natural father. To date my efforts have been unsuccessful.

1. [X] I checked in telephone directories for listings. The details of my attempts are:

    4/2/90 I went to the public library and checked in the Anchorage telephone book. There was one listing for F.M. Michaels, and no other listings for either F. or Fred Michaels.
    4/2/90 I called the number listed for F. Michaels, 907/999-9999. A man who identified himself as Frank Michaels answered. He had never heard of Fred Michaels.

2. [X] I checked with directory assistance. The details of my attempts are:

    I called directory assistance at 907/555-1212 on 4/1/90. There were no listings for Fred Michaels or F. Michaels.

3. [X] I checked with friends and relatives. The details of my attempts are:

    4/12/90 I called Fred Michaels' sister, Karen Bradford. She has not talked to Fred in six years and does not know where he is.
    4/14/90 I wrote a letter to Fred Michaels' brother, Michael Michaels. The letter was returned from the post office marked "moved, left no forwarding address."

    I do not know any other friends or relatives of Fred Michaels.

4. [X] I checked with former employers. The details of my attempts are:

    I called Bossco on 4/6/90 at 907/999-8888. The receiptionist, Kathleen Smith, said Fred Michaels quit three years ago. The last she heard, he was planning to move to Spain. She did not have a forwarding address for Fred Michaels.

GUARDIANSHIP OF (Name):	Case Number:
BRIAN TIMOTHY MICHAELS	

5. ☒ I checked the last known residence address. The details of my attempts are:

   I sent a letter to Fred Michaels at 1 Cold Street, Anchorage, Alaska on 4/1/90. It was returned on 4/11/90 from the post office marked "address unknown, not deliverable." I do not have any other address for Fred Michaels.

6. ☒ I checked with voter registration records. The details of my attempts are:

   I sent a letter to the registrar of voters in Anchorage, Alaska on 4/1/90. They wrote back saying Fred Michaels was not registered to vote there. Copies of correspondence are attached.

7. ☒ I checked with the motor vehicles department. The details of my attempts are:

   I sent a letter to the Alaska motor vehicles department on 4/1/90, requesting information on Fred Michaels and F. Michaels. There is no one registered under either name in Alaska. Copies of correspondence are attached.

8. ☒ Other (specify):

   I wrote to the U.S. Navy on 4/4/90. Fred Michaels was not a member of the Navy at any time. Copies of correspondence are attached.

I declare under penalty of perjury under the laws of the state of California that the foregoing is true and correct.

Date: 4/29/90

SUSAN STEVENSON
....
(TYPE OR PRINT NAME)

Susan Stevenson
_____
(SIGNATURE)

BACK

ATTACHMENT 14 TO PETITION FOR APPOINTMENT OF GUARDIAN OF MINOR

NP

E. Consent of Proposed Guardian, Nomination and Waiver of Notice Form

YOU'RE NOW READY TO PREPARE a form called the "Consent of Guardian, Nomination and Waiver of Notice." Completing this form will help you understand the process of notifying relatives and getting their written consents to the guardianship. This is actually three forms put together on one page. Despite three forms being compressed into one, it is very easy to prepare and understand. There are separate instructions for each part.

> **CAPTION:** CONSENT OF GUARDIAN, NOMINATION AND WAIVER OF NOTICE
>
> Fill in the caption following the general instructions in Chapter 3, Section D1.
>
> Where you seek guardianship of more than one minor, use one form for each child, listing the name of each minor on a separate form.
>
> There are three boxes entitled "CONSENT OF PROPOSED GUARDIAN," "NOMINATION OF GUARDIAN" and "WAIVER OF NOTICE AND CONSENT." After you finish filling in the form, check the boxes applying to each part of the form you completed.

1. Consent of Proposed Guardian

In the first part of the form, you—the proposed guardian—sign a simple statement in which you agree to be guardian. Obviously, this is implied if you're the one petitioning for the guardianship. But the form is designed to include the possibility that someone such as a parent or adult relative is asking the court to appoint another adult who agrees to be guardian. You need to complete this part even though you are asking to have yourself appointed guardian.

Just below the caption, you will find a small box and the words "CONSENT OF PROPOSED GUARDIAN." Check this box, as well as the corresponding box in the caption. Next check the box next to the word "person," "estate," or both, depending on the type of guardianship you are seeking. Then fill in the date and your full name, and sign just above the words "Signature of proposed guardian." You have now completed the Consent of Proposed Guardian form.

2. Nomination of Guardian

In the second part of the form, the guardian may be nominated by one or both of the minor's parents.[6] Whether you'll fill in the Nomination of Guardian depends on your situation. Although it isn't mandatory that a parent nominate a proposed guardian, it is desirable. A judge will be more likely to grant the guardianship if the minor's parents approve of it, so your nomination as guardian is an extremely important part of the guardianship process. Filling out the Nomination of Guardian portion of the form is very easy. What should be done carefully is obtaining signatures of the minor's parents. (Section F in this chapter discusses in detail the issues you'll need to consider when you seek their signatures on the form.)

Whenever a parent agrees with the guardianship and is willing to nominate you as guardian, this part of the form should be used.[7] If both parents will

---

[6] In the rare situation where someone is donating a gift to the minor and you are seeking guardianship of the minor's estate, the adult who gives the gift would make the nomination.

[7] Parents who refuse to nominate you as guardian are very likely to oppose the guardianship unless they have

nominate you as guardian, fill out a separate Nomination of Guardian for each of them.

If you haven't discussed the guardianship with the minor's parents, but think they might go along with it, complete this part of the form. If you are certain that the minor's parents won't approve of the guardianship, you do not need to complete this part of the form. But bear in mind that if the parents are likely to contest the guardianship, you will need to see an attorney.

To complete the form, first check the "NOMINATION OF GUARDIAN" box, as well as the corresponding box in the caption.[8]

If a parent will be nominating you as guardian, check the box next to the words "a parent of the minor." In the rare situation where you are seeking guardianship of the estate because an adult is donating a gift to a minor, check the box next to the words "donor of a gift to the minor."

After the words "I nominate (name and address)," fill in your name and residence address. Then check the boxes next to the words "person," "estate," or both, depending on the type of guardianship you are seeking. Below this, you will again find a sentence that begins "I nominate (name and address)." The form has this language twice for the unusual situation in which a parent nominates one person as guardian of the minor's person and another as guardian of the minor's estate. Ignore the second nomination unless you and someone else are being nominated for these two different types of guardian of the same minor. If that's your situation, fill in the requested information for the other guardian.

Print or type the date and name of the person making the nomination at the left of this part of the form. You will later have the person making the nomination sign above the word "Signature" on the right. For now, this part of the form is complete.

3. Waiver of Notice and Consent

In the third and last part of the form, any or all of the minor's relatives may indicate that they consent to the proposed guardianship and agree to give up the right to be notified at all stages of the proceeding, which will make things easier for you. The minor may not sign this form.[9] Again, as discussed, although it isn't necessary to have this form signed, doing so will save you the trouble of having legal notices served on the minor's relatives, including the parents if they are making the nomination.

The final portion of the form begins about two-thirds down the page. Check the box just before the words "WAIVER OF NOTICE AND CONSENT," as well as the corresponding box in the caption. Fill in the name to the left of the signature line and relationship to the minor of each person to the right side of each signature line. If applicable, list the parent making the nomination first, then the other living parent willing to agree and waive notice. Then, using the Guardianship Notification Worksheet you began completing in Section B of this chapter as a guide, list the names of all adult relatives whose signatures can be obtained.[10]

If you need more space to list all the relatives, check the box next to the words "Continued on attachment" at the bottom left of the form. Then prepare a continuation of the form on an Additional Page Judicial Council form provided in Appendix D or a plain piece of typing paper. (See Chapter 3, Section D3 for instructions on how to prepare attachment pages.) Label the additional page "Attachment to Waiver of Notice and Consent" at the top. On the attachment, continue listing the minor's relatives, following the same format as the original Waiver of Notice and Consent.

---

abandoned their child, are in jail, or otherwise are out of the picture. If the minor's parents oppose the guardianship, you will need to consult an attorney. (See Chapter 13.)

[8]If a deceased parent has nominated you to be guardian in a will, you do not need to fill out this part of the form, unless the other parent is alive and willing to sign the nomination.

[9]A minor who is over 12 years of age must be served personally with notice of the guardianship. We tell you how to do this in Chapter 6, Section F. A minor who is under 12 does not have to be served.

[10]Signatures may also be obtained for anyone presently having legal custody of the minor, anyone nominated the minor's legal guardian, and anyone who has physical custody of the minor (not including you).

ATTORNEY OR PARTY WITHOUT ATTORNEY (Name and Address):	TELEPHONE NO.:	FOR COURT USE ONLY
NEIL DAVID ELLIS 2863 My Street Martinez, CA 94553	415/555-1212	
ATTORNEY FOR (Name): In Pro Per		

SUPERIOR COURT OF CALIFORNIA, COUNTY OF CONTRA COSTA
STREET ADDRESS: 725 Court Street
MAILING ADDRESS: P.O. Box 911
CITY AND ZIP CODE: Martinez, CA 94553
BRANCH NAME:

GUARDIANSHIP OF THE [X] **PERSON** [X] **ESTATE OF (NAME):**
ANN MARIE ELLIS
Minor

[X] CONSENT OF PROPOSED GUARDIAN [X] NOMINATION OF GUARDIAN [X] WAIVER OF NOTICE AND CONSENT	CASE NUMBER:

[X] CONSENT OF PROPOSED GUARDIAN

I consent to serve as guardian of the [X] person [X] estate of the minor.

Dated: 3/31/92

NEIL DAVID ELLIS   /s/ Neil David Ellis
(Type or print name)   (Signature of proposed guardian)

[X] NOMINATION OF GUARDIAN

I am [X] a parent of the minor [ ] donor of a gift to the minor. I nominate (name and address):

NEIL DAVID ELLIS
2863 My Street, Martinez, CA 94553
as guardian of the [X] person [X] estate of the minor.

I nominate (name and address):

as guardian of the [ ] person [ ] estate of the minor.

Dated: 3/31/92

ANDREW ELLIS
(Type or print name)   (Signature)

[X] WAIVER OF NOTICE AND CONSENT

I am entitled to notice in this proceeding. I waive notice of hearing of the petition for appointment of guardian of minor and consent to appointment of the guardian as requested.

(Type or print name)	(Signature)	(Relationship to minor)
Andrew Ellis		Father
Sarah Ellis-Smith		Sister
Helen Peterson		Maternal Grandmother
Richard Peterson		Maternal Grandfather
Karen Ellis		Paternal Grandmother

[ ] Continued on attachment.

Form Approved by the Judicial Council of California
Effective January 1, 1981
GC-211(81)

CONSENT OF GUARDIAN, NOMINATION, AND WAIVER OF NOTICE

You're now ready to go back to the caption at the top of the page and make sure you have checked the boxes for the parts of the form you've completed. Set this form aside for now. You will later come back to it, when you're ready to obtain signatures from the minor's relatives.

F. Discussing the Guardianship with the Minor's Relatives

IF YOU HAVEN'T ALREADY TOLD the minor's relatives about the guardianship, it's now time to think about doing this. But don't put down this book and contact any relatives yet. This section gives you an overview of why you'll be talking to the relatives, and what you'll be saying to them.

You aren't required to discuss the guardianship with any of the minor's relatives, but it's generally a good idea for two reasons:

1. If any relatives agree with the guardianship, you may be able to get their signatures on the Waiver of Notice and Consent form that you filled out in Section E of this chapter. If they sign this form, you won't need to have them served with legal papers.

2. If a relative isn't in favor of the guardianship, you'll have more time to prepare yourself for a possible challenge to your appointment as guardian. (If a relative objects to the guardianship by filing papers with the court or showing up at the hearing, you will need to consult a lawyer—see Chapter 13.)

How you approach the minor's relatives is extremely important. You might want to call them on the telephone or get together with them in person. You might even choose to write a letter, especially if they don't live nearby. No matter what method you choose for bringing up the guardianship, make sure you do it in a friendly and open way. Since you are seeking a guardianship because you believe it's best for the minor, communicate these intentions. If you get the idea that the minor's relatives aren't going to cooperate, don't push the matter. You aren't required to get any signatures on the Waiver of Notice and Consent, and it isn't even essential that both parents sign the Nomination part of the form. It just makes things a little easier for you if you can obtain the signatures.

Example: Susan wants to become the guardian of her sister's only child, Annie, who is five years old. Susan's sister is in favor of the guardianship, because she is going through personal problems and cannot care for her daughter. She is willing to sign legal documents nominating Susan as guardian, and waiving her right to notice of the guardianship. Susan's parents also agree with the guardianship and are willing to waive their right to legal notification, which Susan knows because they have discussed the guardianship at great length. Susan decides not to ask Annie's father if he'll sign documents consenting to the guardianship, because she has never gotten along well with him. Susan plans to have him served with the guardianship papers instead. Susan contacts Annie's paternal grandparents, but they are unwilling to sign legal documents, so she must have them served as well.

1. Talking with the Minor's Relatives

Here are some things to keep in mind when you tell the minor's relatives that you're going to seek a legal guardianship:

- Be prepared. Know what a legal guardianship is, and how you get one. If they ask you questions, answer them as best you can. It might help to show them this book, as it may address their questions or concerns.
- Carefully and respectfully explain why the guardianship would be best for the minor. It helps to be diplomatic. For example, it would not be a good idea to say: "Your daughter is a terrible mother, and I bet she had a lousy childhood." On the other hand, it might be helpful to say: "She's found that taking care of her child is too much of a responsibility right now, and I'm happy to help out by taking the child in and being his legal guardian."
- Talk over any concerns the relatives have, such as your willingness to let them visit the minor.
- Let them know that you'd like their signature on the Waiver of Notice and Consent part of the form. Tell them that by signing the form they're saying that they agree with the guardianship, and don't need to be formally notified of any legal proceedings.

- Never try to pressure a relative into signing a Waiver of Notice and Consent form. Remember that if you can't get a relative's signature, it simply means that you'll have to arrange to have her served with guardianship papers.

2. Special Considerations for Talking with the Minor's Parents

When you talk to the minor's parents, find out if they are willing to nominate you as guardian, and to waive their right to formal notice of the guardianship proceeding. Getting the parents' support may not be a problem, as the minor's parents have probably suggested the guardianship or at least are in favor of it.

But what if you fear for the welfare of the child,[11] the minor's parents don't know of your plans and may be hostile when they find out? In these situations you should obviously be very careful in how you bring up the guardianship. After all, if a parent gets nervous and leaves the area with her child, your plans to obtain a legal guardianship will amount to nothing. In addition to the tips for talking to relatives listed in Section F1 above, here are some suggestions for dealing with the minor's parents:

- Reassure the minor's parents that you are not taking their child away from them. In the case of a guardianship of a minor's person, explain that you are seeking legal custody of the minor, but you are *not* attempting to adopt the minor. If the parents later want to have the guardianship ended, they (or even you) can petition the court to do so.
- Be reasonable. Explain why the guardianship would be best for everyone concerned, without blaming, insulting, or implying that the parents have done something wrong.
- Remind the minor's parents that you want to do what's best for their child. Let them know that you want to help out, and you believe a guardianship will be best for their child.

G. Obtain Signatures from Relatives on the Nomination and Waiver of Notice Forms

YOU ARE NOW READY to make photocopies and obtain signatures on the last two parts of the three-part Consent of Guardian, Nomination and Waiver of Notice and Consent form. You'll need:
- Two copies of the form for each parent who will be signing the Nomination or Waiver of Notice and Consent; and
- Two copies for each relative who will be signing a Waiver of Notice and Consent.

1. Obtain Signatures from the Minor's Parents

If possible, you should get the minor's living parents to sign the Nomination of Guardian form.[12] Using the suggestions for approaching the minor's parents in Section F2 above, ask them to sign both the Nomination of Guardian and the Waiver of Notice and Consent form. If both parents are willing to sign, you either will need to add an extra signature line in the space above the printed line of the Nomination of Guardian, or have them each sign a photocopy of the form.

Once you have these signatures, don't let the signed original forms out of your hands until you file them with the court. For example, if you're going to be obtaining Waiver of Notice and Consent signatures from the minor's relatives, make sure you send out photocopies of the form, not the originals.

---

[11]Remember that if the minor is in danger of abuse or neglect, you will need to take immediate action to protect him. If you aren't sure whether the minor would be in danger if you don't get a legal guardianship, you can call a local agency for more information and possible intervention. Check the phone book under your county's agencies for "Children's Emergency Services," "Children's Protective Services," "Child Abuse Reporting," or a similar heading.

[12]If you do not know where one or both of the minor's parents are, you need not obtain their signatures. However, you will need to make reasonable efforts to locate the parents to notify them of the guardianship proceedings following the guidelines in Section C of this chapter. In the rare situation where the guardianship is for the minor's estate, and a donor of a gift is making the nomination, you should have the donor sign the Nomination of Guardian.

2. Obtain Signatures from the Minor's Other Relatives

As we have emphasized, each and every one of the people listed in Part 1 of the Guardianship Notification Worksheet must be served with formal legal papers unless they sign a Waiver of Notice and Consent form or can't be found. If any relatives voluntarily sign a Waiver of Notice and Consent form, you will be free of the requirement to send them documents about the guardianship proceeding. So, as you can see, obtaining these signatures can save you a good deal of time and trouble. Here is how to do it.

Make two photocopies of the unsigned Waiver of Notice and Consent form for *each* of the minor's relatives you listed on the form. Contact each relative and tell her about the guardianship, following the suggestions in Section F1 in this chapter. If a relative supports the guardianship, ask her to sign a copy of the Waiver of Notice and Consent. Do this in person if possible, and by mail if that's not possible. If she wants a copy of the form, give one to her.

It is not necessary that every relative entitled to notice sign the same Waiver of Notice and Consent form. For example, if you are going to mail the form to out-of-state relatives for their signatures, send an unsigned form. That way, if they don't return it to you, you won't risk losing the signatures you already obtained. Naturally, if you are going in person to obtain signatures from more than one person, they can sign the same form.

Once you have obtained all the signatures you can get, you have completed this form. For now, put all original signed copies of the form in a safe, convenient place.

H. Continue Filling in the Worksheet

AS YOU'VE GONE THROUGH the process of talking to the minor's relatives and getting their signatures on the Waiver of Notice and Consent, you may have filled in more of the Guardianship Notification Worksheet. If not, here is the time to catch up. You can now fill in Items 4 and 5. (You'll complete the Guardianship Notification Worksheet fully by the end of Chapter 6.)

Item 4: In this item, answer whether each relative is willing to sign a Waiver of Notice and Consent. This applies to the third section of the Consent of Guardian, Nomination and Waiver of Notice form that you filled out in Section E of this chapter. For each relative, indicate whether they will sign—or already have signed—a Waiver of Notice and Consent. When you obtain a signature, also jot down the date it was signed. In the form, we remind you that certain relatives may not sign because they are under age 18.

Item 5: As you've learned, all relatives must be served, except those who signed a Waiver of Notice and Consent and those who can't be located. For each relative, write down "yes" if they need to be served, and "no" if they do not need to be served because they either can't be found or have signed a Waiver of Notice and Consent. Note that the form already contains information about serving the minor and her brothers and sisters. Underneath this information, fill in whether they need to be served.

You may now put the Guardianship Notification Worksheet aside and go on to Chapter 5. Again, keep this worksheet handy, as you will find it useful when you fill out other forms.

CHAPTER 5

PREPARING FORMS TO FILE FOR A GUARDIANSHIP

A.	Petition for Appointment of Guardian of Minor	5/2
B.	Declaration Under Uniform Child Custody Jurisdiction Act (Guardianship of a Minor's Person Only)	5/16
C.	Notice of Hearing	5/21
D.	(Proposed) Order Dispensing Notice	5/21
E.	(Proposed) Order Appointing Guardian of Minor	5/25
F.	(Proposed) Letters of Guardianship	5/30
G.	Prepare Supplemental Documents if Required	5/30
H.	When You Need a Guardianship Right Away	5/32

IF YOU HAVEN'T ALREADY READ CHAPTER 3 ("Getting Started"), do so now. That chapter contains basic information on how to get organized, how to prepare legal forms and how to apply to have court fees waived. We also tell you how to find out in which court to file your guardianship papers, and what information you'll need to obtain from that court. At this point we assume that you are familiar with the material in Chapter 3. Of course, remember that you can always refer back to Chapter 3 for a review—there's no reason to memorize everything.

In Chapter 4 ("Notifying Minor's Relatives and Obtaining Their Consents"), you began filling out documents required for the legal guardianship. You're now about to complete the rest of the forms required to file for a guardianship. But first, here are a few words of encouragement. You'll need to complete several legal forms to obtain a guardianship, but you can usually complete the process by yourself. The step-by-step instructions here will take you through each form and help you complete each procedure. As long as you're patient—and willing to spend a little time preparing and double-checking your work, you shouldn't have any trouble.

Here's an overview of the steps you'll take:

Step 1: If you skipped Chapter 1 or Chapter 3, turn to them before filling in the forms in this chapter.

Step 2: Read the instructions and complete the forms in Chapter 4.

Step 3: Complete the rest of the documents you'll need to file for a legal guardianship:

- **Petition for Appointment of Guardian of Minor.** This form must be completed following the instructions in Section A. If you are seeking guardianship of a minor's estate or person and estate, you will periodically refer to Chapter 10 to complete the petition.

- **Declaration Under Uniform Child Custody Jurisdiction Act.** This form is only completed if you are seeking guardianship of a minor's person. Instructions for completing it are in Section B.

- **Notice of Hearing.** This form, which lists information about when and where the guardianship hearing will take place, must be completed following the instructions in Section C.

- **(Proposed) Order Dispensing Notice.** You only complete this form if you could not locate some relatives, or you obtained their signatures on a Waiver of Notice and Consent form. Instructions for completing it are in Section D.

- **(Proposed) Order Appointing Guardian of Minor.** This form must be completed following the instructions in Section E.

- **(Proposed) Letters of Guardianship**. This form must be completed following the instructions in Section F.
- **Supplemental documents** may be required by your local court. A list and samples of some of these documents are contained in Section G.

Step 4: If you need a guardianship of a minor's person right away (within six weeks), turn to Chapter 7, where you will find instructions on completing temporary guardianship documents.

Step 5: Once you have completed the forms in this chapter, turn to Chapter 6, which tells you how to file and serve your papers.

A. Petition for Appointment of Guardian of Minor

TO BEGIN GUARDIANSHIP PROCEEDINGS, a "petition" must be filed with the court. The Petition for Appointment of Guardian of Minor is the document in which you summarize why you should be appointed the minor's guardian. Since you are the person filing the Petition for Appointment of Guardian of Minor, you are referred to as the "petitioner" in the proceedings.

The following instructions are complete if you are seeking guardianship of a minor's person only. If, however, you are seeking guardianship of a minor's estate or guardianship of both a minor's person and estate, you will occasionally need to turn to Chapter 10, Section B for instructions as noted.

Before you begin, have handy the Guardianship Notification Worksheet you began completing in Chapter 4. You will need to refer to this worksheet periodically.

CAPTION: PETITION FOR APPOINTMENT OF GUARDIAN OF MINOR

Fill in the caption following the general instructions in Chapter 3, Section D1.

At the bottom of the caption, check the boxes to indicate whether you are seeking guardianship of the person, estate, or both. Make sure you know exactly what type of guardianship you are seeking. This is discussed in detail in Chapter 1, Section E.

Leave the case number blank. You will be assigned a case number when you file your documents with the court.

Item 1: After the words "Petitioner (name)" fill in your full first, middle and last names. This means that you are the person who is filing for the guardianship.[1]

Item 1a: Skip this item if you are only seeking guardianship of the minor's estate. If you are seeking guardianship of the minor's person or person and estate, fill in your full first, middle and last names, followed by your address. This indicates that you are the proposed guardian of the minor's person.

Item 1b: Skip this item if you are only seeking guardianship of the minor's person. If you are seeking guardianship of the minor's estate or person and estate, fill in your full first, middle and last names, followed by your address. This indicates that you are the proposed guardian of the minor's estate.

Item 1c: If you are seeking guardianship of more than one minor, check this box. You can petition to be guardian of two or more on the same petition only if the minors are full- or half-brothers or sisters. If you wish to be appointed guardian of two or more minors who are not related, you will need to file a separate petition for each one. If you are seeking guardianship

---

[1] Throughout this book, the instructions refer to only one petitioner. However, it's quite possible that you are seeking to be guardian jointly with someone else (such as a spouse). If that's your situation, fill in the names of all petitioners wherever one petitioner's name is requested, unless instructed otherwise.

of two or more minor brothers and sisters, you'll have to add extra pages called "Attachment 1c" to the petition. These attachments are used to provide the information called for in Items 2 through 11 for each additional minor. Appendix D includes an "Attachment 1c to Petition for Appointment of Guardian of Minor: Information on Additional Minors." It is printed in exactly the same format as Items 2 through 11 of this petition. Simply make a copy of Attachment 1c for each additional minor, and fill in the information for that minor in the same way you fill in Items 2 through 11 for the first minor, following the instructions below.

Item 1d: If you are seeking guardianship of a minor's estate or person and estate, turn to Chapter 10, Section B for instructions on how to complete this item.

If you are seeking guardianship of a minor's person only, check only the first box before 1d (1) "bond not be required." Then cross off the words "for the reasons stated in attachment 1d," and fill in the words "pursuant to Probate Code Section 2322." This code section says that guardian of the person does not have to file a bond unless the court specifically requires it.[2] Leave the rest of this item blank.

Item 1e: If you are seeking guardianship of a minor's person only, skip this item. If you are seeking guardianship of a minor's estate or person and estate, turn to Chapter 10, Section B for instructions on how to complete this item.

Item 1f: If you are seeking guardianship of a minor's estate only, skip this item. This item only applies to guardianships of the minor's person or person and estate, but normally this box is not checked. It is used where a guardian intends to either move the minor out of California or to insist that a minor 14 years or older receive other than emergency medical treatment against the minor's wishes. A guardian cannot do either of these without a specific court order, which will require the help of an attorney. (See Chapter 13.)

Item 1g: A number of people must get written notice of the guardianship proceeding unless they signed the Waiver of Notice and Consent, or you are unable to locate them. Look at the Guardianship Notification Worksheet for information needed to complete this item. Then check this box if you could not locate one or more relatives entitled to notice, after you searched for them following the guidelines in Chapter 4, Section C. More information about having notice waived will be given in the instructions for Item 14, where you will complete an Attachment 14.

Item 1h: Leave this item blank unless one of the following apply:

- The minor is 12 years of age or older, and will be at the guardianship hearing; or
- You are seeking guardianship of a minor's estate, and the only money you'll be receiving on behalf of the minor are public benefit payments such as Aid to Families with Dependent Children (AFDC), General Assistance from a county, or Supplemental Security Income and State Supplemental Program (SSI/SSP) benefits paid through the Social Security Administration; and the minor does not receive more than $300 per month in addition to these benefits; *and* the entire amount of assets belonging to the minor does not exceed $5,000 (excluding clothes and ordinary household items); *and* any money you receive on behalf of the minor will be spent for her benefit. If you complete this item, you will request that you not be required to file periodic accountings with the court, which will make your job as guardian of a minor's estate much easier.

If you are in either of these situations, complete an Attachment 1h following the instructions in Chapter 3, Section D3, using the following sample as a guide.

Item 2: If you are seeking guardianship of more than one minor in one Petition for Appointment of Guardian of Minor, you must fill out separate Items 2-11 for each minor. See the discussion in Item 1c above, and use the form provided in Appendix D entitled "Attachment 1c to Petition for Appointment of Guardian of Minor: Information on Additional Minors."

---

[2] In the extremely rare case where a judge would require bond for the guardian of a minor's person only, she would make the order at your court hearing. This petition would not have to be amended.

ATTORNEY OR PARTY WITHOUT ATTORNEY *(Name and Address)*:	TELEPHONE NO.:	FOR COURT USE ONLY
PATRICIA ANN LEE 2 West Street Santa Ana, CA 92702	714-555-1212	
ATTORNEY FOR *(Name)*: In Pro Per		

SUPERIOR COURT OF CALIFORNIA, COUNTY OF ORANGE
STREET ADDRESS: 700 Civic Center Drive West
MAILING ADDRESS: P.O. Box 838
CITY AND ZIP CODE: Santa Ana, CA 92702
BRANCH NAME:

GUARDIANSHIP OF (NAME):
DANIEL FRANK LEE
                                                                            MINOR

PETITION FOR APPOINTMENT OF GUARDIAN OF [x] **MINOR** [ ] **MINORS**
[x] **Person** [ ] **Estate**

CASE NUMBER:

1. Petitioner *(name)*: PATRICIA ANN LEE   requests that
   a. *(name and address)*: PATRICIA ANN LEE
      2 West Street, Santa Ana, CA 92702

   be appointed guardian of the **person** of the minor and Letters issue upon qualification.
   b. *(name and address)*:

   be appointed guardian of the **estate** of the minor and Letters issue upon qualification.
   c. [ ] the proposed guardian be appointed for several minors who are brothers and sisters. The information requested in items 2–11 for each additional minor is supplied in attachment 1c.
   d. (1) [X] bond not be required ~~for the reasons stated in attachment 1d~~ pursuant to Probate Code Sec. 2322
      (2) [ ] $_____ bond be fixed. It will be furnished by an authorized surety company or as otherwise provided by law. *(Specify reasons in attachment 1d if the amount is different from the minimum required by Probate Code, § 541.)*
      (3) [ ] $_____ in deposits in a blocked account be allowed. Receipts will be filed. *(Specify institution and location)*:
   e. [ ] authorization be granted under section 2590 of the Probate Code to exercise independently the powers specified in attachment 13.
   f. [ ] orders relating to the powers and duties of the proposed guardian of the person under sections 2351-2358 of the Probate Code be granted *(specify orders, facts, and reasons in attachment 1f)*.
   g. [ ] an order dispensing with notice to the persons named in attachment 14 be granted.
   h. [X] other orders be granted *(specify in attachment 1h)*.

2. The minor is *(name)*: DANIEL FRANK LEE   [ ] married [X] unmarried.
   (present address): 2 West Street   *(telephone)*: 714-555-1212
   Santa Ana, CA 92702

3. Date of minor's birth: 11/1/79
4. Petitioner is
   a. [X] related to the minor as *(specify)*: Paternal grandmother
   b. [ ] a minor 12 years of age or older.
   c. [ ] other person on behalf of minor *(specify)*:
5. The proposed guardian is
   a. [X] nominee (affix nomination as attachment 5).
   b. [X] related to minor as *(specify)*: Paternal grandmother
   c. [ ] other *(specify)*:

6. a. [X] The person having legal custody of the minor is *(name and address)*:
   BRIAN LEE
   800 East Way, San Francisco, CA 94102

   b. [X] *(Complete only if this person is one other than the person having legal custody.)* The person having care of the minor is *(name and address)*:
   PATRICIA ANN LEE
   2 West Street, Santa Ana, CA

7. The minor
   a. [X] is not [ ] is a patient in or on leave of absence from a state institution under the jurisdiction of the State Department of Mental Health or the State Department of Developmental Services *(specify state institution)*:

   b. [X] is neither receiving nor entitled to receive [ ] is receiving or entitled to receive benefits from the Veterans Administration *(estimate amount of monthly benefit payable)*: $

Do NOT use this form for a temporary guardianship.   *(Continued on reverse)*

Form Approved by the
Judicial Council of California
GC-210 [Rev. January 1, 1993]*

**PETITION FOR APPOINTMENT OF
GUARDIAN OF MINOR**

Probate Code, § 1510
*Use of form GC-210 (revised 1/1/89) is authorized until 12/31/93 if petitioner is not a minor, or if item 4b is corrected by changing "14" to "12."

GUARDIANSHIP OF (Name): DANIEL FRANK LEE MINOR	CASE NUMBER:

8. Petitioner [ ] has no knowledge [X] has knowledge that the minor is receiving public assistance benefits, or that there are any adoption, juvenile court, marriage dissolution, domestic relations, custody, or other similar proceedings affecting the minor (specify in attachment 8).

9. [ ] Petitioner, with intent to adopt, has accepted or intends to accept physical care or custody of the minor.

10. [ ] A person other than the proposed guardian has been nominated by [ ] will [ ] other nomination (nomination affixed in attachment 10) (specify name and address):

11. Character and estimated value of property of the estate
    Personal property: $ _____
    Annual gross income from
    [ ] real property: $ _____
    [ ] personal property: $ _____
    Total: $ _____
    Real property: $ _____

12. Appointment of a guardian of the [X] person [ ] estate of the minor is necessary and convenient.

13. [ ] Granting the proposed guardian of the estate powers to be exercised independently under section 2590 of the Probate Code would be to the advantage and benefit and in the best interest of the guardianship estate. Powers and reasons are specified in attachment 13.

14. [ ] Notice to the persons named in attachment 14 should be dispensed with under section 1511 of the Probate Code because [ ] they cannot with reasonable diligence be given notice (specify names and efforts to locate in attachment 14)
    [ ] the giving of notice would be contrary to the interest of justice (specify names and reasons in attachment 14).

15. (Complete this section only for a petition, other than one for appointment of a guardian of the estate only, filed by a person who is not related to the minor and who has not been nominated as guardian by a parent under section 1500 of the Probate Code.)
    a. [ ] Petitioner is the proposed guardian and will promptly furnish all information requested by any agency referred to in section 1543 of the Probate Code.
    [ ] Petitioner is not the proposed guardian. A statement by the proposed guardian that he or she will promptly furnish all information requested by any agency referred to in section 1543 of the Probate Code is affixed as attachment 15a.
    b. The proposed guardian's home [ ] is [ ] is not a licensed foster family home.
    c. [ ] The proposed guardian has never filed any petition for adoption of the minor [ ] except as specified in attachment 15c.

16. [X] A Declaration Under Uniform Child Custody Jurisdiction Act (UCCJA) is filed with this petition. (The declaration must be filed if this petition requests appointment of a guardian of the person. See Judicial Council form MC-150.)

17. [X] Filed with this petition are the following (see Judicial Council forms GC-211 and GC-110):
    [X] Consent of Proposed Guardian   [X] Waiver of Notice and Consent
    [X] Nomination of Guardian   [ ] Petition for Appointment of Temporary Guardian

18. The names, residence addresses, and relationships of the father, mother, spouse, and all relatives within the second degree of the minor so far as known to petitioner are as follows:

    RELATIONSHIP AND NAME   RESIDENCE ADDRESS
    a. Father: Brian Lee   800 East Way
                                         San Francisco, CA 94102

    b. Mother: Ruth Simmons Lee - deceased

    c. Spouse: N/A

    d. Sister: Alice Lee   800 East Way
                                         San Francisco, CA 94102

    e. [X] List of names and addresses continued in attachment 18.

19. [X] Number of pages attached: 5

Date: 4/4/93

▶ *Patricia Ann Lee*
(SIGNATURE OF PETITIONER*)

▶ _____
(SIGNATURE OF PETITIONER*)

I declare under penalty of perjury under the laws of the State of California that the foregoing is true and correct.
Date: 4/4/93

PATRICIA ANN LEE
(TYPE OR PRINT NAME)

▶ *Patricia Ann Lee*
(SIGNATURE OF PETITIONER*)

* All petitioners must sign the petition. Only one need sign the declaration.

GC-210 [Rev. January 1, 1993]   **PETITION FOR APPOINTMENT OF GUARDIAN OF MINOR**   Page two

GUARDIANSHIP OF (Name): _____ Case Number: _____

ATTACHMENT 1h
to Petition for Appointment of Guardian of Minor:
Request for Additional Orders

[ ] <u>REQUEST FOR ORDER WAIVING SERVICE BY MAIL OF ORDER APPOINTING GUARDIAN OF MINOR</u>

    1. The minor who is the subject of this guardianship proceeding is at least 12 years of age, and will attend the hearing on this petition.

    2. The minor has received notice of the guardianship proceeding. The original proof of service is or will be filed with the court by the time of the guardianship hearing.

    3. An extra copy of the Order Appointing Guardian of Minor will be available to the minor at the hearing.

    4. It would be an unnecessary inconvenience to mail the minor a copy of the Order Appointing Guardian of Minor before Letters of Guardianship issue.

[ ] <u>REQUEST FOR ORDER WAIVING ACCOUNTINGS (Probate Code §2628)</u>

    1.[ ] This petition is for the guardianship of the [ ] estate or [ ] person and estate of_____.

    2.[ ] Petitioner is or will be receiving the following public benefit payments on behalf of the minor:

        [ ] Aid to Families with Dependent Children (AFDC);

        [ ] General Assistance from _____
            County; or

        [ ] Supplemental Security Income and State Supplemental Program
            (SSI/SSP) benefits paid through the Social Security Administration.

3.[ ] The minor receives:

    [ ] less than $300 per month in addition to these benefits; or

    [ ] no additional money per month in addition to these benefits.

4. The entire assets belonging to the minor does not exceed $5,000 (excluding clothes and ordinary household items).

5. Any money petitioner will receive on behalf of the minor will be spent for the benefit of the minor.

6. It would be an unnecessary inconvenience to complete accountings for the minor's estate, and such accountings should be waived pursuant to Probate Code §2628.

For each minor, fill in the name, current street address (not post office box), city, state, zip code and telephone number (including the area code) in the spaces indicated. Also, check the box next to the word "unmarried" if the minor is unmarried (or if the marriage was annulled). If the minor is married, check the box next to "married." Remember, you can obtain guardianship of a minor's estate but not the minor's person if the minor is or has been married, and that marriage was not annulled.

Item 3: Fill in the minor's date of birth.

Item 4: Check only one box, whichever applies:

Check the first box if you are related to the minor, and list the relationship. Be specific, such as, "maternal aunt" if you're the minor's mother's sister, or "paternal grandmother" if you're the minor's father's mother.

Leave the second box blank. This is intended to be checked only by a minor over age 12 who is filing for the guardianship on her own.[3]

Check the third box if you're not related to the minor by blood or marriage. Then, after the words "other (specify)," briefly describe your relationship with the minor. This might be "best friend of minor's deceased mother," or just "adult friend of minor." If either of the minor's parents specifically nominated you in writing to be the minor's guardian, state that as well. For example, you might use a description such as "nominated by minor's deceased father in his will."

Item 5: Note that you may need to check more than one box in this item.

Check the first box if either or both of the minor's parents nominated you in writing to be the minor's guardian, or if someone who's giving property to the minor nominated you in writing to be the guardian of that part of the minor's estate. You will have to attach a copy of the written nomination as "Attachment 5." This could be a copy of a letter from a parent asking you to care for the minor, or a copy of a will which nominates you as guardian.[4] If you have obtained signatures of one or both of the minor's parents on the Nomination of Guardian section of the three-part Consent of Guardian, Nomination and Waiver of Notice form (Chapter 4), you don't need to attach a copy as long as you file the signed Nomination of Guardian form with the court.

Check the second box if you are a relative of the minor, and indicate the relationship, just as you did in the first box in Item 4.

Check the third box if you're not a relative of the minor and you haven't been nominated in writing by the minor's parents. Then fill in the information just as you did in the third box in Item 4.

Item 6: This two-part item is located on the right side of the form, across from Items 3 through 5.

Item 6a: Check this box if any living person has legal custody of the minor. Unless a court decree of divorce or legal separation has given "legal custody" to one parent, this would be both parents if they are still alive, or the surviving parent. Note that many California courts typically award "legal custody" to both parents even if one parent has physical custody. Get copies of a court decree of divorce or legal separation if you aren't sure who has legal custody. List the names and addresses of one or both individuals having legal custody of the minor.[5]

Item 6b: Check this box if the person who is taking care of the minor is different from the one who has legal custody. Then list the name and address of the person with whom the minor is living. Where you're seeking guardianship of the minor's person, if the minor is already living with you, list your own name and address.

Item 7a: This item asks if the minor is either a patient of or on leave from an institution which is operated by the California Department of Mental Health or the State Department of Developmental Services. Check the first box next to the words "is not," if the minor is not a patient in an institution for the mentally disabled or severely disabled. Check the second box next to the word "is," if the minor is a

---

[3]This book does not cover situations where the minor is the one seeking the guardianship. See Chapter 13 for how to do your own research, or how to find and deal with attorneys.

[4] If the parent or, for guardianship of a minor's estate only, the person who gave the minor a gift, is available and willing to sign a nomination form, the better practice is to file a separate Nomination of Guardian. (See Chapter 4, Section E.)

[5]Even if the minor is living with you, you do not have legal custody of the minor unless you have been granted that right by a court. However, when you become the minor's guardian, you will then have legal custody.

patient in such an institution, or even on leave from one. If you checked the second box in this item, you should see an attorney. (See Chapter 13.)

Item 7b: Children of disabled or deceased veterans are eligible and may be receiving Veterans' Administration benefits. (See Chapter 2, Section C6, for more information about these benefits.) Check the first box next to the words "is not," if the minor is neither receiving nor entitled to receive benefits from the Veterans' Administration. Check the second box next to the word "is," if the minor is receiving or is entitled to receive benefits from the Veterans' Administration. Then list the monthly amount in the space indicated.

CAPTION: PAGE TWO OF THE PETITION FOR APPOINTMENT OF GUARDIAN OF MINOR

In capital letters fill in the minor's first, middle and last names after the words "GUARDIANSHIP OF."

Leave the case number blank since it hasn't been assigned yet.

Item 8: This item asks if the minor is receiving welfare benefits, and if there are any adoption, juvenile court, divorce, or other custody proceedings relating to the minor. Specific situations are discussed in more detail below.

- *Public Assistance Benefits:* Welfare payments supporting minors are not made directly to them, but to a parent or other adult under a program such as Aid to Families with Dependent Children (AFDC). A portion of these benefits are considered to belong to the minor even though someone else receives them. (See Chapter 2, Section C3, for more information on public assistance benefits.)
- *Divorce:* Any divorce proceedings between the minor's parents, whether in the process or final, must be listed. Even divorces which occurred years ago should be listed since a final divorce decree can be reopened to change custody, support and visitation arrangements.
- *Adoption:* All pending adoption proceedings involving the minor must be listed. For example, if you are seeking a guardianship to prevent a minor from being finally placed in a foster home or adopted, you must state that such proceedings are going on.
- *Juvenile Court Action:* List all juvenile court cases involving the minor. This includes pending juvenile court cases, and all cases made final, including those which resulted in an order making the minor either a "dependent of the juvenile court" or "ward of the juvenile court." List all criminal juvenile cases, including those in which the juvenile is on probation.
- *Pending Custody Proceedings:* List all pending custody proceedings affecting the minor, such as a custody suit between unmarried parents.

Important: If you know of any case of the type listed above which has been filed but not yet finally decided by a court, see a lawyer for advice on how it may affect your petition for guardianship. In some instances, such as pending adoptions, the cases must be consolidated. We do not recommend doing your own guardianship if there are open cases of any kind affecting the child's legal status, unless both parents, if living, are not claiming rights to custody of the minor—for example, both parents have abandoned their child or consent to the guardianship by nominating you as guardian.

If any of the proceedings listed above apply, you must obtain copies of the legal documents. In Item 8, check the first box next to the words "has no knowledge" if you are sure that the minor is *not* receiving public assistance benefits such as welfare, and you know that there are *not* any adoption, juvenile court, divorce, or other custody proceedings relating to the minor.

Check the second box next to the words "has knowledge" if you know that the minor is receiving public assistance benefits or that there are any pending adoption, juvenile court, divorce, or other custody proceedings involving the minor.

If you checked the second box, you must prepare an attachment to the form following the instructions in Chapter 3, Section D3. Label the document "Attachment 8 to Petition for Appointment of Guardian of Minor" at the top. You can refer to our sample for an example of how this is done. If the minor is receiving public assistance, state the type and amount of benefits being received, the name and address of the person receiving benefits, and the name of the county or other governmental agency paying the benefits.

If the minor is being affected by any of the types of court proceedings mentioned above, on Attachment 8 state the name and type of each case, the name of the court (including state and county), the case number and a brief description of the status of the case or how it was resolved. If the parents are divorced and still living, you still must list the divorce case in Attachment 8. State that it is a closed divorce case, and give the date of the final divorce decree. Refer to the accompanying sample as a guide.

Item 9: Check this item only if you eventually hope to adopt the minor, even if you haven't yet filed a petition for adoption.[6] When you check this item, it guides the court investigator or social services department in conducting the investigation.

Item 10: Except for very rare situations, you will leave this item blank. It asks whether anyone besides you has been nominated guardian. For example, a parent may nominate a guardian of the minor's person or estate, and a donor of a gift may nominate a guardian in a will or other document. If a person *other than you* has been nominated for a guardianship either of the minor's person or estate, contact an attorney.

(See Chapter 13.) The law requires that the first person nominated be given preference for guardianship unless the person is found to be unsuitable.[7] If this is your situation, check the first box, and either the box next to the word "will" or "other nomination." Then list the name and address of the other person nominated in the space provided. You also would have to attach a copy of the nomination as "Attachment 10."

Item 11: If you are seeking guardianship of a minor's person only, skip this item. If you are seeking guardianship of a minor's estate or person and estate, turn to Chapter 10, Section B to complete this item.

Item 12: Check one or both boxes next to the words "person" and "estate," whichever apply. In this item you simply state that it is proper for the court to appoint you as guardian of the minor's person, estate, or both.

Item 13: If you are seeking guardianship of a minor's person only, skip this item. If you are seeking guardianship of a minor's estate, or person and estate, turn to Chapter 10, Section B to complete this item.

Item 14: If you checked Item 1g of this form, you will need to complete this item. If you did not check Item 1g, skip to Item 15.

To complete this item, you again will need to look at the Guardianship Notification Worksheet. If you were unable to locate one or more relatives, check the first box next to the words "they cannot with reasonable diligence be given notice." You will then have to add an Attachment 14 explaining your efforts to locate each person. Fortunately, you should have already completed a Due Diligence Declaration for each relative you couldn't locate, following the instructions in Chapter 4. If for some reason you didn't complete Due Diligence Declarations for all missing relatives for whom you searched, turn to Chapter 4, Section D1 and do it now.

---

[6]If you do file a petition to adopt the minor, the guardianship proceeding should be consolidated with the adoption proceeding and transferred to the court's Family Law Division.

[7]It is possible that one person would be nominated guardian of a minor's person, and another person nominated guardian of the estate of the same minor. In this case, there might not be a conflict between the two guardianships. This is, however, beyond the scope of this book.

SHORT TITLE: Guardianship of DANIEL FRANK LEE	CASE NUMBER:

ATTACHMENT 8
TO PETITION FOR APPOINTMENT OF GUARDIAN OF MINOR

1. I have applied for and will start receiving AFDC payments in the amount of approximately $___ per month on behalf of the minor starting in May, 1992.

2. I know of two legal proceedings affecting the minor:

(a) The minor is involved in Orange County Juvenile Court Case No. XXX. This case involves an incident where the minor was allegedly caught shoplifting in a grocery store. The minor is presently on probation. His probation officer is Jackie Z.

(b) The minor's parents, Brian Lee and Ruth Simmons Lee (now deceased) were divorced on April 30, 1980. The dissolution took place in Santa Clara Superior Court, Case No. YYY. The minor's mother was awarded custody, and the minor's father was given visitation rights.

3. I do not know of any other public assistance benefits which the minor is receiving, or any other legal proceedings affecting the minor, except for those described in this Attachment 8.

(Required for verified pleading) The items on this page stated on information and belief are *(specify item numbers, not line numbers)*:

This page may be used with any Judicial Council form or any other paper filed with the court.   Page 2 of 5

Form Approved by the Judicial Council of California
MC-020 [New January 1, 1987]

ADDITIONAL PAGE
Attach to Judicial Council Form or Other Court Paper

CRC 201, 501

Do not check the second box next to the words "the giving of notice would be contrary to the interest of justice," which refers to situations in which you want to avoid notifying a person whose whereabouts are known. If there is a relative you can locate but don't want to notify for what you think are very good reasons, you will need to consult a lawyer. (See Chapter 13.)

Example: Baby Judy's grandmother is planning to seek a guardianship of Judy's person. Judy's unmarried mother (the grandmother's daughter) is 15 years old, and agrees with the guardianship. Judy's father (who is not listed on her birth certificate) is also 15 years old. Both he and his parents have made it clear that they want nothing to do with Judy or her family. They have sent a letter to Judy's grandmother requesting that she never contact them, and tell no one who the father is since it only causes pain and hard feelings. In their letter they also suggest that she put the baby up for adoption. With the help of a lawyer, Judy's grandmother obtains permission from a judge which allows her not to list or serve Judy's father or his parents in the guardianship documents.

Item 15: As the instructions on the form indicate, you only need to complete this item (15a-c) if all three of the following are true:

1) You are only seeking guardianship of the minor's person; *and*

2) You are not related to the minor; *and*

3) You were not nominated guardian by one or both parents of the minor.[8]

Skip this item if:
- You are only seeking guardianship of the minor's estate; *or*
- You are related to the minor; *or*
- You were nominated in writing by a parent of the minor to be the minor's guardian.

Item 15a: If this item applies to you, check the first box. It says that you, the petitioner, are the proposed guardian, and that you'll give information to agencies—such as local social services agencies—that might request it. If such information is ever requested, which is unlikely unless you seek to adopt the minor, it would probably be similar to the information an investigator would request. (See Chapter 8.)

Do not check the second box unless you, the petitioner, are not also the proposed guardian.[9]

Item 15b: Check the first box next to the word "is" only if your home is a licensed foster care home. If you do not contract with government agencies such as counties to temporarily take children into your home, and are not licensed for this, check the second box next to the words "is not."

Item 15c: Check the first box. If you have never filed a petition for the minor's adoption, go on to Item 16. If you have filed a petition for the minor's adoption, also check the box next to the words "except as specified." You then also need to prepare a continuation of the form following the instructions for preparing attachments in Chapter 3, Section D3. Label the top of the attachment "Attachment 15c to Petition for Appointment of Guardian of Minor: Information on Petition for Adoption of Minor." In Attachment 15c, you must include information about the adoption proceeding. If your adoption petition was denied, see a lawyer, since a judge will want to know why you still should be appointed the child's guardian.

Item 16: Skip this item if you are only seeking guardianship of a minor's estate. If you are seeking guardianship of a minor's person, or guardianship of both a minor's person and estate, check this box. Then fill in the words "See Attachment 16." You will fill out the form referred to in this item later, in Section B of this chapter.

Item 17: This item tells the court what other separate legal documents you are filing at the same time as the Petition for Appointment of Guardian of Minor. If, as you usually would be, you are filing the three-part Consent of Guardian, Nomination and Waiver of

---

[8]Remember that to be nominated by a parent as the minor's guardian, the parent will need to sign a legal document such as the Nomination of Guardian (see Chapter 4, Section E), a will naming you as the minor's guardian, or other legal document.

[9]This book assumes that you, the petitioner, are also the proposed guardian. However, if you, the petitioner, are not also the proposed guardian—you must prepare an Attachment 15a following the instructions in Chapter 3, Section D3. On the attachment type in the words "I am the proposed guardian and will promptly furnish all information requested by any agency referred to in Section 1543 of the Probate Code." Then put a signature line for the proposed guardian to sign, and obtain the proposed guardian's signature.

Notice form discussed in Chapter 4 (as a substitute for serving close relatives of the minor with legal papers), or a Petition for Appointment of Temporary Guardian discussed in Chapter 7, check the first box in this item.

Then check any of the four boxes which follow, as they apply. The first three boxes all refer to the three-part Consent of Guardian, Nomination and Waiver of Notice form. (See Chapter 4, Section E, where this form is discussed and step-by-step instructions are given for completing it.)

Check the first box next to "Consent of Proposed Guardian." Make sure you have completed and signed this portion of the form following the instructions in Chapter 4, Section E1.

Check the second box next to "Nomination of Guardian" if you have completed this section of the form and obtained signatures of one or both of the minor's parents.

Check the third box next to "Waiver of Notice and Consent" if you have completed this section of the form and obtained signatures of some or all of the minor's relatives.

Check the fourth box only if you will be filing a Petition for Appointment of Temporary Guardian. (See Chapter 7 for information and instructions on how to petition for a temporary guardianship.)

Item 18: Look at the Guardianship Notification Worksheet to complete this item. Then list the name and address of each of the minor's close relatives (maternal grandparents, paternal grandparents, brothers and sisters, spouse and children). If you do not know a name or address for a particular relative, fill in the word "unknown." If a relative has died, fill in the word "deceased." If the minor's mother and father are listed on his birth certificate, make sure you list them, even if you do not know where they are.

Important: It is essential that you list all known names and addresses. If you know the name or address of a parent or spouse, but do not list them, that person may later claim the guardianship was not properly obtained and ask the court to end it.

Item 18a: After the word "Father," list the minor's father's name. If he is dead, put the word "deceased" after his name. If you do not know who the father is, fill in "unknown." You will then need to supply some proof of this, by attaching a copy of the minor's birth certificate labeled "Attachment 18a."[10] At the right, under the words "RESIDENCE ADDRESS," fill in the minor's father's address. If you do not know his address, put in the word "unknown."

Item 18b: After the word "Mother," list the minor's mother's name. If she is dead, put the word "deceased" after her name. At the right, under the words "RESIDENCE ADDRESS," fill in the minor's mother's address. If you do not know where she is, fill in the word "unknown."

Item 18c: This item only applies to guardianships of a minor's estate, in the rare situation where the minor is married. If this does not apply, skip this item. Otherwise, after the word "Spouse," list the minor's spouse's name. If the spouse is dead, follow the name with the word "deceased." At the right, under the words "RESIDENCE ADDRESS," fill in the minor's spouse's address, or the word "unknown," if that information is not available.

Items 18d, 18e and Attachment 18: Beginning with the blank Item 18d, list all of the minor's living grandparents, brothers and sisters and children in the same format as Items 18a-c. If there is more than one additional living relative, check Item 18e. You then will need to prepare a continuation of the form on a separate page. You can use a blank piece of paper or an Additional Page Judicial Council form provided in Appendix D. (See Chapter 3, Section D3 for how to complete attachments.) Label the page "Attachment 18 to Petition for Appointment of Guardian of Minor: Additional Names and Addresses of Minor's Relatives" at the top. At the left of the page type in the words "Relationship and Name," and at the right type in "Residence Address." Then list each living relative and address. You can refer to our sample for the format.

---

[10]Some courts (such as Santa Clara) require a copy of the minor's birth certificate, while others do not. To play it safe, attach a copy of the birth certificate.

Item 19: Check the box. If you are not attaching any additional pages, fill in the word "None." Otherwise, count up and enter the number of total pages to be attached. If you include any pages which are double-sided photocopies, count each side as a separate page. A checklist of possible attachment follows. The attachments all should be stapled (in numerical order) to the Petition for Appointment of Guardian of Minor before you file it with the court. If you are seeking guardianship of a minor's person or person and estate, leave this item blank until you complete the Declaration Under Uniform Child Custody Jurisdiction Act following the instructions in Section B.

CHECKLIST OF POSSIBLE ATTACHMENTS TO PETITION FOR APPOINTMENT OF GUARDIAN OF MINOR*

- ☐ Attachment 1c: Information on additional minors. (A form is provided in Appendix D.)
- ☐ Attachment 1d: Information on bond requirements.
- ☐ *Attachment 1f: Information on special orders for guardianship of a minor's person. (This material is beyond the scope of this book.)*
- ☐ Attachment 1h: Request for additional orders waiving service of Order Appointing Guardian of Minor and waiving accountings. (A form is provided in Appendix D.)
- ☐ Attachment 5: Copy of nomination of proposed guardian.
- ☐ Attachment 8: Information on minor's public assistance benefits, and court proceedings affecting minor. (A completed sample is provided.)
- ☐ *Attachment 10: Copy of nomination of a person other than the proposed guardian. (This material is beyond the scope of this book.)*
- ☐ *Attachment 13: Information on additional powers for guardianship of a minor's estate. (This material is beyond the scope of this book.)*
- ☐ Attachment 14: Declaration of due diligence for people you could not locate. (A completed sample is provided in Chapter 4, Section D1. A form is provided in Appendix D.)
- ☐ Attachment 15a: Statement by proposed guardian other than petitioner regarding willingness to furnish information to agencies.
- ☐ Attachment 15c: Information on a petition for adoption of minor.
- ☐ Attachment 16: Declaration Under Uniform Child Custody Jurisdiction Act. (Instructions and a completed sample are provided in Section B of this chapter. A form is provided in Appendix D.)
- ☐ Attachment 18: Additional names and addresses of minor's relatives. (A completed sample is provided.)
- ☐ Attachment 18a: Copy of the minor's birth certificate, showing proof that the minor's father is unknown.

*Some or possibly all of these Attachments may be required. See the instructions for each item number. Attachments in the checklist which are italicized are for situations beyond the scope of this book, and you probably will need to consult an attorney if you need to include any of them.

SHORT TITLE: Guardianship of DANIEL FRANK LEE	CASE NUMBER:

ATTACHMENT 18
TO PETITION FOR APPOINTMENT OF GUARDIAN OF MINOR:
ADDITIONAL NAMES AND ADDRESSES OF MINOR'S RELATIVES

RELATIONSHIP AND NAME	RESIDENCE ADDRESS
f. Brother: Eric Lee	Unknown
g. Paternal Grandfather: Dan Lee	2 West Street Santa Ana, CA 92702
h. Maternal Grandmother: Rose Smith	400 East Street Cleveland, Ohio 44118
i. Maternal Grandfather: Hank Smith	400 East Street Cleveland, Ohio 44118

(Required for verified pleading) The items on this page stated on information and belief are *(specify item numbers, not line numbers)*:

This page may be used with any Judicial Council form or any other paper filed with the court.   Page 3 of 5

Form Approved by the
Judicial Council of California
MC-020 [New January 1, 1987]

ADDITIONAL PAGE
Attach to Judicial Council Form or Other Court Paper

CRC 201, 501

Finally, fill in today's date in the space near the first two signature lines at the bottom of the page. If more than one person is petitioning to be the minor's guardian, each of you must sign on the first two signature lines.

In the box at the bottom, only one petitioner needs to sign. Again, fill in today's date. To the left of the signature line, type or clearly print your name in capital letters, and finally sign your name. You're now ready to prepare the next form.

B. Declaration Under Uniform Child Custody Jurisdiction Act (Guardianship of a Minor's Person Only)

SKIP THIS ENTIRE SECTION if you are only seeking guardianship of a minor's estate. But if you are seeking guardianship of a minor's person, or person and estate, you must complete a two-page form called a Declaration Under Uniform Child Custody Jurisdiction Act. This form—which we refer to as the UCCJA Declaration—will be attached to the petition as Attachment 16.

The UCCJA Declaration gives information about you, the minor, and the minor's custody situation. You may recall that you listed information about divorce, adoption, juvenile court and other custody proceedings involving the minor in Item 8 of the petition.[11] But even though some of the information on the UCCJA Declaration is repetitious, you must complete it if you want to be appointed guardian of a minor's person.

> **CAPTION:** DECLARATION UNDER UNIFORM CHILD CUSTODY JURISDICTION ACT
>
> At the top of the form fill in the words "Attachment 16 to Petition for Appointment of Guardian of Minor."
>
> Fill in the caption following the general instructions in Chapter 3, Section D1.
>
> Leave the case number blank. You will be assigned a case number when you file your documents with the court.

Item 1: Leave this item blank. It states that you are involved in a legal action to determine custody of the minor.

Item 2: This item applies if the minor has allegedly been abused. If so, the minor's address and the address of the person alleging the abuse may remain confidential in all court documents.

Item 3: List the number of minors for whom you are seeking guardianship. You are given room in this item to fill in information for up to two minors. If you are seeking guardianship of more than two minors, you must add attachment pages. (This is covered below in Item 3c.)

Item 3a: In the spaces provided, fill in the minor's complete first, middle and last names, place and date of birth, and sex. Or check the box if the address is to remain confidential (see Item 2).

Below that are boxes for you to list all the places where the minor has lived for the past five years unless, of course, the minor is under five years of age. If you don't know the exact dates, give the closest approximation, after the words "estimated dates." Start with the place the minor is now living, and then continue listing the rest in reverse chronological order.

---

[11] As stated earlier, if there are any pending court actions affecting the minor, other than a final divorce decree of the minor's parents, you should consult a lawyer. (See Chapter 13.)

For each time period, indicate the months and
rs on each side of the word "to" and make sure
 the second date you fill in is the same as the first
 in the box above. For example, if the minor now
s with you and has been since June 1987, the left-
d box in the first row would read "6/87 to
sent." In this example, 6/87 is when the child
ved, so the information on the line below that
uld read "5/86 to 6/87" if the child lived at the
vious address between May 1986 and June 1987.
Period of Residence: In the first column, list the
month and year the minor began living at each
ddress, and the month and year the minor moved
rom that address.
Address: For each period of residence, fill in the
he street address, city and state where the minor is
or was living.
Person child lived with: For each period of
esidence, fill in the names of the adults with
whom the minor is or was living, along with their
current address. Of course, if the minor is living
with you, list your address again in this column.
Relationship: For each period of residence, fill in
he relationship of the person with whom the
minor lived. For example, this might be "mother
nd father," "maternal uncle" or "stepmother."
Item 3b: If you are only seeking guardianship of
 minor, skip this item. Otherwise, fill in the name,
e and date of birth, and sex of an additional
or. If this minor has lived at the same address as
minor listed in Item 3a, check the box next to the
ds "Residence information is the same as given
ve for the minor listed in 3a." Otherwise, provide
 information requested following the instructions
Item 3a.
Item 3c: If you are seeking guardianship of one
wo minors, skip this item. If you are seeking
rdianship of three or more minors, check this box.
 must prepare an attachment to the form following
 instructions in Chapter 3, Section D3. Label the
ument "Attachment 3c to Declaration Under
form Child Custody Jurisdiction Act" at the top.
n give the same information for each additional
or that is asked for in Items 3a and 3b.

> **CAPTION:** PAGE TWO OF THE DECLARATION UNDER UNIFORM CHILD CUSTODY JURISDICTION ACT
>
> In capital letters fill in the minor's first, middle and last names after the words "GUARDIANSHIP OF."
> Leave the case number blank since it hasn't been assigned yet.

Item 4: This item requires information on any other legal proceeding involving the minor in which you have participated, such as litigation, divorce, adoption, guardianship, or juvenile court. Your involvement may have been either as a party (such as petitioner, respondent, plaintiff or defendant), or as a witness. You must include proceedings in other states. If you have not been involved in any such proceeding as a party or witness, simply check the "No" box and skip to Item 5.

If you have participated in other such proceedings, check the "Yes" box. You must then fill in the requested information in Items 4a-d:

Item 4a: If this item applies to you, fill in the names of all minors for whom you're seeking guardianship who were involved in a legal proceeding in which you participated.

Item 4b: You are considered the "declarant" in this item. Check the box next to the word "party" if you were a plaintiff, defendant, petitioner or respondent in a legal proceeding involving the minor. For example, one of these terms applies if you sought custody of the minor or someone else sought custody from you. If you only testified as a witness in court or in a deposition, check the box next to the word "witness."

Item 4c: Fill in the name of the court where the proceeding took place, followed by the state and county or city. For example, this might be "Superior Court of California, Santa Clara County, North County (Palo Alto) Branch," or "Pennsylvania Court of Common Pleas, Philadelphia County." If you know the case number, list that as well.

Item 4d: Fill in the date the court entered its most recent order, judgment, or decree regarding custody of the child. If you don't know it, call the court and ask the clerk to check the file. Also make arrangements with the clerk to get copies of these court documents.

To get copies, you will probably need to send a fee to the court, along with a self-addressed, stamped envelope.

Item 5: List any court proceedings—other than those listed in Item 4—involving custody of the minor. If you don't know of any, check the box next to the word "No," box and skip to Item 6.

If you do know of other proceedings, check the box next to the word "Yes." You must then fill in the requested information in Items 5a-d:

Item 5a: Fill in the names of all minors involved in any custody proceedings.

Item 5b: Check the box that applies to indicate whether the other proceeding affecting the minor is a divorce (or "dissolution of marriage"), another guardianship, an adoption, or some other kind of proceeding, such as a juvenile court case for dependency.

Item 5c: Fill in the name and location of the court. (See the instructions for Item 4c above.)

Item 5d: Fill in a brief description about the current status of the proceeding. Here are a few examples:

"Final judgment of dissolution of marriage granted to Petra Petitioner in 5/91, custody awarded to Reginald Respondent."

"Minor named ward of the Juvenile Court in 6/89, jurisdiction terminated in 6/90."

If the case has been filed but there is no final decision on it, fill in the words "Case is pending." However, as indicated earlier, if any custody proceeding affecting the minor is still pending, you should seek a lawyer's advice before going any further.

Item 6: If anyone other than you has physical custody of the minor, has visitation rights under a divorce or other decree, or merely claims to have the right to custody or visitation of the minor, you must check the "Yes" box and provide specific information regarding this item. Normally, this would be one or both of the minor's parents, even if the parents are not vigorously insisting on their right to visit or care for the child.[12] If none of these situations applies, check the "No" box, and skip the instructions for the rest of this item.

If you checked the "Yes" box, complete Items 5a-c:

Items 6a-c: In these large boxes (a, b and c), list information on up to three people who claim or have the right to custody or visitation. List the names and addresses of any individuals in the spaces provided and check whether that person "Has physical custody," "Claims custody rights," or "Claims visitation rights." In the space below that, list the name of the minor.

Now fill in the date and your name in the spaces provided, and sign your name.

Item 7: Check the box. If you are not attaching any additional pages, fill in the word "None." Otherwise, count up and enter the number of total pages to be attached.

Finally, attach this document to the Petition for Appointment of Guardian of Minor as Attachment 16. Make sure you have listed the correct number of attachment pages in Item 19 of the petition.

getting legal custody of the minor. If the guardianship is contested, consult a lawyer. (See Chapter 13.)

---

[12] As discussed many times earlier, you should not attempt to do a guardianship proceeding yourself if you are aware of a parent or other person who opposes it or who insists on

PREPARING FORMS TO FILE FOR A GUARDIANSHIP

ATTACHMENT 16 TO PETITION FOR APPOINTMENT OF GUARDIAN OF MINOR

ATTORNEY OR PARTY WITHOUT ATTORNEY *(Name and Mailing Address)*:	TELEPHONE NO.:	FOR COURT USE ONLY
PATRICIA ANN LEE 2 West St. Santa Ana, CA 92702	714/555-1212	

ATTORNEY FOR *(Name)*: In Pro Per

SUPERIOR COURT OF CALIFORNIA, COUNTY OF ORANGE
STREET ADDRESS: 700 Civic Center Drive West
MAILING ADDRESS: P.O. Box 838
CITY AND ZIP CODE: Santa Ana, CA 92702
BRANCH NAME:

CASE NAME:
Guardianship of DANIEL FRANK LEE

DECLARATION UNDER UNIFORM CHILD CUSTODY JURISDICTION ACT (UCCJA)	CASE NUMBER:

1. **I am a party** to this proceeding to determine custody of a child.
2. ☐ Declarant's present address is not disclosed. It is confidential under Civil Code section 5158. The address of children presently residing with declarant is identified on this declaration as confidential.
3. *(Number)*: One (1) minor children are subject to this proceeding as follows:
   (Insert the information requested below. The residence information must be given for the last FIVE years.)

a. Child's name	Place of birth	Date of birth	Sex
DANIEL FRANK LEE	Cleveland, OH	11/1/76	Male

Period of residence	Address	Person child lived with *(name and present address)*	Relationship
6/87 to present	2 West St. Santa Ana, CA 92702 ☐ Confidential	PATRICIA ANN LEE 2 West St., Santa Ana	Paternal grandmother
5/86 to 6/87	800 East Way San Francisco, CA 94102	BRIAN LEE 800 East Way San Francisco, CA	Father
2/84 to 5/86	20 West Avenue Cleveland, OH 44118	BRIAN LEE 800 East Way San Francisco, CA	Father
to			
to			

b. Child's name	Place of birth	Date of birth	Sex
☐ Residence information is the same as given above for child a. *(If NOT the same, provide the information below.)*			

Period of residence	Address	Person child lived with *(name and present address)*	Relationship
to present	☐ Confidential		
to			
to			
to			

c. ☐ Additional children are listed on Attachment 3c. *(Provide requested information for additional children on an attachment.)*

(Continued on reverse)

Form Approved by the
Judicial Council of California
MC-150 [Rev. January 1, 1993]

**DECLARATION UNDER
UNIFORM CHILD CUSTODY JURISDICTION ACT (UCCJA)**

Civil Code, § 5158
Probate Code, §§ 1510(f), 1512

SHORT TITLE: Guardianship of DANIEL FRANK LEE	CASE NUMBER:

4. Have you participated as a party or a witness or in some other capacity in another litigation or custody proceeding, in California or elsewhere, concerning custody of a child subject to this proceeding?
   [X] No [ ] Yes *(If yes, provide the following information:)*

   a. Name of each child:

   b. Capacity of declarant: [ ] party [ ] witness [ ] other *(specify)*:
   c. Court *(specify name, state, location)*:

   d. Court order or judgment *(date)*:

5. Do you have information about a custody proceeding pending in a California court or any other court concerning a child subject to this proceeding, other than that stated in item 4?
   [ ] No [X] Yes *(If yes, provide the following information:)*

   a. Name of each child: DANIEL FRANK LEE

   b. Nature of proceeding: [X] dissolution or divorce [ ] guardianship [ ] adoption [ ] other *(specify)*:

   c. Court *(specify name, state, location)*: Santa Clara Superior Court, San Jose, CA

   d. Status of proceeding: Final judgment of dissolution of marriage granted to Ruth Simmons Lee, Petitioner 4/30/80

6. Do you know of any person who is not a party to this proceeding who has physical custody or claims to have custody of or visitation rights with any child subject to this proceeding?
   [X] No [ ] Yes *(If yes, provide the following information:)*

a. Name and address of person	b. Name and address of person	c. Name and address of person
[ ] Has physical custody [ ] Claims custody rights [ ] Claims visitation rights	[ ] Has physical custody [ ] Claims custody rights [ ] Claims visitation rights	[ ] Has physical custody [ ] Claims custody rights [ ] Claims visitation rights
Name of each child	Name of each child	Name of each child

I declare under penalty of perjury under the laws of the State of California that the foregoing is true and correct.

Date: 4/4/93

PATRICIA ANN LEE
(TYPE OR PRINT NAME)

▶ *Patricia Ann Lee*
(SIGNATURE OF DECLARANT)

7. [X] Number of pages attached after this page: None

NOTICE TO DECLARANT: You have a continuing duty to inform this court if you obtain any information about a custody proceeding in a California court or any other court concerning a child subject to this proceeding.

MC-150 [Rev. January 1, 1993]

**DECLARATION UNDER
UNIFORM CHILD CUSTODY JURISDICTION ACT (UCCJA)**

C. Notice of Hearing

THE NOTICE OF HEARING FORM tells everyone entitled to notice when and where the guardianship petition will be heard in court. When you file your papers with the court, the clerk will give you a hearing date and place. This information will be written or stamped on the Notice of Hearing form.

CAPTION: NOTICE OF HEARING

Fill in the caption following the general instructions in Chapter 3, Section D1.

Check the boxes next to the words "Guardianship," "Person" and/or "Estate" (as appropriate), and "Minor."

After the words "NOTICE OF HEARING," check the box just before the word "Guardianship."

Leave the case number blank since it hasn't been assigned yet.

Item 1: After the words "NOTICE is given that (name)," in capital letters fill in your full first, middle and last names exactly as you entered them on the Petition for Appointment of Guardian of Minor. Just below, after the words "(representative capacity, if any)," enter the words that apply: "proposed guardian of the person," or "proposed guardian of the estate," or "proposed guardian of the person and estate." Just below this, after the words "has filed (specify)," enter the words "Petition for Appointment of Guardian of Minor—" followed by the words "person," "estate," or "person and estate" as appropriate.

Item 2: Skip this item if you are only seeking guardianship of a minor's person. This item is only relevant to the guardian of a minor's estate or person and estate, but normally, it is left blank. It is used only when you ask for permission to take unusual or speculative action with the minor's assets, for which you will need assistance from an attorney. (See the instructions in Section A of this chapter for Item 1e of the Petition for Appointment of Guardian of Minor.)

Item 3: Leave this blank for now. This is the space for specific information on the time and place of the hearing that you will obtain from the clerk. As noted, the clerk will fill in this part of the form when you file it, listing the hearing date and time, the courtroom in which the hearing will be held (by checking the box next to "Dept.," "Div.," or "Rm.," depending on whether the court refers to its courtrooms by department, division, or room number).

Immediately below Item 3, fill in the court's street address again, even though it's already listed in the caption at the top of the form.

Below the court's street address is a space for the date. Leave this blank for now—the court clerk will later stamp it in. Check the box before the words "Clerk, by" to indicate that the clerk will be signing the original Notice of Hearing. Do not put an X next to the word "Attorney," since only a licensed attorney or a court clerk can sign the original. After the words "This notice was mailed on (date)," again leave the date blank. On the same line, after the words "at (place)," fill in the name of the city in which the courthouse is located.

Leave the rest of the front side of the form blank. When you file the Notice of Hearing with the court, the clerk will date the form and sign on the line after the words "Clerk, by."

Also leave the back of the form blank for now. The back of the form is a proof of service, which tells how documents were mailed to people entitled to notice of the guardianship. You will complete the proof of service later, after you file your papers with the court. But make sure that you photocopy the back of the form when you make copies.

D. (Proposed) Order Dispensing Notice

AS DISCUSSED, it is not necessary to notify any of the minor's relatives of the guardianship proceeding if:

- They have signed a Waiver of Notice and Consent form; and
- Their whereabouts are unknown although you've diligently tried, without success, to locate them. Remember that you must genuinely be unable to find out the name or location of the person, rather than be unwilling.

You may skip this entire section if no relatives signed a Waiver of Notice and Consent form *and* you have the names and addresses of all of the minor's living relatives listed on the Guardianship Notification Worksheet.

ATTORNEY OR PARTY WITHOUT ATTORNEY (NAME AND ADDRESS):	TELEPHONE NO.:	FOR COURT USE ONLY
JOHN BRUCE RIVERA 100 Fine Road Napa, CA 94559	(707) 555-1212	
ATTORNEY FOR (NAME): In Pro Per		

SUPERIOR COURT OF CALIFORNIA, COUNTY OF NAPA
STREET ADDRESS: Courthouse, Room 3
MAILING ADDRESS: P.O. Box 880
CITY AND ZIP CODE: Napa, CA 94559
BRANCH NAME:

[X] GUARDIANSHIP [ ] CONSERVATORSHIP OF THE [X] PERSON [X] ESTATE OF
(NAME):
HERMAN DONALD MEAD   [X] Minor [ ] Conservatee

CASE NUMBER:

NOTICE OF HEARING
[X] Guardianship [ ] Conservatorship [ ] Limited Conservatorship

> This notice is required by law. This notice does not require you to appear in court, but you may attend the hearing if you wish.

1. NOTICE is given that (name): JOHN BRUCE RIVERA
   (representative capacity, if any): proposed guardian of the person and estate
   has filed (specify): Petition for Appointment of Guardian of Minor-Person and Estate

   reference to which is made for further particulars.

2. [ ] The petition includes an application for the independent exercise of powers under section 2590 of the Probate Code. Powers requested are [ ] specified below [ ] specified in attachment 2.

3. A hearing on the matter will be held

on (date):	at (time):	in [ ] Dept:	[ ] Div:	[ ] Rm.:

   located at (address of court): Courthouse, Napa, CA 94559

   Dated: . . . .   [X] Clerk, by _____, Deputy
                                                    [ ] Attorney _____
                                                                   (Signature)

   This notice was mailed on (date): . . . ., at (place): . . . ., California.

   (Continued on reverse)

Form Approved by the
Judicial Council of California
Revised Effective January 1, 1981
GC-020(81)

**NOTICE OF HEARING
GUARDIANSHIP OR CONSERVATORSHIP**

To get permission from a judge to waive notice for relatives, you must prepare one more form—an Order Dispensing Notice. Before you begin filling out this form, have handy the Guardianship Notification Worksheet and all completed copies of the Due Diligence Declaration (Attachment 14 to Petition for Appointment of Guardian of Minor). You will need to refer to these forms.

> **CAPTION:** ORDER DISPENSING NOTICE
>
> Fill in the caption following the general instructions in Chapter 3, Section D1.
>
> Do not check the boxes next to the words "CONSERVATORSHIP" or "Conservatee," as these boxes only are used in conservatorship proceedings.
>
> Leave the case number blank since it hasn't been assigned yet.

Item 1: After the words "THE COURT FINDS that a petition for (specify)," fill in the words "Guardianship of the person," "Guardianship of the estate," or "Guardianship of the person and estate" depending on the type of guardianship you are seeking.

Item 1a: This item only applies if you have been able to get *all* of the minor's living relatives entitled to notice to sign a Waiver of Notice and Consent form. Using the Worksheet for Notifying Minor's Relatives as a guide (Chapter 4, Section B), determine if you obtained all these signatures. If this is not your situation, skip this item. If you have obtained *all* the signatures, check the first box. Then check the boxes before the words "waived notice," "consented to the appointment" and "guardian."

Item 1b: This item only applies if there are relatives of the minor who could not be located. If this does not apply to you, skip this item. In Chapter 4, Section D1, you completed a Due Diligence Declaration for each of the minor's relatives who could not be located despite your diligent efforts. (These declarations are attached to the petition as Attachment 14). Check the box next to "b" and list each of the missing relatives' names and relationship to the minor in the blank space provided.

Item 1c: This item only applies to the rare situation where you propose not giving notice to a relative for some reason other than being unable to locate her. If this is your situation, see a lawyer, since it is very difficult to get a judge to waive such notice to relatives. (See Chapter 13 for information on finding and dealing with lawyers.)

Item 1d: Skip this item.

Item 1e: This item only applies if you have been able to get some, but not all, of the minor's living relatives who are entitled to notice to sign a Waiver of Notice and Consent form described in Chapter 4. Look at the Guardianship Notification Worksheet for a listing of everyone entitled to notice. If only certain relatives signed the Waiver of Notice and Consent forms, check the box next to "e" and fill in the words: "The following people who are entitled to notice have waived notice and consented to the appointment of the proposed guardian:" and then list their names and relationship to the minor.

Item 2: After the words "THE COURT ORDERS that notice of hearing on the petition for (specify)," again fill in the kind of petition you have filed: "Guardianship of the person," "Guardianship of the estate," or "Guardianship of the person and estate."

Item 2a: Leave this item blank.

Item 2b: Check the box. Then in the space provided list the names of:

- All of the minor's relatives who signed a Waiver of Notice and Consent form; and
- All of the minor's relatives you cannot locate.

The form is now complete. Leave the date and signature line blank. The judge will fill these in if and when she signs the order. As emphasized, the judge should do away with required notice for all relatives who signed a Notice of Waiver and Consent. As discussed in Chapter 4, depending on your thoroughness in searching for missing relatives, and how close they are to the minor, a judge may or may not sign the Order Dispensing Notice for those relatives.

ATTORNEY OR PARTY WITHOUT ATTORNEY (NAME AND ADDRESS):	TELEPHONE NO.:	FOR COURT USE ONLY
SANDRA ELIZABETH FREEMAN 28 Commuter Blvd. Los Angeles, CA 90012	213/555-1212	
ATTORNEY FOR (NAME): In Pro Per		

SUPERIOR COURT OF CALIFORNIA, COUNTY OF LOS ANGELES
STREET ADDRESS: 111 North Hill Street
MAILING ADDRESS: P.O. Box 151
CITY AND ZIP CODE: Los Angeles, CA 90053
BRANCH NAME:

[X] GUARDIANSHIP [ ] CONSERVATORSHIP OF (NAME):

JANE MELISSA FOX   [X] Minor [ ] Conservatee

ORDER DISPENSING NOTICE	CASE NUMBER:

1. THE COURT FINDS that a petition for (specify): GUARDIANSHIP OF THE ESTATE
   has been filed and

   a. [ ] all persons entitled to notice of hearing have [ ] waived notice [ ] consented to the appointment of the proposed [ ] guardian [ ] conservator.

   b. [X] (for guardianship only) the following persons cannot with reasonable diligence be given notice (names):

       James Fox (Minor's father)
       Susan Fox (Minor's paternal grandmother)
       Clancy Fox (Minor's paternal grandfather)

   c. [ ] (for guardianship only) the giving of notice to the following persons is contrary to the interest of justice (names):

   d. [ ] good cause exists for dispensing with notice to the following persons referred to in section 1460(b) of the Probate Code (names):

   e. [X] other (specify): The following people who are entitled to notice have waived notice and consented to the appointment of the proposed guardian:
       Jennifer Freeman (Minor's mother)
       Alexander Freeman (Minor's maternal grandfather)
       Henry Fox (Minor's brother)

2. THE COURT ORDERS that notice of hearing on the petition for (specify): GUARDIANSHIP OF THE ESTATE

   a. [ ] is not required except to persons requesting special notice under section 2700 of the Probate Code.
   b. [X] is dispensed with to the following persons (names):
       James Fox, Susan Fox, Clancy Fox, Jennifer Freeman,
       Alexander Freeman, and Henry Fox.

Dated: . . . .
                                                                Judge of the Superior Court

Form Approved by the
Judicial Council of California
Effective January 1, 1981
GC-021(81)

ORDER DISPENSING WITH NOTICE
GUARDIANSHIP OR CONSERVATORSHIP

E. (Proposed) Order Appointing Guardian of Minor

IN ORDER TO BECOME THE MINOR'S GUARDIAN, the judge must sign an order appointing you.

CAPTION: ORDER APPOINTING GUARDIAN OF MINOR

Fill in the caption following the general instructions in Chapter 3, Section D1.

Check the boxes to indicate whether you are seeking guardianship of the person, estate, or both.

Leave the case number blank. You will be assigned a case number when you file your documents with the court.

Item 1: In this item you give information about when the hearing will be held, and who will attend. If there are any changes or additions, they may be filled in at the hearing by the judge or clerk.

Item 1a: Leave this item blank, unless you know the name of the judge or commissioner who will be hearing the guardianship case. If so, fill in the name.

Item 1b: This item may be left blank. It will be completed at the hearing.

Item 1c: Check this box. Then fill in your full first, middle and last names.

Item 1d: Check this box. Then after the words "Attorney for petitioner (name)," fill in your full first, middle and last names, followed by the words "appearing In Pro Per."

Item 1e: Ordinarily this item is left blank, except for the rare situation where the minor for whom you are seeking the guardianship has his own attorney. If he does, fill in the attorney's name. If the minor is being represented separately by an attorney, there's a good likelihood that the guardianship will be contested and you'll need the help of a lawyer. (See Chapter 13.)

Item 2a: If no relatives signed a Waiver of Notice and Consent form *and* you have the names and addresses of all of the minor's living relatives listed on the Guardianship Notification Worksheet, check the first box before the words "All notices required by law have been given." This means you will be having all of the relatives served with notice of the guardianship.

If you completed an Order Dispensing Notice following the instructions in Section D of this chapter, check the second box next to the words "Notice of hearing to the following persons." Skip the next box, before the words "has been." Check the box next to the words "should be dispensed with (names)." In the space provided, list the names of each person listed in Item 2b of the Order Dispensing Notice.

Item 2b: Depending on the type of guardianship you are seeking, check the boxes before the words "person," "estate," or both.

Item 2c: Leave this item blank. It corresponds to Item 1e of the Petition for Appointment of Guardian of Minor, which was also left blank.

Item 2d: Ordinarily this item is left blank, except for the rare situation when an attorney has been appointed to represent the minor—not you, the petitioner. If an attorney is representing the minor, check the box and fill in the attorney's name and the amount the attorney is charging. If the minor is being represented by an attorney, the guardianship will likely be contested, and you also should consult an attorney. (See Chapter 13.)

Item 2e: In Chapter 3, Section B3, you called the clerk and obtained information about the guardianship investigator. Complete this item only if a court-appointed investigator will be conducting an investigation. Investigation policies vary depending on the court, but often an investigator is appointed by the court if you are seeking guardianship of the minor's person and are related to the minor by blood. If so, check the box and then fill in the investigator's name, title, address and telephone number. If you don't have this information, call the probate court clerk, say what kind of guardianship you are seeking (person, estate, or both) and what your relationship is to the minor. If a court investigation will be required, get the name, title, address and telephone number of the court investigator.

Item 3a: If you are only seeking guardianship of a minor's estate, skip this item. If you are seeking guardianship of a minor's person or person and estate, fill in your full name, address and telephone number in the spaces provided. After the words "is appointed guardian of the person of (name)," fill in the minor's full first, middle and last names.

> **CAPTION:** PAGE TWO OF THE ORDER APPOINTING GUARDIAN OF MINOR
>
> After the words "GUARDIANSHIP OF (NAME)," in capital letters fill in the minor's full first, middle and last names.
>
> Leave the case number blank since it hasn't been assigned yet.

Item 3b: If you are only seeking guardianship of a minor's person, skip this item. If you are seeking guardianship of a minor's estate or person and estate, fill in your full name, address and telephone number in the spaces provided. After the words "is appointed guardian of the estate of (name)," fill in the minor's full first, middle and last names.

Item 3c: Check the box in this item only if you checked the second box in Item 2a of this form, and listed relatives of the minor you could not locate.

Item 3d: To complete this item, you will need to look at Item 1d of the Petition for Appointment of Guardian of Minor.

Check the first box if you checked the first box of Item 3d of the petition.

Check the second box if you checked the second box of Item 3d of the petition. Then fill in the amount of bond requested in Item 3d of the petition.

Check the third box if you checked the third box of Item 3d of the petition. Then fill in the name of the financial institution and the amount to be deposited, as indicated in Item 3d of the petition.

Item 3e: Skip this item unless the minor is being represented separately by an attorney. If this is the situation, check the first box if the minor's parents will be paying the minor's legal fees. Or check the second box if the minor's estate will be paying the minor's legal fees. Then after the words "to (name)," fill in the name of the lawyer who is representing the minor, and the amount of legal fees in the blank provided. If legal fees are to be paid as soon as the guardianship is granted, check the first box before the word "forthwith." If any other payment arrangements have been made, check the second box before the words "as follows," and list the arrangements in the space provided.

Item 3f: Skip this item. It corresponds to Item 1e of the Petition for Appointment of Guardian of Minor, which was also left blank.

Item 3g: Skip this item. It corresponds to Item 1f of the Petition for Appointment of Guardian of Minor, which was also left blank.

Item 3h: Skip this item.

Item 3i: If you completed Item 1h of the Petition for Appointment of Guardian of Minor, check this box and complete an Attachment 3i to the order following the instructions in Chapter 3, Section D3, using the following sample as a guide.

Item 3j: Skip this item if you are only seeking guardianship of a minor's person. If you are seeking guardianship of a minor's estate or person and estate, you'll need to look at Item 11 of the petition. If the minor does not own any real property or personal property other than cash or bank accounts, skip this item. Otherwise, check the box. Then call the court clerk, explain that you are petitioning for a guardianship and ask the for the name and address of the probate referee (sometimes called the "inheritance tax referee"). Fill in that information in the space provided.

Item 4: Count the number of boxes you checked in Item 3, and fill in that number.

Item 5: Check the box and fill in the number of pages attached. If you are not attaching any additional pages, fill in the word "None."

Leave the date and signature line blank. These will be completed at the hearing by the judge or her clerk.

PREPARING FORMS TO FILE FOR A GUARDIANSHIP 5 / 27

ATTORNEY OR PARTY WITHOUT ATTORNEY (NAME AND ADDRESS):	TELEPHONE NO.:	FOR COURT USE ONLY
PATRICIA ANN LEE 2 West Street Santa Ana, CA 92702	714/555-1212	
ATTORNEY FOR (NAME): In Pro Per		

SUPERIOR COURT OF CALIFORNIA, COUNTY OF ORANGE
STREET ADDRESS: 700 Civic Center Drive West
MAILING ADDRESS: P.O. Box 838
CITY AND ZIP CODE: Santa Ana, CA 92702
BRANCH NAME:

GUARDIANSHIP OF THE [X] PERSON [ ] ESTATE OF (NAME):
DANIEL FRANK LEE   Minor

CASE NUMBER:

ORDER APPOINTING GUARDIAN OF [X] **MINOR** [ ] **MINORS**

1. The petition for appointment of guardian came on for hearing as follows (check boxes c, d, and e to indicate personal presence):
   a. Judge (name):
   b. Hearing date: Time: [ ] Dept.:   [ ] Div.:   [ ] Room:
   c. [X] Petitioner (name): PATRICIA ANN LEE
   d. [X] Attorney for petitioner (name): PATRICIA ANN LEE appearing In Pro Per
   e. [ ] Attorney for minor (name, address, and telephone):

2. THE COURT FINDS
   a. [ ] All notices required by law have been given.
      [X] Notice of hearing to the following persons [ ] has been [X] should be dispensed with (names):
          James Fox, Susan Fox, Clancy Fox, Jennifer Freeman
          Alexander Freeman, and Henry Fox.
   b. Appointment of a guardian of the [X] person [ ] estate of the minor is necessary and convenient.
   c. [ ] Granting the guardian powers to be exercised independently under section 2590 of the Probate Code is to the advantage and benefit and in the best interest of the guardianship estate.
   d. [ ] Attorney (name):   has been appointed by the court as legal counsel to represent the minor in these proceedings. The cost for representation is $ _____
   e. [X] The appointed court investigator, probation officer, or domestic relations investigator is (name, title, address, and telephone): Ira Investigator
          700 Civic Center Drive West
          Santa Ana, CA 92702
          714/999-9999

3. THE COURT ORDERS
   a. (name): PATRICIA ANN LEE
      (address): 2 West Street   (telephone): 714/555-1212
                 Santa Ana, CA 92702
      is appointed guardian of the person of (name): DANIEL FRANK LEE
      and Letters shall issue upon qualification.

(Continued on reverse)

Do NOT use this form for a temporary guardianship.
Form Approved by the
Judicial Council of California
Revised Effective January 1, 1981
GC-240(81)

ORDER APPOINTING GUARDIAN OF MINOR

GUARDIANSHIP OF (NAME): DANIEL FRANK LEE Minor	CASE NUMBER:

ORDER APPOINTING GUARDIAN OF MINOR   Page 2

3. **THE COURT ORDERS** (continued)
   b. (name):

      (address):   (telephone):

      is appointed guardian of the estate of (name):

      and Letters shall issue upon qualification.

   c. [X] Notice of hearing to the persons named in item 2a is dispensed with.

   d. [X] Bond is not required.
      [ ] Bond is fixed at $ _____ to be furnished by an authorized surety company or as otherwise provided by law.
      [ ] Deposits shall be made at (specify institution): _____ in the amount of $ _____ and receipts filed.

   e. [ ] For legal services rendered on behalf of the minor, [ ] parents of the minor [ ] minor's estate shall pay to (name):   the sum of $ _____
      [ ] forthwith [ ] as follows (specify terms, including any combination of payors):

   f. [ ] The guardian of the estate is granted authorization under section 2590 of the Probate Code to exercise independently the powers specified in attachment 3f [ ] subject to the conditions provided.

   g. [ ] Orders are granted relating to the powers and duties of the guardian of the person under sections 2351-2358 of the Probate Code as specified in attachment 3g.

   h. [ ] Orders are granted relating to the conditions imposed under section 2402 of the Probate Code upon the guardian of the estate as specified in attachment 3h.

   i. [X] Other orders are granted as specified in attachment 3i.

   j. [ ] The inheritance tax referee appointed is (name and address):

4. Number of boxes checked in item 3:   3

5. [X] Number of pages attached: 1

Dated: . . . .   _____
                                                      Judge of the Superior Court
                                                      [ ] Signature follows last attachment

GUARDIANSHIP OF (Name): _____ Case Number: _____

ATTACHMENT 3i

to Order Appointing Guardian of Minor: Additional Orders

[ ] <u>ORDER WAIVING SERVICE BY MAIL OF ORDER APPOINTING GUARDIAN OF MINOR</u>

    [ ] Service by mail of the Order Appointing Guardian of Minor on _____, a minor over the age of 12 who is the subject of this guardianship proceeding, is waived, since the minor personally appeared at the hearing and was advised of the nature of the Order Appointing Guardian of Minor.

[ ] <u>ORDER WAIVING ACCOUNTINGS (Probate Code §2628)</u>

    [ ] Accountings for the estate of _____ are waived, since the income of the estate consists of public assistance benefits of the type stated in Probate Code §2628. Pursuant to Probate Code §2628, the minor's estate does not exceed $5,000 (excluding clothes and ordinary household items), and the minor receives no more than $300 per month in addition to public assistance benefits.

F. (Proposed) Letters of Guardianship

THE LETTERS OF GUARDIANSHIP FORM is the document that states that you have the court's authority to act as guardian. Although it is an extremely important document, you'll find it very easy to prepare.

> **CAPTION:** LETTERS OF GUARDIANSHIP
>
> Fill in the caption following the general instructions in Chapter 3, Section D1.
> Where you seek guardianship of more than one minor, use one form for each child, listing the name of each minor on a separate form.
> Leave the case number blank. You will be assigned a case number when you file your documents with the court.

On the left side of the form, next to the words "STATE OF CALIFORNIA, COUNTY OF," fill in the county in which you are filing the guardianship action.

Item 1: In capital letters, after the word "(Name)," fill in your full first, middle and last names. Check the box or boxes next to the words "person," "estate," or both, depending on the type of guardianship you are seeking. After the words "of (name)," in capital letters fill in the minor's full first, middle and last names.

Items 2a-2d: Leave Items 2a-2c blank. They apply to situations where you are seeking powers beyond those ordinarily granted, for which you need an attorney's assistance.

Leave the rest of the left side of the form blank, including the date, and proceed to Item 3 on the right side of the page.

Item 3: Fill in the date and place you are completing the form. Then sign your name on the signature line. In this item, you promise to fulfill the duties of a guardian.

Item 4: Leave this item blank. The clerk will fill out this item, which simply says that it is a certified copy of the original Letters of Guardianship in the court's file.

G. Prepare Supplemental Documents if Required

DEPENDING ON YOUR SITUATION and the court in which you are filing, you may need to prepare one or a number of additional local court forms. Copies of local forms are not supplied in this book, so you must contact your court to arrange to obtain copies. Here is information about many—but not all—local forms. Call your local court to find out its requirements.

1. Larger Courts May Require Declaration for Filing and Assignment

In some counties, a special form is required if you want your case to be filed in a branch court—which may be closer and more convenient—rather than the main court. Branch courts are discussed in Chapter 3, Section B1, along with information about where to file your papers. If you will be filing in a branch court, call the court clerk and ask if there is a local declaration for filing and assignment form, and find out how to obtain a copy. These forms are self-explanatory and easy to complete.

2. Some Courts Require Form Listing Address Information

You may need to complete a form that gives the current addresses of the proposed guardian and minor. The form in Appendix D in the back of the book entitled Notification to Court of Address of Guardian/Ward contains substantially the same information as any of the local court forms. Chapter 11, Section D1 gives instructions on how to complete the Notification to Court of Address of Guardian/Ward form, and provides a completed sample. However, many courts require that you use their local forms, so to be on the safe side, check with the court and find out if one is required.

PREPARING FORMS TO FILE FOR A GUARDIANSHIP

ATTORNEY OR PARTY WITHOUT ATTORNEY (NAME AND ADDRESS):	TELEPHONE NO.:	FOR COURT USE ONLY
BARBARA FAITH JOHNSON 10 Some Street Redding, CA 96001	(916) 555-1212	
ATTORNEY FOR (NAME): In Pro Per		

SUPERIOR COURT OF CALIFORNIA, COUNTY OF SHASTA
STREET ADDRESS: 1500 Court Street
MAILING ADDRESS: P.O. Box 880
CITY AND ZIP CODE: Redding, CA 96099
BRANCH NAME:

GUARDIANSHIP OF (NAME):

SUSAN BETH SIMPSON   Minor

LETTERS OF GUARDIANSHIP
[X] Person   [X] Estate

CASE NUMBER:

STATE OF CALIFORNIA, COUNTY OF SHASTA

1. (Name): BARBARA FAITH JOHNSON
   is appointed guardian of the [X] person [X] estate of (name):

   SUSAN BETH SIMPSON

2. ☐ Other powers have been granted and conditions have been imposed as follows:
   a. ☐ powers to be exercised independently under section 2590 of the Probate Code as specified in attachment 2a *(specify powers, restrictions, conditions, and limitations)*.
   b. ☐ conditions relating to the care and custody of the property under section 2402 of the Probate Code as specified in attachment 2b.
   c. ☐ conditions relating to the care, treatment, education, and welfare of the minor under section 2358 of the Probate Code as specified in attachment 2c.
   d. ☐ other *(specify in attachment 2d)*.

Dated: . . . .

Clerk, by _____, Deputy

☐ Number of pages attached:

SEAL

3.   **AFFIRMATION**

I solemnly affirm that I will perform the duties of guardian according to law.

Executed on (date): . June 10, 1991 . . . .
at (place): . Redding, California . . . .

Barbara Faith Johnson
(Signature of appointee)

4.   **CERTIFICATION**

I certify that this document and any attachments is a correct copy of the original on file in my office, and that the letters issued to the person appointed above have not been revoked, annulled, or set aside and are still in full force and effect.

Dated: . . . .

Clerk, by _____, Deputy

SEAL

Form Approved by the
Judicial Council of California
Effective January 1, 1981
GC-250(81)

LETTERS OF GUARDIANSHIP

3. Sacramento Superior Court Requires Information about Civil Litigation Cases

If you are filing your guardianship in the Sacramento Superior Court, you must complete a short form that states whether the minor has been or is involved in a lawsuit in which money damages are claimed. If the minor is involved in such a case, you must name the county in which the case is pending along with the court case number. Call the court and find out how to obtain a copy of this form.

4. San Mateo Superior Court Requires Guardianship Affidavit

If you are filing your guardianship in the San Mateo Superior Court, and seeking guardianship of a minor's person or person and estate, you must complete a short form that gives information about you and the minor, as well as:

- Specific reasons why a guardianship is necessary; and
- Facts telling how you're able to provide an environment that would be good for the minor, and would meet any special needs she might have. Following is a completed sample.

5. Santa Clara Superior Court Requires Declaration in Support of Petition

If you are seeking guardianship of a minor's person or person and estate in the Santa Clara Superior Court, you must submit a statement that covers:

- Complete legal names and dates of birth for you and all of the people who will be living with the minor.
- Why a guardianship is needed. Give specifics about why both parents are unable to care for the minor.
- A brief discussion of your background, including your education, employment and status of your health.
- A description of your housing situation, and what living space will be available for the minor.
- A discussion of the minor's development and whether she has any special emotional, psychological, educational or physical needs. If the minor has any special needs, include an explanation of your ability to provide for them.
- The name of the minor's school or day care center and telephone number, if any.
- How the minor will be supported. For example, you may expect to receive AFDC, money from the minor's parents, or plan to support the minor yourself.[13]

In the declaration, cover each of the points as clearly as possible in plain English. You can either use lined paper or a Declaration form, both of which are contained in Appendix D. Following is a completed sample.

H. When You Need a Guardianship Right Away

IF YOU NEED A GUARDIANSHIP sooner than six weeks from the date you file your papers with the court, you may be able to obtain a temporary guardianship to go into effect sooner—usually within five days. In addition to the documents you prepared in this chapter, you will need to prepare papers for a temporary guardianship and file them with the court following the instructions in Chapter 7.

---

[13] A minor's parents are obliged to support the minor even if a legal guardianship exists (CC §§196, 242, 244). However, in the real world, not all parents are conscientious about making support payments.

IN THE SUPERIOR COURT OF THE STATE OF CALIFORNIA

IN AND FOR THE COUNTY OF SAN MATEO

IN THE MATTER OF THE)
GUARDIANSHIP OF)
)
) Case No. 100
DEAN GREEN)
) GUARDIANSHIP
) AFFIDAVIT
MINOR(S))

Name of Minor(s): DEAN GREEN   Date of Birth: 4/12/87

Proposed   Relation to
Guardian(s): RAE GRAY   Minor(s): Maternal Aunt

Home Phone: 415/555-1212   Business Phone:

Please type or print your answers to the following, using attachments as necessary.

The reasons a guardianship is necessary (BE SPECIFIC):
Dean Green, my five-year old nephew, has been living with my family for the last six months. His mother is very ill with terminal cancer and cannot care for him. She has signed a Nomination of Guardian form, and agrees with the guardianship. Dean's father is dead.
Dean will be old enough to attend kindergarten this fall, and I need a legal guardianship to register him in school.

Facts showing proposed guardian's ability to provide an environment which would be beneficial to the minor(s) as well as meet any special needs:
Dean has been very close to me and my family all his life. He gets along with my daughter, Alice, who was born 9/30/87. We live in a 3-bedroom house. Dean and Alice each have their own rooms. We also have a small den which serves as a playroom, and there is plenty of space for Dean.
Dean's mother agrees that the guardianship would be best for Dean since she is too ill to care for him. My husband and I are willing and able to care for and support Dean until he reaches age 18.
Dean is getting special counseling from Dr. White, a psychologist who comes to his daycare center once a week. Dr. White agrees with the guardianship.
(Continued on reverse)

I certify (or declare) under penalty of perjury under the laws of the State of California that the foregoing is true and correct and that this affidavit is executed on <u>July 16, 1991</u> at <u>Menlo Park</u>, California.
                    (Date)   (Place)

<u>RAE GRAY</u>   <u>Rae Gray</u>
(Type or print name)   (Signature of affiant)

(To be submitted for filing with the County Clerk with all petitions for guardianships of person only or of person and estate.)

```
Rae Gray
123 King Street
Santa Clara, CA 94510



Appearing in Pro Per
```

SUPERIOR COURT OF CALIFORNIA

CITY AND COUNTY OF SANTA CLARA

GUARDIANSHIP OF:	)	NO. 12345
	)	
	)	
DEAN GREEN,	)	DECLARATION OF RAE GRAY
	)	IN SUPPORT OF PETITION FOR
Minor	)	APPOINTMENT OF GUARDIAN OF MINOR
	)	
_____	)	

DECLARATION

I, Rae Gray, declare that I am the petitioner and proposed guardian in this guardianship case, and further declare:

1. My legal name is Rae Gray, and my birthdate is January 2, 1955. I am the maternal aunt of Dean Green, the minor in this guardianship case.

2. The other people who presently are and will be living with me and Dean Green are (1) my husband, Fred Gray, whose birthdate is March 22, 1954, and (2) my daughter, Alice Gray, whose birthdate is September 30, 1987.

3. A guardianship is needed for Dean Green because his mother is very ill with terminal cancer and cannot care for him. She has signed a Nomination of Guardian form. Dean Green's father is dead. Dean Green has been living with my family and me for the last six months. He will be old enough to attend school this fall, and I need a legal guardianship to register him.

4. I graduated from Heights High School in 1973. I work as a secretary for Company Incorporated. I am in excellent health.

5. I live in a 3-bedroom house with my husband, daughter and Dean Green. My husband and I share one bedroom, and the children each have their own bedrooms. We have a small den which serves as a playroom, and there is plenty of space for Dean Green in our home.

6. Dean Green does not have any special emotional, psychological, educational, or physical needs except for the need for counseling about his mother's illness which was recommended by his teacher, Mary Wu. He has been seeing a psychologist, Dr. White, who comes to his day care center once a week.

7. Dean Green attends Children's Day Care Center. The telephone number is (415) 555-1212.

8. Dean Green's mother will help support him by paying $75.00 per month from her disability check. My husband and I will provide whatever supplemental support he needs. If my sister becomes unable to contribute any money, my husband and I are willing and able to support Dean Green completely until he reaches age 18.

I declare under penalty of perjury under the laws of the State of California that the foregoing is true and correct.

Dated: 2/21/90   *Rae Gray*
                         (Rae Gray)

CHAPTER 6

FILING AND SERVING THE GUARDIANSHIP PAPERS

A.	Check Your Work	6/1
B.	File Guardianship Documents and Get a Hearing Date	6/1
C.	Local Court Forms May Be Required After You File Your Papers	6/6
D.	What, When and How Papers Are Served	6/7
E.	Use Guardian Notification Worksheet to Determine Who Must Be Served	6/8
F.	Personal Service and Notice and Acknowledgment of Receipt	6/11
G.	Having Documents Served by Mail	6/16
H.	Copy and File Proofs of Service and Possibly Notice of Hearing	6/20
I.	Complete the Guardianship Notification Worksheet	6/21

A. Check Your Work

AFTER YOU HAVE FILLED OUT AND SIGNED the initial guardianship documents following the instructions in Chapters 4 and 5, review them carefully. Make sure the correct attachments are numbered and fastened to the appropriate documents. Be sure that all the proper boxes are checked, everyone's name is spelled correctly and any necessary signatures have been obtained.

1. Call the Court

When all your documents are ready for filing, call the clerk in the court's probate department. Tell the clerk that you are filing a guardianship petition, and that you want to verify that you've completed all the required paperwork. Identify the documents you have prepared, and ask if others are required.[1] If the court's local rules require any additional forms, arrange to get copies. You usually can get forms either by going to court, or through the mail by sending a letter to the court explaining what forms you want, and enclosing a self-addressed, stamped envelope. Check in advance whether there is a charge for these additional forms—if so, it will be a small fee. Finally, ask how many copies of all guardianship documents are required by the court. Some courts only need the original completed forms, while others keep the original and one or possibly more additional copies.

B. File Guardianship Documents and Get a Hearing Date

AT LAST YOU'RE READY TO COPY YOUR PAPERS and file them with the court. Chapter 3 gives general rules on how to file your papers with the court. Here is an explanation of some specifics.

1. Photocopy Documents

The documents you'll file for the guardianship are listed in the following chart. Regardless of whether you take or mail your documents to the court, always keep an extra copy of each document at home, in case something happens to the ones you're filing. Remember that you're better off having too many copies than not enough. (See Chapter 3, Section E1 for general guidance on copying documents.)

---

[1] If the clerk will not give you this information, check a copy of the court's local probate rules. See Chapter 13, Section D3.

You'll need an extra copy of the Petition for Appointment of Guardian of Minor—including all attachments—and the Notice of Hearing for each person and agency that must be served. Section E of this chapter discusses which people and agencies must be served. You may either skip to Section E now and figure out how many people and agencies must be served, or estimate the number of copies you'll need by looking at the Guardianship Notification Worksheet, which lists relatives and agencies to be served.

2. Take or Send Guardianship Documents to Court

Now that you've made photocopies of the completed forms, you are ready to file them with the court clerk. You may either take or mail your documents to the court, following the instructions in Chapter 3, Section E. When your documents are filed, you will be assigned a case number. At that time, you will also request a hearing date following the instructions in Section B3 below. If you will be applying for a waiver of court fees and costs, also read the Section B2a just below.

a. Applying for a Waiver of Court Fees and Costs

Skip this section unless you have a very low income and are applying to have court fees and costs waived. If you are applying for a fee waiver, you should have prepared and copied the necessary documents. (See the accompanying list.)

By law, you may file your guardianship papers with the court at the same time as the fee waiver request, without paying a filing fee. Some clerks may tell you that you'll have to wait a few days for a judge to grant the fee waiver before you can file your guardianship papers. If this happens, be polite but firm. Tell the clerk that you are entitled to file your papers under Rule 985 of the California Rules of Court. If for some reason the clerk still will not file your papers, ask to speak with a supervisor, and give the supervisor the same information.

If you file your documents in person, you may have to take the fee waiver documents to be reviewed and filed by a clerk in a different department or courtroom from the probate court's filing desk. To find out the procedure, call or go to the probate department, and ask the clerk where to file your fee waiver documents.

Once an Application for Waiver of Court Fees and Costs form has been filed, the court must decide whether to grant the request within five days. If the court doesn't deny your request within that five-day period, your fees and costs are automatically waived (CRC 985(e)). If your fee waiver request is granted, the court might send you a document entitled "Notice of Waiver of Court Fees and Costs," which indicates that your request was granted. However, in the real world, courts usually don't send out this form. If your fee waiver request is denied, the Order on Waiver of Court Fees and Costs will be marked to indicate this. You will then have to pay court fees and costs within 10 days.

If you don't get any notification from the court within a week after you file your fee waiver documents, call the clerk to find out whether your fees were waived.

b. (Proposed) Orders and Letters Will Not Be Returned

When you give your documents to the court clerk, he will stamp and return most of them. However, orders —which require a judge's signature—and Letters of Guardianship or Letters of Temporary Guardianship will not be returned to you. At the hearing, the judge will decide whether to sign the orders, and whether you will be named guardian. Once she does, you will get copies of the signed papers as long as you submitted extra photocopies. To alert you to these forms, they are referred to as "proposed" documents in the instructions.

GUARDIANSHIP DOCUMENTS TO BE FILED WITH THE COURT

Depending on your situation, you may be filing all or just some of these documents:

You Must File:	**Number of Copies Needed***
☐ Consent of Proposed Guardian, Nomination and Waiver of Notice, three-part form (Chapter 4, Section E)[2]	Original + 2
☐ Petition for Appointment of Guardian of Minor (Chapter 5, Section A)[3]	Original + 2 + one for each person entitled to notice
☐ Notice of Hearing (Chapter 5, Section C)	Original + 2 + one for each person entitled to notice
☐ (Proposed) Order Appointing Guardian of Minor (Chapter 5, Section E)	Original + 2 + one for each minor over age 12
☐ (Proposed) Letters of Guardianship (Chapter 5, Section F)	Original + 2 + any additional copies needed for agencies (4-5 recommended)

You May File:

☐ (Proposed) Order Dispensing Notice (Chapter 5, Section D)	Original + 2

Fee Waiver Documents, if you have a very low income and are applying for a waiver of court fees and costs (Chapter 3, Section F1):

☐ Application for Waiver of Court Fees and Costs	Original + 2
☐ (Proposed) Order on Application for Waiver of Court Fees and Costs	Original + 2

Supplemental documents, if required, Chapter 5, Section G):

☐ Declaration for Filing and Assignment	Original + 2
☐ Notification to Court of Address on Guardianship	Original + 2
☐ Information re: Civil Litigation Cases (Sacramento County)	Original + 2
☐ Guardianship Affidavit (San Mateo County)	Original + 2
☐ Declaration in Support of Petition (Santa Clara County)	Original + 2

Additional documents for a temporary, guardianship, if applicable (Chapter 7):

☐ Petition for Appointment of Temporary Guardian (if required)	Original + 2 + one for each person entitled to notice
☐ Notice of Hearing (for Temporary Guardianship if required by local rules)	Original + 2 + one for each person entitled to notice (if required)
☐ (Proposed) Order for Appointment of Temporary Guardian	Original + 2
☐ (Proposed) Letters of Temporary Guardian	Original + 2 + any additional copies needed by agencies

*The 2 copies listed include one that you leave at home when you take or send your papers to the court. You may need at least one additional copy of all documents if the court's local rules require it.

---

[2] If you haven't obtained any signatures on the Nomination of Guardian or Waiver of Notice and Consent portions of the form, you must still complete and sign the Consent of Proposed Guardian section.

[3] The Declaration Under Uniform Child Custody Jurisdiction is attached to the petition as Attachment 16. It is required for all petitioners seeking guardianship of a minor's person or person and estate.

3. Obtain a Hearing Date

When you file your guardianship papers with the court, get a date and time when you and the minor will appear in court before a judge[4] who decides whether to grant the guardianship. This court appearance is called a "hearing." You must appear in court with the minor, even if it seems like a formality because everyone involved is in favor of the guardianship. At the hearing, you will tell the judge why a guardianship is needed, and that you want that responsibility. The judge will probably ask you and the minor a few questions before making a decision.

Generally, the court clerk will either assign you a date, or ask you to choose a hearing date when you file your papers. Sometimes clerks automatically assign you a hearing date unless you ask to choose your own. If you make it clear from the start that you want to select a date, you'll probably have better luck getting a date and time convenient for you. Follow the guidelines in this section about the timing of the hearing.

Ask the clerk to fill in Item 3 of the Notice of Hearing with the date, time and location of the hearing. The clerk also should date and sign the original Notice of Hearing in the space below Item 3 provided for this purpose. Some clerks stamp in the hearing information or affix printed labels. Sometimes clerks will only complete one Notice of Hearing, and ask you to "conform" the rest of the copies, meaning that you must write in the same information on additional copies of forms. Some courts may require you to fill out a simple local form specifically requesting a hearing date.

The clerk should return the *original* Notice of Hearing to you without filing it.

a. When Should the Hearing Be?

Be sure to request that your hearing be scheduled at least 45 days after the date you file your guardianship papers.[5] Getting a hearing date several weeks away allows time to have the guardianship papers served and proofs of service completed and filed with the court. Also, many counties' local court rules require that all guardianship applications be reviewed by an investigator associated with the court, social services department of the county, or probation department. (The guardianship investigation is discussed in Chapter 8.)

Note: In a few counties, the clerk will not give you a court date until the guardianship investigation is completed, particularly if it is being investigated by a probation officer.

b. Obtaining a Hearing Date over the Phone

If you mail in your papers to be filed by the court and the clerk inadvertently forgets to give you a hearing date, in most counties you can call the court clerk and get one, rather than having to go back to court to have the date assigned. Tell the clerk the case number, which will be stamped on your papers once they've been filed with the court. Tell the clerk that you have filed a guardianship petition, and would like to obtain a hearing date. Follow the instructions in Section 3a just above for selecting the court date.

c. Local Rules May Require Investigation Before a Hearing Date is Assigned

It is possible that you may not get a hearing date when you file your papers, because the court's policy requires an investigation to be completed before the hearing date may be assigned. If this is your court's policy, you'll need to wait until the investigation is completed before you can obtain a hearing date. (See Chapter 8 for more information on the guardianship investigation.)

---

[4]In some counties a probate commissioner hears guardianship cases. For purposes of obtaining a guardianship, the probate commissioner has the same authority as a judge.

[5]If you can't wait this long, you may need to file for a temporary guardianship in addition to a general guardianship. For example, a school or medical provider might require you to have a guardianship before allowing school enrollment or authorizing a medical treatment. Instructions for preparing and filing forms for a temporary guardianship are given in Chapter 7.

d. Check to See if You Have Original Notice of Hearing

Most courts do not accept the original Notice of Hearing until everyone entitled to notice has been served. When you file the Notice of Hearing, check to see if you have the original signed document. You can tell which is the original because the copies should be stamped with the clerk's name rather than signed. If you're not sure, ask the clerk which is the original. If the clerk gives the original Notice of Hearing back to you, make sure you keep it in a safe place. You will need to file it with the court along with proofs of service after everyone entitled to notice has been served.

4. Follow Local Court Procedures

Different courts have special procedures for guardianship cases. If you want to obtain a guardianship, you will have to follow the court's local rules—regardless of your opinion about them. For example, when you file your documents you may be required to:
- Be fingerprinted;
- Have your guardianship documents reviewed by a court investigator or examiner before they're filed; or
- Fill out documents pertaining to the guardianship investigation. (See Chapter 8 for more information about investigations.)

You can check with the court clerk or the local Probate Policy Manual before filing your documents to find out if the court follows any special procedures.

5. Continuing (Postponing) the Hearing Date

If you want the hearing date rescheduled—called "continued" in legalese—read this section very carefully. If you don't follow your court's local procedures, you could end up having to file another petition—and pay the expensive filing fees all over again.

Here are several reasons why you might need to postpone the hearing date once it has been set:
- You cannot have the minor's relatives served in time;
- Someone objects to the guardianship, and you need time to find a lawyer;
- The investigation is not completed in time; or
- It's impossible for you to appear in court on that date (usually because some urgent matter has come up).

a. Check Local Procedures

If you need to continue the hearing, call the clerk at the probate court. Explain that you want to continue the guardianship hearing and get a new date. Local procedures vary depending on the court, and this book does not cover them in detail. They should be outlined in the court's Probate Policy Manual and local rules.

Here are some of the ways continuances are handled at different courts:
- The clerk may give you a new date over the telephone and ask for a letter confirming the new date.
- You may be required to complete an amended Notice of Hearing with the new hearing date and have it served by mail on everyone entitled to notice.
- You may need to get the new date by appearing at the scheduled hearing and requesting it at that time.
- You may be required to submit a formal motion for continuance to the court, which would require additional research or an attorney's help. (See Chapter 13.)

6. Amending the Petition for Appointment of Guardian of Minor

If, after filing your Petition for Appointment of Guardian of Minor, you become aware of any proceedings that affect the minor that weren't disclosed in the petition you already filed with the court, you must amend it within 10 days of the time you find out about the proceedings. This includes adoptions, juvenile court matters, marriage, divorce, or other similar proceedings affecting the minor (PC §1512). In addition, if you find that you have made a serious error or the situation set out in any document has changed, file an amended document right away.

(Chapter 3, Section E4 discusses how to prepare and file amended documents.)

If you file an amended petition, it must contain a full set of attachments, including the UCCJA Declaration for guardianship of a minor's person. If you originally petition for one type of guardianship and wish to add another, you must also complete a new Consent of Proposed Guardian, Nomination, and Waiver of Notice form.

Note: Depending on local rules, you may be required to continue the hearing date if the amended documents are not served on everyone entitled to notice well in advance of the hearing date. The amount of time required would depend on the court. Check your court's local policies.

C. Local Court Forms May Be Required After You File Your Papers

LOCAL COURT RULES SOMETIMES REQUIRE you to complete additional forms *after* you file the initial guardianship papers. These additional local court forms usually are for those seeking guardianship of a minor's person, and pertain to screening or investigating the prospective guardian.

If the clerk gives you more forms to complete when you file your guardianship papers, look at them carefully before leaving the court. The forms probably will be self-explanatory, but if you are confused by something, you might be able to get additional information from the clerk. However, understand that court clerks can't answer every question you might have. By law, they're forbidden to direct you in any way that might be considered giving legal advice—only lawyers can do that. If you do need more help, the court clerk may refer you to a local service that gives free or low-cost legal assistance. (Or see Chapter 13 for information about doing your own research or finding a lawyer.)

Make sure you understand from the start when all forms are due back at the court, and follow those deadlines carefully. For example, if a form must be completed and returned within 10 days and you don't get it back for 11 or 12, you may lose your scheduled hearing date. That could mean a lot of extra work, since you'd have to obtain a new hearing date and have those entitled to notice served again.

Because local rules vary widely, we cannot give you information on all possible forms that may be required. However, here are some of the forms the clerk may give you to fulfill local requirements:

1. Information for Court Investigation

In some counties, there are special forms for anyone seeking appointment as guardian of a minor's person. For example, the Fresno Superior Court has a four-page Guardianship Questionnaire that asks for information about the minor, the minor's natural parents and personal information about you and your plans to care for the minor. This questionnaire may seem overwhelming at first, but with a little patience, you shouldn't have trouble completing it. Some helpful samples for completing this questionnaire are the declarations for the San Mateo and Santa Clara Superior Courts in Chapter 5, Section G.

2. Special Form for Agencies Entitled to Notice

Some counties have special forms you must send to agencies to notify them of the guardianship. For example, the Alameda Superior Court has a form that must be completed and sent to the county's local social services agency, the Child Protective Services. It is used to screen the potential guardian for reports of prior child abuse or neglect, then returned to the court.

D. What, When and How Papers Are Served

WHEN SOMEONE PERSONALLY DELIVERS or sends legal documents by mail, this formal notice is called "service of process." When someone entitled to notice receives these documents, she has been "served." Depending on the legal requirements, service is done:
- By mail (documents are sent by regular U.S. mail);
- By personal service (documents are either personally handed to or left near the person); or
- By Notice and Acknowledgment of Receipt (documents are mailed to the person along with a special form saying that the papers were received; the recipient signs and mails back the form).

Having documents properly served is an essential part of the process of obtaining a guardianship. The reason for this is simple: a person who is being affected by the guardianship has a constitutional right to be notified of the proceedings. She may contest your appointment as guardian by filing papers with the court or appearing before the judge at the hearing. Before you can have a court hearing on the guardianship, the court must be assured that everyone entitled to know about the hearing was given notice, waived the right to notice, or cannot be located.

There are specific rules about how documents must be served for the service to be legally valid. As the person petitioning for the guardianship, you cannot serve papers yourself. The person who serves papers must be over 18 years old and must not be involved in the legal action. If you don't follow service rules to the letter, you will have to start over again—rescheduling your case for a new hearing date and having everyone served all over again—even if only one person was served incorrectly.

1. What Papers Must Be Served?

Copies of these two documents must be served on every person and agency entitled to notice of the guardianship proceeding:

- Petition for Appointment of Guardian of Minor—including all of the attachments; and
- Notice of Hearing.

Make sure you have one copy of each of the papers for every person or agency entitled to service, plus one for yourself and one extra for the court, if required.

2. When Must Papers Be Served?

The guardianship papers must be served at least 20 days before the date listed in the Notice of Hearing in the box in Item 3. That means that documents served by mail must be mailed at least 20 days before the hearing date, and documents personally served must be received at least 20 days before the hearing date.[6] (Service by mail is discussed in detail in Section G. Personal service is covered in Section F.)

If you do not comply with these requirements, the guardianship will not be heard on the scheduled hearing date. To be safe, have the papers served immediately after you file them with the court. (If papers are not served properly or on time, see Section B5 in this chapter, which gives important information about having a hearing continued.)

3. Who May Serve the Papers?

The law forbids you, the person filing for the guardianship, from serving the papers yourself. Fortunately, service can be carried out by any other person 18 years of age or older who is not involved in the guardianship proceeding—meaning they're not listed anywhere on the Petition for Appointment of Guardian of Minor. This could be a friend, family member, acquaintance, or employee. Or, for a fee, you can hire a professional process server or marshal or sheriff's deputy to serve the papers.

When service is made through the mail, it's fine to ask a friend or relative to do it. The legal assumption is that papers are received when they are properly

---

[6]Some courts only require 15 days notice for service by mail, while others specifically require 20 days notice (notably, Merced and Stanislaus). To play it safe, we advise you to give at least 20 days notice.

deposited in the U.S. mail. There's no reason to pay a professional to mail your papers.

However, arranging to have someone personally served can be a little tricky. If you anticipate that there might be problems serving the minor's parents or anyone else entitled to personal service, hire a professional process server or marshal or sheriff's deputy.[7] Then, if anyone later questions the validity of the service in court, a process server's testimony tends to be much more persuasive than that of a friend or relative who may be biased about the outcome.

Good professional process servers are commonly quick and resourceful at serving evasive people. They are usually a little more expensive than marshals or sheriffs, but the money you'll save in having the papers served faster may justify the extra expense, since you won't have to go back to court for a new hearing date. Some process servers charge a flat fee for service in a geographical area, while others charge for each attempted delivery and additional amounts for each mile they travel to attempt service. You can get information about the fees by calling the process servers before you hire them.

To find a good process serving firm in the area where the person requiring service lives or works, get a recommendation from a paralegal or attorney, if you know one. Or you can check the Yellow Pages for process servers. You will need to give the process server copies of the papers to be served, and the date by which service must be completed. Since the process server won't be familiar with the person she's serving, you'll need to help out by providing as much detailed information as possible, such as the best hours to find the person at home or work, and a general physical description. It's even better if you can provide a recent photograph.

Some people choose to have a marshal or deputy sheriff serve their papers. However, this choice may mean it takes longer to have papers served because these offices tend to be busy and law enforcement officers only serve papers during regular business hours. If you only have a few weeks before your guardianship hearing date, it's probably best to use a professional process server. If you choose to have a marshal or deputy serve the papers, call the marshal's office or civil division of the county sheriff's office to find out who serves court papers in your county.[8] You then go into that office with copies of the papers to be served, pay a fee (usually under $20) for each person to be served, and fill out a form giving information such as the best hours to find the person at home or work, and a general physical description.

As we said earlier, you can have a friend, relative, or other person who is 18 years or older and not involved in the guardianship proceeding serve copies of the guardianship papers. But only have a non-professional serve papers personally if the person being served will not be upset by receiving the guardianship papers. It's not a good idea to put people you know in the middle of a conflict.

E. Use Guardian Notification Worksheet to Determine Who Must Be Served

AS DISCUSSED, CERTAIN RELATIVES of the minor must receive legal notice of the guardianship proceeding unless they sign a Waiver of Notice form or you cannot locate them. In addition to these relatives, certain agencies also may be entitled to notice of the guardianship. Each of the relatives and agencies entitled to notice must be served at least 20 days before the hearing date. To avoid problems later on, you must make sure everyone entitled to notice is served correctly. The way to do this is by using the Guardianship Notification Worksheet to figure out who must be served and how.

---

[7] If you expect service problems because someone may contest the guardianship, you will need to see a lawyer. However, if someone entitled to personal service is difficult or uncooperative, is in jail or another institution, have a professional do the job.

[8] Marshals are the enforcement officers for some counties who serve court papers Some counties, such as Los Angeles, have marshals' offices separate from sheriffs' offices. But in many other counties, especially in Northern California, the sheriff is designated as the marshal for—among other things—serving papers.

1. Which Relatives Must be Served?

In Chapter 4, you began to fill in Part 1 of the Guardianship Notification Worksheet. Now you'll use that worksheet to figure out which relatives must be served.

In Item 5, for each relative, you answered the question "Need to have served?" Each of the relatives for whom you answered "yes" must be served. If you submitted an Order Dispensing Notice, do not serve those listed on it. At the hearing, the judge will decide whether to grant the order—for now, you will have to assume that service will not be required. Anyone for whom the Order Dispensing Notice is signed does not have to be served, so for them Item 5 should be answered "no."

Item 6 of the Guardianship Notification Worksheet gives a summary of how each person must be served, and refers to the section in this chapter that gives service instructions. Here is a more detailed explanation of service requirements for people who have not signed a Waiver of Notice and Consent or for whom an Order Dispensing Notice is not signed:

- *Minor*. A minor who is 12 years of age or older must be personally served with notice of the guardianship, and cannot sign a document waiving the right to service. A minor who is younger than 12 does not get served with notice of the guardianship, except if she has a child. If the minor must be served, gently explain that as part of the guardianship procedure, someone other than you will be giving her copies of legal papers.
- *Minor's mother*. The minor's mother may either be served personally or by Notice and Acknowledgment of Receipt (documents are mailed to the person along with a special form saying that the papers were received; the recipient signs and mails back the form).
- *Minor's father*. The minor's father may either be served personally or by Notice and Acknowledgment of Receipt.
- *Minor's maternal grandparents*. The minor's maternal grandparents are served by mail.
- *Minor's paternal grandparents*. The minor's paternal grandparents are served by mail.
- *Minor's spouse*. The minor's spouse is served by mail.
- *Minor's sisters and brothers*. The minor's siblings are served by mail if they are 12 years or older. If they are between the ages of 12 and 18, you must also have their parents served by mail. In most instances, you serve their parents anyhow since they're the same parents as the minor for whom you're seeking guardianship. But occasionally the minor may have a half-brother or sister whose other parent must be served. Minors under 12 years of age do not have to be served.
- *Minor's children*. The minor's children do not need to be served. However, you'll need to serve the child's other parent by mail.
- *Anyone presently having legal custody of the minor*. If the minor has a legal guardian or someone other than the parents has legal custody, he may either be served personally or by Notice and Acknowledgment of Receipt.
- *Anyone nominated minor's legal guardian*. Anyone besides you who has been nominated as the minor's legal guardian may be served either personally or by Notice and Acknowledgment of Receipt.
- *Anyone having physical custody of the minor*. Anyone other than you who has physical custody of the minor must be served by mail.

2. Which Agencies Must be Served?

You may be required to serve one or more agencies with notice of the guardianship because by law, certain agencies may be required to investigate your appropriateness as guardian. Other agencies are entitled to notice so they can better monitor benefits to which the minor may be entitled. All agencies are served by mail.

As you go through each agency listed in this section, fill in Part 2 of the Guardianship Notification Worksheet. Indicate whether each agency needs to be served, and fill in the names and addresses of those that do. A completed sample is shown in Section I2 of this chapter.

a. Local Social Services Agency

If you are seeking guardianship of a minor's person, you must serve the local agency that screens every proposed guardian for a history of child abuse or neglect. Additionally, in some counties the local agency also conducts an investigation. (See Chapter 8 for information about investigations.)

The front pages of the telephone book should list county services. Look for a heading such as "Children's Emergency Services," "Children's Protective Services," "Social Services," "Probation Department" or "Welfare Department." Call the number and explain that you are filing guardianship papers with the court and need the address of the local agency that screens guardianships for the court. You may need to make several calls to track down the correct address.

b. Court Investigator

In some counties, an investigator of the superior court in which you file the guardianship will conduct an investigation, which is done in addition to the social services screening. If you don't already have the name and address of the court investigator who handles guardianships, call the court and ask for this information. (See Chapter 8 for information about investigations.)

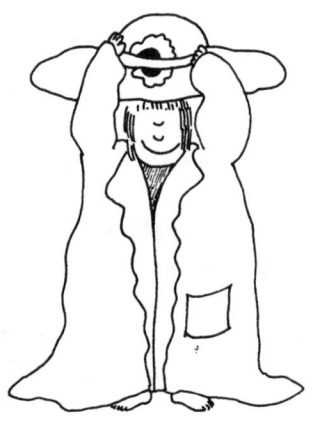

c. State Director of Social Services

If you are not a blood relative of the minor and you are seeking guardianship of the minor's person, you must serve the State Director of Social Services. Step-parents are not blood relatives, nor are uncles or aunts who are only related to a minor by marriage. If you're not sure whether you're a blood relative of the minor, go ahead and have the State Director of Social Services served by mail—just in case it's required. Here is the address:

Director of Social Services
ATTN: M.S. 19-31
744 "P" Street
Sacramento, CA 95814

d. Directors of Mental Health and Developmental Services

Look at the Petition for Appointment of Guardian of Minor you filed with the court. If you answered "yes" to Item 7a (checked the second box), you must serve the Director of Mental Health (if the minor is a patient of or on leave from a state mental hospital), or the Director of Developmental Services (if the minor is developmentally disabled).[9] (PC §1461). Here are their addresses:

Director of Mental Health
State of California
ATTN: Legal Offices
1600 Ninth Street, Room 151
Sacramento, CA 95814

Director of Developmental Services
State of California
ATTN: Office of Legal Affairs
1600 Ninth Street, Room 240
Sacramento, CA 95814

e. Veterans' Administration

Now look at Item 7b of the Petition for Appointment of Guardian of Minor that you filed with the court. If you answered yes to Item 7b (checked the second box), you must serve the office of the Veterans' Administration (PC §1461.5). If you happen to know

---

[9]This is very rare. If the minor is developmentally disabled, and you are a board and care, treatment, or habilitation facilities provider, spouse or employee, there are additional service requirements if you're also not the minor's parent. This is beyond the scope of this book. (See Chapter 13 for information on finding and dealing with lawyers.)

the claim number for the veteran, note it on the outside of the envelope.

In California, there are three regional offices of the Veterans' Administration. Use the office closest to the court in which you are filing the guardianship. If you're not sure which one to use, call the Veterans' Administration.

The Northern California address is:

Veterans' Administration
Regional Office - Northern California
Office of the Veterans' Administration
211 Main Street
San Francisco, CA 94105

There are two Southern California addresses. Use the Los Angeles address if the court is north of Riverside. Use the San Diego address if the court is located in or south of Riverside.

Veterans' Administration
Regional Office - Los Angeles
11000 Wilshire Blvd.
Los Angeles, CA 90024

or

Veterans' Administration
Regional Office - San Diego
2022 Camino Del Rio North
San Diego, CA 92108

F. Personal Service and Notice and Acknowledgment of Receipt

YOU HAVE USED THE GUARDIANSHIP NOTIFICATION WORKSHEET to figure out who—if anyone—must be served personally or by notice and acknowledgment of receipt. Remember that minors 12 years of age and older must be served personally.[10] Bear in mind that you cannot give the documents to the minor yourself, and she cannot sign a document waiving her right to notice.

---

[10]If the minor is under 12 years of age, she does not have to be served unless she has a child, in which case she should be served personally.

1. How to Have Documents Served Personally

For personal service, copies of the Petition for Appointment of Guardian of Minor and Notice of Hearing must be handed to or left for each person by a process server. If a minor is being served, let him know that someone other than you will be giving him legal documents about the guardianship. A few kind and reassuring words are probably in order, so he knows what to expect.

If you hire a law enforcement officer or a registered process server, she will know how to serve someone personally. But if you use a relative, neighbor or friend, you need to give careful instructions. Give the server a detailed description of the person to be served (for example, "mid-40s, graying hair, about 5'10," medium build, and wears horn-rimmed glasses"). Provide a photograph if you have one.

If a non-professional is serving the papers for you, it's best for him to serve the person at home. Service can be made at the person's workplace, but we recommend you use a professional server if that's necessary, unless the person is agreeable about being served. The server shouldn't disturb anyone very early or very late in the day. Your server should understand that personal service is not complete if he simply leaves the papers on the person's porch, or in the mailbox (which, incidentally, is illegal under Postal Service regulations).

The server must give copies of the legal papers to the person being served. This, of course, means that the server must actually see the person and be able to talk to him, regardless of whether the person is willing to take the papers. Once the server sees and identifies the person, and is close enough to complete the service, it doesn't matter if the person gets angry, tries to run away, refuses to take the papers, or even rips them up. The server can put the papers on the ground as close as possible to the person's feet, saying something like "This is for you," or "You have been served," and leave.

Under no circumstance should the server pick up the papers once they have been served in this manner. If he does, the service will be invalidated and will have to be done again. And he should never try to force anyone to take the papers—it's unnecessary and may subject the server (or even you) to a lawsuit for assault or battery.

2. How to Have Documents Served by Notice and Acknowledgment of Receipt

Anyone entitled to personal service who is over age 18 may be served by mail instead, if she is willing to sign and immediately return to you a document saying she received notice of the guardianship proceeding. This document is called a Notice and Acknowledgment of Receipt. By law, the person being served is allowed 20 days to send the signed form back to you, so you might not have enough time before the hearing date to have service done this way. Also, unless a relative is extremely responsible and cooperative (and for some reason chose not to sign a Waiver of Notice and Consent), you should have documents served personally on anyone entitled to personal service.[11] (See Section F1 above.)

If you're not sure you'll get the signed document back promptly, you could try this method of service, but be prepared to have the person served personally if he doesn't return the Notice and Acknowledgment of Receipt at least 20 days before the hearing date. If possible, contact the person you are serving to let them know about the guardianship proceeding and to make sure they're willing to sign the Notice and Acknowledgment of Receipt.

Even though you prepare the documents being served, someone else must put them in the mail and sign a Proof of Service. You will need a separate Notice and Acknowledgment of Receipt for each person to whom you're sending notice of the guardianship.

---

[11]There is no penalty for failing to sign and return the Notice and Acknowledgement of Receipt back within 20 days—or at all—for guardianship cases. So it's up to the recipient as to whether he wants to sign and return it to you.

a. Notice and Acknowledgment of Receipt Form

CAPTION: NOTICE AND ACKNOWLEDGMENT OF RECEIPT

Fill in the caption following the general instructions in Chapter 3, Section D1.

TO: Just under the caption there is a dotted line after the word "TO."

Fill in the full first and last names of the person being served. If more than one person is being served, you must complete a separate Notice and Acknowledgment of Receipt for each person, even if all of them live at the same address.

Dated: Fill in the date the documents will be served. At the right is a signature line and the words "(Signature of sender)." Sign your name on this line.

Item 1: Leave this item blank.

Item 2: Check only the last box entitled "Other: (Specify)." Then list the full title of each document you are serving, such as the Petition for Appointment of Guardian of Minor and Notice of Hearing.

Leave the rest of the form blank. The person to whom you send the documents must date and sign the form and return it to you to show that she has received them.

b. Copy and Have Notice and Acknowledgment of Receipt Sent

Make two copies of the Notice and Acknowledgment of Receipt, and keep one for your records. Then put the following in an envelope, with the correct amount of postage affixed, addressed to the person being served:

- Signed original and one copy of the Notice and Acknowledgment of Receipt;
- A self-addressed, stamped envelope; and
- One copy of each of the documents you listed in Item 2 of the Notice and Acknowledgment of Receipt.

You might want to prepare a cover letter to the person being served so the procedure will not seem threatening, especially if for some reason you haven't yet discussed the guardianship. Your cover letter might go something like the sample letter which follows.

NAME AND ADDRESS OF SENDER:	TELEPHONE NO.:	For Court Use Only:
JOYCE MARGARET YU 19 North Avenue Fairfield, CA 94533	707/555-1212	

Insert name of court, judicial district or branch court, if any, and Post Office and Street Address:
SUPERIOR COURT OF CALIFORNIA, COUNTY OF SOLANO
600 Union Avenue, Hall of Justice
P.O. Box 1
Fairfield, CA 94533

GUARDIANSHIP OF (Name):

JOHN TODD YU

Minor

NOTICE AND ACKNOWLEDGMENT OF RECEIPT	Case Number: 12345

TO: KIM YU
(Insert name of individual being served)

This summons and other document(s) indicated below are being served pursuant to Section 415.30 of the California Code of Civil Procedure. Your failure to complete this form and return it to me within 20 days may subject you (or the party on whose behalf you are being served) to liability for the payment of any expenses incurred in serving a summons on you in any other manner permitted by law.

If you are being served on behalf of a corporation, unincorporated association (including a partnership), or other entity, this form must be signed by you in the name of such entity or by a person authorized to receive service of process on behalf of such entity. In all other cases, this form must be signed by you personally or by a person authorized by you to acknowledge receipt of summons. Section 415.30 provides that this summons and other document(s) are deemed served on the date you sign the Acknowledgment of Receipt below, if you return this form to me.

Dated: 8/10/92

Joyce Margaret Yu
(Signature of sender)

ACKNOWLEDGMENT OF RECEIPT

This acknowledges receipt of: (To be completed by sender before mailing)
1. ☐ A copy of the summons and of the complaint.
2. ☐ A copy of the summons and of the Petition (Marriage) and:
   ☐ Blank Confidential Counseling Statement (Marriage)
   ☐ Order to Show Cause (Marriage)
   ☐ Blank Responsive Declaration
   ☐ Blank Financial Declaration
   ☒ Other: (Specify) Petition for Appointment of Guardian of Minor
   Notice of Hearing

(To be completed by recipient)

Date of receipt: _____
(Signature of person acknowledging receipt, with title if acknowledgment is made on behalf of another person)

Date this form is signed: _____
(Type or print your name and name of entity, if any, on whose behalf this form is signed)

Form Approved by the Judicial Council of California
Revised Effective January 1, 1975

NOTICE AND ACKNOWLEDGMENT OF RECEIPT

CCP 415.30, 417.10;
Cal. Rules of Court,
Rule 1216

> SAMPLE
>
> August 10, 1992
>
> Kim Yu
> 2 Anyplace
> Calcity, CA 99999
>
> Re: Guardianship of John Todd Yu
>   Case No. 12345
>
> Dear Kim:
>
> I've enclosed documents letting you know that I intend to become John's legal guardian. As you know, I've been taking care of John for almost a year now, and it would be best to go to court to make the guardianship official.
>
> I'd appreciate it if you would sign the enclosed original Notice and Acknowledgment of Receipt, showing that you've been given notice of the guardianship proceeding. Then return it to me in the enclosed self-addressed, stamped envelope. I need to get a signed copy of the Notice and Acknowledgment of Receipt to the court right away, so please send it back to me as soon as possible.
>
> I hope everything is going well with you. Please call me if you have any questions.
>
> Sincerely,
>
> Joyce Margaret Yu
>
> Enclosures

After you have assembled all of the above documents and made sure that you have an extra copy of everything for your files, have someone else mail them. The envelope, with correct postage attached, should simply be put in a U.S. mailbox. The person who mails the papers must be at least 18 years old, must not be involved in the guardianship, and must live or work in the city where the mailing occurs.

Do not have the papers served by certified or registered mail, since this kind of mail must be signed for before delivery. If the recipient isn't home when the envelope arrives, she must make a special trip to the post office—which can lead to further delays.

3. Complete Proof of Service for Personal Service or by Notice and Acknowledgment of Receipt Form

Once the papers have been served, you must complete a Proof of Service for Personal Service or By Notice and Acknowledgment of Receipt form. This form is a declaration by someone (other than you) stating how and when the documents were served. After the form is filled in, the person who served the papers must sign it.

You can use this form for people who either were served personally, or by Notice and Acknowledgment of Receipt. For each person served, complete a separate proof of service form. Here's how to complete it.

		FOR COURT USE ONLY
PARTY WITHOUT AN ATTORNEY *(Name and Address):* GEORGIA ANNA FRANKLIN 100 East Street Berkeley, CA 94703 In Pro Per	TELEPHONE NO: 415/555-1212	
NAME OF COURT: ALAMEDA SUPERIOR COURT STREET ADDRESS: 1225 Fallon MAILING ADDRESS: CITY AND ZIP CODE: Oakland, CA 94612 BRANCH NAME: Northern		
GUARDIANSHIP OF THE [X] PERSON [X] ESTATE OF (NAME): SHARON DANIELLE TURNER MINOR		
PROOF OF SERVICE FOR PERSONAL SERVICE OR BY NOTICE AND ACKNOWLEDGMENT OF RECEIPT (CCP SECTIONS 415.10, 415.30)	CASE NUMBER 1000	

I declare that:

1. At the time of service I was at least 18 years of age and not a party to this legal action.
2. I am a resident of or employed in the county where the mailing occurred, if service was by mail.
3. My business or residence address is: 400 West Way, Alameda, CA 94550

4. I served copies of the following paper(s) in the manner shown:
    - [X] Petition for Appointment of Guardian of Minor
    - [X] Notice of Hearing (Guardianship)
    - [ ] Other [list exact titles of paper(s)]:

5. Manner of service:

    a. [X] Personal Service. I personally delivered these papers to:

      (1) Name of person served: Howard Turner

      (2) Address where served: 222 Third Street
          Alameda, CA 94550

      (3) Date served: 6/16/90

      (4) Time served: 2:00 p.m.

    b. [ ] By mailing copies by first-class mail, postage prepaid, along with two copies of a Notice and Acknowledgment of Receipt and a self-addressed, stamped envelope to:

      (1) Name of person served: _____

      (2) Address to which documents were mailed: _____

      (3) Date documents were mailed: _____

      (4) City and state where mailing occurred: _____

      (5) The completed Notice and Acknowledgment of Receipt is attached.

I declare under penalty of perjury under the laws of the State of California that the foregoing is true and correct.

Date: 6/16/90

EMMA FRAND   *Emma Frand*
(TYPE OR PRINT NAME)   (SIGNATURE OF PERSON WHO SERVED PAPERS)

PROOF OF SERVICE FOR PERSONAL SERVICE
OR BY NOTICE AND ACKNOWLEDGMENT OF RECEIPT

CAPTION: PROOF OF SERVICE FOR PERSONAL SERVICE OR BY NOTICE AND ACKNOWLEDGMENT OF RECEIPT

Fill in the caption following the general instructions in Chapter 3, Section D1.

Item 1: Leave this item blank. It simply states that the person who served the documents is at least 18 years old and not involved in the guardianship action.

Item 2: Leave this item blank.

Item 3: Fill in the business or residence address of the person who served the documents. If the documents were served by mail along with a Notice and Acknowledgment of Receipt, make sure this address is in the same county where the mailing occurred.

Item 4: Check the boxes that apply, depending on which papers were served. Check the first box if the Petition for Appointment of Guardian of Minor was served. Check the second box if the Notice of Hearing (Guardianship) was served. Check the third box entitled "OTHER" if any other documents were served, and list the full name of each document served.

Item 5a: Check this box if the person was personally served. If the person was served by mail along with a Notice and Acknowledgment of Receipt, skip this item and go on to Item 5b.

Item 5a(1): Fill in the name of the person served. If more than one person was served, complete a separate Proof of Service for each person, even if they live at the same address.

Item 5a(2): Fill in the address where the person was served.

Item 5a(3): Fill in the date the person was served.

Item 5a(4): Fill in the time the person was served.

Item 5b: Check this box if the person was served by mail along with two copies of a Notice and Acknowledgment of Receipt and a self-addressed, stamped envelope. Skip this item if the person was personally served.

Item 5b(1): Fill in the name of the person served. If more than one person was served, complete a separate Proof of Service for each, even if all of them live at the same address.

Item 5b(2): Fill in the address to which the documents were mailed.

Item 5b(3): Fill in the date the documents were mailed.

Item 5b(4): Fill in the city and state where the documents were mailed. This must be the county where the person mailing them either lives or works.

Item 5b(5): Staple to the Proof of Service the original Notice and Acknowledgment of Receipt that was signed both by the sender and the person who received the documents.

Item 6: Leave this item blank.

Finally, have the person who served the documents fill in the date, sign the form on the signature line and print his or her full name on the line provided. Instructions on how to file proofs of service with the court are covered in Section H in this chapter.

G. Having Documents Served by Mail

USING THE GUARDIANSHIP Notification Worksheet as a guide, write or type on envelopes the names and addresses of every person and agency who must be served. If two people are being served at the same address, prepare a separate envelope for each one. Place a copy of the Petition for Appointment of Guardian of Minor and Notice of Hearing in each envelope, and seal the envelopes.

After you have affixed the correct amount of postage to each envelope and made sure that you have an extra copy of everything for your files, have someone mail the envelopes for you. The person who serves the papers must be at least 18 years old, must not be involved in the guardianship proceeding, and must live or work in the city where the mailing occurs. The envelopes should simply be put in a mailbox—do not have them sent by certified or registered mail. It's an unnecessary expense, and can create delays if the recipient isn't home to sign for the mail.

1. Complete Proof of Service

Once service has taken place, complete a Proof of Service by Mail form. This form is a declaration by someone (other than you) stating how and when the documents were served. After the form is filled in, the person who serves the papers must sign it.

You may either use the Proof of Service by Mail form following the instructions in Section G1a, or—if you have the original Notice of Hearing—the back of the Notice of Hearing form following the instructions in Section G1b. You can call your court to find out if it requires the back of the Notice of Hearing. You do not need to fill out both forms.

a. Proof of Service by Mail Form

There is a Proof of Service by Mail form in the back of this book in Appendix D.[12] You may use one Proof of Service by Mail form for everyone who was served by mail, as long as the envelopes were deposited by one person at the same time.[13] Here's how to complete it.

CAPTION: PROOF OF SERVICE BY MAIL

Fill in the caption following the general instructions in Chapter 3, Section D1.

Item 1: Leave this item blank.

---

[12] This Proof of Service by Mail form may be used whenever you have any document served on someone by mail.
[13] A different form is used for anyone served by Notice and Acknowledgment of Receipt, even though it is also mailed. Instructions are in Section F2 of this chapter.

Item 2: Leave this item blank. But note that the person who served the documents must have mailed them from the county where she either lives or works.

Item 3: Fill in the business or residence address of the person who served the documents.

Item 4: Check the boxes that apply, depending on which papers were served. Check the first box if the Petition for Appointment of Guardian of Minor was served. Check the second box if the Notice of Hearing (Guardianship) was served. Check the third box entitled "OTHER" if any other documents were served, and list the full name of each document served.

Item 5a: Fill in the date that the documents were mailed.

Item 5b: Fill in the city and state where the documents were mailed. Again, remember this must be in the county where the person mailing the documents either lives or works.

Item 6: In the blank space, fill in the name and address of each person to whom documents were mailed. If you need additional space, check the box at the bottom of the item that reads "Additional names and addresses on reverse." Then at the top of the back of the form, type in the name and number of the guardianship case. Beneath that, list the additional names and addresses. If you do this, remember to photocopy both sides of the form when you make copies for filing with the court.

Item 7: Leave this item blank.

Finally, have the person who served the documents fill in the date, sign the form on the signature line and print his or her full name on the line provided. Instructions for how to file proofs of service with the court are covered in Section H in this chapter.

b. Back of Notice of Hearing

When you prepared the Notice of Hearing, you left the back of the form blank. If you have the original signed Notice of Hearing, you may use the proof of service on the back. If the clerk filed the original signed Notice of Hearing, instead complete the Proof of Service By Mail following the instructions in Section G1a of this chapter.

Here's how to complete the back of the Notice of Hearing form.

PARTY WITHOUT AN ATTORNEY (*Name and Address*): GEORGIA ANNA FRANKLIN 100 East Street Berkeley, CA 94703 In Pro Per	TELEPHONE NO.: 415/555-1212	FOR COURT USE ONLY

NAME OF COURT: ALAMEDA SUPERIOR COURT
STREET ADDRESS: 1225 Fallon
MAILING ADDRESS:
CITY AND ZIP CODE: Oakland, CA 94612
BRANCH NAME: Northern

GUARDIANSHIP OF THE [X] PERSON [X] ESTATE OF (NAME):
SHARON DANIELLE TURNER, MINOR

PROOF OF SERVICE BY MAIL
(CCP SECTIONS 1013a, 2015.5)

CASE NUMBER: 1000

I declare that:

1. At the time of service I was at least 18 years of age and not a party to this legal action.
2. I am a resident of or employed in the county where the mailing occurred.
3. My business or residence address is: 400 West Way, Alameda, CA 94550

4. I served copies of the following paper(s) in the manner shown:
   [X] Petition for Appointment of Guardian of Minor
   [X] Notice of Hearing (Guardianship)
   [ ] Other [list exact titles of paper(s)]:

5. Manner of service: by placing true copies in a sealed envelope addressed to each person whose name and address is given below and depositing the envelopes in the United States Mail with the postage fully prepaid.
   a. Date of deposit: 6/14/90
   b. Place of deposit (city and state): Alameda, California

6. Name and address of each person to whom documents were mailed:

Ruth Turner
100 Any Street
Alameda, CA 94550

Elizabeth Smith
6 City Blvd.
Oakland, CA 94612

Bill Turner
100 Any Street
Alameda, CA 94550

Jan Smith
10 Metropolitan Ave.
Oakland, CA 94610

Cynthia Jackson
900 Some Street
Berkeley, CA 94710

[ ] Additional names and addresses on reverse.

I declare under penalty of perjury under the laws of the State of California that the foregoing is true and correct.

Date: 6/14/90

EMMA FRAND
(TYPE OR PRINT NAME)

Emma Frand
(SIGNATURE OF PERSON WHO SERVED PAPERS)

NP

PROOF OF SERVICE BY MAIL

| ☒ GUARDIANSHIP ☐ CONSERVATORSHIP OF (NAME): REBECCA DIANA STONE | ☒ Minor ☐ Conservatee | CASE NUMBER: 12345 |

NOTICE OF HEARING—GUARDIANSHIP OR CONSERVATORSHIP
CLERK'S CERTIFICATE OF ☐ POSTING ☐ MAILING

Page 2

I certify that I am not a party to this cause and that a true copy of the foregoing Notice of Hearing—Guardianship or Conservatorship

1. ☐ *(for sales under section 2543(c) of the Probate Code only)* was posted at (address):

2. ☐ was mailed, first class, postage fully prepaid, ☐ with a copy of the petition (title):

   in a sealed envelope addressed to each person whose name and address is given below.
I certify that the notice was posted or mailed and this certificate was executed on (date): . . . .
at (place): . . . . , California.

Clerk, by _____, Deputy

PROOF OF SERVICE BY MAIL

I am over the age of 18 and not a party to this cause. I am a resident of or employed in the county where the mailing occurred. My residence or business address is:
25 Some Street, Antioch, CA 94555

I served the foregoing Notice of Hearing—Guardianship or Conservatorship ☒ with a copy of the petition (title):
   Petition for Appointment of Guardian of Minor
by enclosing a true copy in a sealed envelope addressed to each person whose name and address is given below and depositing the envelope in the United States mail with the postage fully prepaid.

(1) Date of deposit: 12/7/90   (2) Place of deposit (city and state): Antioch, CA

I declare under penalty of perjury under the laws of the State of California that the foregoing is true and correct and that this declaration is executed on (date): 12/9/90 . . . . . at (place): Antioch, CA . . . . . .

Emma Frand
(Type or print name)

Emma Frand
(Signature of declarant)

NAME AND ADDRESS OF EACH PERSON TO WHOM NOTICE WAS MAILED

Frederick Stone
1 West Street
Anycity, CA 94901

Jane Doe
25 East Avenue
Somecity, CA 99999

Nina Smith
22 South Street
Anycity, CA 94901

John Stone
1 West Street
Anycity, CA 94901

John Doe
100 North Lane
Somecity, CA 99999

Joanne Stone
1 West Street
Anycity, CA 94901

Penelope Doe
2001 Space Street
Anothercity, CA 99000

☐ List of names and addresses continued on attachment.

> **CAPTION:** PAGE TWO OF THE NOTICE OF HEARING
>
> Check the boxes before the words "GUARDIANSHIP" and "MINOR," and fill in the minor's name after the words "GUARDIANSHIP OF."
>
> Fill in the case number.

Clerk's Certificate of Posting/Mailing: The first section, entitled "CLERK'S CERTIFICATE OF POSTING/MAILING," is usually not completed. Some courts have a policy of allowing the clerk to serve documents by mail, if you give the clerk copies and self-addressed, stamped envelopes. If your court provides this service and you want the clerk, rather than a friend or family member, to serve the documents by mail, complete this section. Otherwise skip to the next section entitled "PROOF OF SERVICE BY MAIL."

If the court clerk will be mailing your documents, check the box in the heading before the word "MAILING."

Item 1: Leave this item blank.

Item 2: Check both boxes in this item. In the space provided, fill in the full name of the petition to be served (for example, Petition for Appointment of Guardian of Minor).

Leave the date, place and clerk's signature line blank. The clerk will complete these at the time of mailing. However, make sure you complete the last section entitled "NAME AND ADDRESS OF EACH PERSON TO WHOM NOTICE WAS MAILED."

Proof of Service by Mail: Complete this section if an adult other than the court clerk is mailing papers for you.

After the words "My residence or business address is," fill in the home or business address of the person who mailed the documents.

Check the box before the words "with a copy of the petition (title)." Then in the space provided, fill in the full name of the petition to be served (for example, Petition for Appointment of Guardian of Minor).

Item (1): Fill in the date the documents were mailed.

Item (2): Fill in the city and state where the documents were mailed.

In the spaces indicated, fill in the date, city and state where this form will be signed by the server. Then fill in the name of the person who completed the service.

Finally, complete the section below.

Name and Address of Each Person to Whom Notice Was Mailed: Always complete this section, regardless of who serves the papers. Fill in all the names and addresses of everyone to whom papers were or will be mailed. If you need more room, check the box at the bottom of the page before the words "List of names and addresses continued on attachment." Then prepare an attachment entitled "Attachment to Notice of Hearing," following the instructions in Chapter 3, Section D3. List the names and addresses of any additional people served.

Finally, have the process server or court clerk sign on the appropriate line. Instructions on how to file proofs of service with the court are covered in Section H in this chapter.

H. Copy and File Proofs of Service and Possibly Notice of Hearing

YOU'RE NOW READY TO PHOTOCOPY THE PROOFS OF SERVICE and file them with the court. You'll also file the original signed Notice of Hearing, if you have it. (See Section G in this chapter.) These papers should be filed at least five days before the hearing date, not including weekends or holidays.

Make at least two or three copies of each proof of service. If you have the original Notice of Hearing and completed the proof of service on the back, also make two or three copies of it. If the court already has the original signed Notice of Hearing, file only the proofs of service with the court. Note that you should not use the proof of service on the back of the Notice of Hearing form unless you have the original.

You are now ready to file these documents with the court, following the instructions in Chapter 3. Make sure that you obtain a date-stamped copy of each paper from the court. If you send the documents by mail, keep an extra copy for your records in case the form is lost in the mail or misplaced at court.

Important: When you file the proofs of service, make sure the original Notice of Hearing is filed with the court. If you don't have the original Notice of Hearing, ask the clerk to check the court file to see if it was previously filed.

I. Complete the Guardianship Notification Worksheet

ONCE YOU RECEIVE YOUR PROOFS OF SERVICE back from the court, you may complete the Guardianship Notification Worksheet.

1. Worksheet—Part 1: Relatives

Item 7: If you haven't already filled in the date each person was served, put in this information. If you've submitted an Order Dispensing Notice, because either you couldn't locate someone or he signed a Waiver of Notice and Consent, leave this item blank for that person.

Item 8: Fill in the date the proof of service was filed with the court. You'll find this stamped in the upper right-hand corner of each filed proof of service.

2. Worksheet—Part 2: Agencies

If you haven't already filled in the date each agency was served, fill in this information. Then fill in the date the proof of service was filed with the court. You'll find this stamped in the upper right-hand corner of each filed proof of service.

GUARDIANSHIP NOTIFICATION WORKSHEET
PART I. RELATIVES

(1) NAMES AND ADDRESSES OF MINOR'S RELATIVES AND OTHER PEOPLE ENTITLED TO NOTICE	(2) NEED TO LOCATE?	(3) DATE LOCATED	(4) WILL SIGN WAIVER OF NOTICE & CONSENT?	(5) NEED TO HAVE SERVED?	(6) SERVICE TYPE, IF NEED TO HAVE SERVED	(7) DATE SERVED OR ORDER DISPENSING NOTICE	(8) DATE FILED PROOF OF SERVICE
Minor MOLLY DENISE SCHWARTZ 60 W. West Street Oakland, CA 94612	No	—	Cannot sign since under 18	Only if 12 or over, or if minor has a child	Personal (Chapter 6, Section F)	—	—
Minor's mother ANGELA NATALIE SCHWARTZ 100 N. North Street Byron, CA 94514	No	—	Yes	No	Personal or Notice and Acknowledgment of Receipt (Chapter 6, Section F)	6/6/90 order signed	—
Minor's father JERRY SCHWARTZ 800 S. South Street San Diego, CA 92138	Yes	5/14/90	Yes	No	Personal or Notice and Acknowledgment of Receipt (Chapter 6, Section F)	6/6/90 order signed	—
Minor's maternal grandparents (mother's parents) BETTY BROWER NATE BROWER 9 Bright Street Boston, MA 02131	No No	— —	No No	Yes Yes	Mail (Chapter 6, Section G)	5/8/90 5/8/90	5/18/90 5/18/90
Minor's paternal grandparents (father's parents) PENNY SCHWARTZ, Deceased BRIAN SCHWARTZ 200 E. West Way Pittsburg, PA	— Yes	— 5/22/90	— No	— Yes	Mail (Chapter 6, Section G)	— 5/24/90	— 5/26/90
Minor's spouse—can only petition for guardianship of the estate	—	—	Can sign only if 18 or over	—	Mail, and also serve parents, if under 18 (Chapter 6, Section G)	—	—

Page 1 of 3

GUARDIANSHIP NOTIFICATION WORKSHEET
PART I. RELATIVES (continued)

(1) NAMES AND ADDRESSES OF MINOR'S RELATIVES AND OTHER PEOPLE ENTITLED TO NOTICE	(2) NEED TO LOCATE?	(3) DATE LOCATED	(4) WILL SIGN WAIVER OF NOTICE & CONSENT?	(5) NEED TO HAVE SERVED?	(6) SERVICE TYPE, IF NEED TO HAVE SERVED	(7) DATE SERVED OR ORDER DISPENSING NOTICE	(8) DATE FILED PROOF OF SERVICE
Minor's sisters and brothers (include their ages; if parents not listed elsewhere on worksheet, list their names and addresses) DANA SCHWARTZ (Age 20) 1 E. East Ave. New York, NY 10003 MICK SCHWARTZ (Age 4) 100 N. North St. Byron, CA 94514	No No	— —	Can sign only if 18 or over Yes No	Only if over 12 (and serve parents if under 18) No No (serving parents)	Mail, if over 12. Serve parents, if under 18 (Chapter 6, Section G)	6/6/90 order signed —	— —
Minor's children (if child's other parent not listed elsewhere on worksheet, list name and address)	—	—	Cannot sign since under 18	—	Not required, but must serve both of child's parents	—	—
Anyone presently having legal custody of minor (not including you)	—	—	—	—	Personal or Notice and Acknowledgment of Receipt (Chapter 6, Section F)	—	—
Anyone nominated minor's legal guardian (not including you)	—	—	—	—	Personal or Notice and Acknowledgment of Receipt (Chapter 6, Section F)	—	—
Anyone who has physical custody of minor (not including you)	—	—	—	—	Mail (Chapter 6, Section G)	—	—

GUARDIANSHIP NOTIFICATION WORKSHEET
PART II. AGENCIES

NAME AND ADDRESS OF AGENCIES ENTITLED TO NOTICE (SEE CHAPTER 6, SECTION E2)	NEED TO HAVE SERVED?	SERVICE TYPE, IF NEED TO HAVE SERVED	DATE SERVED	DATE FILED PROOF OF SERVICE
Local Social Service Agency CHILD PROTECTIVE SERVICES Sylvia Smith-Jooo 401 Broadway Oakland, CA 94607	Yes	Mail (Chapter 6, Section G)	5/8/90	5/18/90
Court Investigator JUDITH SCHINDLER, COURT INVESTIGATOR Administration Building 1221 Oak Street, Room 20 Oakland, CA 94612	Yes	Mail (Chapter 6, Section G)	5/8/90	5/18/90
State Director of Social Services Attn: M.S. 19-31 744 "P" Street Sacramento, CA 95814	Yes	Mail (Chapter 6, Section G)	5/8/90	5/18/90
Director of Mental Health	No	Mail (Chapter 6, Section G)	—	—
Director of Developmental Services	No	Mail (Chapter 6, Section G)	—	—
Veterans Administration Regional Office - Northern California Office of the Veterans' Administration 211 Main Street San Francisco, CA 94105	Yes	Mail (Chapter 6, Section G)	5/8/90	5/18/90

CHAPTER 7

TEMPORARY GUARDIANSHIPS OF A MINOR'S PERSON

A.	When to Seek a Temporary Guardianship	7/1
B.	Overview of the Temporary Guardianship Process	7/2
C.	Call the Court	7/3
D.	Complete the Regular Guardianship Documents	7/4
E.	Complete Temporary Guardianship Documents	7/4
F.	Filing Documents, Serving Papers, Obtaining Letters of Temporary Guardianship	7/14
G.	How to Extend the Temporary Guardianship	7/15

AS YOU HAVE LEARNED, you don't have the right or power to act as a minor's legal guardian until you are appointed guardian by the court. The fact that you've filed and had the necessary guardianship papers served does not give you any legal status as the minor's guardian pending the court's approval of the guardianship. You must attend a hearing and formally be appointed before you have any legal rights to act as the minor's guardian.

Fortunately, in urgent situations, an emergency measure can easily be taken—a temporary guardianship can be obtained before the regular guardian is appointed. It usually takes less than five days from the date papers are filed in court to obtain the temporary guardianship. A temporary guardian is not a substitute for a regular guardian, but is someone who serves for a short period of time, often until the regular guardian is appointed. The regular guardian and the temporary guardian are usually, although not necessarily, the same person.

A temporary guardian generally has only the duties and responsibilities that are "necessary to provide for the temporary care, maintenance and support" of the minor (PC §2252).[1] A temporary guardian has the same responsibilities as a regular guardian to make decisions about medical treatment for a minor. (See Chapter 11, Section C3.) A temporary guardian should not move the minor out of California without prior permission from the court.

In this chapter, we cover only temporary guardianships of a minor's person, not temporary guardianships of a minor's estate. A judge will probably not allow a proposed guardian to manage a minor's financial affairs without proof there is extraordinary good reason to do so. If you want a temporary guardianship of a minor's estate, see a lawyer. (See Chapter 13 for information on how to find and hire a lawyer.)

A. When to Seek a Temporary Guardianship

THERE ARE SOME SITUATIONS in which you need guardianship powers right away, before the hearing date for the regular guardianship, which is usually about six weeks from the date you file your petition. For example:

- The minor may require needed but non-emergency medical treatment before the hearing. As we saw in Chapter 2, Section C2, a child does not need a guardian to obtain emergency medical care.

---

[1] A temporary guardian may be given additional powers with the court's permission. How to obtain such additional powers is beyond the scope of this book.

- You need a temporary guardianship to qualify to receive public assistance.[2]
- The minor's school will not allow her to enroll without you having obtained a formal guardianship, and the minor would miss school while the hearing is pending.
- The minor's mother wants to go into the armed services, which all require that the child must be in someone else's legal custody while she is in the service.
- The minor's parents have deserted her, and no one has legal authority to make decisions on the minor's behalf.
- The court calendar is congested, and you cannot get a hearing date before you need to make an important decision about a minor's care or schooling.

In any of these, and other urgent situations, you may apply to the court for a temporary guardianship.[3] The temporary guardianship gives you guardianship powers for a limited time—usually 30 days or up until the time of the hearing, whichever is earlier. A temporary guardianship of a minor's person can usually be obtained within about five days of filing your papers with the court.

1. If a Temporary Guardianship is Granted at the Regular Guardianship Hearing

Occasionally, people who seek regular guardianships and attend the guardianship hearing are granted temporary guardianships. Usually this is on the recommendation of the investigator, who feels something should be taken care of before the regular guardianship is granted. For example, the minor might first need to get counseling, or a change in the living arrangements might be required—such as the minor getting her own bedroom. Or possibly the guardianship hearing must be continued because the judge wants someone who couldn't be located served, and a temporary guardianship is desirable in the meantime.

If only a temporary guardianship is granted at the regular guardianship hearing and the hearing is continued to another date, you will need to prepare and submit to the judge an Order Appointing Temporary Guardian, and obtain Letters of Temporary Guardianship following the instructions in this chapter.

Note: If the judge did not actually grant the temporary guardianship, but simply recommended that you file ex parte papers for a temporary guardianship, you will also need to complete the Petition for Appointment of Temporary Guardian and follow all the steps in this chapter for obtaining a temporary guardianship.

B. Overview of the Temporary Guardianship Process

THIS CHAPTER TAKES YOU THROUGH THE STEPS of obtaining a temporary guardianship of a minor's person. Here is a brief overview:

Step 1: Call the court and find out specific local procedures for obtaining a temporary guardianship.

Step 2: Complete the forms needed to obtain a regular guardianship in Chapters 4 and 5.[4]

Step 3: Following the instructions in this chapter, complete three additional forms: Petition for Appointment of Temporary Guardian, Order Appointing Temporary Guardian, and Letters of Temporary Guardianship. You may also need to complete a Notice of Hearing, depending on your court's procedures.

Step 4: If the minor's parents are available and willing, have them sign an attachment to the Petition

---

[2] County agencies cannot deny public assistance benefits to eligible temporary guardians (*Timmons v. McMahon*, 235 Cal. App. 3d 512 (1991)). This used to be a problem temporary guardians frequently faced.

[3] A temporary guardianship may also be obtained either during an appeal to a higher court of an order in a guardianship case, or while someone who was appointed guardian has had his powers suspended by the court. Both these situations involve contested and technical proceedings in which an attorney is essential. Therefore, a temporary guardianship under either of these circumstances is beyond the scope of this book. (See Chapter 13 for information on how to hire an attorney.)

[4] Temporary guardianship papers can only be filed if the regular guardianship papers have already been filed, or are being filed at the same time. Temporary guardianship papers should be filed as soon as you realize that a temporary guardianship is needed.

for Appointment of Temporary Guardian nominating you as temporary guardian and waiving their right to notice.

Step 5: Make copies and then file both the regular guardianship and temporary guardianship papers with the court.

Step 6: Unless the temporary guardianship is heard "ex parte" (without a hearing) or the court orders otherwise, have the minor's living parents and the minor, if 12 or over, served with notice of the temporary guardianship.

Step 7: Attend a hearing, if it is required. Often temporary guardianships are obtained ex parte. In some counties, temporary guardianship documents are taken to the judge and signed right away.

Step 8: Obtain issued Letters of Temporary Guardianship from the court clerk.

Step 9: If you need to extend the guardianship, follow the instructions for obtaining an ex parte order to extend the temporary guardianship.

C. Call the Court

BEFORE YOU GET STARTED filling in the temporary guardianship documents, you will need to call the court. Each court has its own special procedures for obtaining a temporary guardianship, and you will need to understand your particular court's procedures.

There is usually a special probate court clerk who handles procedural questions. You may be required to call that clerk during certain hours of the day. If the court clerk cannot give you the information, consult the local Probate Policy Manual. Or you can ask for the name and number of the clerk of the probate judge or commissioner who handles guardianships, if that clerk is different from the one you've already talked to.

Explain that you are filing a temporary guardianship pending the hearing on a regular guardianship petition. Then find out:

- **Are temporary guardianship petitions heard ex parte?** If a petition is heard ex parte (pronounced "ex-partay"), you don't need to have copies of your papers served on anyone. Often the "hearing" consists only of a judge reviewing your documents. Court policies vary, so you will need to find out the local rules.

- **Do the minor's parent or the minor need to be served?** Each court decides whether the minor's natural parents and the minor—if age 12 or over—must be served with notice of the temporary guardianship petition (PC §2250(c)). If service is required, they will need to be served personally five days before the scheduled temporary guardianship hearing. Some courts routinely waive service requirements for the parents and minor. However, each court has the discretion to require that the parents and minor must be served, and that additional people be served, which is especially likely if you think the guardianship may be contested.[5] Some courts don't require personal service of the parents, but instead require the parents to be notified by telephone a day or two before the hearing.

- **When and how are temporary guardianship petitions heard?** Find out the days and times guardianship petitions are heard, the location, the judge or commissioner who will hear and decide on them, and how you may schedule your petition. If you need to have the minor and his parents served, you'll need to allow enough time to accomplish that. In some areas, you simply bring your papers to the judge when they are complete. Others want to put the temporary guardianship matter on the court calendar to be heard by a judge later.

- **Where are temporary guardianship documents filed?** Some courts require that you file your temporary guardianship documents along with your regular guardianship papers. Others have you bring them to a special room after you've already filed your regular guardianship papers. Very often, temporary guardianship papers are left with the judge's clerk to be reviewed.

- **How long will it take for the judge to rule on the temporary guardianship?** Some courts take several days to decide on temporary guardianships, while others decide on them immediately. If the

---

[5]If either the temporary guardianship or the regular guardianship is contested, consult an attorney. (See Chapter 13.)

minor or his parents must be served, it will probably take a little longer.

D. Complete the Regular Guardianship Documents

AS WE HAVE EMPHASIZED, temporary guardianship papers can be filed only if the regular guardianship papers have either already been filed, or are being filed at the same time. Complete the regular guardianship documents following the instructions in Chapters 4 and 5.

E. Complete Temporary Guardianship Documents

YOU WILL NEED TO FILL IN THREE OR FOUR FORMS in addition to the regular guardianship papers. These documents are similar to those you completed in Chapter 5, so you should find them easy to complete.

1. Petition for Appointment of Temporary Guardian

The Petition for Appointment of Temporary Guardian is the basic document in which you summarize reasons why you urgently need to be appointed temporary guardian. This form is similar to the Petition for Appointment of Guardian of Minor you completed in Chapter 5, Section A. However, it is simpler because it requires mostly specific information about why you need to be appointed temporary guardian pending the regular guardianship hearing.

Important: Before you begin filling in this form, you will need to complete the Petition for Appointment of Guardian of Minor following the instructions in Chapter 5, Section A. Refer to that completed form to fill in this document.

CAPTION: PETITION FOR APPOINTMENT OF TEMPORARY GUARDIAN

Fill in the caption following the general instructions in Chapter 3, Section D1.

Where you seek guardianship of more than one minor, use one form for each child, listing the name of each minor on a separate form.

Check the box entitled "GUARDIAN," then check the box next to the word "person" to indicate you are seeking temporary guardianship of the minor's person.

Leave the case number blank, unless a case number has been assigned because you already filed regular guardianship documents with the court.

Item 1: After the word "Petitioner (name)," fill in your full first, middle and last names. This means that you are the person who is filing for the temporary guardianship.

Item 1a: Again fill in your full first, middle and last names, followed by your address. This indicates that you are the proposed guardian of the minor's person. Then check the boxes before the words "guardian" and "ward."[6]

Item 1b: Leave this item blank. It applies only to temporary guardianships of a minor's estate, which is beyond the scope of this book.

---

[6]This form, as well as several others, is a multi-purpose one used for conservatorships as well as guardianships. You will always leave the boxes applying to the words "conservator" and "conservatee" blank.

Item 1c: Check only the first box before the words "bond not be required." Then cross off the words "for the reasons stated in attachment 1c," and fill in the words "pursuant to Probate Code Section 2322." This code section says that guardian of the person does not have to file a bond unless the court specifically requires it.[7] Leave the rest of this item blank.

Item 1d: Normally this box should not be checked. It is used where a temporary guardian intends to exercise powers beyond those she is ordinarily allowed to exercise, such as moving the minor out of state or insisting the minor receive non-emergency medical treatment against his will. These sorts of powers are almost never granted as part of a temporary guardianship. Contact an attorney if you think you may need these extraordinary powers.

Item 1e: Skip this item if the minor is under 12 years of age. If the minor is 12 years or older, you ordinarily cannot obtain a temporary guardianship until at least five days after you have copies of the Petition for Appointment of Temporary Guardian personally served on the minor.

If the minor is 12 or older, and it is essential that you obtain the temporary guardianship within less than five days, check this box and explain why you need the temporary guardianship so urgently on a separate attachment page. Follow the instructions for attachments in Chapter 3, Section D3, and label it "Attachment 1e to the Petition for Appointment of Temporary Guardian."

Explaining why you can't wait five days actually shouldn't be difficult. If the minor is at least 12 years old, you've probably already discussed the situation with him at length, and he wants you to proceed with the temporary guardianship. In the attachment you might state something like: "The minor's school year will begin in three days, and I am unable to enroll him in the school district in which we live without having first obtained a temporary guardianship. The minor is 15 years old and of sound mind. I have discussed this Petition for Appointment of Temporary Guardian with him, and he is anxious that I proceed, and that the Letters of Temporary Guardianship be issued. I have been regularly caring for the minor, who has been living with me for the past six months."

Item 1f: In this item you will ask the judge to waive notice requirements for the parents if you either can't locate the minor's parents within five days, or the minor's parents are around and are willing to sign a document authorizing you to serve as temporary guardian. If neither of these situations applies, skip this item.

Otherwise, check the box. Then follow the instructions for preparing an attachment set out in Chapter 3, Section D3, and label it "Attachment 1f to the Petition for Appointment of Temporary Guardian."

If you can't locate the minor's parents within five days, state this in your own words on the attachment. For example, you might state: "The minor's father is unknown. The minor's mother abandoned her three years ago, and I do not know how to find her before the temporary guardianship petition will be heard. Since this is an urgent situation, I request that an order be granted dispensing with notice to the minor's parents," or "The minor's mother is dead, and the minor's father is in the army and stationed in Germany. I cannot locate and have the minor's father served before the temporary guardianship petition will be heard. Since this is an urgent situation, I request that an order be granted dispensing with notice to the minor's parents."

If the parent or parents approve of the temporary guardianship and are willing to sign a document saying so, type or write these words on a blank piece of paper: "I, [parent's name], am a parent of [minor's name], the subject of this temporary guardianship. I nominate [your name] as temporary guardian of the person of [minor's name], and request that no bond be required. I also waive notice of the hearing of the Petition for Appointment of Temporary Guardian." Have the parents sign and date the document, and attach it to the petition.

Item 2: Check the first box before the word "ward." Then, in the spaces provided, fill in the minor's full name, address and telephone number. As indicated earlier, if you are seeking temporary guardianship of more than one minor, fill out a separate form for each minor.

---

[7] In the extremely rare case where a judge would require bond for the guardian of a minor's person only, she would make the order at your court hearing. This petition would not have to be amended.

ATTORNEY OR PARTY WITHOUT ATTORNEY (NAME AND ADDRESS):	TELEPHONE NO.:	FOR COURT USE ONLY
PATRICIA ANN LEE 2 West Street Santa Ana, CA 92702	714/555-1212	

ATTORNEY FOR (NAME): In Pro Per

SUPERIOR COURT OF CALIFORNIA, COUNTY OF ORANGE
STREET ADDRESS: 700 Civic Center Drive West
MAILING ADDRESS: P.O. Box 838
CITY AND ZIP CODE: Santa Ana, CA 92702
BRANCH NAME:

TEMPORARY [X] GUARDIANSHIP [ ] CONSERVATORSHIP OF (NAME):
DANIEL FRANK LEE   [X] Minor [ ] Conservatee

PETITION FOR APPOINTMENT OF TEMPORARY
[X] GUARDIAN [ ] CONSERVATOR
[X] Person [ ] Estate

CASE NUMBER: 123

1. Petitioner (name): PATRICIA ANN LEE requests that
   a. (name and address): PATRICIA ANN LEE
      2 West Street, Santa Ana, CA 92702
      be appointed temporary [X] guardian [ ] conservator of the person of the
      proposed [X] ward [ ] conservatee and Letters issue upon qualification.
   b. (name and address):

      be appointed temporary [ ] guardian [ ] conservator of the estate of the
      proposed [ ] ward [ ] conservatee and Letters issue upon qualification.
   c. [X] bond not be required for the reasons stated in attachment 1c. pursuant to Probate Code Section 2322.
      [ ] bond be fixed at $ _____ to be furnished by an authorized surety company or as otherwise provided by law (specify reasons if the amount is different from the minimum required by section 2320 of the Probate Code).
      [ ] deposits at (specify institution):
      in the amount of $ _____ be allowed. Receipts will be filed.
   d. [ ] the powers specified in attachment 1d be granted in addition to the powers provided by law.
   e. [ ] an order be granted dispensing with notice to the proposed [ ] ward [ ] conservatee for the reasons stated in attachment 1e.
   f. [ ] other orders be granted (specify in attachment 1f).
2. The proposed [X] ward [ ] conservatee is (name): DANIEL FRANK LEE
   (present address): 2 West Street   (telephone): 714/555-1212
   Santa Ana, CA 92702
3. The proposed [X] ward [ ] conservatee requires a temporary [X] guardian [ ] conservator to [X] provide for temporary care, maintenance, and support [ ] protect property from loss or injury because (facts are [X] specified below [ ] specified in attachment 3):

   I am the minor's paternal grandmother. I have been taking care of Daniel, who lives with me in Santa Ana, California, for the past six months. Daniel's natural mother is deceased. Daniel's natural father lives in San Francisco, California, where he is undergoing treatment in a drug rehabilitation program. I have discussed both the regular guardianship and the temporary guardianship with Daniel's father over the telephone, and he agrees that both would be best for Daniel. He has signed a Nomination of Guardian form.
   Daniel has been attending Academic High School for the last six months, and has been doing well. Daniel has been selected to represent his school in a spelling competition in New York, and I just discovered that I must be his legal guardian to authorize this trip. Daniel's father is in a hospital and cannot be reached within 1 week, when Daniel will be leaving.   (Continued on reverse)

Form Approved by the
Judicial Council of California
Effective January 1, 1981
GC-110(81)

**PETITION FOR APPOINTMENT OF
TEMPORARY GUARDIAN OR CONSERVATOR**

TEMPORARY [X] GUARDIANSHIP ☐ CONSERVATORSHIP OF (NAME): DANIEL FRANK LEE [X] Minor ☐ Conservatee	CASE NUMBER: 123

PETITION FOR APPOINTMENT OF TEMPORARY GUARDIAN OR CONSERVATOR — Page 2

4. The temporary [X] guardianship ☐ conservatorship is required
   - [X] pending the hearing on the petition for appointment of a general [X] guardian ☐ conservator.
   - ☐ pending an appeal pursuant to section 2750 of the Probate Code.
   - ☐ during the suspension of powers of the ☐ guardian ☐ conservator.

5. Character and estimated value of the property of the estate
   - Personal property: $_____
   - Annual gross income from
     - ☐ real property: $_____
     - ☐ personal property: $_____
     - Total: $_____
   - Real property: $_____

6. ☐ CHANGE OF RESIDENCE OF PROPOSED CONSERVATEE
   - a. ☐ Petitioner requests that the residence of the proposed conservatee be changed to (address):

     The proposed conservatee will suffer irreparable harm if his or her residence is not changed as requested and no means less restrictive of the proposed conservatee's liberty will suffice to prevent the harm because *(precise reasons are* ☐ *stated below* ☐ *stated in attachment 6a)*:

   - b. ☐ The proposed conservatee must be removed from the State of California to permit the performance of the following nonpsychiatric medical treatment essential to the proposed conservatee's physical survival. The proposed conservatee consents to this medical treatment. *(Facts and place of treatment are* ☐ *specified below* ☐ *specified in attachment 6b.)*

   - c. *(change of residence only)* The proposed conservatee
     - ☐ will attend the hearing.
     - ☐ is able but unwilling to attend the hearing, does not wish to contest the establishment of a conservatorship, does not object to the proposed conservator, and does not prefer that another person act as conservator.
     - ☐ is unable to attend the hearing because of medical inability. An affidavit or certificate of a licensed medical practitioner or an accredited religious practitioner is affixed as attachment 6c.
     - ☐ is not the petitioner, is out of state, and will not attend the hearing.

   - d. ☐ *(change of residence only)* Filed with this petition is a proposed Order Appointing Court Investigator *(see Judicial Council form GC-330).*

7. Petitioner believes the proposed [X] ward ☐ conservatee ☐ will [X] will not attend the hearing.
   Petition submitted ex parte.
8. [X] Number of pages attached: None

Dated: 4/10/92

Patricia Ann Lee
(Signature of petitioner)

I declare under penalty of perjury under the laws of the State of California that the foregoing is true and correct and that this declaration is executed on (date): 4/10/92 at (place): Santa Ana, CA

PATRICIA ANN LEE
(Type or print name)

Patricia Ann Lee
(Signature of petitioner)

Item 3: This item is the most important part of the Petition for Appointment of Temporary Guardian. Check the boxes before the words "ward" and "guardian." Then check the box before the words "provide for temporary care, maintenance and support." Leave the box blank next to the words "protect property from loss or injury." This applies only to guardianships of a minor's estate, which is beyond the scope of this book.

Finally, unless you need more room than the blank space provided, check the box before the words "specified below." If you need more room, check the box before the words "specified in attachment 3," and add an additional page following the instructions in Chapter 3, Section D3. In the blank space or on Attachment 3, explain why a temporary guardianship is necessary now, and why you cannot wait until the hearing date several weeks away. Be as detailed and specific as possible, and list dates, times and places where appropriate. State facts, rather than mere conclusions. Here are a few examples:

Example 1: "I am the sister of the minor's mother. I am taking care of Jacques, who has been living with me in Stockton, California for the past three months. Jacques' natural father is deceased, and his mother resides out of state in Harrisburg, Pennsylvania. I have discussed both the guardianship and the temporary guardianship with Jacques' mother over the phone, and she approves of both. Jacques has severe food allergies (to wheat, eggs, dairy products and sugar), and has just begun undergoing treatments. His doctor is unwilling to continue the treatments without the approval of a legal guardian. I need a temporary guardianship to authorize those medical treatments."

Example 2: "I am Jill's father's brother, and have taken care of and lived with Jill for the past two months. Jill's parents are both on a one-year sabbatical in New Zealand. I live in a school district different from that in which Jill's parents reside, and wish to enroll her for school here. Classes in Morescience High School in our district resume on September 10th, only two weeks away. I have just been informed that to enroll Jill there, I must be her legal guardian. There is insufficient time to have the Petition for Appointment of Guardian of Minor heard within that period. I have spoken to Jill, who is 16 years old, and she wants me to obtain a temporary guardianship as soon as possible. In addition, her parents will be signing and returning a Nomination of Guardian and Waiver of Notice and Consent of the legal guardianship within the next two weeks."

> **CAPTION:** PAGE TWO OF THE PETITION FOR APPOINTMENT OF TEMPORARY GUARDIAN
>
> Check the box next to the word "GUARDIANSHIP," and in capital letters fill in the minor's full first, middle and last names. Check the box next to the word "Minor."
>
> Leave the case number blank, unless a case number has been assigned because you already filed regular guardianship documents with the court.

Item 4: You'll check three boxes in this item. On the first line, check the box before the word "guardianship." On the next line, check the box before the words "pending the hearing on the petition..." and in that same line check the box before the word "guardian." These indicate you are seeking a temporary guardianship only while you're waiting for your hearing date for the regular guardianship.

Item 5: Leave this item blank. It applies only to temporary guardianships of a minor's estate, which is beyond the scope of this book.

Item 6: Leave all parts of this item (6a-d) blank. The item applies to conservatorship proceedings only.

Item 7: In Section C of this chapter, you called the court clerk to find out whether temporary guardianships are heard ex parte, meaning a hearing is not required. If you have not obtained this information already, call the court clerk and find it out before you complete this item.

If a hearing is not required, check the box before the word "ward," and before the words "will not attend the hearing." Below that, fill in the words "Petition submitted ex parte." Obviously, in this situation, the minor does not need to go to court for a hearing—and neither do you.

If a hearing is required, check the box next to the word "ward." Then check the box next to the word "will," to indicate the minor will attend the hearing. The minor's attendance at the temporary guardianship hearing is required in many counties, and is always advisable when a temporary guardianship petition is heard unless it's handled ex parte.

Item 8: Check the box. If you are not attaching any additional pages, fill in the word "None." Otherwise, count up and enter the number of total pages to be attached.

Finally, put today's date in the two places indicated near the lines for each of the two signatures at the bottom of the page. Just above the space for the second signature, fill in the name of the city (or county if it is an unincorporated area) in which you happen to be when you sign the form. To the left of the space for the second signature, type or clearly print your name. Finally, sign your name in both places.

2. (Proposed) Order Appointing Temporary Guardian

You will also have to prepare a proposed order for the judge to sign, appointing you as the minor's temporary guardian pending the hearing.

CAPTION: ORDER APPOINTING TEMPORARY GUARDIAN

Fill in the caption following the general instructions in Chapter 3, Section D1.

Where you seek guardianship of more than one minor, use one form for each child, listing the name of each minor on a separate form.

Check the box entitled "GUARDIANSHIP," then check the box next to the word "person" to indicate you are seeking temporary guardianship of the minor's person, fill in the minor's name and check the box before the word "Minor."

Check the box entitled "GUARDIAN."

Leave the case number blank, unless a case number has been assigned because you already filed regular guardianship documents with the court.

Item 1: Regardless of whether you attend a hearing for the temporary guardianship, always check the box before the word "guardian" on the first line.

Item 1a: If you are submitting your temporary guardianship papers to a judge without a required hearing, fill in the words "Submitted ex parte" in Item 1a after the space for the judge's name, and skip to Item 2.

If a hearing is required, or you have been appointed temporary guardian following a court hearing for a regular guardianship, fill in the judge's name.

Item 1b: Fill in the date, time and location of the temporary guardianship hearing.

Item 1c: Check the first box and fill in your full first, middle and last names. Check the second box, then after the words "Attorney for petitioner (name)," fill in your full first, middle and last names, followed by the words "appearing In Pro Per."

Item 1d: Check the first box and in the blank provided, fill in the minor's full first, middle and last names.

Ordinarily the second box in this item is left blank, except for the rare situation where the minor for whom you are seeking the guardianship has his own attorney. If he does, fill in the attorney's name. (If the minor is being represented separately by an attorney, there's a good likelihood that the guardianship will be contested and you'll need the help of a lawyer. See Chapter 13.)

Item 2a: In this item, indicate whether anyone will be, or should be, served with notice of the temporary guardianship hearing. As discussed in Section C, each court has its own policies for service and for whether an appearance is required at the hearing.

Check the first box only if you skipped Items 1e *and* 1f of the Petition for Appointment of Temporary Guardian, meaning that you plan to serve the minor's parents and the minor if he is 12 or over.

Check the second box next to the words "Notice of time and place of hearing" and also next to the words "should be dispensed with" if you completed Item 1e or 1f of the Petition for Appointment of Temporary Guardian. This indicates that there is no requirement for advance notice of any hearing. This is because either no separate hearing will be set for your temporary guardianship petition, or the parents can't be located within a few days or have signed a document agreeing to the temporary guardianship.

ATTORNEY OR PARTY WITHOUT ATTORNEY (Name and Address):	TELEPHONE NO.:	FOR COURT USE ONLY
PATRICIA ANN LEE 2 West Street Santa Ana, CA 92702	714/555-1212	
ATTORNEY FOR (Name): In Pro Per		

SUPERIOR COURT OF CALIFORNIA, COUNTY OF ORANGE
STREET ADDRESS: 700 Civic Center Drive West
MAILING ADDRESS: P.O. Box 838
CITY AND ZIP CODE: Santa Ana, CA 92702
BRANCH NAME:

TEMPORARY [X] GUARDIANSHIP [ ] CONSERVATORSHIP OF THE [X] PERSON [ ] ESTATE OF (NAME):
DANIEL FRANK LEE   [X] Minor [ ] Conservatee

ORDER APPOINTING TEMPORARY [X] GUARDIAN [ ] CONSERVATOR

CASE NUMBER: 123

---

1. The petition for appointment of temporary [X] guardian [ ] conservator came on for hearing as follows (*check boxes c and d to indicate personal presence*):
    a. Judge (name): Submitted ex parte

    b. Hearing date: Time: [ ] Dept.:   [ ] Div.:   [ ] Room:

    c. [ ] Petitioner (name):
       [ ] Attorney for petitioner (name):

    d. [ ] Minor [ ] Conservatee (name):
       [ ] Attorney for [ ] minor [ ] conservatee (name):

2. THE COURT FINDS
    a. [X] Notice of time and place of hearing has been given as directed by the court.
       [ ] Notice of time and place of hearing [ ] has been dispensed with [ ] should be dispensed with.

    b. [X] It is necessary that a temporary [X] guardian [ ] conservator be appointed to [X] provide for temporary care, maintenance, and support [ ] protect property from loss or injury
       [X] pending the hearing on the petition for appointment of a general [X] guardian [ ] conservator.
       [ ] pending an appeal pursuant to section 2750 of the Probate Code.
       [ ] during the suspension of powers of the [ ] guardian [ ] conservator.

    c. [ ] To prevent irreparable harm, the residence of the conservatee must be changed. No means less restrictive of the conservatee's liberty will prevent irreparable harm.

    d. [ ] The conservatee must be removed from the State of California to permit the performance of nonpsychiatric medical treatment essential to the conservatee's physical survival. The conservatee consents to this medical treatment.

    e. [ ] The conservatee need not attend the hearing on change of residence or removal from the State of California.

(Continued on reverse)

Form Approved by the
Judicial Council of California
Effective January 1, 1981
GC-140(81)

**ORDER APPOINTING
TEMPORARY GUARDIAN OR CONSERVATOR**

TEMPORARY [X] GUARDIANSHIP ☐ CONSERVATORSHIP (NAME): DANIEL FRANK LEE [X] Minor ☐ Conservatee	CASE NUMBER: 123

ORDER APPOINTING TEMPORARY GUARDIAN OR CONSERVATOR — Page 2

3. THE COURT ORDERS
   a. (name): PATRICIA ANN LEE

   (address): 2 West Street, Santa Ana, CA 92702   (telephone): 714/555-1212

   is appointed temporary [X] guardian ☐ conservator of the person

   of (name): DANIEL FRANK LEE   and Letters shall issue upon qualification.

   b. (name):

   (address):   (telephone):

   is appointed temporary ☐ guardian ☐ conservator of the estate

   of (name):   and Letters shall issue upon qualification.

   c. ☐ Notice of hearing is dispensed with.

   d. [X] Bond is not required.
      ☐ Bond is fixed at $_____ to be furnished by an authorized surety company or as otherwise provided by law.
      ☐ Deposits shall be made at (specify institution): _____ in the amount of $_____ and receipts filed.

   e. ☐ The conservator is authorized to change the residence of the conservatee to (address):

   f. ☐ The conservator is authorized to remove the conservatee from the State of California to the following address to permit the performance of nonpsychiatric medical treatment essential to the conservatee's physical survival (address):

   g. ☐ The conservatee need not attend the hearing on change of residence or removal from the State of California.

   h. ☐ In addition to the powers granted by law, the temporary conservator is granted other powers. These powers are ☐ specified below ☐ specified in attachment 3h.

   i. ☐ Other orders as specified in attachment 3i are granted.

   j. ☐ Unless modified by further order of the court, this order expires on (date):

4. Number of boxes checked in item 3: 2
5. [X] Number of pages attached: None

Dated: . . . .   _____
       Judge of the Superior Court
       ☐ Signature follows last attachment

Item 2b: Check five boxes in this item. Check the boxes before the words "It is necessary that a temporary," and before the word "guardian." Then check the box before the words "provide for temporary *[next line]* care, maintenance, and support." Don't check the box before the words "protect property from loss or injury," as it only applies to temporary guardianships of a minor's estate.

On the next line, check the boxes before the words "pending the hearing on the petition..." and "guardian." Leave the rest of the item blank. (The other two boxes apply only for temporary guardianships pending appeal or suspension of some other guardian's powers—situations in which an attorney should be consulted.)

Items 2c-e: Leave all parts of these items (2c-e) blank. They apply to conservatorship proceedings only.

> **CAPTION:** PAGE TWO OF THE ORDER APPOINTING TEMPORARY GUARDIAN
>
> Check the box next to the word "GUARDIANSHIP," and in capital letters fill in the minor's full first, middle and last names. Check the box next to the word "Minor."
>
> Leave the case number blank, unless a case number has been assigned because you already filed regular guardianship documents with the court.

Item 3a: Fill in your name, address and telephone number in the spaces provided. Then check the box before the word "guardian." After the words "of (name)" fill in the minor's full first, middle and last names.

Item 3b: Leave this item blank. It applies only to temporary guardianships of a minor's estate, which is beyond the scope of this book.

Item 3c: This item applies only if you checked the second box in Item 2a, indicating that service should not be required on the people entitled to service—generally the minor, if 12 or over, and her parents. If you checked the second box in Item 2a, also check this box to indicate that you will not need to have anyone served with notice of the hearing.

Item 3d: Check the first box only, before the words "Bond is not required."

Items 3e-h: Leave Items 3e-h blank. They apply to conservatorship proceedings only.

Item 3i: Normally this item is not checked. (See instructions for Item 1d of the Petition for Appointment of Temporary Guardian.)

Item 3j: Leave this item blank. This is the date the temporary guardianship should expire—up to 30 days from the date it was obtained. The judge will fill it in at the hearing. If all goes well, the temporary guardianship should be replaced by a regular guardianship.

Item 4: Count the number of boxes you checked in Item 3, and fill in that number.

Item 5: Check the box. If you are not attaching any additional pages, fill in the word "None." Otherwise, count up and enter the number of total pages to be attached.

The form is now complete. The date and signature will be filled in by the judge who signs the order.

3. (Proposed) Letters of Temporary Guardianship

The Letters of Temporary Guardianship is the document which says you have permission to serve as the minor's temporary guardian.

ATTORNEY OR PARTY WITHOUT ATTORNEY (NAME AND ADDRESS):	TELEPHONE NO.:	FOR COURT USE ONLY
PATRICIA ANN LEE 2 West Street Santa Ana, CA 92702	714/555-1212	

ATTORNEY FOR (NAME): In Pro Per

SUPERIOR COURT OF CALIFORNIA, COUNTY OF ORANGE
STREET ADDRESS: 700 Civic Center Drive West
MAILING ADDRESS: P.O. Box 838
CITY AND ZIP CODE: Santa Ana, CA 92702
BRANCH NAME:

TEMPORARY [X] GUARDIANSHIP [ ] CONSERVATORSHIP OF (NAME):
DANIEL FRANK LEE   [X] Minor [ ] Conservatee

LETTERS OF TEMPORARY [X] GUARDIANSHIP [ ] CONSERVATORSHIP
[X] Person [ ] Estate

CASE NUMBER: 123

STATE OF CALIFORNIA, COUNTY OF ORANGE

1. **(Name):** PATRICIA ANN LEE
   is appointed temporary [X] guardian
   [ ] conservator of the [X] person
   [ ] estate of (name): DANIEL FRANK LEE

2. [ ] Other powers have been granted or restrictions imposed on the temporary
   [ ] guardian [ ] conservator as
   [ ] specified below [ ] specified in attachment 2.

3. These Letters shall expire
   [ ] thirty days after the appointment of the
   temporary [ ] guardian [ ] conservator
   (specify expiration date):
   or upon earlier notice of appointment of a general guardian or conservator.
   [ ] other date *(specify):*

   Dated: . . . .
   Clerk, by _____, Deputy

   [ ] Number of pages attached:

   SEAL

4. **AFFIRMATION**

   I solemnly affirm that I will perform the duties of temporary [X] guardian [ ] conservator according to law.

   Executed on (date): 4/10/92
   at (place): Santa Ana, CA

   Patricia Ann Lee
   (Signature of appointee)

5. **CERTIFICATION**

   I certify that this document and any attachments is a correct copy of the original on file in my office, and that the Letters issued to the person appointed above have not been revoked, annulled, or set aside and are still in full force and effect.

   Dated: . . . .
   Clerk, by _____, Deputy

   SEAL

Form Approved by the
Judicial Council of California
Effective January 1, 1981
GC-150(81)

**LETTERS OF TEMPORARY
GUARDIANSHIP OR CONSERVATORSHIP**

CAPTION: LETTERS OF TEMPORARY GUARDIANSHIP

Fill in the caption following the general instructions in Chapter 3, Section D1.

Where you seek guardianship of more than one minor, use one form for each child, listing the name of each minor on a separate form.

Check the box next to the word "GUARDIANSHIP," and in capital letters fill in the minor's full first, middle and last names. Check the box next to the word "Minor."

Check the box entitled "GUARDIANSHIP," then check the box next to the word "person" to indicate you are seeking temporary guardianship of the minor's person.

Leave the case number blank, unless a case number has been assigned because you already filed regular guardianship documents with the court.

On the left side of the form, next to the words "STATE OF CALIFORNIA, COUNTY OF," fill in the county in which you are filing the guardianship action.

Item 1: In the blank after the word "(Name)," fill in your full first, middle and last names. Then check the box before the word "guardian." Check the box before the word "person." Finally, fill in the minor's full first, middle and last names following the words "estate of (name)," even though you do not check the "estate" box to the left of them—the blank for the minor's name applies to all types of guardianships.

Item 2: Leave this entire item blank. It applies only if you have been granted powers beyond those ordinarily granted for temporary guardianships (such as subjecting her to involuntary non-emergency medical treatment), for which you need an attorney's assistance.

Item 3: Leave this item blank. The judge will fill it in at the hearing.

Leave the rest of the left side of the form blank, including the date, and proceed to Item 4.

Item 4: Check the box before the word "guardian." Fill in the date and place you are completing the form. Then sign your name on the signature line. In this item, you promise to fulfill the duties of a temporary guardian.

Item 5: Leave this item blank. The clerk will fill out this item, which simply says that it is a certified copy of the original Letters of Temporary Guardianship in the court's file.

4. Notice of Hearing (If Service Is Required)

If you do not need to have the minor or her parents served, you may skip this section and go on to Section F. However, if they must be served, prepare a Notice of Hearing following the instructions in Chapter 5, Section C, with these exceptions:

Item 1: After the words "(representative capacity, if any)," enter the words "proposed temporary guardian of the person." Just below this, after the words "has filed (specify)," enter the words "Petition for Appointment of Temporary Guardian."

Item 3: Fill in the information in the box about the date, time and place of the hearing.

F. Filing Documents, Serving Papers, Obtaining Letters of Temporary Guardianship

IF THE MINOR'S PARENTS ARE AVAILABLE and agree with the temporary guardianship, prepare and have them sign an Attachment 1f to the Petition for Appointment of Temporary Guardian. Obtaining these signatures can be helpful in getting the temporary guardianship petition approved. You're now ready to file your papers with the court.

1. Filing Temporary Guardianship Papers with the Court

If you are filing your temporary guardianship documents at the same time as the regular guardianship petition, proceed to Chapter 6.

If you have already filed regular guardianship documents, make at least two or three copies of all documents (depending on whether the court requires an extra copy, and whether you are sending the documents to court by mail), plus one for the minor and her parents, if service is required on them.

Before you file your papers, make sure you know when and where to take the temporary guardianship documents, according to the information you gathered in Section C of this chapter.

If you are submitting your temporary guardianship documents ex parte, let the clerk know it's an urgent matter. Clerks can and do submit papers to judges more quickly if they feel the case needs immediate attention. Ask the clerk when you can expect the judge to sign the Order Appointing Temporary Guardian. Generally this takes one to five days, depending on the court's size and local procedures.

2. Serve Temporary Guardianship Papers and Complete Proofs of Service (If Required)

If your court requires service on anyone—generally the minor if 12 or over, and her parents—have them served with copies of the Notice of Hearing and Petition for Appointment of Temporary Guardian (including any attachments). Usually personal service will be required, but some courts may allow notification of the parents or other relatives by telephone. If you have documents served, also complete a proof of service for each person and immediately file it with the court. (Chapter 6 gives instructions on how to have documents served and how to complete proofs of service.)

3. Attend Hearing (If Required)

If a hearing is required, attend it along with the minor. At the hearing, the judge will decide whether to grant the temporary guardianship, and if so, will sign the Order Appointing Temporary Guardian. (General information about court hearings is contained in Chapter 9.)

If the judge asks how long you want the temporary guardianship to last, tell him you would like it to run until the date the regular guardianship is scheduled to be heard. If this is more than 30 days away, the judge should grant the temporary guardianship for 30 days, and you will need to have it extended before the regular guardianship is heard. (See Section G of this chapter.)

4. Obtain Issued Letters of Temporary Guardianship

If you attended a hearing, there the judge usually signs and gives you copies of the Order Appointing Temporary Guardian. In larger courts, the judge may sign the order after the hearing, so you may need to return to court to pick it up.

If the temporary guardianship papers were submitted ex parte, on the date the clerk told you the judge would sign the Order Appointing Temporary Guardian, call the clerk to find out if it's been signed. If the judge hasn't signed the order, ask politely if he knows why. It may just be a technical error. If not, and the judge refuses to sign it, you may either have to wait until your scheduled hearing date to get a regular guardianship or get help from a lawyer.

Once your Order Appointing Temporary Guardian has been signed by a judge, you will still need to have the court clerk issue Letters of Temporary Guardianship. The letters will be your proof for any agencies, health care providers and others, that you can act as temporary guardian. You obtain Letters of Temporary Guardianship in the same way as regular Letters of Guardianship, by submitting the signed Order Appointing Temporary Guardian to the clerk. (See Chapter 9, Section E.)

G. How to Extend the Temporary Guardianship

A TEMPORARY GUARDIANSHIP LASTS up to 30 days (PC §2257). However, you may need the temporary guardianship to extend for a longer period of time, generally because the hearing on the regular guardianship is set for more than 30 days away. If so, you can submit an ex parte request for an order extending the temporary guardianship.

Call the court and find out how to submit an ex parte motion for an order extending a temporary guardianship pending the regular guardianship hearing. The procedure may be similar to the procedure for obtaining a temporary guardianship. Usually you submit your documents to the judge or her clerk, and either wait for the signature or return in a day or two to pick up the signed order. The court may require that the minor's parents and others be notified about the motion, possibly by telephone. If advance notice is necessary, find out the method of notice required, and how far in advance of the hearing it must be done.

1. Ex Parte Motion, Declaration and Order Extending Temporary Guardianship

In this document you state why an extension of the temporary guardianship is needed, and leave room for the judge to sign an order extending the guardianship. Use the accompanying sample as a guide.

2. Filing Documents, Serving Papers, Obtaining Order and Letters

Following the guidelines in Chapter 3, Section E, make copies of the Ex Parte Motion, Declaration and Order Extending Temporary Guardianship, and file it with the court at least 5 days before the Letters of Temporary Guardianship expire. If your court requires notification or service, follow those requirements. (How to serve documents and prepare proofs of services is covered in Chapter 6.)

To obtain new Letters of Temporary Guardianship, follow the instructions in Section F4, by submitting the signed order to the clerk. If you need to have the Letters of Temporary Guardianship extended again, follow the instructions in this section again.

PARTY WITHOUT AN ATTORNEY *(Name and Address)*: RUTH MARCI NORTON 100 Any Street Nevada City, CA 95959 In Pro Per	TELEPHONE NO: 916/555-1212	FOR COURT USE ONLY
NAME OF COURT: NEVADA SUPERIOR COURT STREET ADDRESS: Courthouse MAILING ADDRESS: 201 Church Street CITY AND ZIP CODE: Nevada City, CA 95959 BRANCH NAME:		
GUARDIANSHIP OF THE PERSON OF (NAME): JANICE LYNN NORTON MINOR		
EX PARTE MOTION, DECLARATION AND ORDER EXTENDING TEMPORARY GUARDIANSHIP	CASE NUMBER 1000	

MOTION

Petitioner moves the court for an order extending the duration of the temporary guardianship of the person of __JANICE LYNN NORTON__

This motion is made on the grounds that the temporary guardianship is due to expire before a regular guardian is appointed, and it would be in the best interests of the minor for the temporary guardianship to be extended for reasons set out in the declaration of the temporary guardian.

DECLARATION OF TEMPORARY GUARDIAN

1. Petitioner (name): __RUTH MARCI NORTON__ is the duly appointed, qualified, and acting temporary guardian of the person of __JANICE LYNN NORTON__.
2. Petitioner has been acting as temporary guardian since __February 19__, 19 __92__.
3. The temporary guardianship is due to expire on __March 21__, 19 __92__.
4. The hearing on the regular guardianship is set for __April 1__, 19 __92__.
5. The best interests of the ward require the extension of the temporary guardianship until __April 1__, 19 __92__, or for thirty days, whichever is sooner because:

As temporary guardian, I am responsible for making decisions about Janice's educational and personal needs. There is no one else to make these decisions for her. Janice is 12 years old and needs an adult to care for her. I have been nominated guardian by Janice's mother. Extending the temporary guardianship will allow the smooth supervision of Janice's needs until a regular guardianship is established.

I declare under penalty of perjury under the laws of the State of California that the foregoing is true and correct. Executed this __15th__ day of __March__, 19 __92__ at __Nevada City__, California.

....RUTH MARCI NORTON.................... *Ruth Marci Norton*
(TYPE OR PRINT NAME)   (SIGNATURE OF DECLARANT)

ORDER

The court having considered the motion and good cause appearing, IT IS ORDERED that the temporary guardianship of the person of _____ is extended until _____, 19_____, or for thirty days, whichever is sooner.

Dated:... _____
                                                          (JUDGE OF THE SUPERIOR COURT)

EX PARTE MOTION, DECLARATION AND ORDER EXTENDING TEMPORARY GUARDIANSHIP

NP

CHAPTER 8

THE GUARDIANSHIP INVESTIGATION

A.	Each Court Has Its Own Policies for Investigations	8/1
B.	Investigation Procedure	8/2
C.	Tips on Dealing with the Investigator	8/3
D.	The Investigator's Report	8/3
E.	Fees for the Investigation	8/4
F.	If the Investigator Recommends Against Granting Guardianship	8/4
G.	If the Investigator Recommends Granting Temporary Guardianship	8/4

AS DISCUSSED, A LEGAL GUARDIANSHIP is set up to take care of the best interests of a minor. You may recall that county agencies are always required to do a routine check of proposed guardians of minors' persons. The county agency checks for prior reports of suspected or actual neglect or abuse of minors (PC §1516), and advises the court if there is any such record.[1] By law, each county sets guidelines on whether a more extensive investigation is conducted to obtain information about the proposed guardian and her relationship with the minor. Some courts don't bother with investigations at all, others waive investigations if the proposed guardian is related to the minor or seeking guardianship of the minor's estate, and still others conduct full investigations of all proposed guardians of the minor's person.

The word "investigation" might sound scary, but the process really isn't. Usually, somebody from either the court or a county agency contacts the proposed guardian and arranges a convenient time to come to the house for an interview. At the arranged time, the investigator talks to the guardian and to the minor—unless the minor is too young to talk. For guardianship of a minor's person, whoever conducts the investigation would want to see where the minor would be living, and to know whether the proposed guardian is in a position to adequately care for the minor. Some investigators meet with the proposed guardian and minor more than once. Often investigators speak with the minor's natural parents as well. After the interviews, the investigator provides a written report to the court about her findings, and recommends whether she thinks the guardianship should be granted.

A. Each Court Has Its Own Policies for Investigations

AS WE HAVE EMPHASIZED, EACH COURT SETS ITS OWN POLICIES for guardianship investigations. If you haven't done so already, check with your court to find out whether an investigation is required for your guardianship case. Call the court and say you are seeking a guardianship, and specify whether it is for the minor's person, estate, or both. Let the clerk know whether you are related to the minor (by blood), and ask whether an investigation is required. If so, find out what agency or court investigator will conduct the investigation. Make sure a copy of the guardianship papers are sent to that investigator, if they haven't been mailed already.[2]

---

[1] The county agency—usually the local social services agency—must be served with notice of the guardianship of a minor's person. This service requirement is covered in Chapter 6, Section E2.

[2] Some local courts require service on the investigating agency at least 30 days before the scheduled hearing date. If you haven't had the agency served by then, check your court's service requirements. (If you need to continue the case, see Chapter 6, Section B5.)

1. Guardianship of a Minor's Person

Screenings by the local social service agency for reports of abuse or neglect are always required for a proposed guardianship of a minor's person. Additionally, an investigation is often required when the proposed guardian is not a close relative of the minor. Many counties require investigations no matter how close the relationship between the proposed guardian and minor. Courts have different rules about who is considered a close relative. For example, one court might consider a stepparent a relative, while another might not. All courts will consider blood-related grandparents, aunts and uncles to be relatives, but courts will vary on how closely related a cousin must be (for example, first, second or third cousin).

Investigations are not meant to resolve custody disputes, so investigators do not decide who will be the best guardian in a contested situation. When guardianships are contested, the matter should be referred to the court's family services division for resolution.

2. Guardianship of a Minor's Estate

Most courts waive investigations for guardianship of a minor's estate. However, depending on the circumstances of the guardianship and the amount of assets involved, the court could require an investigation even if you are only seeking guardianship of a minor's estate. For example, an investigation might be required if the court has questions about your ability to handle the minor's assets, or if there is a dispute about the ownership of the minor's property.

B. Investigation Procedure

AS WE HAVE EMPHASIZED, INVESTIGATIONS VARY from one county to another, so we cannot tell you exactly what will happen in your county. This section provides an overview of how investigations generally are handled.

1. Who Conducts the Investigation?

If the proposed guardian is related to the minor (by blood), the investigation may be conducted by a special probate court investigator, a probation officer, or a domestic relations investigator (PC §1513). Proposed guardians who are not related to the minor are generally investigated by a local social services agency.

2. Investigator May Check Background Sources

The investigator may choose to look at the minor's school records, medical and psychological records and written summaries, probation records, and public and private social service records (PC §1513(e)).

Depending on local policies, the investigator may also check into your background. For example, the investigator may obtain information by:
- Discussing the guardianship with the minor's living parents, if they are available to be interviewed;
- Contacting relatives entitled to notice of the guardianship, and interviewing them about how they feel about you being appointed guardian;
- Talking with the minor's day care or school teachers and counselors to get information about the minor's academic performance and behavior;
- Talking with neighbors;
- Checking your background for instances of child abuse and neglect; and
- Requiring that you be fingerprinted, and checking into your record for prior offenses.

3. Some Courts Use Questionnaires

To help assess whether to grant a guardianship, some courts require prospective guardians to fill out extensive questionnaires. These typically ask for personal information about your education, employment, marital history, health, criminal record, housing and who lives with you. Generally, you will need to answer questions about why you are seeking the guardianship, and how you plan to care for the minor. These questionnaires may seem long (four pages or so) and intimidating, but they really are not difficult to complete.

4. Home Interviews

Before the hearing date, the investigator may want to conduct at least one interview at your home. Some investigators will meet with you more than once, others just schedule one interview. The investigator will talk with you, probably your spouse (if you have one living with you), and the minor—unless he is too young to talk. The investigator may want to talk with you and the minor separately.

At the interview, you may be asked to provide some personal information about such things as your marital status, your own children, employment, education, health, how you plan to take care of the minor or his assets and your means of financial support. The investigator may want to discuss why a guardianship is needed, and why you want to be the guardian. You may be asked how long you've known the minor, and how long the minor has been living with you, if the minor is presently living with you. In addition, the investigator may want the names of several references.

If you are seeking guardianship of a minor's person, the investigator may want to see where the minor will be living, whether you have adequate space and a comfortable place for the minor to live, and if the minor has enough clothing, toys and room to play. The investigator should discuss any special educational, emotional, psychological or physical needs the minor may have. Investigators often want to look at the minor's report cards and other school reports, so have these handy.

If you are seeking guardianship of a minor's estate, the investigator may want information about your experience with managing finances. The investigator may also want some information about your own financial situation.

C. Tips on Dealing with the Investigator

WHEN YOU MEET WITH THE INVESTIGATOR, bear in mind that she is not looking for ways to trick you. The best approach is to be honest, relaxed and to do your best to answer all questions. Remember, both you and the investigator want what's best for the minor.

If the minor is old enough to understand, let him know that someone will be talking to both of you about the guardianship. Explain that he hasn't done anything wrong, and that he'll be talking to someone who wants to make sure you'll be taking good care of him. Let him know the investigator wants to make sure you're the one he wants to take care of him, and it's okay to tell how he feels about it.

What if there is something in your background that you're not proud of? It's quite possible that an unfortunate event from your past may not even come up, especially if it happened a long time ago and no one is likely to contest the guardianship. But if the investigator asks about something that you're worried about, be honest in your answer. If the investigator later finds out you haven't been honest, she may not not trust other information you've given, and may not give a favorable recommendation to the court.

It's unlikely that an investigator will hold your past against you if your situation has changed, and past events don't have a bearing on your ability to care for the minor. For example, if you were convicted of shoplifting when you were a teenager, and haven't been arrested or convicted since then, it's unlikely that an investigator would hold the shoplifting conviction against you. But if you're still having frequent run-ins with the law, an investigator may be hesitant to recommend you as guardian.

D. The Investigator's Report

AFTER THE INVESTIGATION IS COMPLETED, and before the hearing date, the investigator writes a report to the court recommending whether the guardianship should be granted. The report briefly discusses the circumstances that made the guardianship necessary, and your relationship with the minor. If the minor has any special emotional, psychological, educational and developmental needs, the investigator will assess whether you can meet them.

The investigator's report will discuss the type of relationship you and the minor have. For example, the report would include the length of time you and the minor have known one another, or have been close. If the minor is living with you, the investigator would discuss what led to that arrangement, and how it seems to be working out.

Generally, the report includes a summary of your attitudes about the guardianship, and how you plan to care for the minor or his estate. For guardianships of a minor's person, the report might discuss whether you can support the minor, or if you've made other arrangements. The report also should include the minor's natural parents' future plans. Finally, the investigator makes a recommendation to the court about whether the guardianship should be granted. Judges almost always follow the investigator's recommendation.

Depending on local policies, the report may be sent to the court in advance of the hearing date, or it may not be filed until that very day. Some investigators also send copies of the report to the proposed guardian. If you haven't received a copy several days before the hearing date, call the court and find out if it is in the file, and how you can get a copy. If it's not available in the court file until the day of the hearing, make sure you arrive a little early so you can look at the report before the hearing begins.

Note: The investigator's report is confidential, meaning that not everyone can get a copy of it. However, it may be read by anyone who has been served with notice of the guardianship proceeding (PC §1513(d)).

E. Fees for the Investigation

INVESTIGATION COSTS VARY FROM COUNTY TO COUNTY, and typically are in the $150 range. Costs of the investigation may be charged to:
- Either or both of the minor's parents;
- Whoever has physical custody and care of the minor;
- The proposed guardian or court-appointed guardian;
- The minor's estate (if you're seeking guardianship of the minor's estate or person and estate); or
- Some other person, depending on the financial situation (PC §1513.1).

If you are the only one caring for the minor, and he does not have an estate, it's likely that you will be required to pay the investigator's fees. However, any or all of the investigation fees may be waived on the basis of hardship. For example, if you applied for and were granted a waiver of court fees and costs, this would cover the costs of an investigation. (See Chapter 3, Section F.)

Important: In cases where an investigation is conducted, you generally cannot obtain Letters of Guardianship until the investigation has been paid for. The clerk may require a copy of the paid receipt for the investigation before issuing Letters of Guardianship.

F. If the Investigator Recommends Against Granting Guardianship

IN ALL PROBABILITY, the investigator will recommend that you be appointed guardian. But in the rare instance when she recommends against it, but you believe you are qualified anyhow, you will need assistance from a lawyer. (See Chapter 13.)

G. If the Investigator Recommends Granting Temporary Guardianship

OCCASIONALLY, INVESTIGATORS ARE HESITANT to recommend a permanent guardianship because they feel the situation may not be best for the minor unless it changes somewhat. For example, the minor may have special educational needs that aren't being met, and a change in school programs is recommended. Or the minor may need to see a therapist or social worker to help with psychological problems. Perhaps a proposed guardian may be required to see a counselor to deal with an alcohol problem.

In such instances, investigators may recommend a temporary guardianship, and a review of both the guardian and minor—often in about six months—to see if the conditions have been met. (Information on temporary guardianships is given in Chapter 7.)

CHAPTER 9

THE HEARING: PREPARING, ATTENDING AND WHAT TO DO AFTERWARDS

A.	Getting Ready for the Hearing	9/1
B.	Make Sure Your Hearing is on the Court Calendar	9/3
C.	The Day of the Hearing	9/3
D.	Attend the Hearing	9/4
E.	Getting the Letters of Guardianship Issued by the Clerk	9/7

THIS CHAPTER DISCUSSES THE COURT HEARING, at which a judge decides whether to appoint you as the minor's guardian. Going to a hearing in a courtroom may sound scary to you. But it can be quite easy, as long as you and the minor are prepared.

A. Getting Ready for the Hearing

IT'S A GOOD IDEA for you to read or reread this chapter at least two weeks before the hearing date. That way, you won't be scrambling around just before the hearing, trying to figure out forms and procedures. If you follow the chapter's guidelines and instructions, you shouldn't have problems handling the hearing yourself.[1] Here are instructions about how to prepare for the court hearing.

1. Prepare Yourself

Several days before the hearing, review all the documents you've filed with the court—especially the Petition for Appointment of Guardian of Minor. You may want to make a few notes about the specific information you've filled out in the petition, and to be familiar with any facts on which you based your statements. For example, if the minor is on probation in a juvenile court case, know the facts and status of the case and have copies of any documents that have been filed in court.

If an investigation was conducted and you haven't received a copy of any report by the investigator, you may want to go to the courthouse and ask to see it, which you have a right to do. (More information on the investigation is contained in Chapter 8.)

Be ready to answer the judge's questions about why the guardianship is necessary, as well as your relationship with the minor, your ability to care for the minor or his assets, and how the minor's parents and other relatives feel about you being guardian. You may want to make notes about what you plan to say on the stand, since it's not advisable to read from this book when you're in front of the judge. (See Section D, which tells more about what to say in front of the judge.)

2. Gather Documents

You'll need copies of all of the papers you've sent to the court, as well as any supporting documents and any notes you've prepared. You might not be asked to show the judge any of these papers. However, if you don't have them with you, it easily could mean a delay of the guardianship. You may want to put these documents into labeled file folders or an accordion file.

---

[1] Remember that you should see a lawyer well before the hearing date if you have any reason to believe the guardianship will be contested. Chapter 13 discusses how to find a lawyer.

Organize the documents so that you can quickly find any one of them. The documents you'll need are listed below.

WHAT TO BRING TO THE HEARING

- ☐ Any notes you've made to prepare for the guardianship proceeding;
- ☐ Copies of all guardianship papers you filed with the court;
- ☐ Birth certificate of the minor;
- ☐ Death certificates of the minor's parents or other relatives entitled to notice of the guardianship proceeding;
- ☐ Copies of any court documents affecting the minor, such as adoption, juvenile court, divorce, or other custody orders;
- ☐ Copies of all proofs of service (Chapter 6);
- ☐ Extra copy of the unsigned Letters of Guardianship (Chapter 5, Section F); and
- ☐ Extra copy of the proposed Order Appointing Guardian of Minor (Chapter 5, Section E), if the minor is age 12 or over.

3. Double-Check What You've Done

Before you go in for the guardianship hearing, make sure you have:

- Completed all documents in Chapters 4, 5 and 6 and filed them with the court.
- Filled in and submitted a proposed Order Appointing Guardian form to the court clerk following the instructions in Chapter 6, so that it will already be in the file for the judge to sign.[2]
- Served everyone entitled to notice as instructed in Chapter 6.
- Completed and filed proofs of service with the court as discussed in Chapter 6.[3]
- Made arrangements to bring the minor to the guardianship hearing.
- Filled in a Proof of Service by Mail of Order Appointing Guardian—if the minor is at least 12 years old—if necessary, after following the instructions in Section E5 of this chapter.

4. Prepare the Minor

It's important that you take time to talk to the minor about what's going to happen in court. Tell her that you will be going to court to get legal documents saying that you're responsible for taking care of her. Reassure her that although you and she are going to court, you're not having a trial, and that your court appearance probably will last only a few minutes in front of a judge. Let her know that she hasn't done anything wrong, and that you're glad to be taking care of her.

If she has questions or fears, let her know that she won't be asked hard questions by an attorney like she may have seen in TV shows or movies. Most likely, the judge will be kind, talk to her gently, and ask her a few questions like: "Do you understand that Ms. Guardian here is asking me to allow her to take care of you just like a mother?" or something similar. Let her know she should tell the truth to the judge.

Note: It's likely that the judge will almost automatically approve the guardianship, assuming it is an uncontested proceeding where the minor's parents agree to the guardianship or can't reasonably be located, and that none of the minor's other relatives object. If you anticipate someone will contest the guardianship, consult an attorney well before the hearing date. (See Chapter 13.)

---

[2] Many courts require that you submit a proposed Order Appointing Guardian to the court when you file your petition, or several days before the hearing date. Some courts will refuse to hear your case if they don't have a proposed Order Appointing Guardian in the file several days before the hearing date. So if you haven't already sent the proposed order to the court, call the clerk and find out if you can bring it to the hearing with you. (If you must continue the case, see Chapter 6, Section B5, which tells you how.)

[3] If for some reason you have not filed the proofs of service with the court in advance of the hearing date, you may be able to bring the originals—along with copies for your files—to the hearing. Call the court clerk and find out.

A. Make a Trip to the Courthouse (Optional)

If you have time, an extra trip to the courthouse can make the hearing go much more easily. Several days before the hearing, we suggest you and the minor go to the very courtroom where the hearing will be held. If the minor is frightened about appearing before a judge, showing him the courtroom and letting him know what will happen there can make the whole experience less intimidating.

You might find it helpful to go to the court a week or so before your case will be heard, at a time when the courtroom is empty, or when other guardianship cases are scheduled. Call the probate court to find out when guardianships are normally heard. Explain that you are seeking a guardianship, and you want to go to court beforehand to hear how other cases are done. Then find out what dates and in what department the cases will be heard. In larger counties, the courtroom may be in a different building from the place you filed your documents.

B. Make Sure Your Hearing is on the Court Calendar

IN CHAPTER 6, SECTION B3, we discuss how to request and obtain a hearing date from the court clerk. This date is listed on the Notice of Hearing, and served along with other necessary papers on the minor's relatives and agencies entitled to notice of the guardianship.

Call the court clerk a few days before the hearing and ask her to confirm that the case is still "on calendar," meaning it is scheduled to take place as planned. If you don't know in which courtroom the judge would hear the case, ask the clerk for this information. Make sure you know exactly where and when you should arrive for the hearing. Find out as much information as possible over the phone, so you won't be hurried on the day of the hearing.

If the clerk says your case isn't on calendar, give the case number and name of the case, and ask him to locate the file. If the Petition for Appointment of Guardian of Minor, Notice of Hearing, filled-out proof of services and other necessary papers all are in the file, the case should be set for hearing. If all your paperwork is in order, ask the clerk to add the matter to the court's list of cases to be heard. You may need to be persistent with the clerk, and ask to speak to his supervisor if he seems unreasonably uncooperative.

But if all your papers aren't in the file or aren't filled out correctly, find out what went wrong. It's possible that you made a mistake in completing or serving the papers. Or maybe you forgot to send in some required document. Make sure you understand exactly what you need to fix. If necessary, go to the clerk's office to look at the case file, and see what's missing or incorrect. In the rare situation where you took or sent documents to the court and they never made it to the file, you may be able to get your case put on calendar by going into the court and showing the court clerk your file-stamped copies of documents, or by providing duplicates.

Unless your guardianship case is on calendar, you can't go into court and have it heard by a judge. If for any reason your case is not scheduled to be heard when you thought it should have been, you must contact the court clerk about getting a new hearing date, following the instructions in Chapter 6, Section B5. Then you'll need to prepare a new Notice of Hearing, and have copies of it, the Petition for Appointment of Guardian of Minor and any other necessary documents served again on *everyone* entitled to notice of the guardianship. (Chapter 6 discusses how to have guardianship papers served.)

C. The Day of the Hearing

AT LAST YOU'RE READY to attend the hearing. Remember that going through a court hearing is easier than you might expect. Make sure you have followed the instructions for preparing yourself and the minor for the hearing.

1. Before You Leave Home

Appearances might count, so dress cleanly and neatly. If you own any, wear business-type clothing. Make sure the minor is dressed neatly and comfortably. Give yourself enough time to get to the courthouse well before your case is scheduled to be heard so you can find the right place. Arrive at least half an hour before the scheduled hearing time if you know where you're going, and give yourself even more time if you're not familiar with the building.

Before you leave home, double-check that you have ready everything listed in Section A above. Also remember to bring along a checkbook or cash to obtain certified Letters of Guardianship. The cost will be approximately $15 for five certified Letters of Guardianship—unless your court costs and fees were waived. (See Chapter 3, Section F and Chapter 6, Section B2a.)

Note: If you are seeking guardianship of a minor's estate, you cannot obtain Letters of Guardianship from the clerk until you've first obtained a bond in an amount the judge will order at the hearing, unless bond is waived. (See Chapter 10, Section C1.)

2. Find the Courtroom

Most counties have more than one Superior Court judge. Each judge has his own courtroom, called a "department," which is identified by a number or letter such as Department 1 or Department A. In some counties, you go straight to the assigned courtroom for your hearing. In some of the larger counties, you may need to go to a special department (often called a "master calendar department") to find out to which courtroom your case has been assigned.

Usually you'll find a list of cases to be heard that day posted outside the assigned courtroom. If you can't find one, go to the clerk's office and ask to see a copy of the calendar for any guardianship or probate cases scheduled to be heard in that department. Look at this listing to see when your case will be called.

3. Guardianship Investigation

In some courts, a formal investigation is not required, but an investigator comes to the courtroom and meets with the proposed guardian and minor before the hearing. If this happens, the investigator will talk to you briefly about the guardianship.

If a formal investigation was conducted and you were not sent a copy of the report, you may be able to see it before the hearing. Sometimes the investigator's report is not filed until the day of the hearing. Check with the clerk or bailiff before the hearing begins to see if a copy of the report is in the case file. (For a detailed discussion of guardianship investigations, see Chapter 8.)

4. Videotape of Guardian's Responsibilities

A few counties—for example, Alameda and San Francisco—require proposed guardians to watch a video that explains the guardian's duties. If required by the county where you're filing, you must attend.

D. Attend the Hearing

WHEN YOU GET TO THE PROPER COURTROOM for your hearing, tell the clerk or bailiff you are there. You may be required to sign in, or to fill out an additional form listing your name and the name of the guardianship case. If the minor cannot keep quiet while you're waiting for your turn, it's fine for you and the minor to wait outside the courtroom. In some courthouses, it's possible that there is a special room for children waiting, complete with toys and books. Check with the clerk or bailiff to find out if your courtroom has such a facility. If you will be outside the courtroom, tell the clerk or bailiff your situation and where you will be, and ask them to get you when your case is called.

1. Appearing Before the Judge

If you're waiting in the courtroom, you may get to watch others go before you. In some counties, other types of cases will be heard first, but you might have an opportunity to see a guardianship case take place before yours. Usually guardianship hearings last less than five minutes.

When your case is called, stand up and answer: "Ready, your Honor." You and the minor should go right on up to the table in front of the judge's bench. You may get sworn in by the bailiff, by declaring that you promise to tell the truth. You can take time to arrange yourself and your papers, so relax. Always call the judge "Your Honor."

First identify yourself by giving your name and saying that you are the petitioner and proposed guardian. Then identify the minor, and indicate that he is the one for whom you're seeking the guardianship.[4] Speak slowly and clearly, and loud enough for the courtroom reporter to hear—he will be typing in this information for the court records. You will probably need to spell out your name and the minor's.

Many judges will ask you questions to get the information they want, but some will just tell you to begin. If the judge simply wants you to start, explain why the guardianship is needed, how long you've known the minor, and how you plan to handle your duties as guardian. If you're seeking guardianship of a minor's estate, briefly summarize what assets she has, why it is necessary to manage them, and that you are able and willing to do so. The judge may have some questions about service of the guardianship papers, or want more information about why notice should be dispensed with if you claim that certain relatives can't be located.

When the judge asks questions, it is only to become better informed and satisfied that the best legal solution is reached. Try to stay relaxed—and just answer briefly and exactly what is asked. There's no need to volunteer information that is not asked for.

After you are finished, the judge may ask the minor a few simple questions like: "Do you understand that Ms. _____ here wants me to allow her to take care of you as if she were your mother? Is this okay with you?" The judge may ask the minor why her parents are unable to care for her and how she feels about it.

When you and the minor are finished talking, and the judge has no more questions, he will recite the orders being made in your case. He will probably complete and sign the original Order Appointing Guardian right there. If you submitted an Order Dispensing Notice, he should also sign that, unless he believes you didn't try hard enough to locate the minor's relatives. If that's the situation, the judge would probably continue the case. (See Section D2b.)

Note: It's possible that even if the judge approves the guardianship, she may not sign the Order Appointing Guardian right away. This is especially common in large counties. Also, it may take some time—a few minutes to a few hours—for the judge to give the court file back to the clerk. You may be able to get the Order Appointing Guardian signed by the judge, and get file-stamped copies from the clerk on the same day as your hearing. But if you're less lucky, you may have to come back to court a day or so later for that step.

If the judge signed any orders, the clerk should hand stamped copies to you. If the minor is at least 12 years old, she should also get a copy of the Order Appointing Guardian of Minor.

Before you leave the courtroom, make sure you take with you:

- Copy of signed Order Appointing Guardian;
- Copy of signed Order Dispensing Notice, if you want notice of the guardianship waived for any relatives who either signed a Waiver of Notice and Consent or could not be located; and
- Unissued Letters of Guardianship and copies.

You should have sent all of these documents to the court when you initially filed your papers with the court. If the judge signs the Order Appointing Guardian but neglects to give any of the listed documents back to you, check with the bailiff or clerk before you leave the courtroom. He should be able to locate them in your file.

2. Trouble-Shooting Guide

Usually you will not have trouble with the guardianship hearing. However, it will probably make you feel better if you have a little information about what to do if something does go wrong.

a. Before the Hearing Begins

People who work in the court sometimes forget that they are there to serve the public. It usually does no

---

[4] The minor may be referred to as the proposed "ward." This term refers to a minor who has a legal guardian.

good to remind them. Rather, if the clerk, bailiff, or even the judge is less than helpful or polite, just keep calm and quietly but firmly pursue your goal. You have a right to be there and a right to represent yourself.

If someone is making things difficult for you, there may be an underlying problem you can correct to make things go more smoothly. Ask what is the matter, and try to get a clear idea about the problem. If necessary, ask to speak to another clerk or to a supervisor. There's no reason to get upset—what is important is to correct the problem. Double-check everything with the help of this book.

b. After the Hearing Begins

This is a scary time for something to go wrong, but don't worry. You have an excellent escape hatch that you can use if all else fails. It is called the "continuance." A continuance simply postpones a hearing to a later date. When you want a hearing rescheduled, you "continue" it to a later date.

If the judge won't grant the guardianship yet, it may mean he thinks you have left out something essential. Politely ask the judge to explain, as it is likely that you can give additional testimony that will solve the problem. If things go very wrong and you can't figure out what your problem is, or if you get into any kind of situation you can't handle, you can still ask for a continuance. You can pause for a moment to collect your thoughts. Then politely tell the judge: "Your Honor, I request that this matter be continued two weeks *[or longer if you need additional time]*, so that I may have time to seek advice and further prepare this case for presentation." During the next recess (when the court is not in session), see if the clerk or bailiff can help you. If you are able to figure out what went wrong and how to correct it, you'll need to arrange to appear at another hearing to be held on a new "continued" date.

If the judge is very difficult, it's possible that he might not grant a continuance, which means that you'll have to start the process all over again.[5] If that happens, seek the help of a lawyer so you don't end up in the same situation again. (See Chapter 13.)

Note: If the judge continues the case, you will not have to serve new notices of hearing unless the problem is that not everyone was properly served. If everyone was properly served, they either will be there to hear the judge set the new court date, or by not appearing, will have given up the right to be told about it.

c. When There's a Dispute over Custody or Visitation Rights

In very rare circumstances, you may arrive at the hearing thinking everything will go smoothly, and find yourself face-to-face with a parent, relative, or other adult who either wants custody of the minor or wants visitation rights. If you're in this unfortunate situation, it's unlikely that the judge will hear the guardianship that day.[6] In larger counties, the case will probably be transferred to the family law department. It is suggested that you consult a lawyer to help work out a custody or visitation rights dispute. (See Chapter 13.)

d. If the Judge Won't Sign the Order Appointing Guardian

If the judge grants your petition, but refuses to sign the Order Appointing Guardian, this means the judge thinks there is something wrong with your proposed order. Listen carefully to what the judge says is wrong. At the recess, if you still don't understand, ask the clerk what is wrong (or look at the clerk's docket sheet, a public record). Occasionally, a judge will make an order that is different from the proposed order you prepared and submitted prior to the hearing. If so, you will have to prepare a new proposed order after the hearing and submit it to the court clerk for the judge to sign. Do it as soon as

---

[5] If there was a personal problem with your individual judge, there is a way to avoid a judge who doesn't seem to like you, or people who represent themselves in court. If you are really up against the wall, it is possible to file a document called a Peremptory Challenge (one time only), which forces the court to give you another judge (CCP §170.6). This should be regarded as an extreme emergency measure, not likely to create goodwill for you at the courthouse. Needless to say, this is beyond the scope of this book.

[6] If a parent or other relative wants an order granting visitation rights, this might easily be resolved with an order specifying such rights. However, this is beyond the scope of this book.

possible, and mail or bring it to the court for the judge's signature.

2. If the Judge Will Only Sign a Temporary Order

Occasionally, a judge will not sign an Order Appointing Guardian because he has questions or is hesitant about allowing the guardianship. This could be because the guardianship investigation raised some issues that he wants taken care of—such as counseling for the minor, or a change in living situation. It's possible, however, that the judge will sign an order appointing you temporary guardian, and set another hearing to decide on the permanent guardianship. If this happens, you will need to fill in documents for a temporary guardianship and submit them to the judge to sign. Instructions on how to file for a temporary guardianship are covered in Chapter 7.

E. Getting the Letters of Guardianship Issued by the Clerk

BEFORE YOU LEAVE THE COURTHOUSE, you may be able to obtain issued Letters of Guardianship—the court document that confirms your authority to act as guardian.[7] Until you obtain issued Letters of Guardianship, you are not considered the minor's guardian, even if the judge signed an order appointing you guardian.

1. Write in the Judge's Changes on Copies of Order Appointing Guardian

Before the clerk will issue Letters of Guardianship, there should be a signed Order Appointing Guardian from the judge in the file. If the judge made any changes to the proposed order, make sure these changes are made on all the copies. If they haven't been made, write in the same changes on the copies before you file them with the court clerk.

2. Take Letters of Guardianship to Clerk

To obtain issued Letters of Guardianship, take or send to the filing clerk:
- Unissued Letters of Guardianship and copies;
- Copy of signed Order Appointing Guardian of Minor;
- Original and copies of a completed and signed Proof of Service By Mail of Order Appointing Guardian of Minor and copies, if you completed this form after reading and following the instructions in Section E5 of this chapter;
- Copy of signed Order Dispensing Notice; and
- Check or cash to pay for issued Letters of Guardianship (the cost is approximately $3.00 per copy).

As indicated earlier, you should do this while you're at the court for the hearing if possible, instead of mailing the forms to the court, in case there is some problem with the papers. That will save you from having to make an extra trip to court.

The clerk will file any orders and Proof of Service, and return file-stamped copies to you. The clerk will then issue the original Letters of Guardianship. The clerk also will provide you with as many certified copies as you request, on payment of several dollars for each of them, unless your court costs and fees were waived by the court. (See Chapter 3, Section F and Chapter 6, Section B2a.)

3. Proof of Payment of Investigation May be Required

If an investigation was conducted, before the clerk will issue Letters of Guardianship, she may require proof that the costs of the investigation were paid in full. You may either need to show a receipt, or obtain Letters of Guardianship after the clerk has reviewed the file.

---

[7] If you need to send the Order Appointing Guardian to the court after the hearing to be signed and returned to you, follow these instructions after you receive the signed order. You can either obtain signed Letters of Guardianship by going to the clerk's office in person, or sending your request to the court following the instructions in Chapter 3, Section F.

4. Special Procedures for Guardianship of a Minor's Estate

Skip this section if you were only appointed guardian of a minor's person. If you were appointed guardian of a minor's estate or person and estate, read this section. Also read Chapter 10, Section C, which gives important information and forms you'll need to complete the process of becoming guardian and obtaining Letters of Guardianship.

a. You May Need to Obtain Bond or Establish Blocked Account

If you are required to obtain bond or set up a blocked account (see Item 3d in the Order Appointing Guardian of Minor), you will have to do so before you can obtain issued Letters of Guardianship from the clerk. (Instructions are contained in Chapter 10, Section C.)

b. You May Need to Sign Instructions about Managing the Estate

In some counties, before the court clerk will issue Letters of Guardianship, you may need to sign a document with general instructions from the court as to how you must manage the minor's estate. This is required in Alameda, Contra Costa, San Bernardino and Santa Clara counties. The instructions document should either have been given to you by the judge or clerk at the hearing, or should be available to you from the clerk. If the clerk doesn't ask for a signed copy of these instructions, you don't need one.

5. Special Procedure if the Minor Is 12 or Older

You may skip this section if the minor is under 12 years of age. However, if the minor is 12 years of age or older, you might need to prepare one new document, depending on whether or not you carefully followed instructions previously in the book.

The law requires that the minor be notified in writing before Letters of Guardianship are issued. Naturally, if the minor attended the guardianship hearing, it doesn't make sense for you to go home and have documents mailed to the minor, since the minor already knows about it, and should have been given a copy of the Order Appointing Guardian at the hearing.

Fortunately, you probably have already solved this problem, if you completed Item 3i in the Order Appointing Guardian of Minor. (See Chapter 5, Section E.) If the judge signed the Order Appointing Guardian—including Item 3i—you may skip the rest of this section.

If the minor is at least 12 years old and a judge does not grant Item 3i of the the Order Appointing Guardian of Minor, you cannot get Letters of Guardianship until you prepare a Proof of Service By Mail of Order Appointing Guardian of Minor, and have that order served on the minor.

First, have a friend or relative over the age of 18 mail a copy of the Order Appointing Guardian to the minor who is 12 years of age or older.[8] Instructions for having documents served are in Chapter 6. Then complete the Proof of Service By Mail of Order Appointing Guardian of Minor.

a. Proof of Service By Mail of Order Appointing Guardian of Minor

This document states that the Order Appointing Guardian was served on the minor.

---

[8] The Order Appointing Guardian of Minor may be served personally instead of mailed to the minor. If documents are served personally, instead complete a Proof of Service for Personal Service following the instructions in Chapter 6, Section F.

ATTORNEY OR PARTY WITHOUT ATTORNEY (NAME AND ADDRESS):	TELEPHONE NO.:	FOR COURT USE ONLY
JENNIFER BETH PADILLA 5000 Any Way Santa Cruz, CA 95060	408/555-1212	

ATTORNEY FOR (NAME): In Pro Per

SUPERIOR COURT OF CALIFORNIA, COUNTY OF SANTA CRUZ
STREET ADDRESS: 701 Ocean Street
MAILING ADDRESS: Courthouse, Room 110
CITY AND ZIP CODE: Santa Cruz, CA 95060
BRANCH NAME:

[X] GUARDIANSHIP [ ] CONSERVATORSHIP OF THE [X] PERSON [X] ESTATE
OF (NAME):
ELIZA VICTORIA WILSON [X] Minor [ ] Conservatee

PROOF OF SERVICE BY MAIL OF ORDER APPOINTING [X] GUARDIAN [ ] CONSERVATOR	CASE NUMBER: 200

PROOF OF SERVICE BY MAIL
(Personal delivery also permitted. Probate Code, § 1466)

I am over the age of 18 and not a party to this cause. I am a resident of or employed in the county where the mailing occurred. My residence or business address is:

25 Some Street, Santa Cruz, CA 95060

I served the Order Appointing [X] Guardian [ ] Conservator by enclosing a true copy in a sealed envelope addressed to each person whose name and address is given below and depositing the envelope in the United States mail with the postage fully prepaid.

(1) Date of deposit: 9/22/91   (2) Place of deposit (city and state): Santa Cruz, CA

I declare under penalty of perjury under the laws of the State of California that the foregoing is true and correct and that this declaration is executed on (date): 9/22/91 . . . . . at (place): Santa Cruz, CA . . . . .

EMMA FRAND
(Type or print name)   (Signature of declarant)

NAME AND ADDRESS OF EACH PERSON TO WHOM NOTICE WAS MAILED

a. [X] Ward 14 years of age or older: Eliza Victoria Wilson
5000 Any Way
Santa Cruz, CA 95060

b. [ ] Conservatee:

c.

[ ] List of names and addresses continued in attachment.

Do NOT use this form for personal delivery permitted in lieu of mailing by section 1466 of the Probate Code.

Form Approved by the
Judicial Council of California
Revised Effective January 1, 1981
GC-030(81)

**PROOF OF SERVICE BY MAIL
OF ORDER APPOINTING
GUARDIAN OR CONSERVATOR**

CAPTION: PROOF OF SERVICE BY MAIL OF ORDER APPOINTING GUARDIAN OF MINOR

Fill in the caption following the general instructions in Chapter 3, Section D1.

Check the box entitled "GUARDIANSHIP," as well as boxes next to the words "PERSON," "ESTATE," or both. Check the box next to the word "MINOR."

After the words "PROOF OF SERVICE BY MAIL OF ORDER APPOINTING," check the box before the word "GUARDIAN."

After the words "My residence or business address is," fill in the business or residence address of the person who served the Order Appointing Guardian of Minor.

Check the box between the words "I served the Order Appointing" and "Guardian."

Item 1: Fill in the date the Order Appointing Guardian of Minor was mailed to the minor.

Item 2: Fill in the city and state where the Order Appointing Guardian of Minor was mailed to the minor.

Fill in the date and place the document will be signed. In the spaces provided, fill in the name of the person who mailed the documents and have them sign.

Item a: Check this box, and fill in the name and address of each minor who is at least 12 years of age.

CHAPTER 10

GUARDIANSHIP OF A MINOR'S ESTATE

A.	How to Use This Chapter	10/1
B.	Completing Estate Items in the Petition for Appointment of Guardian of Minor Form	10/2
C.	After the Guardianship Hearing	10/5
D.	Consult Other Resources to Meet Court Reporting Requirements	10/6
E.	Using Funds from the Estate for Support of the Minor	10/9
F.	Ongoing Responsibilities for the Guardian of a Minor's Estate	10/10

AS YOU LEARNED IN CHAPTER 1, a guardian of a minor's estate handles assets and property belonging to the minor. A guardianship of the estate often is not needed if the minor only owns a small amount of money or assets (usually $5,000 or less). If you haven't already read Chapter 1, Sections D and E, please do so now, since that will help you determine what type of guardianship you need. This chapter only applies if you are seeking guardianship of a minor's estate or both person and estate. References to "estate" guardianships in this chapter include guardianships of the estate and person and estate.

This chapter shows you how to complete the forms necessary to obtain a guardianship of a minor's estate. To become guardian of a minor's estate, you follow almost the same procedures as for a guardianship of a minor's person. This is straightforward and you should have little difficulty doing it on your own. This chapter provides an overview of what's involved in guardianship of a minor's estate, but it doesn't explain how to do these procedures in detail. You will need to consult other resources or seek the help of a legal professional once you obtain the estate guardianship.[1] (See Chapter 13.)

A. How to Use This Chapter

HERE ARE SOME SUGGESTIONS about how to use this chapter. This advice applies whether or not you are seeking guardianship of both a minor's person and estate, or only guardianship of the minor's estate:

Step 1: Follow the instructions and complete the forms in Chapters 4 and 5. These are necessary to go to court to request a guardianship. You will be referred back to Section B of this chapter to complete specific items pertaining to the minor's estate in the Petition for Appointment of Guardian of Minor form.

Step 2: Follow the instructions in Chapter 6 for filing guardianship papers with the court and having relatives and agencies served.

Step 3: Follow the instructions in Chapter 9 for appearing in court and being appointed guardian. Chapter 9 also tells what to do after the hearing.

Step 4: After the hearing, also read Section C of this chapter. If you need to post bond, make deposits or set up blocked accounts before Letters of Guardianship will be issued, follow the instructions for doing so. Once you obtain Letters of Guardianship, read Section C5 and arrange for the transfer of assets, if applicable.

Step 5: Do your own legal research or arrange to hire a legal professional to help you handle the minor's estate and fulfill the legal reporting requirements. To help you understand and evaluate

---

[1] *The Conservatorship Book,* by Lisa Goldoftas and Carolyn Farren (Nolo Press) covers in detail financial accountings and some court appearances.

how a legal professional can help you, an overview of the court's requirements is set out in Section D.

Step 6: If you want to use funds from the minor's estate to support the minor, read Section E of this chapter.

Step 7: Carefully read Section F of this chapter. There you will find an overview of your duties as guardian of a minor's estate, and your ongoing reporting responsibilities to the court. You will also need to read Chapter 11, which gives you a general overview of a guardian's responsibilities.

B. Completing Estate Items in the Petition for Appointment of Guardian of Minor Form

MOST INSTRUCTIONS FOR THE PETITION for Appointment of Guardian of Minor are covered in Chapter 5, Section A. However, Items 1d, 1e, 11 and 13, which pertain only to the guardianship of a minor's estate, are covered in this section.

> **CAPTION:** PETITION FOR APPOINTMENT OF GUARDIAN OF MINOR
>
> Remember to check the boxes to indicate whether you are seeking guardianship of the estate or person and estate.

Item 1d: This item deals with the requirement that the guardian of a minor's estate post a "bond" (PC §2320). A bond is basically a financial guarantee that the estate will be reimbursed if the guardian takes improper actions, such as stealing or mishandling estate funds.

If you want to be appointed guardian of the minor's estate, you will not have to post a bond if:

- Both living parents nominate you as guardian and agree to waive bond and the court doesn't require otherwise (PC §§1500(a), 2324); or
- The estate consists of property given by another person (either while alive or through a will), and that person has requested waiver of the bond, either in a written nomination of guardian or in a will (PC §§1501, 2324).

If either of the above applies, check only 1d (1) "bond not be required for the reasons stated in Attachment 1d." Then prepare an "Attachment 1d" following the instructions in Chapter 3, Section D3, and label it "Attachment 1d to Petition for Appointment of Guardian of Minor: Information on Bond Requirements" at the top. On Attachment 1d, state in plain and concise language why you think bond is not required, and document your reasons. For example, if a donor of property nominates you and waives bond, you might type, "Dennis Manning left real estate to the minor in his will and requested that no bond be required. A copy of the will follows this attachment." Or if both parents have waived bond and nominated you as guardian, you might type, "Petitioner was nominated guardian by both parents, who requested that no bond be required. A copy of the nomination follows this attachment."[2]

If you don't qualify to have bond waived, your task becomes a little more complicated. Here's why. When attorneys handle guardianships, bond is usually acquired from surety companies—companies willing to guarantee the guardian's actions in exchange for the payment of an annual premium (usually ranging anywhere from fifty to several hundred dollars). If the minor and estate are damaged, sureties generally may be sued for reinforcement within four years after the guardian stops serving. It's likely the sureties would then sue the guardian for reimbursement.

Unfortunately, most surety companies will not bond guardians who represent themselves in court without an attorney. A guardian who needs bond and cannot obtain it from a surety company may:

- obtain bond from personal sureties—such as friends or relatives (the bond amount must be twice as much as the amount required were a surety company used); or

---

[2]If the parents nominated you by signing a Nomination of Guardian as set out in Chapter 4, Section E, you will also need a document stating that the parents waive bond. On a blank piece of typing paper, type in the words "I, [parent's name], am a parent of [minor's name], the subject of this guardianship. I nominate [your name] as guardian of the [estate or person and estate] of [minor's name], and request that no bond be required." Have the parents sign and date the document, and make it the next page of this attachment.

- deposit non-estate-money, certificates of deposit or certain bonds with the court clerk or assign an interest in financial accounts to the court clerk.
- place funds from the minor's estate in a "blocked account"—an account that requires written permission from the court before the guardian can withdraw funds or remove assets. The amount of bond required is reduced by the sum held in blocked accounts.

Check 1d (2) "$_____ bond be fixed" if you don't qualify to have bond waived. You will then have to calculate the amount of the bond needed:

- If a surety company is used or deposits made with the court clerk, the bond amount equals the estimated value of the minor's personal property, plus the estimated yearly gross income from real estate, personal property and public benefits.
- If the surety is a personal one—such as a friend or relative—the bond equals twice the amount required for a surety company (PC §2320).

To figure out the amount of bond, fill in the figures on the small worksheet that follows, using our instructions and checking the example provided. (You'll need these figures again in Item 11, so write them in on the worksheet, or on a separate piece of paper).

WORKSHEET FOR CALCULATING BOND

Personal property: $_____

Annual gross income from
Real property: $_____
Personal property: $_____

TOTAL:
(if using surety company or
making deposits with clerk)* $_____

*If personal sureties are used, this amount must be **doubled**.

Personal property: In this blank, list the total estimated value of the minor's assets other than real estate: all bank accounts, vehicles, stocks, jewelry, antiques and all other property. Do not have these assets appraised, because someone called a "probate referee" will be appointed by the court to appraise them (regardless of any appraisal you've had done already), so you will end up paying to have the property appraised twice.[3]

Important: If, aside from cash or money in bank or similar accounts, the minor does not own anything of value except to her—such as clothes and old toys—just list the total of cash and bank accounts owned in the space provided for the value of personal property. If you list a dollar amount for any personal property other than cash or money in bank accounts, that property will have to be appraised, and the estate must pay for the appraisal. Naturally this would be an unnecessary expense for old clothes and toys.

Annual gross income from real property: If the minor receives any income from real estate (for example, rent), list the amount of the annual gross income (total yearly amount received before taxes).

Annual gross income from personal property: If the minor receives any income from personal property (for example, interest on savings accounts), or public benefits, such as Social Security, indicate the amount of the annual gross income from that (total yearly amount received before taxes).

Total: Add the amounts of the personal property, the real property income, and the personal property income. Enter the total in the space provided.

Example: Mindy Minor has belongings worth approximately $11,000 (that do not bring in any income) a $10,000 bank account that pays 5% interest per year, and a house that rents out for $600 a month. The amount of bond, if issued by a surety company, is calculated as follows:

---

[3] With court permission, you can hire an independent appraiser, rather than a probate referee, to appraise a "unique, artistic, unusual, or special item of tangible personal property." (PC §8904(a)). The procedure for doing this is beyond the scope of this book.

Personal property:
  Personal possessions ($11,000) +
  Cash in bank account ($10,000) = $21,000

Annual gross income from rental
property ($600/month rental
income x 12 months) = $7,200

Annual income from bank account
(5% of $10,000) = $500
                                                 _____
TOTAL BOND REQUIRED = $28,700

Next, fill in the amount of bond needed. If you plan to deposit some funds or assets in blocked accounts, deduct that sum from the amount of bond required.

Example: Let's use the example of Mindy Minor mentioned above. Recall that $28,700 total bond is required. Mindy Minor has $10,000 cash in a bank account. If the $10,000 stays in a blocked account, the amount of bond would be reduced to $18,700 ($10,000 lower than the original $28,700).

If you're planning to use personal sureties, fill in double the amount required when a surety company is used and prepare an Attachment 1d following the instructions in Chapter 3, Section D3. In Attachment 1d, specify that "Bond will be furnished by personal sureties. As provided in Probate Code Section 2320(b), the amount of bond is for twice the amount required for a bond given by a surety company."

If you are petitioning for guardianship of the estate of more than one minor (they must be full- or half-brothers and sisters or you must petition for each separately), add the figures for each minor's property to get the total amount of the bond.

Item 1d (3) applies if the minor's estate includes money or assets that you plan to keep in blocked accounts during the guardianship. You can enter into a special agreement with a bank, trust company or other financial institution to "block" an account. Blocked accounts require written permission from the court before the guardian can withdraw funds or remove assets. Some guardians prefer to establish blocked accounts because the amount of bond required is reduced by the sum in the blocked account—and annual premiums the estate would have to pay a surety company also decrease.

Assets in a blocked account typically are money or securities, but they could also include personal property such as jewelry to be held in a bank's safety deposit box. If you want to set up a blocked account as an alternative to bond, you will need to specify the name and location of the financial institution in which you expect to have the blocked account. Generally this will be the place where the account or asset is located already—otherwise, you may not be able to transfer assets without court approval. Call the financial institution and explain that you are seeking guardianship of a minor's estate and want to set up a blocked account. Then find out the procedures and fees—if any—for doing this. (Instructions on how to set up a blocked account after the judge signs an order appointing you guardian are contained in Section C2 of this chapter.)

If any money will be deposited in a blocked account, check 1d (3) and fill in the amount in the space provided in the sentence "$_____ in deposits in a blocked account be allowed." In the blank that follows, fill in the name and address of the financial institution where the blocked account will be.

Item 1e: Do not check this box. This item is checked only when you wish the court to allow you to undertake certain unusual or speculative actions in handling the minor's estate. As a guardian of the minor's estate, you normally cannot legally enter into any but the simplest investments. For example, money usually must be invested in a savings account, and real estate must be rented out for reasonable market value. If, however, you wish to operate a farm, sell off and purchase other investment property, borrow money against the minor's property for investment, lend money, exercise stock options, or hire employees on the minor's behalf, you must first apply to the court for special authority to do so, and explain why it is necessary (PC §§2590, 2591). This authority is known as "independent powers." This book does not cover such situations. If you think that you, as guardian of the minor's estate, will require authority to do any sophisticated investing, consult an attorney. (See Chapter 13.)

Item 11: List the total estimated value of what the minor owns. The instructions given above for Item 1d show you how to calculate the amount of bond needed; you now can use that same information in this item. If you did not calculate bond in Item 1d, follow the instructions above for completing the Worksheet for Calculating Bond printed in this book.

Then simply copy the figures from that worksheet and check the appropriate boxes. If the minor owns real estate, also indicate the total estimated value of the minor's real estate in the last blank provided.

Item 13: Usually, this box is not checked. The instructions to Item 1e above discuss the need for court permission to undertake certain unusual or speculative investments when handling the minor's property. If you wish to seek this sort of permission, see a lawyer.

C. After the Guardianship Hearing

AT THE GUARDIANSHIP HEARING, the judge may name you as the minor's guardian, but require that you obtain bond or set up a blocked account before Letters of Guardianship will be issued. This section tells you how to go about fulfilling those requirements, and what to do once you've completed them.

1. Obtaining Bond

If you are required to post a bond, the amount of it will be reflected in the order the judge signed at the hearing.[4]

a. Surety Company

Remember that most surety companies will not bond guardians unless they are represented by an attorney. Surety companies are listed in the yellow pages under "Bond" or "Surety." If you successfully obtain bond through a surety company, get a completed Bond on Qualifying and Order document from the surety company. You may reimburse yourself from the estate for money you spend out of your own pocket for guardianship bond premiums. Keep copies of all receipts and documents pertaining to the bond. (Chapter 11, Section F2, gives information on reimbursement for such expenses.)

b. Personal Sureties

To use personal sureties, you must find a minimum of two friends, relatives or business associates willing to serve. You cannot be one of the sureties. Everyone willing to serve should understand that they may be held personally liable for any damages caused by your improper actions—regardless of whether your mistakes were intentional or accidental. Although sureties may later seek reimbursement from you, they stand to lose the full amount of bond if you mismanage the estate.

All those you select must meet these requirements (Code of Civil Procedure §995.510):

- They must be California residents who own their homes or other real estate in California.
- They cannot be lawyers or officers of a California court.
- For bonds of $10,000 or less, each personal surety's net worth must be at least the amount of required bond in personal property, real estate or both. Their net worth is calculated over and above all debts and liabilities and excludes property exempt from enforcement of a money judgment.[5]
- For bonds over $10,000, three or more personal sureties may be used. Each personal surety's net worth may be less than the amount of bond as long as the total worth of all sureties is twice the amount of bond. Again, net worth is calculated over and above all debts and liabilities and excludes property exempt from enforcement of a money judgment.

Many courts have these two local forms, which you must prepare, photocopy and file with the court:

---

[4]Don't obtain bond before the hearing, because the judge might raise or lower it from the amount you requested in the petition.

[5]If there is a money judgment against any of the proposed sureties, you'll need to research exemptions. See *Collect Your Court Judgment,* by Gini Scott, Stephen Elias and Lisa Goldoftas (Nolo Press).

- *Bond (Personal) on Qualifying and Order:* This sets out the surety's willingness to provide bond. It must be signed by a judge before being effective.
- *Declaration of Personal Surety:* A separate declaration must be prepared for each surety. The document gives information about the surety's assets and helps a judge decide if the surety is qualified.

If your court doesn't have these forms, see *The Conservatorship Book,* by Lisa Goldoftas and Carolyn Farren (Nolo Press).

2. Establishing Blocked Accounts

The judge may have reduced the amount of bond required by allowing some assets to be placed in blocked accounts with a financial institution. You must obtain written permission from the court before your can withdraw funds from these accounts.[6]

If you asked for a blocked account as an alternative to all or partial bond, the name and location of the financial institution in which you expect to have the blocked account should have been specified in Item 3d of the Order Appointing Guardian of Minor.

To establish the blocked account, take a copy of the order to the financial institution, which will need to complete some paperwork to designate the account as blocked. Ask for a signed receipt showing the balance in the account and indicating that it is a blocked account. You must provide this document to the court to prove that the account is blocked. Make several copies of the blocked account receipt before you file it with the court. You may take it to the court for filing at the same time you file any bond.

3. Making Deposits With the Court

If you plan to make deposits with the court, contact the court and find out its procedures. The court should have its own agreement form for authorizing deposits. (If you must provide the deposit agreement, see *The Conservatorship Book,* by Lisa Goldoftas and Carolyn Farren (Nolo Press).)

4. Obtain Issued Letters of Guardianship

Once you have obtained any bond or set up blocked accounts that were required, follow the instructions in Chapter 9, Section E, for obtaining issued Letters of Guardianship. Remember to also take or send to the court the original receipts showing you have obtained bond or set up blocked accounts. Make sure you keep copies of those receipts.

5. Arrange to Have Assets Transferred

If a guardianship of the estate was necessary so the minor could inherit or receive assets, they may be obtained once Letters of Guardianship are issued. The institution or agency holding the assets will require certified Letters of Guardianship. Contact them to find out their procedures.

Assets with title will need to be transferred either to your name, as guardian of the estate, or the minor's estate itself. Such assets include real estate, vehicles, stocks, bonds, securities, businesses, money market accounts, mutual funds. Contact the title company, business or financial institution that is holding the assets and arrange to have them transferred. If you need help having assets with title transferred, see a lawyer or do your own legal research. (See Chapter 13.)

D. Consult Other Resources to Meet Court Reporting Requirements

YOU WILL BE REQUIRED to file at least one document with the court within 90 days after the date Letters of Guardianship are issued. In this section we give you a brief overview of the court's reporting requirements. You can consult a resource that covers these requirements, such as *The Conservatorship Book,* by Lisa Goldoftas and Carolyn Farren (Nolo Press). Or

---

[6]The order can generally be submitted ex parte, and a hearing may not be required. For step-by-step instructions, see *The Conservatorship Book,* by Lisa Goldoftas and Carolyn Farren (Nolo Press) or seek an attorney's help to withdraw funds from a blocked account. (See Chapter 13.)

hire a legal professional. Paralegals specializing in the probate area may be your best bet, since they should be familiar with the court's special rules for financial reporting requirements. Or you can seek the help of a probate attorney.[7] (See Chapter 13 for information on legal professionals.)

Most courts have Probate Policy Manuals that govern that court's specific accounting requirements for guardianships. You will generally have to complete documents setting a hearing at which you must appear, unless the court grants otherwise. Following is an overview of the procedures.[8]

1. Probate Referee Appraises Non-Cash Property

If the minor owns any real estate or personal property other than cash or accounts in financial institutions, the court will require that such property be appraised. You must use an independent court-appointed appraiser, called a "probate referee" or an "inheritance tax referee" in some counties. The court must give specific approval for written appraisals from someone else before the appraisals will be accepted. Otherwise, the court-appointed probate referee must appraise the minor's non-cash property. For the appraisal, the minor's estate will be charged a fee of one-tenth of one percent of the total value of the assets appraised with a minimum of $75 and generally a maximum of $10,000 (PC §609). The referee may also receive his actual and necessary expenses, such as mileage for driving to inspect real estate.

TIMELINE OF REPORTING REQUIREMENTS FOR GUARDIANSHIP OF A MINOR'S ESTATE

- *Within 3 Weeks from Date Letters of Guardianship are Issued:* Suggested date for filing Application and Order Appointing Probate Referee form with the court, if required.

- *90 Days After Letters of Guardianship are Issued:* Inventory & Appraisement Due.

- *After 90 Days from Date Letters of Guardianship are Issued:* May petition court for compensation for yourself or to pay for the help of a lawyer; the court's local rules may require that you wait one year.

- *1 Year After Letters of Guardianship are Issued:* First Accounting due.

- *Anniversary Each 1-2 Years After Letters of Guardianship are Issued (or as Directed by the Court):* Accountings due.

- *When Guardianship is No Longer Needed:* Final Accounting and termination documents due; a hearing may be required. The court must give permission for the guardianship to end.

---

[7] Although a bookkeeper or accountant may be useful in helping you establish a financial recordkeeping system, she will probably not know the legal requirements for reporting on estate guardianships—they do not conform to standard accounting methods.

[8] If the minor is living with someone else, you may need that person's help in preparing the accounting records if money was spent on the minor's support. Arrange this in advance, and make sure that adult keeps track of receipts and expenditures following the guidelines in Sections F1 and F2 of this chapter.

The probate referee does not need to appraise money (including bank accounts, savings and loan and credit union accounts, certificates of deposit, U.S. savings bonds and money market funds held in a brokerage house). However, the probate referee will need to appraise all other personal property, including stocks and bonds (even if its value is listed in the open stock exchange), jewelry, annuity policies, real estate, vehicles, promissory notes, business interests, coin collections, antiques and other personal possessions.

To obtain the services of a probate referee, you will need to file an Application and Order Appointing Probate Referee form with the court. We suggest you do this within three weeks of the date Letters of Guardianship are issued.

2. Inventory and Appraisement

Within 90 days of the date you obtain Letters of Guardianship of the minor's estate, you must prepare and file with the court a Judicial Council form entitled "Inventory and Appraisement." In this form you give the court an inventory of all money,[9] goods or other property coming into your hands as guardian. If the only property you're holding for the minor is money—including bank accounts—or U.S. savings bonds with a fixed redemption value, you don't need to have it appraised, but you still need to file an inventory. If there is property in the estate other than money and U.S. savings bonds, you will need to obtain a court-appointed referee to determine the value of the property. (Section D1 just above discusses probate referees.)

3. Petitioning the Court for Compensation

You may petition the court for compensation for your services any time after the Inventory and Appraisement is filed, but it must be no sooner than 90 days of the date Letters of Guardianship were issued. If you use an attorney, you may also petition the court to compensate him for his services. Many courts require that you wait an entire year before you can be compensated, so you may make this request when you file your First Accounting as described in Section D4 just below. (Compensation is covered in more detail in Chapter 11, Section F.)

4. First Accounting

One year after the Letters of Guardianship are issued, you must file a First Accounting with the court and possibly attend a hearing. The First Accounting shows what income was received and spent during the year, what money and property you are currently handling for the minor, and any reimbursements or compensation you have received as a guardian. (See Section D3 just above and Chapter 11, Section F.)

Local court accounting requirements vary, but all courts insist that you keep extremely accurate records. Some courts require a receipt for each expenditure, or only for expenditures exceeding a certain amount (often $20 or more). Some courts require original bank statements.

Note: If the guardianship estate has not had any activity for the entire year, you can advise the court and generally obtain a waiver of accounting for one year.

5. Periodic Accountings

Beginning with the two-year anniversary of the date that Letters of Guardianship were issued (one year after the First Accounting is due), you must file an accounting with the court. You may also need to appear in court for a hearing on the accounting. Some courts require accountings every year, while other courts require them every two years. Depending on the court's local rules as well as the amount and nature of the estate, accountings may be required more or less frequently.

Each accounting will contain the same information described in the First Accounting in Section D4 just above, but it will be entitled "Second Accounting" (and so on for each year), and will provide current information about the minor's assets. If the

---

[9] In the context of this chapter, the term "money" includes bank accounts, savings and loan and credit union accounts, certificates of deposit, U.S. savings bonds and money market funds held in a brokerage house.

guardianship estate has been inactive for the entire year, you can advise the court and generally obtain a waiver of account for that year.

6. Documents Must be Filed to End Guardianship

A guardianship of a minor's estate can be terminated when it's no longer needed,[10] such as when:
- The minor reaches age 18 or dies;
- The assets of the estate are used up; or
- The guardianship is no longer in the minor's best interests.

To end a guardianship of a minor's estate, documents requesting the guardianship be terminated must be filed with the court along with a final accounting and documents signed by the minor stating she has received the assets that belong to her. The court may also require that you attend a hearing.

E. Using Funds from the Estate for Support of the Minor

IF YOU BECOME GUARDIAN OF A MINOR'S ESTATE, you may also be able to get court permission to use estate funds to support the minor. This varies greatly according to the situation, but here is a broad outline of how it usually works.

1. Guardians Who Are Parents

The law requires that parents support their minor children, regardless of whether their children are living with them (CC §§196, 242, 244). Parents must typically support an unmarried child who is over 18 years of age, is a full-time high school student and is not self-supporting (CC §196.5). If you are a parent of a minor and also guardian of the minor's estate, you usually cannot use funds from the estate for the support of your child unless you have received specific permission from the court to do this. The authorization would have to be in the form of a court order.[11]

2. Guardians Who Are Not Parents

If you are guardian of the person and estate of a minor whose parents have died or cannot support her, you usually can use funds from the minor's estate to support and take care of her and to provide her with an education. However, you must first go to court and obtain an order allowing you to use the estate's funds either on an ongoing basis or for a given purpose (PC §2422).[12]

Example 1: Dawn is named guardian of her nephews, Hal and Homer. The boys' parents die in an automobile crash, and Dawn obtains legal guardianships of her nephews' persons and estates. Dawn is a single mother of three children and cannot possibly support her nephews. Fortunately, Hal's and Homer's parents left them substantial assets. With the help of a lawyer, Dawn asks the court for permission to use a reasonable amount of the money from the boys' estate on an ongoing basis for their support and education. Her motion is granted. As required for a guardianship of the estate, Dawn is responsible to the court for periodic accountings.

Example 2: Gerry's mother and father are divorced, and his father has left the area and remarried. For the first few years after he remarries, Gerry's father sends child support payments, but then Gerry's mother and father informally agree that the child support payments aren't needed anymore. Gerry's mother dies suddenly, and her assets pass to Gerry. Gerry's grandparents obtain guardianship of his person and estate, notifying Gerry's father of the guardianship proceeding as required by law. Gerry's father contacts the grandparents and says that he'd be willing to resume paying child support. However, Gerry's grandparents don't like Gerry's father, and

---

[10]Termination of guardianships is discussed in more detail in Chapter 12.

[11]This book does not cover the procedure for obtaining an order. If this is your situation, you will need to do your own research or hire an attorney. (See Chapter 13.)

[12]We do not cover the procedure for obtaining an order in this book. If this is your situation, you will need the help of an attorney. See Chapter 13, which gives you information on finding and dealing with lawyers.

they tell him they don't want his child support money. Because Gerry's grandparents both are retired and on a limited income, they seek permission from the court to use the estate's assets to support Gerry. A judge denies their request on the basis that Gerry's father can and should be paying child support. Gerry's grandparents then make arrangements to receive child support payments from his father.

F. Ongoing Responsibilities for the Guardian of a Minor's Estate

A GUARDIAN OF AN ESTATE must keep in contact with the court until the guardianship ends. A guardian's responsibilities are covered in general in Chapter 11, which you should read and follow. In addition, you may want to use the services of a legal professional to help set up and maintain the minor's estate. (See Chapter 13.)

This section provides a brief overview of your legal responsibilities as guardian of a minor's estate. It does not give you investment advice or other suggestions about how to manage the minor's property. As an estate guardian, you must manage and protect the assets of the estate honestly and for the best interests of the minor. And just to make sure you do, the court requires you to keep it updated about the minor's property and how you've been managing it.

If you are authorized to spend money from the minor's estate to support him (see Section E of this chapter), you must use it to provide for the "comfortable and suitable support, maintenance and education" of the minor (PC §2420). You also are required to manage the minor's assets prudently, and not take any risks, such as speculative investing. In addition, you may not combine your funds with the minor's, and you may not mismanage or do anything illegal with the minor's assets, including borrowing money for your personal use, even if you intend to pay it back.[13]

---

[13] It is illegal to "borrow" money from the estate without a court order, and is considered embezzlement, regardless of your intentions to pay it back.

1. Minor's Assets and Accounts Must be Kept Separate

It is absolutely fundamental to your role as a guardian that all of the minor's assets and accounts are always kept separate from yours and everyone else's.

All assets belonging to the minor, including those with title, must either be in the name of the estate or in your name specifically as guardian of the estate. In Section C4 of this chapter are instructions for having assets transferred. Even if an asset is listed in your name as guardian of the minor's estate, remember that you are handling it for the minor—it does not belong to you.

All of the minor's accounts must be kept in the name of the minor's estate, and may not be mixed with your own. As guardian, you have authority to make deposits and withdrawals. Whenever you set up an account as estate guardian, you must provide the financial institution with a certified copy of the Letters of Guardianship. The account must be in the name of the minor's estate, with you being authorized to sign as guardian of the minor. For example, the name on the account for the minor, Mary Jones, is "Estate of Mary Jones," and the authorized signer on the account is "Joe Evans, Guardian of the Estate of Mary Jones."

Note: Some banks charge special fees to process guardianship bank accounts. These fees typically run about 1/10 of 1 percent of the amount in the account simply to open it (commonly called an "acceptance fee"), and the same percentage to close the account. It's worth checking around with different banks for one with a policy of charging little or nothing extra.

2. Carefully Manage the Minor's Assets

At the beginning of this section, we said that you must manage the minor's finances prudently, and not take any risks. Here are some general guidelines for taking care of the estate.

a. Save Receipts

You must account to the court for all expenditures you make on behalf of the minor or his estate, so keep all receipts, no matter how small the amount. You will need information on the breakdown of these expenditures for periodic accountings required by the court that tell how you managed the estate's assets. Depending on the court's policies, you may also need copies of the actual receipts. Keep the receipts in a safe, organized place such as in an envelope or file folder. Even though the court may never ask to see the original receipts, you're better off safe than sorry.

If you are authorized to spend the estate's money to support the minor (see Section E in this chapter), keep copies of receipts for any funds you spent on her upkeep. Depending on what the court authorized, this might include costs of the minor's food, housing, education, clothing, or medical care.

If you are not authorized to spend the estate's money to support the minor, expenditures can only pertain to your management of the estate. For example, this might include insurance premiums on the minor's assets, accountants' fees, or payments made to settle a claim.

b. Keep Original Documents from Financial Institutions

Keep all statements, correspondence and other documents you get from financial institutions. Some courts require that you attach *original* bank statements to your financial accountings, to minimize the possibility that you could alter those documents.

c. Keep Accurate Accounting Records

We suggest you record every transaction you make on behalf of the minor's estate, no matter how small. Make sure you have an accurate means of record-keeping. You might want to consult with an accountant or bookkeeper about establishing a good system, and then have it reviewed periodically.[14] Generally, reasonable accountant's fees can be paid directly by the estate. Keep copies of all receipts—you will need to give the court a breakdown and proof of these expenditures.

---

[14] If possible, hire someone who is familiar with accounting requirements for guardianships. The probate court does not follow standard accounting principles in its reporting requirements. You might also want to hire a legal assistant or attorney. (See Chapter 13.)

d. Maintain Adequate Insurance for the Minor's Assets

You must maintain adequate insurance against fire, theft or other possible hazards on any valuable estate property that might require it. For example, if the minor's estate includes a house and a vehicle, you would need to insure both of them. Federally-insured banking facilities always should be used to deposit the minor's funds because they are considered stable. See a lawyer if you have any questions about whether to insure property the minor owns. (See Chapter 13.)

e. Avoid Conflict of Interest

Never get into transactions in which your own financial interests and those of the estate could conflict. Make sure that you never personally profit from the financial transactions of the estate. For example, do not purchase assets from the estate without paying a fair price. If you have any doubt about a transaction, seek court approval before undertaking it. (See Section F4 in this chapter.)

f. Filing Tax Returns

As guardian of the minor's estate, you have full authority to prepare, sign and file tax returns on behalf of the minor and the minor's estate. You may claim exemptions for the minor under applicable tax laws (PC §2461). You can hire an accountant if you don't want to complete the tax returns yourself, and pay for these services directly out of the minor's estate. Keep copies of all receipts; you will need to give the court information about these expenditures.

3. Maintain Adequate Bond

When you petition to be guardian of a minor's estate, you are almost always required to post bond unless both parents waive it. This is a sort of financial guarantee that would reimburse the estate if you stole or misappropriated estate assets. (How to apply for a bond is discussed in Section C1 of this chapter. Information on seeking reimbursement by the estate for bond premiums is covered in Section F6 of this chapter and in Chapter 11, Section F.)

During the entire time of the guardianship, you must have the appropriate bond amount. If the assets of the estate increase or decrease substantially, you must adjust the amount of bond by going to court for an order allowing the change in the amount of bond. (See *The Conservatorship Book,* by Lisa Goldoftas and Carolyn Farren. Or see Chapter 13 for information on how to find and deal with lawyers.)

4. Getting Court Approval

As guardian of a minor's estate, you are not given freedom to do whatever you think is appropriate with the estate's assets. It is common for a guardian of a minor's estate to be a little uncertain about the legal or ethical propriety of an transaction. Since a guardian can sometimes be held personally liable for mismanaging a minor's estate, it pays to be cautious. Fortunately, if you are concerned about a questionable transaction, you can always ask the court beforehand for legal permission to undertake that action (PC §2403). You must follow certain procedures and give notice to people entitled to it before you can undertake any substantial financial transactions such as:

- Selling, purchasing or undertaking any action that involves the estate's real property (PC §2501, PC §§2463-2464);[15]
- Compromising or settling a claim against the estate for more than $25,000 (PC §2502);
- Becoming personally involved in a transaction, such as settling a claim by the minor against you or changing the terms of a debt you owe to the minor or her estate (PC §2503);
- Settling a wrongful death or personal injury claim (PC §2504);
- Borrowing money on behalf of the estate (PC §§2550); or

- Purchasing an automobile for the minor. That might require proof of car insurance and court approval.

This book does not cover the procedures for obtaining court approval of estate transactions. (See *The Conservatorship Book,* by Lisa Goldoftas and Carolyn Farren. Or see Chapter 13 for information on how to find and deal with lawyers.)

5. Receiving Benefits and Reporting to Agencies

Sometimes a guardianship of a minor's estate includes receiving and expending money or benefits from an agency that requires periodic accountings to show how the money has been spent. In such a situation, you must comply with the organization's requirements.

For example, the Veterans' Administration is almost certain to require these accountings. Social Security and other agencies may also require them. These reports do not get filed with the court. However, you may want to attach them as exhibits to your accountings. (See Sections D4 and D5 in this chapter for general information on accounting requirements.)

6. Reimbursements and Compensation of the Guardian

With court approval, a guardian may be reimbursed or compensated for expenses incurred personally in taking care of a minor's estate, or for time spent taking care of a minor's estate. (See Chapter 11, Section F.)

7. Minors Cannot Sign Contracts

Minors are normally not permitted to make contracts on their own (CC §1556). If they do, these contracts are not usually legally valid. As guardian, you are not responsible for any contracts the minor might sign, unless you enter into the contract as a co-signer.[16]

---

[15] Court approval is not mandatory if a lease is being extended, renewed, or modified, as long as its unexpired term is two years or less and the monthly rental amount is less than $750, or the lease is month-to-month. A guardian also does not need a court order to maintain or make repairs on the house where the minor lives (PC §2457).

[16] In certain situations the minor may obtain counseling or medical treatment without a guardian's consent, and the guardian is not liable for the cost of such services. (CC §§25.9, 34.5, 34.7-34.10.)

CHAPTER 11

NOW THAT YOU'RE A GUARDIAN: RIGHTS AND RESPONSIBILITIES

A.	What to Do with Letters of Guardianship	11/1
B.	Responsibilities of Guardians of a Minor's Estate	11/1
C.	Responsibilities of Guardians of a Minor's Person	11/1
D.	Responsibilities to the Court	11/3
E.	Transferring the Guardianship to Another California Court	11/5
F.	Reimbursements and Compensation of the Guardian	11/12
G.	If the Guardianship Is Contested After You are Appointed	11/13

YOU PROBABLY TURNED TO THIS CHAPTER because you have obtained a court-ordered legal guardianship. Congratulations! You have undoubtedly put in time and effort to accomplish this task. Now that you're a guardian, you have certain rights and responsibilities. These will vary, depending upon whether you are guardian of a minor's person, estate, or both.

Note: You may notice that the minor for whom you're a guardian is referred to as a "ward" in legal documents or by the court. This is simply the legal terminology for a minor who has a legal guardian.[1]

A. What to Do with Letters of Guardianship

LETTERS OF GUARDIANSHIP are legal proof that you are the guardian of a minor. Any time you need to show anyone that you are the minor's legal guardian, simply provide a copy of the Letters of Guardianship. Naturally, if you obtained a guardianship because an agency or institution insisted on one, you should now take or send it a copy of the Letters of Guardianship.

It's possible to make photocopies of the Letters of Guardianship, but you may have problems getting others to accept them as legal proof of your status, since photocopies are not considered official copies of court documents and could be altered. It's better to get certified copies stamped with the court's seal by following the instructions in Chapter 9, Section E. Each copy costs about $3.00, but all are free if you cannot afford to pay court fees and they were waived by the court. Keep extra certified copies in a convenient, safe place.

B. Responsibilities of Guardians of a Minor's Estate

IF YOU ARE GUARDIAN OF A MINOR'S ESTATE ONLY, you may skip only Section C in this chapter, but you will need to read all of Chapter 10. If you are guardian of both a minor's person and estate you will need to read both this entire chapter and Chapter 10.

C. Responsibilities of Guardians of a Minor's Person

THE DISCUSSION IN THIS SECTION only covers responsibilities of a guardian of a minor's person.

---

[1] In the context of a legal guardianship, a ward is different from a minor who is a dependent of the court, although in both instances the minor may be referred to as a ward.

1. Taking Care of the Minor

As guardian of a minor's person, you have legal custody of the minor. You now have a legal duty to take care of the minor, although it's likely that you were doing this even before being appointed guardian. As guardian, you are responsible for the basic needs of the minor, which includes providing the minor with food, shelter and health care, as well as taking charge of the minor's educational and religious development.[2] And, no doubt, you will also be giving the minor a lot of loving care.

2. Residence for the Minor

As legal guardian, you must have an established residence for the minor in California, usually at your home, but possibly at a boarding school.

You must obtain court permission before you can move the minor to a residence outside of California. That requires filing papers with the court, serving people entitled to notice (PC §2700(a)(18)), attending a hearing and getting an order signed by the court. If you don't obtain an order from the court, it may, at its discretion, require the minor to be returned to California. A legal action could also be brought against you for breaking the law. The court can require guardianship proceedings to be conducted in any other place a minor is living for four or more months (PC §2352(b)). If you plan to move the minor out of California, you'll need to hire a lawyer or do your own legal research. (See Chapter 13.)

3. Medical Treatment

In general, you have the same right as a parent to consent and require medical treatment for the minor. For example, you can take the minor to the doctor or dentist for routine examinations and medical treatment. And of course you have the right to add the minor to your health insurance plan if he qualifies.

There are several exceptions to your right to give consent for the minor's medical treatment.[3] Except in emergencies, surgical procedures usually require the consent of both you and the minor, if she is 14 years of age or older (PC §2353(b)). As guardian, you cannot involuntarily place the minor in a mental health treatment facility unless she is a danger to herself or others or is gravely disabled (PC §2356(a), W&I §5150). There are also laws which prevent a guardian from allowing a minor to be treated with experimental drugs, given convulsive treatment or sterilized. If the minor needs medical or psychological treatment which falls into any of these categories, you will need to obtain an order from the court, which will require the help of an attorney. (See Chapter 13.)

4. Receiving Benefits

As guardian of the minor's person, you may receive for the minor public assistance, Social Security, or other benefits for which he qualifies. Any funds received are to be used for the minor's benefit, and some of these agencies require accountings in which you show how you spent the money.

5. Liabilities

Along with a legal guardianship comes some liability. Like parents, legal guardians may have to pay for a minor's actions. For example:
- If the minor intentionally does something wrong (called "willful misconduct" in legal lingo) which results in the injury or death to another person, or damage to property (such as spraypainting or defacing property), you could be held liable for damages in an amount up to $10,000 (CC §1714.1).
- If the minor shoplifts or steals library materials, you could be held liable for between $50 and $500 plus

---

[2]If you are guardian of the minor's person and estate, the minor's funds cannot be used to support the minor without prior court approval. This subject is covered in more detail in Chapter 10, Section E.

[3]If necessary, you can seek a court order to authorize a specific medical treatment. That procedure is beyond the scope of this book. (See Chapter 13 for information on doing your own research and dealing with attorneys.)

the actual value of the merchandise or books (CC §490.5).[4]

- If you sign the minor's driver's license application[5] or give the minor permission to drive a vehicle—either express or implied—and the minor is involved in an accident, you could be liable to pay for injuries or death as a result of the accident. The amount of damages for one accident could be up to $15,000 for the injury or death of one person and up to $30,000 for the injury or death of everyone involved in the accident. Additionally, you could be liable for property damages up to $5,000 as a result of the accident (Vehicle Code §§17707-17709).

- If the minor injures or kills someone by discharging a firearm, you could be held liable for damages in an amount up to $30,000 for the injury or death of one person, or up to $60,000 for injury or death to more than one person (CC §1714.3). If you were negligent—for example, by leaving a gun where the minor would have access to it—you could have additional liability.

5. Visitation Rights

As emphasized earlier, this book is not intended to resolve disputes over child custody or visitation rights. The minor's parents' visitation rights are not taken away simply because a guardianship was obtained. Even after a guardian has been named, an adult may seek visitation rights by filing papers in the guardianship court case. If this situation arises in any guardianship in which you are involved, you will need to see a lawyer. (See Chapter 13.)

6. Minors Cannot Sign Contracts

Minors are normally not permitted to make contracts on their own (CC §1556). If they do, these contracts are not usually legally valid. As guardian, you are not responsible for any contracts the minor might sign, unless you enter into the contract as a co-signer.[6]

D. Responsibilities to the Court

1. Notify Court About Address Changes

As legal guardian, you must notify the court if either you or the minor move. This simply involves filling out a form, in some instances having copies served, and filing the form with the court. Check your local court rules. Some courts (such as Sacramento and San Francisco) use their own special forms for address changes.

Important: There are special procedures you must follow if you plan to move the minor out of California. (See Section C2 in this chapter.) However, if you are moving the minor to another California county, the guardianship case can be transferred following the procedures in Section E of this chapter.

a. Notification to Court of Address of Guardian/Ward Form

Appendix D at the back of the book contains a form entitled "Notification to Court of Address of Guardian/Ward."[7] This easy-to-use form should be used to notify the court whenever you or the minor moves. Remember to make extra copies before you fill it out—you or the minor might move again.

---

[4] At the court's discretion, you could perform public services instead of paying a fine. Your liabilities are not limited to a $50 to $500 fine if the law allows for other remedies.
[5] The minor's driver's license application can be signed by a parent, legal guardian, or an adult having custody of the minor (Vehicle Code §§17701).

[6] In certain situations the minor may obtain counseling or medical treatment without a guardian's consent, and the guardian is not liable for the cost of such services. (CC §§25.9, 34.5, 34.7-34.10.)
[7] As noted previously, in this context the term "ward" simply refers to a minor who has a legal guardian.

PARTY WITHOUT AN ATTORNEY *(Name and Address)*:	TELEPHONE NO:	FOR COURT USE ONLY
JENNIFER BEATRICE PERKINS 555 Any Street Hollister, CA 95023 In Pro Per	408/555-1212	

NAME OF COURT: SAN BENITO SUPERIOR COURT
STREET ADDRESS: Courthouse, Room 206
MAILING ADDRESS: 440 5th Street
CITY AND ZIP CODE: Hollister, CA 95023
BRANCH NAME:

GUARDIANSHIP OF THE ☒ PERSON ☒ ESTATE OF (NAME):

MARK ROBERT CARLSON
                                                                MINOR

NOTIFICATION TO COURT OF ADDRESS OF GUARDIAN/WARD	CASE NUMBER 501

1. **INFORMATION ABOUT GUARDIAN**
   NAME OF GUARDIAN: JENNIFER BEATRICE PERKINS
   STREET ADDRESS: 555 Any Street
   CITY: Hollister   STATE: CA   ZIP: 95023
   MAILING ADDRESS (If different): (Same)
   CITY: STATE: ZIP:
   PHONE NUMBER (Include area code): (408) 555-1212

2. **INFORMATION ABOUT WARD (MINOR)**
   NAME OF WARD: MARK ROBERT CARLSON
   STREET ADDRESS: 555 Any Street
   CITY: Hollister   STATE: CA   ZIP: 95023
   MAILING ADDRESS (If different): (Same)
   CITY: STATE: ZIP:
   PHONE NUMBER (Include area code): (408) 555-1212

3. **INFORMATION ABOUT COMPLETION OF THIS FORM:**
   NAME: JENNIFER BEATRICE PERKINS
   CAPACITY (e.g., Guardian): Proposed guardian
   STREET ADDRESS: 555 Any Street
   CITY: Hollister   STATE: CA   ZIP: 95023
   MAILING ADDRESS (If different): (Same)
   CITY: STATE: ZIP:
   PHONE NUMBER (Include area code): (408) 555-1212

Date: 1/13/91

JENNIFER BEATRICE PERKINS
(TYPE OR PRINT NAME)

Jennifer Beatrice Perkins
(SIGNATURE OF PERSON COMPLETING FORM)

NP   NOTIFICATION TO COURT OF ADDRESS OF GUARDIAN/WARD

CAPTION: NOTICE TO COURT OF ADDRESS OF WARD/GUARDIAN

Fill in the caption following the general instructions in Chapter 3, Section D1.

Item 1: In the spaces provided, fill in your name. Then enter your current street and mailing address (if different from your street address), your city, state, zip code and telephone number.

Item 2: Fill in the minor's name. If you are the guardian of more than one minor and they are living at the same address, you can enter all of their names in the first space. Otherwise, you will need to copy the form and fill out a separate one for each minor. Next, enter the minor's current street and mailing address (if different from the street address), city, state, zip code and telephone number.

Item 3: You will be filling in most of the same information here as requested in Item 1. In the first space, fill in your name. In the second space, fill in your capacity in the guardianship—guardian of the person, guardian of the estate, or guardian of the person and estate. Next enter your street and mailing address (if different from your street address), your city, state, zip code and telephone number.

Fill in the date the form was completed. Type or print your name, and sign your name in the spaces provided.

You have now completed the form. Make copies of the Notification to Court of Address of Guardian/Ward and file them with the court following the instructions in Chapter 3, Section E.

Court Proceedings and Special Notice

During the guardianship, you might need to go to court to obtain permission to do something. This typically applies only to guardianships of the estate (see Chapter 10), but occasionally it may be needed for guardianships of the person if you want to:

- Have the guardianship case transferred to a different California court (the procedure is covered in Section E in this chapter);
- Move the minor outside of California (see Section C2 in this chapter);
- Place the minor in a mental health treatment facility (see Section C3 in this chapter); or
- Insist a minor receive involuntary medical treatment (see Section C3 in this chapter).

If you go to court to obtain permission to do anything listed above, you must serve all the relatives listed on the Guardianship Notification Worksheet as well as anyone who filed a document requesting special notice of these hearings (PC §2700). This request should have mailed to you by the person filing such a Request for Special Notice. You will also need to follow specific procedures for filing papers, attending a hearing and obtaining an order. We do not give instructions for most of those types of court proceedings in this book. (See Chapter 13 for information about doing your own legal research and hiring a lawyer.)

E. Transferring the Guardianship to Another California Court

IF YOU AND THE MINOR MOVE to another county, you may need to obtain a guardianship in a court in that county.[8] Certain agencies (for example, public assistance agencies in some counties) may require a guardianship in their own county before they will give benefits.

---

[8] This process for transferring the guardianship to another court may be followed either before or after the guardian has been appointed by the court.

As petitioner or guardian, you are entitled by law to have the guardianship transferred to another court, as long as it is in the best interests of the minor and her estate. You will need to complete and have several forms served, appear at a court hearing, and pay court fees to have the case transferred. Here's how to have your guardianship case transferred.

1. Call the Court

Call the court from which you are transferring the case—**not** the new court to which you want the case moved. Say you're filing a petition to have the guardianship proceeding transferred, and ask:

- If you can obtain a hearing date over the phone. If you can get a hearing date, obtain one at least 25 days away—you'll need to have papers served at least 20 days before the hearing takes place. If you can't get the hearing date now, you will get one when you file your papers with the court.
- What fees the old court charges for transferring your case, and whether the fees must be paid when you file your papers. If you are guardian of a minor's estate, the fees for transferring the case will be paid out of the minor's estate.

Note: A larger fee (usually between $75 and $130) must also be paid to the new court when your papers are transferred.

You're now ready to complete the forms required to have the case transferred.

2. Complete Petition for Transfer of Guardianship Proceeding

In this petition, you tell the court why the guardianship case should be transferred to another court.

> **CAPTION:** PETITION FOR TRANSFER OF GUARDIANSHIP PROCEEDING
>
> Fill in the caption following the general instructions in Chapter 3, Section D1.

Item 1: In the blanks, fill in your name and the county where you want the case transferred. If the new court has a district or branch name, put it after the name of the county (for example, Santa Clara, North County Branch). Then in your own words state why the case should be transferred. For example, this might be "Andrew Smith and I moved to Santa Clara County in May 1989. I applied for AFDC, and was informed that I cannot obtain benefits unless the guardianship is transferred to this county. It would be in the minor's best interests for me to obtain AFDC benefits to help support him."

Item 2: Check the first box before the word "guardian" if you have already been appointed guardian by the court and have obtained issued Letters of Guardianship. Check the second box before the words "proposed guardian" if you have petitioned to be guardian but have not yet been appointed. Then check the box next to the words "person," "estate" or both, depending on the type of guardianship. In the blank space, fill in the minor's name exactly as it appears on the other guardianship papers.

Item 3: Skip this entire item (3, 3a and 3b) if you are the guardian or proposed guardian of the minor's person only. Otherwise, check the first box before the word "guardian" if you have already been appointed guardian of the minor's estate by the court and have obtained issued Letters of Guardianship. Check the second box before the words "proposed guardian" if you have petitioned to be guardian of the minor's estate but have not yet been appointed.

Item 3a: Check this box only if the space provided gives enough room for you to list the estate's property. Then list and briefly describe each piece of property, tell its approximate value and where it is located.

Item 3b: Check this box if you need additional space to list the minor's property. Prepare and label an Attachment 3a to this petition, following the instructions in Chapter 3, Section D3. Then list and briefly describe each piece of property, tell its approximate value and where it is located.

Item 4: In the space provided, fill in your name and current residence address.

PARTY WITHOUT AN ATTORNEY (Name and Address):	TELEPHONE NO:	FOR COURT USE ONLY
ANGELO MARTIN FREDERICKS 222 Any Street Yreka, CA 96097 In Pro Per	916/555-1212	

NAME OF COURT: SISKIYOU SUPERIOR COURT
STREET ADDRESS: 311 4th Street
MAILING ADDRESS: P.O. Box 338
CITY AND ZIP CODE: Yreka, CA 96097
BRANCH NAME:

GUARDIANSHIP OF THE ☒ PERSON ☐ ESTATE OF (NAME):

JOE GEORGE FREDERICKS

MINOR

PETITION FOR TRANSFER OF GUARDIANSHIP PROCEEDING

CASE NUMBER: 2001

1. Petitioner (name): ANGELO MARTIN FREDERICKS requests that this guardianship proceeding be transferred to the Superior Court of the State of California, County of SHASTA.
   Such transfer would be in the best interests of the ward for the following reason(s):
   The minor and I are moving to Redding, California on 9/1/91. In order to register him in school and obtain welfare benefits, I need a guardianship in Shasta County, the county in which we'll be living.

2. Petitioner is the ☒ guardian or ☐ proposed guardian of the:
   ☒ person ☐ estate of JOE GEORGE FREDERICKS.

3. ☐ Petitioner is the ☐ guardian or ☐ proposed guardian of the estate in this proceeding. The character, value, and location of the estate's property:
   a. ☐ is as follows:

   b. ☐ is described in Attachment 3a.

4. The guardian's name and address are: ANGELO MARTIN FREDERICKS, 222 Any Street, Yreka, CA 96097

5. The ward's name and address are: JOE GEORGE FREDERICKS, 222 Any Street, Yreka, CA 96097

6. The names, residence addresses and relationships of the ward's father, mother, spouse and all relatives within the second degree of the ward so far as known to petitioner are as follows:
   a. Father: Gene Fredericks, 440 Another Street, Yreka, CA 96097
   b. Mother: Ann Fredericks, Deceased
   c. Spouse: None
   d. Brother: Andrew Fredericks, 111 City Street, Los Angeles, CA 90012
   e. ☒ List of names and addresses continued as Attachment 6.

7. A request for special notice:
   a. ☒ has not been filed.
   b. ☐ has been filed, and notice of hearing on this petition will be given by law to: _____

8. Petitioner requests an order transferring this proceeding to the Superior Court of the State of California, County of SHASTA.

I declare under penalty of perjury under the laws of the State of California that the foregoing is true and correct.

Date: 8/3/91

ANGELO MARTIN FREDERICKS
(TYPE OR PRINT NAME)

Angelo Martin Fredericks
(SIGNATURE OF PETITIONER)

NP   **PETITION FOR TRANSFER OF GUARDIANSHIP PROCEEDING**

Item 5: In the space provided, fill in the minor's name and current residence address.

Item 6: In this item, list the names and addresses of the minor's close relatives. Follow the instructions for listing these relatives covered in Item 18 of the Petition for Appointment of Guardian of Minor in Chapter 5, Section A.

Item 7: In addition to the relatives listed in Item 6 just above, anyone who has filed a document with the court requesting special notice of further hearings must get a copy of this petition. If you aren't sure whether someone filed a request for special notice, call the court. Give the clerk the case name and file number, and ask her to pull the file and see if special notice was requested. (See Section D2 of this chapter.) If so, get the names and addresses of anyone who filed a request for special notice.

Item 7a: If no request for special notice was filed, check this box.

Item 7b: If special notice was filed any time after you filed your initial guardianship papers, check this box and in the space provided fill in the name and address of each person who requested the special notice.

Item 8: In the blank after the words "County of" again fill in the name of the county where you want the case transferred. If the new court has a district or branch name, put it after the name of the county.

Sign and date the form in the spaces indicated, and print or type your name.

3. Complete (Proposed) Order for Transfer of Guardianship Proceeding

Before the guardianship proceeding can be transferred to another court, a judge must sign an order allowing this to happen.

CAPTION: ORDER FOR TRANSFER OF GUARDIANSHIP PROCEEDING

Fill in the caption following the general instructions in Chapter 3, Section D1.

Item 1: In this item, give information about when the hearing will be held and who will attend. If there are any changes or additions, they may be filled in at the hearing by the judge or clerk.

Item 1a: This item is left blank, unless you know the name of the judge or commissioner who will be hearing the guardianship case. If so, fill in the name.

Item 1b: If you obtained the hearing date and location from the court clerk, fill in this information in the spaces provided.

Item 1c: Check this box. Fill in your full first, middle and last names.

Item 1d: Check this box. Then after the words "Attorney for petitioner (name)," fill in your full first, middle and last names, followed by the words "appearing In Pro Per."

Item 1e: Ordinarily this item is left blank, except for the rare situation where the minor has an attorney representing him independently. If he does, check the box and fill in the attorney's name, address, and phone number.

Item 2a: Check the first box before the words "All notices required by law have been given." This means you will be having all of the people listed in Items 6 and 7 of the Petition for Transfer of Guardianship Proceeding served with notice of the hearing.

Item 2b: In the first space fill in the minor's name exactly as it appears on the other documents already filed with the court. In the second space fill in the case number of the guardianship case in the court from which it is being transferred. In the last blank after the words "County of," fill in the name of the county where you want the case transferred. If the new court has a district or branch name, put it after the name of the county.

Item 3: In the blank provided, again fill in the name of the county where you want the case transferred. If the new court has a district or branch name, put it after the name of the county.

Leave the date and judge's signature line blank. These will be filled in at the hearing.

PARTY WITHOUT AN ATTORNEY (Name and Address):	TELEPHONE NO:	FOR COURT USE ONLY
ANGELO MARTIN FREDERICKS 222 Any Street Yreka, CA 96097 *In Pro Per*	916/555-1212	

NAME OF COURT: SISKIYOU SUPERIOR COURT
STREET ADDRESS: 311 4th Street
MAILING ADDRESS: P.O. Box 338
CITY AND ZIP CODE: Yreka, CA 96097
BRANCH NAME:

GUARDIANSHIP OF THE ☒ PERSON ☐ ESTATE OF (NAME):
JOE GEORGE FREDERICKS
MINOR

ORDER FOR TRANSFER OF GUARDIANSHIP PROCEEDING	CASE NUMBER: 2001

1. The Petition for Transfer of Guardianship Proceeding came on for hearing as follows (check boxes c, d and e to indicate personal presence):

   a. Judge (name):

   b. Hearing Date: 8/8/91 Time: 9:00 am ☒ Dept: 1   ☒ Div.: 1   ☒ Room: 1

   c. ☒ Petitioner (name): ANGELO MARTIN FREDERICKS

   d. ☒ Attorney for petitioner (name): ANGELO MARTIN FREDERICKS, appearing In Pro Per

   e. ☐ Attorney for ward (name, address and telephone):

2. THE COURT FINDS

   a. ☒ all notices required by law have been given.

   b. Transfer of the Guardianship of JOE GEORGE FREDERICKS,

   Case Number 2001, from this court to the Superior Court of the State of California,

   County of SHASTA is in the best interests of the ward.

3. THE COURT ORDERS that this proceeding be transferred to the Superior Court of the State of California, County of SHASTA.

Dated: ....

_____
(JUDGE OF THE SUPERIOR COURT)

NP **ORDER FOR TRANSFER OF GUARDIANSHIP PROCEEDING**

4. Complete Notice of Hearing

Complete a Notice of Hearing following the instructions in Chapter 5, Section C, with these exceptions:

Item 1: If you have been appointed guardian or temporary guardian by the court, after the words "(representative capacity, if any)," enter the words "guardian of the person," "guardian of the estate," or "guardian of the person and estate," or the word "temporary," before each of these types of guardianships if that applies. If you have not been appointed guardian, indicate that you are "proposed guardian of the person," "proposed guardian of the estate," or "proposed guardian of the person and estate."

Just below this, after the words "has filed (specify)," enter the words "Petition for Transfer of Guardianship Proceeding."

Item 3: Fill in the information in the box about the date, time and place of the hearing if you obtained these over the phone. Otherwise, have the clerk fill in this information when you file your papers with the court.

5. Copy and File Documents with the Court

You are now ready to copy the documents. Make at least two to three photocopies of each document, depending on whether the court requires an additional copy. In addition, make one copy each of the Notice of Hearing and Petition for Transfer of Guardianship Proceeding for each person listed in Items 6 and 7 of the Petition for Transfer of Guardianship Proceeding.

File the documents following the instructions in Chapter 3, Section E2. If you have not already obtained a hearing date, get one from the clerk. The date should be at least 25 days away to give you enough time to get the papers served as required. Make sure all copies of the Notice of Hearing have the date, time and place listed on them. If the clerk gives you the original signed Notice of Hearing, keep it in a safe place; you will need to file it with the court after everyone entitled to notice has been served.

6. Have Papers Served, Complete and File Proof of Service

Have copies of the Notice of Hearing and Petition for Transfer of Guardianship Proceeding served by mail on each person listed in Items 6 and 7 of the Petition for Transfer of Guardianship Proceeding at least 20 days before the scheduled hearing date. Instructions for having documents served by mail are contained in Chapter 6. If you don't have papers served in time, you will need to have the hearing continued. (See Chapter 6, Section B5.)

Finally, complete a proof of service by mail following the instructions in Chapter 6, Section G. Have the person who served the papers sign the proof of service. Make two or three copies, and take or send them to the court at least one week before the hearing date. If you have the original signed Notice of Hearing, also file it with the court.

7. Call the Court to Find Out the Tentative Decision

In most courts, several days before the scheduled hearing date, your petition is sent to the office of the judge or commissioner. First a clerk reviews your papers to make sure everything is in order. Then the judge makes a tentative ruling on your petition—called a "pre-grant decision"—based solely on the papers you've submitted.

Call the court two days before the hearing is scheduled to find out if the judge has made a tentative decision on your petition. In some counties this information is given on a recorded tape either one or two days before the hearing. In other counties you talk to a clerk. If there is a problem with the petition, the clerk can probably tell you what's wrong and what you need to do to fix it.

If the judge tentatively granted your petition, find out from the clerk whether you need to attend the hearing. In some counties, petitions which are granted by the judge ahead of time are not called at the hearing unless someone shows up to contest them. If you do not have any reason to believe the petition would be contested, you may not need to appear at the hearing. Find out from the clerk how you may get copies of the order you submitted once the judge signs it.

8. Attend the Hearing

We advise that you go to court even if the pre-grant decision was in your favor, just in case someone shows up to contest your petition at the last minute. Bring copies of all your documents, including the proofs of service to the hearing. Let the clerk or bailiff know you are present—especially if the petition was tentatively granted by the judge ahead of time, since you may not then be called automatically in court.

At the hearing, the judge will decide whether to allow the case to be transferred. In almost all instances, this is a formality, since there are good reasons to have the case transferred. The judge may simply grant and sign the Order for Transfer of Guardianship Proceeding without asking you any questions. However, the judge may want additional information from you. For example, she may want to make sure you and the minor have moved to the new residence permanently, rather than just staying there for a few months.

Make sure you get a signed copy of the Order for Transfer of Guardianship Proceeding before you leave the court. If an agency requires proof that the case will be transferred to a different court, you may need to show a copy of the signed order.

9. Old Court Transfers Case and Charges Estate Transfer Fees

After the Order for Transfer of Guardianship Proceeding is granted, the court from which the case is being transferred will arrange to have the file transferred to the new court, and transferring fees will be charged to the minor's estate (PC §2216(b)). A few days after the order is granted, call the clerk of the old court to find out when the transfer will be completed.

10. Contact the New Court and Pay Transfer Fees

After the date the transfer should have taken place, call the clerk of the new court and find out if the case was transferred. You will have to pay the new court the same filing fee that would be required if you had filed an original petition there. These fees may be reimbursed by the estate.

If you seek waiver of those fees on the basis that you and the estate can't afford them, you'll have to fill out documents and file them with the new court. (See Chapter 3, Section F). Ask if you will be sent a document in the mail giving you the new case number, or if you can simply get it over the phone. You will need the new case number for any further contact you may have with the new court.

F. Reimbursements and Compensation of the Guardian

WITH COURT APPROVAL, a guardian of the minor's estate or person and estate may be reimbursed or paid for:
- Expenses incurred personally in taking care of a minor or the minor's estate; and
- Time spent taking care of a minor or the minor's estate.[9]

1. Guardianship Expenses

A guardian of a minor's estate is not personally responsible for paying the estate's expenses. The guardian normally is permitted to hire competent professional help—an accountant and perhaps an investment advisor as needed, as long as the expense is reasonably related to the size of the estate. A guardian may also hire an attorney to represent either the minor or her estate, but prior approval from the court should be obtained first.

Typically, the guardian of a minor's estate—or person and estate—may be reimbursed for:

---

[9]It is not common for a court to grant a guardian compensation for taking care of a minor, unless there are extraordinary circumstances. Usually, courts only grant guardianship of a minor's person if the proposed guardian is willing to take on the responsibilities and demands of acting as the minor's parent, so they will not allow compensation for the responsibility.

- Money of her own which she paid for the benefit of the minor's estate.[10]
- Expenses incurred for the support, maintenance and education of the ward, if the guardianship is for the estate and person. This includes maintaining and repairing the place where the minor lives (PC §2457).
- Paying the minor's or estate's debts, if proven to the court to be legitimate and correct.
- The collection, care and administration of the minor's estate (PC §2430(a)(4)).

You should consult an attorney if you have incurred such expenses, or anticipate doing so. (See Chapter 13.)

2. Reimbursement of Court Costs and Bond Premiums

You do not need court approval to reimburse yourself for official court costs paid to the county clerk to obtain the guardianship of the minor's estate. You can simply pay yourself back out of the assets of the estate, and then indicate these expenditures on the accountings you file with the court. You may also reimburse yourself for amounts paid as premiums on your bond. Remember to keep receipts and records of all expenditures and reimbursements for filing with the court in an accounting.

3. Compensation for a Guardian's Time

In some situations, you may be eligible for reasonable compensation from the estate for your services. This would probably be given in situations where you have spent a lot of time tending to the affairs of the estate. To receive compensation, you must petition the court for an order granting compensation. The amount of compensation is typically fixed by local court rule or practice, and usually amounts to a certain percentage of the overall estate. The court may also authorize periodic payments to the guardian for services (PC §2643). The guardian would need to document reasons why compensation should be granted.

You may petition the court for compensation any time after the Inventory and Appraisement is filed[11] (see Section Chapter 10, Section D2), but it must be no sooner than 90 days after the date Letters of Guardianship were issued (PC §2640). Unless you have prior court approval, you cannot compensate yourself for your services. If you plan to petition the court for compensation for your services, arrange to hire an attorney.[12] (See Chapter 13.)

G. If the Guardianship Is Contested After You are Appointed

AT MANY TIMES IN THIS BOOK, we have advised you to see a lawyer if the guardianship is contested before you are appointed guardian. Although unusual, a guardianship could be contested even after the court appoints a guardian. A guardianship could be contested for many reasons, and in a number of ways. For example, an absent parent could simply show up at your doorstep and say she wants her children back. Or a parent or relative could claim you're not doing your job right, and hire an attorney to take the matter to court to end the guardianship. If someone tries to have you removed or suspended as guardian, there are likely to be many legal complications, so you will need to see a lawyer to help sort them out. (See Chapter 13.)

---

[10] With court approval, the guardian may be allowed interest on the amount paid out at the legal rate payable on judgments (PC §2466). You will need to see a lawyer if you wish to seek this type of reimbursement.

[11] Some courts have local rules which require simultaneous filings of a petition for compensation and the Inventory and Appraisement.

[12] Although you must petition the court for compensation no sooner than 90 days after the date Letters of Guardianship were issued, some courts will not allow the money to be disbursed until one year after Letters of Guardianship were issued, after accounting documents have been filed with the court.

CHAPTER 12

ENDING THE GUARDIANSHIP

A.	Termination of the Guardianship	12/2
B.	Resignation of the Guardian	12/8
C.	Contested Situations: Removal or Suspension of the Guardian	12/9

AS YOU KNOW, a guardian has a number of responsibilities and possible liabilities. A guardian of a minor's person must care for the minor by providing a home, taking care of the minor's physical needs, overseeing his education and perhaps managing his agency benefits. A guardian of a minor's estate must prudently handle the minor's assets, maintain bond if required, keep accurate accounting records and make periodic reports to the court.

Perhaps you turned to this chapter because you're serving as a minor's legal guardian, and no longer want the responsibility. It could be that your personal situation has changed and you're no longer in a position to take care of the minor, his estate, or both. Or maybe you turned to this chapter because a guardianship is no longer needed. Possibly the minor's parents are able to care for him, and you want to step down from the guardian position.

A guardianship—unlike the adult-child relationship between a natural or adoptive parent and child—does not last forever. Since a guardianship is set up to take care of a minor or his assets, it generally ends when the minor reaches age 18.[1] Additionally, with permission of the court, a guardian may step down from her position, which generally means that a different adult will take over the position of guardian.[2] Or with permission of the court, the guardianship itself may be ended ("terminated"). When a guardianship terminates, it no longer exists. This can happen when it isn't needed anymore, usually because one or both of the minor's parents can take care of their child or his estate again.

Example 1: Barbara is guardian of the person of her niece, Cathy. Barbara obtained the guardianship when Cathy's widowed mother—a single parent—went into the army, and needed someone else to have legal guardianship. Cathy's mother finishes her time in the service, and returns to California. She wants to regain custody of her daughter, and is a fine parent. Since Cathy's natural mother will resume caring for her, a guardianship is no longer necessary. Barbara goes to court and obtains a termination of the guardianship using the forms in this book.

Example 2: Andrew is guardian of the person of his granddaughter, Patty. Andrew is in his 70's, and is beginning to have serious health problems. He realizes that taking care of Patty is too much work for him, and discusses the problem with other family members. Patty's aunt is in a position of being able to take over as guardian, and she is glad to help out. With the help of a lawyer, Andrew resigns as guardian, and Patty's aunt is appointed successor guardian.

Example 3: Herman is guardian of the person and estate of his cousin, Johnny. When Herman obtained the guardianship, Johnny's estate consisted of approximately $25,000 cash. With the court's permission, he has used money from the estate to support Johnny, and there is approximately $18,000 left. Herman wants to put the money into a blocked account—meaning that he would need a court order to withdraw it. He wants to end the guardianship of the estate so that he doesn't have to make periodic reports to the court, or continue to pay bond premiums. With the help of an attorney, Herman terminates the guardianship of

---

[1] Guardianship of a minor's estate does not end automatically when the minor reaches age 18. See Section A2 of this chapter.

[2] If there is no appropriate adult willing to take over the guardianship and the guardian can no longer serve, the Juvenile Court or a Public Guardian can be appointed to take over.

Johnny's estate. He continues acting as the guardian of Johnny's person.

Note: If the guardian dies, the guardianship itself does not end. Instead, a successor guardian must be appointed. If you are concerned about what will happen to the minor if you die before the minor reaches age 18, you may want to do some estate planning. (See Chapter 1, Section E2a.)

A. Termination of the Guardianship

WHEN A GUARDIANSHIP TERMINATES, it no longer exists. Guardianships of the person may terminate automatically, or they may be ended earlier if the guardian or another interested person files papers with the court and obtains a judge's permission. Guardianships of a minor's estate require filing special forms with the court and a court appearance before they terminate.

1. Automatic Termination of a Guardianship of a Minor's Person

A guardianship of the minor's person terminates automatically when the minor:
- Is legally adopted;
- Reaches age 18;
- Marries;[3] or
- Dies.

If any of these occurs, the guardianship relationship legally terminates. There is no need to go to court to obtain an order—the guardianship ends automatically.

2. Termination of a Guardianship of a Minor's Estate

A guardianship of the minor's estate terminates when:
- The estate is used up; or
- The minor reaches age 18; or
- The minor dies.

A guardianship of the minor's estate does not terminate if the minor marries or is adopted, even though guardianship of the minor's person terminates automatically when either of those happens.

When the estate is used up, or the minor reaches age 18 or dies, the former guardian is required to file a "final account" with the court, itemizing how money was spent and received on the minor's behalf, and what property remains in the estate. After the court approves the final account, the remaining property in the estate must be turned over to the minor or the legal representative of the deceased minor's estate. This procedure is beyond the scope of this book. (See Chapter 13 for information on finding lawyers and doing your own research.)

3. How to Terminate Guardianship of a Minor's Person

The guardian, minor, parent, or other interested person may request that a court order put an end to a guardianship. The forms in this section should be used if one or both of the minor's parents can resume parental duties, making a legal guardian unnecessary. These forms should only be used if the minor will not be in any danger by returning to the care of the parent.

a. Call the Court

Call the court and say you're filing a Petition for Termination of Guardianship. Find out if you can obtain a hearing date over the phone. If you can get a hearing date, obtain one at least 25 days away, since you'll need to have papers served at least 20 days before that date. If you can't get the hearing date now, you will get one when you file your papers with the court. You're now ready to complete the forms required.

b. Complete Petition for Termination of Guardianship

In this petition, you tell the court why the guardianship case should be terminated.

---

[3] A minor under age 18 may marry with the consent of the guardian, if the superior court approves, following premarital counseling. (CC § 4101).

CAPTION: PETITION FOR TERMINATION OF GUARDIANSHIP

Fill in the caption following the general instructions in Chapter 3, Section D1.

Item 1: In the blanks, fill in your name and the minor's name exactly as they appear on the original issued Letters of Guardianship.

Item 2: Fill in the date you were appointed guardian. This is on the original issued Letters of Guardianship.

Item 3: In your own words, tell why a guardianship was necessary when you filed your petition. For example: "The minor's mother was hospitalized for drug addiction, and the minor's father is unknown and has never had contact with her," or "The minor's father is dead. When the guardianship petition was filed, the minor's mother was entering the U.S. Army, and could not have legal custody of her son."

Item 4: In your own words, tell why a guardianship is no longer necessary. For example: "The minor's mother has recovered fully, and is now able to resume caring for her daughter. Copies of written statements by her doctor and psychologist are attached to this petition," or "The minor's mother was honorably discharged from the U.S. Army on 1/11/90, has returned to California, and wishes to resume caring for her son."

Item 5: In your own words, tell why it would be best for the minor for the guardianship to end. For example: "The minor wants to live with his mother, and she can provide a stable family life for him," or "The minor resumed living with his father in Los Angeles, California three months ago, and is happy to be reunited. His father has remarried and is providing a stable family life for him."

Item 6: In this item, list the names and addresses of the minor's close relatives. Follow the instructions for listing these relatives covered in Item 18 of the Petition for Appointment of Guardian of Minor in Chapter 5, Section A.

Item 7: In addition to the relatives listed in Item 6 just above, anyone who has filed a document with the court requesting special notice of further hearings must get a copy of this petition. If you aren't sure whether someone filed a request for special notice, call the court. Give the clerk the case name and file number, and ask her to pull the file and see if special notice was requested. (See Chapter 11, Section D2.) If so, get the names and addresses of anyone who filed a request for special notice.

Item 7a: If no request for special notice was filed, check this box.

Item 7b: If special notice was filed any time after you filed your initial guardianship papers, check this box and in the space provided fill in the name and address of each person who requested the special notice.

Item 8: In the blank, fill in the full name of the minor exactly as it appears in Item 1.

Sign and date the form in the spaces indicated, and print or type your name.

PARTY WITHOUT AN ATTORNEY *(Name and Address):* MURRAY ARTHUR BART 5 Sidewalk Street Los Angeles, CA 90053 In Pro Per	TELEPHONE NO: 213/555-1212	FOR COURT USE ONLY
NAME OF COURT: LOS ANGELES SUPERIOR COURT STREET ADDRESS: 111 North Hill Street MAILING ADDRESS: P.O. Box 151 CITY AND ZIP CODE: Los Angeles, CA 90053 BRANCH NAME:		

GUARDIANSHIP OF THE PERSON OF (NAME):

SUZANNA GINGER GERARD   MINOR

PETITION FOR TERMINATION OF GUARDIANSHIP	CASE NUMBER: 2020

1. Petitioner (name): __MURRAY ARTHUR BART__ is the duly appointed, qualified and acting guardian of the person of __SUZANNA GINGER GERARD__.

2. Petitioner has been acting as guardian since __April 12__, 19__89__.

3. At the time of appointment, a guardianship was necessary for the following reason(s):
   Suzanna's father is unknown. Her mother could not care for her because she was entering the armed services.

4. It is no longer necessary that the ward have a guardianship for the following reason(s):
   Suzanna's mother, Elsa Gerard, received an honorable discharge from the army on August 22, 1990. Suzanna has been living with her since September 2, 1990.

5. The best interests of the ward require termination of the guardianship for the following reason(s):
   Suzanna is happy living with her mother, who is able to provide her with the care she needs. She has returned to the elementary school she started attending. Her mother can provide excellent parenting.

6. The names, residence addresses and relationships of the ward's father, mother, spouse and all relatives within the second degree of the ward so far as known to petitioner are as follows:
   a. Father: __Unknown__
   b. Mother: __Elsa Gerard, 8 Skateboard Lane, Los Angeles, CA 90053__
   c. Spouse: __None__
   d. __Maternal grandmother: Rose Bart, 2 Scarborough, Cleveland, OH 44118__
   e. ☒ List of names and addresses continued as Attachment 6.

7. A request for special notice:
   a. ☒ has not been filed
   b. ☐ has been filed, and notice of hearing on this petition will be given by law to: _____

8. Petitioner requests an order terminating the guardianship of the person of __SUZANNA GINGER GERARD__.

I declare under penalty of perjury under the laws of the State of California that the foregoing is true and correct.

Date: 9/8/90

MURRAY ARTHUR BART   *(signed)* Murray Arthur Bart
........(TYPE OR PRINT NAME)........   (SIGNATURE OF PETITIONER)

PETITION FOR TERMINATION OF GUARDIANSHIP

c. Complete (Proposed) Order for Termination of Guardianship

Before the guardianship proceeding can be terminated, a judge must sign an order allowing this to happen.

CAPTION: ORDER FOR TERMINATION OF GUARDIANSHIP

Fill in the caption following the general instructions in Chapter 3, Section D1.

Item 1: In this item, give information about when the hearing will be held, and who will attend. If there are any changes or additions, they may be filled in at the hearing by the judge or clerk.

Item 1a: This item is left blank, unless you know the name of the judge or commissioner who will be hearing the guardianship case. If so, fill in the name.

Item 1b: If you obtained information from the clerk about the hearing date and location, fill this in in the spaces provided.

Item 1c: Check this box. Fill in your full first, middle and last names.

Item 1d: Check this box. Then after the words "Attorney for petitioner (name)," fill in your full first, middle and last names, followed by the words "appearing In Pro Per."

Item 1e: Ordinarily this item is left blank, except for the rare situation where the minor has an attorney representing him independently. If he does, check the box and fill in the attorney's name, address and phone number.

Item 2a: Check the first box before the words "All notices required by law have been given." This means you will be having all of the people listed in Items 6 and 7 of the Petition for Termination of Guardianship served with notice of the termination hearing.

Item 2b: Fill in the minor's name exactly as it appears on the original issued Letters of Guardianship.

Item 2c: Leave this item blank.

Item 3: Fill in the minor's name exactly as it appears on the original issued Letters of Guardianship. Leave the last line blank. A date will be filled in by the judge.

Leave the date and judge's signature line blank. These will be filled in at the hearing.

d. Complete Notice of Hearing

Complete a Notice of Hearing following the instructions in Chapter 5, Section C, with these exceptions:

Item 1: After the words "(representative capacity, if any)," enter the words "guardian of the person." Just below this, after the words "has filed (specify)," enter the words "Petition for Termination of Guardianship."

Item 3: Fill in the information in the box about the date, time and place of the hearing, if you obtained these over the phone. Otherwise, have the clerk fill in this information when you file your papers with the court.

e. Copy and File Documents with the Court

You are now ready to copy the documents. Following the instructions in Chapter 3, Section E1, make at least two or three photocopies of each document, depending on whether the court requires an additional copy. In addition, make one copy of the Notice of Hearing and Petition for Termination of Guardianship for each person listed in Items 6 and 7 of the Petition for Termination of Guardianship.

File the documents following the instructions in Chapter 3, Section E2. There should not be a filing fee for the petition. If you have not already obtained a hearing date, get one from the court clerk. You may either request one in person if you take in your papers, or in a letter to the court. Remember that the hearing date should be at least 25 days away to give you enough time to get the papers served as required. Make sure all copies of the Notice of Hearing have the date, time and place listed. If the clerk gives you the original signed Notice of Hearing, keep it in a safe place. You will need to file it with the court after everyone entitled to notice has been served.

PARTY WITHOUT AN ATTORNEY *(Name and Address)*:	TELEPHONE NO:	FOR COURT USE ONLY
MURRAY ARTHUR BART 5 Sidewalk Street Los Angeles, CA 90053 *In Pro Per*	213/555-1212	

NAME OF COURT: LOS ANGELES SUPERIOR COURT
STREET ADDRESS: 111 North Hill Street
MAILING ADDRESS: P.O. Box 151
CITY AND ZIP CODE: Los Angeles, CA 90053
BRANCH NAME:

GUARDIANSHIP OF THE PERSON:

SUZANNA GINGER GERARD   MINOR

ORDER FOR TERMINATION OF GUARDIANSHIP

CASE NUMBER: 2020

---

1. The Petition for Termination of Guardianship came on for hearing as follows (check boxes c, d and e to indicate personal presence):

   a. Judge (name):

   b. Hearing Date: 10/2/90 Time: 9:00 am ☒ Dept: 2   ☒ Div.: 2   ☒ Room: 2

   c. ☒ Petitioner (name):   MURRAY ARTHUR BART

   d. ☒ Attorney for petitioner (name):   MURRAY ARTHUR BART, appearing In Pro Per

   e. ☐ Attorney for ward (name, address and telephone):

2. THE COURT FINDS

   a. ☒ all notices required by law have been given.

   b. The guardianship of the person of ___SUZANNA GINGER GERARD___ is no longer necessary.

   c. Termination of the guardianship is in the best interests of the ward.

3. THE COURT ORDERS that the guardianship of the person of ___SUZANNA GINGER GERARD___ is terminated effective _____.

Dated: ....   _____
                                                            (JUDGE OF THE SUPERIOR COURT)

NP   **ORDER FOR TERMINATION OF GUARDIANSHIP**

Have Papers Served at Least 20 Days Before Hearing Date, Complete and File Proof of Service

Have copies of the Notice of Hearing and Petition for Termination of Guardianship served by mail on each person listed in Items 6 and 7 of the Petition for Termination of Guardianship at least 20 days before the scheduled hearing date. Instructions for having documents served by mail are contained in Chapter 6, Section G. If you don't have papers served in time, you must have the hearing continued. (See Chapter 6, Section B5.)

Finally, complete a proof of service by mail following the instructions in Chapter 6, Section G1a. Have the person who served the papers sign the proof of service. Make two or three copies, and take or send them to the court at least one week before the hearing date. If you have the original signed Notice of Hearing, also file it with the court.

Call the Court to Find Out the Tentative Decision

In most courts, several days before the scheduled hearing date, your petition is sent to the office of the judge or commissioner. First a clerk reviews your papers to make sure everything is in order. Then the judge makes a tentative ruling on your petition—called a "pre-grant decision"—based solely on the papers you've submitted.

Call the court two days before the hearing is scheduled to find out if the judge has made a tentative decision on your petition. In some counties this information is given on a recorded tape either one or two days before the hearing. In other counties you talk to a clerk. If there is a problem with the petition, the clerk can probably tell you what's wrong and what you need to do to fix it.

If the judge tentatively granted your petition, find out from the clerk whether you need to attend the hearing. In some counties, petitions which are granted by the judge ahead of time are not called at the hearing unless someone shows up to contest them. If you do not have any reason to believe the petition would be contested, you may not need to appear at the hearing. Find out from the clerk how you may get copies of the order you submitted once the judge signs it.

h. Attend the Hearing

We advise that you go to court even if the pre-grant decision was in your favor, just in case someone shows up to contest your petition at the last minute. Bring copies of all your documents, including the proofs of service to the hearing. Let the clerk or bailiff know you are present—especially if the petition was tentatively granted by the judge ahead of time, since it may not then be called automatically in court.

The minor should attend the hearing with you. If the minor's parent will resume taking care of her child, the parent should attend the hearing as well. If the pre-grant decision was in favor of your petition, immediately let the clerk or bailiff know that you're present, as the judge may skip over your case entirely unless it is contested.

At the hearing, the judge will decide whether to allow the guardianship to be terminated. The judge may simply grant and sign the Order for Termination of Guardianship without asking any questions. However, the judge may ask you for additional information —questioning you or the minor's natural parent about why the guardianship is no longer needed. He may ask the minor if she would rather return to live with her parent or remain with you. The judge may question you, the minor and the natural parent about how the natural parent's situation has changed. The judge will want to make sure the parent is now able to care for the child, even though she couldn't before.

It's possible that the judge could require an investigation before allowing the guardianship to end. If so, he will instruct you on whether and when you must return to court. (Investigations are covered in Chapter 8.) If the judge will not permit the guardianship to end, you will need the help of a lawyer. (See Chapter 13.)

B. Resignation of the Guardian

A GUARDIAN CANNOT SIMPLY DECIDE TO STOP SERVING in that role without first getting an order from the court allowing him to "resign." If a guardian stops acting as guardian without a court's approval, he is still responsible for all the duties and liabilities of a guardian. However, when a guardian resigns with court approval, the guardianship continues and the court names a new person to step in and take over the guardian's duties. Some common reasons a guardian would seek permission from the court to resign are:

- The guardian will be moving out of California and cannot take the minor along, perhaps because work requires moving overseas to a place which is not safe for children;[4] or
- The guardian can't handle the job any longer for personal reasons, perhaps because of very poor health or an inability to handle a difficult minor, and another non-parent is better suited and willing to take on the responsibility. (If a natural parent wants to resume caring for his child, a guardianship may not be needed any longer. See Section A of this chapter.)

Judges do not generally let guardians resign without good reason, and will be reluctant or unwilling to let you resign unless someone else is available to take over. In situations where a guardian must resign quickly, a temporary guardian is sometimes named to take the responsibilities before the next regular guardian can be appointed. In very rare, extreme cases where no one can take over and it would be detrimental for the minor to stay with the present guardian, the court might order the Juvenile Court or a Public Guardian to take over.

The process of resigning as guardian is beyond the scope of this book and will require the help of an attorney. (See Chapter 13.)

C. Contested Situations: Removal or Suspension of the Guardian

A GUARDIAN MAY BE "REMOVED," meaning she is taken out of the position of guardian by court order. When a guardian is removed, the guardianship itself may continue if the court names a successor guardian. Pending a hearing on whether the guardian is to be removed, a guardian's powers can be "suspended," meaning she temporarily does not have the right to act as the minor's legal guardian.

A proceeding to remove a guardian can be initiated by the ward, a parent, or any interested person. This is done by filing and serving the guardian with a copy of a petition for removal of guardian. The procedures for defending against this are beyond the scope of this book. If you are ever served with a petition for removal, see a lawyer right away. (See Chapter 13.)

1. Removal of the Guardian of a Minor's Person

A guardian of a minor's person can be removed for any of the following reasons:
- Failing to perform duties—namely, failing to adequately care for the minor;
- Any other reason which the court determines is detrimental to the minor;
- Involuntarily placing the minor in a mental health facility, subjecting her to involuntary medical treatment, allowing the prescription for or administration of unauthorized experimental drugs or convulsive treatment, or sterilizing the minor, without obtaining prior court approval;
- Being convicted of a felony; or
- Gross immorality. The definition of "gross immorality" would be up to a judge. However, this might include being involved in serious drug use, or being suspected of child abuse.

---

[4] You can move the minor permanently out of the state if you obtain a court order beforehand. (See Chapter 11, Section C2.)

Removal of the Guardian of a Minor's Estate

guardian of a minor's estate can be removed for any the following reasons:
- Being negligent in handling the minor's funds;
- Failing to file the appropriate court documents when required, including the "Inventory and Appraisement" and periodic financial accountings (see Chapter 10, Section D);
- Failing to perform duties, including keeping track of the minor's receipts and expenditures of funds;
- Having a financial interest adverse to the minor, such as buying a company the ward owns for less than it's worth;
- Bankruptcy or insolvency;
- "Gross immorality," such as embezzling the minor's money; or
- Being convicted of a felony.

CHAPTER 13

LAWYERS AND LEGAL RESEARCH

A.	Finding Free Legal Help	13/1
B.	What an Independent Paralegal Can Do	13/2
C.	Finding and Hiring a Lawyer	13/2
D.	Doing Your Own Legal Research	13/5

THIS CHAPTER PROVIDES USEFUL INFORMATION if you need to hire a lawyer or other legal professional, or if you need to do legal research beyond the scope of this book. As noted several times, you should consult an attorney if the guardianship is contested at any point.

Although seeking a lawyer's help isn't essential, a lawyer who has experience in what to say and how to say it may be more skillful than you are in arguing why you should be appointed or retained as guardian.

If your guardianship is not contested, and you just want someone to prepare legal forms or check your work—but not provide legal advice—you may be able to save considerable money by using an independent paralegal instead of a lawyer. (See Section B in this chapter.)

A. Finding Free Legal Help

MANY PROGRAMS THAT USED TO OFFER FREE LEGAL HELP have dwindled in the past few years. But if you have a low income, you may be able to find free legal help with your guardianship. Although the qualifications for "low income" vary from county to county, you may be eligible for free legal help if you qualify for public assistance, or your income is in the range set out in the court fee waiver chart in Chapter 3, Section F1.

1. Legal Aid Offices

Most counties have a legal aid office (often called legal services or legal assistance) available to low-income people for free or low-cost advice, consultation and sometimes representation. As a result of funding cutbacks, not all legal aid offices handle guardianship cases, but you may get a referral from them for free legal assistance, or to attorneys who offer reasonably priced services. To find a local legal aid office, check in the telephone book's white pages under "Legal Aid" or "Legal Services," the yellow pages under "Attorneys," or ask the clerk at your court.

2. County Bar Associations (Volunteer Legal Service Programs)

Some county bar associations have established their own legal service programs or corporations to help low-income people with legal problems by providing free or low-cost legal services.

Increasingly, county bar associations are becoming aware of the need for assistance in obtaining guardianships. For example, the Volunteer Legal Services Corp. run by the Alameda County Bar Association holds a guardianship clinic once a month for low-income people. The clinic provides an overview of guardianships of the person, assists in completing the necessary forms and helps people prepare to represent themselves in court.

Check with your local bar association for information on available legal services and to find out whether your income level qualifies you for assistance. To find a listing for the bar association in your county, check in the phone book or with directory assistance.

3. Resources for Minors

An organization that gives legal information referrals both within and outside the Bay Area, as well as represents minors, is Legal Services for Children, Inc., 1254 Market Street, 3rd Floor, San Francisco, California 94102; telephone (415) 863-3762.

Some county bar associations also assist minors in guardianships and related legal matters. (See Section A2, above.)

B. What an Independent Paralegal Can Do

IT IS COMMON KNOWLEDGE in the legal field that the real experts in preparing legal forms are lawyers' assistants, often called "legal assistants" or "paralegals." Unfortunately, because of strict laws forbidding non-lawyers from practicing law, a consumer typically could not work directly with paralegals employed in law offices—instead, the law office itself had to be hired, at lawyer's rates.

Now, however, an increasing number of paralegals are striking out on their own—as "independent paralegals"—and offering direct assistance to people who are undertaking their own legal tasks.[1] Simple procedures such as uncontested divorces, name changes, bankruptcies and child support modifications are all routinely handled by independent paralegals at a much lower cost than a lawyer would charge. Paralegals cannot give you legal advice, and they cannot represent you in court. They can, however, assist you in preparing your own guardianship documents. If you work with an independent paralegal, you should get your forms typed, and can probably obtain some important tips on local court rules. But you must go to court on your own and represent yourself.

---

[1] For a history of independent paralegals, see *The Independent Paralegal's Handbook*, by Ralph Warner (Nolo Press).

To find independent paralegals in your area, check in the yellow pages of the telephone book under "Paralegal" or "Typing Services." Or you may be able to get a referral to an independent paralegal in your area by contacting:

National Association for Independent Paralegals
635 5th St. West
Sonoma, California 95476
(707) 935-4141
(800) 542-0034

C. Finding and Hiring a Lawyer

LAWYERS—ALSO CALLED ATTORNEYS—are the only people allowed to give legal advice in California. Lawyers must be licensed by passing the California bar examination, which tests their knowledge of different areas of law. Almost all lawyers have gone to law school, but a few have followed special self-study courses and passed the bar without attending law school.

Lawyers who work on their own are called "sole practitioners." But lawyers often set up businesses or partnerships in which they work together, which are called "law firms" or "law offices." Law firms often handle a variety of legal matters, and individual lawyers in the firms tend to specialize in one or a few fields. When you hire a lawyer, it is important that you find someone who specializes in the type of law in which you need help. For example, a corporate or criminal defense lawyer, although backed by many years of legal experience, may well know nothing at all about how to set up a guardianship.

1. What a Lawyer Can Do

It may come as a surprise to realize that lawyers are simply people you hire to work for you. So you're best off hiring someone you trust will work competently for you. There are a variety of ways you can choose to use a lawyer's services, depending on your needs.

Consultation and Advice

You can often arrange to meet with a lawyer to discuss a problem and whether the lawyer can help with it. Frequently these initial consultations are free or relatively reasonably priced. For example, a fee of about $75 to $125 for a consultation is probably common, depending on how long it takes. Find out the consultation fee before you go in. If the fee seems too high, you and a lawyer may be able to agree on a lower price, or shop around until you find an attorney you can afford. Lawyers who give free legal consultations naturally hope to get new clients from the meetings.

At the consultation, a lawyer should listen to the details of your situation, analyze it for you and advise you on your best plan of action. Bring a list of questions you want answered, and make sure the lawyer answers them in a way you understand. Ideally, she will give you more than just conclusions, but will educate you about your whole situation and the alternatives from which you can make your own choices. If you are willing to put in some time and work of your own, using a lawyer as a consultant may be the most worthwhile for you. Talk is relatively cheap and may allow you to avoid more serious—and more expensive—problems later.

Contested Guardianships

Occasionally, guardianships end up being contested in court. Having a lawyer handle a court case is very expensive. Unfortunately, archaic language, forms and courtroom procedures make it difficult for nonlawyers to represent themselves except in Small Claims Court.[2] If you hire a lawyer to represent you in court, you can help make the courtroom procedures less baffling by learning what happens there and why. Some lawyers encourage willing clients to help out with some of the legwork of a case, such as by gathering and organizing documents, which can keep legal fees down.

---

[2]Small Claims Courts can only be used to seek limited amounts of money. They are not used for guardianship proceedings.

c. Checking Your Work

Some people are comfortable preparing all their own guardianship papers following the instructions in this book, but want the security that comes with having someone experienced check the work. You may be able to find a lawyer to do this, but that will probably require shopping around a bit. If you do find a lawyer who is experienced in guardianships, and is willing to check your work, make sure you agree on an hourly rate or flat fee in advance.

2. Finding a Lawyer

Finding a lawyer you trust and who also charges reasonable prices is not always an easy task. There is always the realistic fear that by just picking a name out of the telephone book you may get an attorney who is unsympathetic, or perhaps will charge too much. It is natural to feel a little intimidated, but it may be helpful to remember that a lawyer is simply someone you hire to do legal work for you.

Here are some suggestions for how to find lawyers. We do not recommend one or another source. You may need to check around until you find someone you feel comfortable hiring.

a. Group Legal Practices

A new but rapidly growing aspect of California law practice is the group legal practice program. Some groups, including unions, employers and consumer action groups offer plans to their members for legal work at rates substantially lower than is available through most private practitioners. If you are a member of such a plan, check with it first if you need a lawyer. However, beware of plans which do no more than refer you to a local attorney who will supposedly give you a good price.

b. Legal Clinics

Some law offices specialize in mass-handling simple types of cases such as guardianships which use standardized forms and are relatively straightforward. These firms sometimes use the word "legal clinic" in their title, and usually advertise heavily. Two large

California clinics are Hyatt Legal Services and Jacoby & Meyers Law Offices. Legal clinics charge approximately $400 to $500 for an uncontested guardianship, plus court costs and other fees such as process servers' and court investigator's fees. Be sure that the advertised or quoted price includes everything you think it does.

c. Legal Insurance

So-called legal insurance plans are marketed by companies such as Bank of America, Montgomery Ward, and others. These plans often are offered by mail to credit card customers, and in some cases are sold door-to-door. Many of these plans offer several free legal consultations, a simple will and some letter writing for a monthly charge of less than $10. But when it comes to more complicated matters, including guardianships, you often get a list of local lawyers who will handle the problem at a supposedly discounted fee. The danger is that the free services become a sort of feeder mechanism to produce paying clients. As with any other consumer transaction, you should take the responsibility to carefully check out legal insurance by finding out exactly what you get for your money.

d. Private Attorneys

If you have hired a lawyer who served you well for some other purpose (estate planning, divorce, personal injury), that lawyer may be a good person to contact. If she does not handle guardianships, she may be able to refer you to another good attorney who specializes in them. Or a trustworthy friend, relative or co-worker may know a reliable attorney you can contact.

If you seek help from a lawyer, make sure you find one who has handled guardianships before. This might be a probate attorney[3] or an attorney specializing in family law. These suggestions should make your search a little easier:

- Call referral panels set up by local bar associations. There is often a small fee if you meet with the lawyer for an initial consultation. You may get a good referral from these panels, but be sure to question the lawyer whose name you are given about her experience in handling guardianship cases. Be aware that some lawyers list their names on referral panels because they don't have enough business, or are new and inexperienced. Referral panels claim to screen the people they list—but many do not.
- Consult the ads in the classified section of the newspaper or phone book under "Attorneys." This often gives you a good idea as to price and range of services offered.
- Shop around by calling different law offices and briefly explaining your situation and the kind of help you want. Try to talk to a lawyer personally to get an idea of how friendly and sympathetic he is to your concerns. Ask how much it would cost for a visit, or if an initial consultation would be free.
- Bear in mind that a lawyer does not have to work downtown or in a fancy office to do good legal work. As a general rule, lawyers in big cities and those working in large firms are pricier than lawyers who work in small towns or smaller firms.

3. Agreeing on Legal Fees

Unless attorneys offer free initial consultations, their hourly rates generally range from $75 to $125. Average hourly rates often are slightly higher, with some lawyers charging up to $350 per hour. However, there is seldom any reason to pay a high-end fee, since guardianships are not a difficult area of the law. It is common for people to negotiate and agree on fees before they hire a lawyer—many lawyers are willing to adjust their fees.

Whether you simply hire an attorney to check your paperwork, or to handle the case from beginning to end, you and he should agree on the fee to be charged before any work begins. You might be able to set a flat fee for the entire guardianship procedure, rather than paying an hourly rate. That way, if the attorney is slow in preparing documents or you have to wait at court, you won't have your wallet slowly emptying as the clock ticks on.

Regardless of the fee arrangement, you must pay for court fees, service of process and other fees such as costs of an investigation. Either the attorney will ask

---

[3]You might find a probate lawyer who has handled a number of conservatorships. The forms for guardianships and conservatorships are almost identical, so a lawyer with conservatorship experience should be sufficient.

ou to pay these costs up front, or will advance the costs and bill you later for reimbursement. Most guardianships will require well over $150 in costs since the court filing fees for the guardianship are often over $100, and any fees for a court investigation or service of process will be an additional expense.

Make sure you understand what law office costs you will be expected to pay. For example, some lawyers charge clients for the costs of each photocopy made for a case, as well as postage and long distance telephone calls, while other lawyers include these office costs in their hourly fees.

Lawyers sometimes require a "retainer fee" before they'll start working on your case—usually of at least several hundred dollars. When costs and lawyers' fees are billed, they are deducted from this retainer. If fees exceed the retainer, you are billed for the excess. But if the retainer is more money than the legal fees and costs, you are given a refund. You should be sent bills regularly, regardless of whether or not you give the lawyer a retainer fee. If you have any questions about fees, you can ask the attorney for copies of all bills and records of time spent on your case.

Get the Fee Agreement in Writing

In California, an attorney must give you an agreement in writing if the total amount you pay, including all attorneys' fees, is likely to be more than $1,000. This amount is unlikely in a normal uncontested guardianship case, but it is always a good idea to get the fee arrangement in writing. The law also requires that the written contract clearly explain all charges and services, and that it set out both the lawyer's and client's responsibilities.

Fees tend to be the biggest cause for misunderstanding between a lawyer and client, and a written agreement can go a long way in preventing problems. Make sure you understand the fee agreement before you sign it. In addition to the lawyers' fees, get a clear picture of what costs you will be paying.

D. Doing Your Own Legal Research

DURING THE COURSE OF OBTAINING A GUARDIANSHIP, you may have questions this book does not answer. If you need additional legal information, can't get the answer from a court clerk and don't wish to consult a lawyer, you will need to do some research on your own.

If you decide to delve into the world of legal research, we recommend that you obtain a copy of *Legal Research: How to Find and Understand the Law* by Steve Elias (Nolo Press). This hands-on guide to the law library addresses the research methods discussed here in much more detail and will answer most of the questions that are likely to arise in the course of your research.

1. Citations in This Book

Throughout this book you will encounter numbered references to California law. These are called "citations," and most refer to a set of statutes called the California Probate Code, which is abbreviated as PC. Thus, PC §2551(b) means Probate Code Section 2551, Subsection (b). Another group of references is to Probate Policy Manuals or Memoranda, which set out local rules for specific courts. (See Section D3 below). Citations are included in this book so that you can look them up in the law library if you want. The box that follows explains most citations used in this book.

LEGAL CITATIONS

Abbreviation	Legal Reference
CC	Civil Code
CCP	Code of Civil Procedure
CRC	California Rules of Court
EC	Education Code
PC	Probate Code
W&I	Welfare & Institutions Code
USC	United States Code

Right now these references may seem like gobbledygook to you. But once you've visited the local law library, you'll quickly become familiar with them.

2. How to Do Legal Research

Here is an overview of the steps you'll take to do legal research:

    a. Find a law library.

    b. If you want to find a general discussion of your issue, you will need to check in an encyclopedia, form book, or practice manual (called a background resource). Use the background resource to find references to relevant statutes. (**Note**: If you want to look up specific statutes and already have the citations, you do not need to complete this step.)

    c. Locate and read the statutes.

    d. Locate and read cases that interpret the statutes.

Now that you have a general idea of the steps involved in legal research, let's take a more detailed look at each of them.

a. Find a Law Library

Each California county must have a law library that is open to the public without charge. In larger counties, the law library is fully staffed and maintains a relatively complete collection of books. In smaller counties, the law library may be a small room off the court clerk's office that is only open during certain hours.

Regardless of the size of the library, you will find most law librarians willing and even pleased to give you a hand, as long as you don't ask them to answer legal questions or interpret what you find in the books, since this might be interpreted as practicing law. If you encounter any difficulty because you are not a lawyer, you may need to give a gentle reminder that the law library is paid for out of court filing fees, and that the California constitution requires public access.

Note: Some local public libraries also have quite extensive collections of law and legal research books. Before making a special trip to the law library, you may first want to check with the public library.

b. Consult Background Resources

If you do not have a particular legal citation, or need help with documents or procedures not covered in this book, look in background resources materials which provide general information about the law. These include encyclopedias, form books and practice manuals.

Here are several background resources which you can consult when you begin researching the law and procedures of guardianships:

- *California Family Law Practice and Procedure* (Christian E. Markey, Jr., Editorial Consultant, published by Matthew Bender). This book provides information and samples of guardianship forms and procedures.

- *California Forms of Pleading and Practice* (published by Matthew Bender). If you want guidance on a particular procedure not covered in this book, turn to this attorneys' form book. Look in the "G" or "Guardianship" volume of this multi-volume set to find the information you need.

- *California Probate Procedure* (by Arthur K. Marshall, published by Parker & Sons Publications, Inc.). This three-volume set gives a wide variety of information and forms. Volume 1 provides an overview of guardianship law, and provides citations to statutes and case law. It is somewhat dense, but still quite readable. Volume 2 contains Probate Policy Manuals for many counties. If you use this resource, make sure they are most up-to-date. Volume 3 provides checklists and local forms for use in many counties. Again, make sure these forms are the most current.

c. Read the Law

Background resources, including this book, are only discussions about law and procedure, not the law self. That's why background resources provide you with citations to relevant statutes (laws passed by the California legislature) and court interpretations of these laws. Reading these statutes is a crucial step in doing legal research.

In California, guardianships are governed by a group of statutes called the Probate Code. The Probate Code governs the processes described in this book.

You may find statutes in a single volume of the California Probate Code, or in a section of a book which consists of the California Probate Code and other codes (generally these books also have the Civil Code, Evidence Code, Code of Civil Procedure, some Rules of Court and portions of the Government Code). You usually can find these books in a public library.

There also are multi-volume annotated book sets which give the statutes and information about each statute. They have information about the history of each statute—when it was first passed, when different sections were amended, along with citations of cases and very short summaries of cases in which courts interpreted the statute. The case law summaries are by no means complete, and it's hard to tell from them whether they're related to the particular issue you're researching. Read the case yourself rather than relying on the annotation.

You may still find that reading statutes leaves you less than fully enlightened. They tend to be difficult to understand and, sometimes purposely ambiguous. It also helps to read what courts have said about them, and that's the next step.

4. Read Cases

Case law refers to judges' published opinions about a dispute that was resolved in court. These decisions give important information about how a law has been interpreted. If you can find a case decision in which the facts were similar to your situation, you can get some guidance on how a court might decide your case.[4]

---

[4] If you are interested in learning more about how to analyze a case, see *Case Analysis and Fundamentals of Legal Writing* (West Publishing Co., 1979).

3. Probate Policy Manuals or Memoranda

Although all probate courts follow the basic procedures outlined in the Probate Code, most counties have a few special rules of their own. Many counties have small printed pamphlets called Probate Policy Manuals or Memoranda. These pamphlets tell you things such as when particular forms must be presented to the court, what must be included in court documents and where to call for information.

Call the court clerk and find out if the Probate Policy Manual is available through the court. More often than not, you'll need to go to the library to look at them. Some libraries have books which have Probate Policy Manuals for counties throughout California. Make sure that you look at the Probate Policy Manual for the specific county in which you are filing the guardianship. You don't need to be concerned with other counties' rules.

4. Resources for Additional Copies of Judicial Council Forms

Most of the forms needed for a guardianship are Judicial Council forms. (See Chapter 3, Section C1.) If you need additional or updated copies of these forms, you can obtain them either free or for a small fee from the superior court clerk. Or, if you're going to the law library, ask the librarian if they have copies of Judicial Council forms. Some law libraries keep copies in a special binder, which may be kept behind the librarian's desk. Or you can probably photocopy the forms you need from these resources:

- *California Forms of Pleading and Practice—Judicial Council Forms* (published by Matthew Bender). This book contains the official forms published by the California Judicial Council.
- *West's California Judicial Council Forms* (published by West Publishing Company). This softcover book contains official forms published by the California Judicial Council. Check supplements to make sure you're copying the current forms. If the supplement shows an updated form, you'll need to get it from another source, since the supplements are printed on pages much smaller than regular Judicial Council forms.

APPENDIX A

GLOSSARY OF GUARDIANSHIP TERMS

To handle your own guardianship you'll have to make an effort to understand some of the common legal terms you'll run into along the way. The legal profession uses language which is specialized and sometimes difficult to understand. The plain English definitions in this book are geared toward guardianships. If you find yourself branching out in another area of law, these terms might be used slightly differently.

If you come across a confusing term which isn't defined in this glossary or elsewhere in the book, try a regular dictionary, but be sure to read the entire definition, as specialized legal meanings often are listed last. You also can check *Black's Law Dictionary*, available in all law libraries. Don't be intimidated if the definitions there are hard to understand; that book is notoriously confusing to everyone. A law librarian might be helpful if you can't find a satisfactory definition, as long as you don't ask for legal advice or legal interpretation.

ADULT: A person who has attained the age of majority. In California, this is someone who is 18 years of age or older.

APPOINT: When a court gives someone legal authority and responsibility to fulfill particular duties. For example, a judge appoints a guardian.

BENEFITS: Money or other rights to which someone is entitled, such as welfare, Social Security or insurance.

BOND: A document guaranteeing that a certain amount of money or insurance policy will be paid if a guardian of an estate does not perform her legal duties. A bond usually is issued by a surety company.

CALENDAR: Master list kept by a court that shows when cases are scheduled to be heard in court. To calendar (slang, verb) means to schedule a hearing.

CASE: A legal action that is taken to court. When you file your guardianship papers, a new case, with its own case number, is opened.

CHILD: The natural born daughter or son of a parent. Sometimes the term "child" may refer to a minor.

COMMISSIONER: A lawyer appointed by the county's judges to assist in finding facts, hearing testimony and resolving issues. Court commissioners frequently hear guardianship cases and have the same authority as judges to issue opinions in them.

CONTESTED: A hearing or case is contested when someone objects, either in person or in writing.

CONTINUANCE: The postponement of a hearing, trial or other scheduled court appearance. A continuance may be granted for many reasons, including when someone in the case is not prepared, or needs time to seek the advice of an attorney.

COURT: The place where cases are filed and heard. This term might also refer to a judge. For example, you might say that the guardianship was granted by the court, even though a judge actually made the decision.

CUSTODY (LEGAL): The court-ordered right to have legal authority or physical control of a minor about matters such as medical and educational needs.

CUSTODY (PHYSICAL): The charge and control over a minor, usually when the minor is living with someone. This traditionally is a court-ordered right, but the term is sometimes used to refer to informal custody arrangements.

DISCHARGE: To relieve someone of his duties in a given capacity (e.g., to relieve someone of his responsibility as a guardian). This typically occurs when a minor reaches the age of majority, or when a judge allows a guardian to resign.

DISMISS: To stop a legal action before it reaches a legal conclusion (e.g., to stop a guardianship case before a guardian is appointed).

ESTATE: The possessions, property and liabilities belonging to a minor.

ESTATE (GUARDIANSHIP OF): See **GUARDIANSHIP (OF ESTATE)**.

ESTATE PLANNING: The method of designating how and to whom property is to be transferred after death.

EX PARTE: (Pronounced "ex-partay.") Without notice. Ex parte papers that are filed with a court are not served on anyone.

FOSTER PARENTS: Specially-licensed adults who take minors into their home after being removed from their biological parents' home by a court.

GUARDIAN: An adult who has been given the legal right by a court to control and care for a minor or her property.

GUARDIAN AD LITEM: An adult, usually a close relative or attorney, who is appointed solely for the purpose of appearing on behalf of a minor in a civil lawsuit for money. (This book does not cover guardians ad litem.)

GUARDIANSHIP (OF ESTATE): Legal recognition by a court that an adult has legal responsibility for taking care of a minor's property.

GUARDIANSHIP (GENERALLY): Legal recognition by a court that an adult has legal custody of and is responsible for taking care of a minor or her property.

GUARDIANSHIP (OF PERSON): Legal recognition by a court that an adult has legal custody of and is responsible for taking care of a minor, including responsibility for his physical, medical, educational and health needs.

GUARDIANSHIP (TEMPORARY): Legal recognition by a court that an adult has responsibility for a minor or his estate for a specified, limited time.

HEARING: A legal proceeding (other than a trial) which is held before a judge or court commissioner.

IN PRO PER: Someone who is representing herself in a legal proceeding.

INVESTIGATOR (COURT): Someone who is appointed by the court to look into a case. Depending on the court's policies, this would probably be a probation officer, domestic relations investigator or other court-appointed official.

JUDGE: A public official who has legal authority to hear and decide cases in a court.

LETTERS (OF GUARDIANSHIP): A document issued by the court that designates legal authority.

MAJORITY (AGE OF): The age at which a minor legally becomes an adult. In California this is the age of 18.

MATERNAL: Related through blood ties to someone's mother. For example, a maternal uncle would be the brother of one's mother, and a maternal grandmother would be the mother of one's mother.

MINOR: A person who has not attained the age of majority. In California, this is someone under age 18.

NOMINATE: To name someone for an appointment (for example, a parent may nominate a proposed guardian). Someone who has been nominated is called a nominee.

NOTICE (OF HEARING): Written notification of a legal event (such as a trial or a hearing). By law this notification must be given to any person involved or interested in a legal action.

ORDER: Decision rendered by a judge. This may be after a hearing or after you present papers for the judge to consider.

PAPERS: Legal documents.

PATERNAL: Related through blood ties to someone's father. For example, a paternal uncle would be the brother of one's father, and a paternal grandmother would be the mother of one's father.

PERSON (GUARDIANSHIP OF): See **GUARDIANSHIP OF PERSON)**.

PETITION: In the context of this book, an application or request that a guardianship be established, or authority to undertake a procedure be given.

PETITIONER: In the context of this book, the person who files a petition, generally someone who is seeking guardianship.

PROBATE COURT (OR PROBATE DIVISION OF THE SUPERIOR COURT): A division of the court that handles guardianship cases. The probate court also handles other matters, such as conservatorships, distribution of deceased people's assets, and administration of trusts.

PROCESS (SERVICE OF): See **SERVICE OF PROCESS**.

PROPERTY: Assets someone owns—including real estate, personal belongings (furniture, jewelry, clothing), bank accounts, stocks, bonds, interest in a business, the right to receive benefits and a variety of other tangible and non-tangible things.

REMOVE: To take someone out of an appointed position.

RESIGN: To voluntarily give up an appointed position.

SERVICE OF PROCESS: Delivering court papers to a person or organization entitled to know what is happening in a case. There are detailed laws which specify how and by whom papers must be delivered.

SURETY OR SURETY COMPANY: A person or entity that is liable for another's debts. A surety company usually provides insurance for guardianship of an estate in the form of a bond.

SUSPEND: To temporarily stop someone or something, such as a guardian from her duties.

TEMPORARY GUARDIANSHIP: See **GUARDIANSHIP (TEMPORARY)**.

TERMINATE: To end something, such as a guardianship.

WARD: A minor who is in a court-appointed guardianship.[1]

---

[1] In a different context, which is not covered in this book, the term "ward" refers to a minor over whom a juvenile court has assumed authority.

APPENDIX B

HOW TO OBTAIN BIRTH, DEATH AND MARRIAGE CERTIFICATES

To obtain copies of birth or death certificates, you must contact the vital statistics office in the state in which the birth or death took place. Call or write to the vital statistics office, and arrange to obtain and fill out any required application and pay a fee. The fee shouldn't be more than $12.00 for a certified copy of a certificate, and frequently it will be considerably less (often from $3.00 to $6.00). Some vital statistics offices will process the request over the telephone if you supply a credit card number and pay an additional fee (usually around $5.00). Some offices also accept requests made by fax.

To obtain copies of marriage certificates, you may need to send your request to a different address from the vital statistics office listed below. Call or write the vital statistics office to find out if this is the correct address for obtaining copies of marriage certificates, how to obtain an application (if necessary), and what fee is required.

The address and telephone numbers for each of the vital statistics offices in the United States are:

ALABAMA
Alabama Department of Public Health
Bureau of Vital Statistics
State Office Building
501 Dexter Avenue
Montgomery, Alabama 36130-1701
205/261-5033

ALASKA
Bureau of Vital Statistics
Alaska Department of Health and Social Services
P.O. Box H
Juneau, Alaska 99811
907/465-3393

ARIZONA
Office of Vital Records
Arizona Department of Health Services
1740 West Avenue
P.O. Box 3887
Phoenix, Arizona 85030-3887
602/255-1072

ARKANSAS
Arkansas Department of Health
Division of Vital Records
4815 West Markham Street
Little Rock, Arkansas 72205-3867
501/661-2371

CALIFORNIA
Office of the State Registrar of Vital Statistics
Department of Health Services
410 N Street
Sacramento, California 95814
916/445-2684

COLORADO
Vital Records Section
Colorado Department of Health
4210 East 11th Avenue, Room 100
Denver, Colorado 80220
303/320-8474

CONNECTICUT
Connecticut State Department of Health Services
Vital Records Unit
150 Washington Street
Hartford, Connecticut 06106
203/566-1124

DELAWARE
Office of Vital Statistics
Division of Public Health
P.O. Box 637
Dover, Delaware 19903
302/736-4721

DISTRICT OF COLUMBIA
Vital Records Branch
Government of the District of Columbia
Department of Human Services
425 I Street N.W., Room 3007
Washington, D.C. 20001
202/727-5314

FLORIDA
State of Florida
Department of Health and Rehabilitation Services
Vital Statistics
P.O. Box 210
Jacksonville, Florida 32231-0042
904/359-6900

GEORGIA
Georgia Department of Human Resources
Vital Records Unit
Rooom 217-H, Health Building
47 Trinity Avenue, S.W.
Atlanta, Georgia 30334
404/656-4750

HAWAII
State Department of Health
Research and Statistics Office
Vital Records Section
P.O. Box 3378
Honolulu, Hawaii 96801
808/548-5819

IDAHO
State of Idaho
Department of Health and Welfare
Bureau of Vital Statistics
450 West State Street
State House
Boise, Idaho 83720
208/334-5980

ILLINOIS
Illinois Department of Public Health
Division of Vital Records
605 West Jefferson Street
Springfield, Illinois 62761
217/782-6553

INDIANA
Indiana State Board of Health
1330 West Michigan Street
P.O. Box 1964
Indianapolis, Indiana 46206
317/633-0276

IOWA
Iowa State Department of Health
Vital Records Section
Lucas State Office Building
Des Moines, Iowa 50319
515/281-4944

KANSAS
Kansas State Department of Health and Environment
Office of Vital Statistics
900 S.W. Jackson
Topeka, Kansas 66612-1290
913/296-1400

KENTUCKY
Cabinet for Human Services
Department for Health Services
Office of Vital Statistics
275 East Main Street
Frankfort, Kentucky 40621
606/564-4212

LOUISIANA
Louisiana State Department of Health and Human Resources
Office of Preventive and Public Health Services
Vital Records Registry
P.O. Box 60630
New Orleans, Louisiana 70160
504/568-5152

MAINE
Maine Department of Human Services
Office of Vital Statistics
221 State Street
State House, Station 11
Augusta, Maine 04333
207/289-3184

MARYLAND
Maryland Department of Health and Mental Hygiene
Division of Vital Records
State Office Building
P.O. Box 13146
Baltimore, Maryland 21203
301/225-5971

MASSACHUSETTS
Massachusetts Executive Office of Human Services
Division of Health Statistics and Research
Registry of Vital Records and Statistics
150 Tremont Street, Room B-3
Boston, Massachusetts 02111
617/727-0036

MICHIGAN
Michigan Department of Public Health
Office of the State Registrar and Center for Health Statistics
3428 North Logan Street
P.O. Box 30035
Lansing, Michigan 48909
517/335-8656

MINNESOTA
Minnesota Department of Health
Section of Vital Statistics Registration
717 Delaware Street, S.E.
P.O. Box 9441
Minneapolis, Minnesota 55440
612/623-5121

MISSISSIPPI
Mississippi State Department of Health
Vital Records Office
2423 North State Street
P.O. Box 1700
Jackson, Mississippi 39215-1700
601/960-7981

MISSOURI
Missouri Department of Health
Bureau of Vital Records
P.O. Box 570
Jefferson City, Missouri 65102
314/751-6387

MONTANA
Montana Department of Health and Environmental Sciences
Bureau of Records and Statistics
Cogswell Building
Helena, Montana 59620
406/444-2614

NEBRASKA
Bureau of Vital Statistics
Nebraska State Department of Health
P.O. Box 95007
Lincoln, Nebraska 68509-5007
402/471-2871

NEVADA
Nevada State Department of Human Resources
State Health Division
Section of Vital Statistics
505 East King Street
Carson City, Nevada 89710
702/885-4480

NEW HAMPSHIRE
New Hampshire Division of Public Health
Department of Health and Human Services
Bureau of Vital Records and Health Statistics
6 Hazen Drive
Concord, New Hampshire 03301-6527
603/271-4650

NEW JERSEY
New Jersey State Department of Health
State Registrar, Search Unit
Bureau of Vital Records
CN 360
Trenton, New Jersey 08625
609/292-4087

NEW MEXICO
New Mexico Health and Environment Department
Health Services Division
Vital Statistics Office
P.O. Box 968
Santa Fe, New Mexico 87504-0968
505/827-0121

NEW YORK—New York City
Bureau of Vital Records
New York City Department of Health
125 Worth Street
New York, New York 10013
212/566-8192

NEW YORK—New York State
Bureau of Vital Records
New York State Department of Health
Tower Building
Empire State Plaza
Albany, New York 12237
518/474-3077

NORTH CAROLINA
North Carolina Department of Human Resources
Division of Health Services
Vital Records Branch
P.O. Box 2091
Raleigh, North Carolina 27602-2091
919/733-3526

NORTH DAKOTA
North Dakota State Department of Health
Division of Health Statistics and Vital Records
State Capitol
Bismarck, North Dakota 58505
701/224-4508

OHIO
Ohio State Department of Health
Division of Vital Statistics
Ohio Departments Building, Room G-20
65 South Front Street
Columbus, Ohio 43266-0333
614/466-2533

OKLAHOMA
Division of Vital Records
Oklahoma State Department of Health
N.E. 10th and Stonewall
P.O. Box 53551
Oklahoma City, Oklahoma 73152
405/271-4040

OREGON
Oregon State Department of Human Resources
State Health Division
Vital Statistics Section
State Office Building, Room 101
1400 S.W. 5th Avenue
P.O. Box 116
Portland, Oregon 97207-0231
503/229-5895

PENNSYLVANIA
Pennsylvania Department of Health
Division of Vital Records
101 South Mercer Street
P.O. Box 1528
New Castle, Pennsylvania 16103
717/787-8552

RHODE ISLAND
Division of Vital Statistics
Rhode Island Department of Health
Cannon Building, Room 101
75 Davis Street
Providence, Rhode Island 02908
401/277-2811

SOUTH CAROLINA
South Carolina Department of Health and
Environmental Control
Office of Vital Records and Public Health Statistics
2600 Bull Street
Columbia, South Carolina 29201
803/734-4830

SOUTH DAKOTA
South Dakota Department of Health
Center for Health Statistics
Joe Foss Building
523 East Capitol
Pierre, South Dakota 57501-3182
605/773-3355

TENNESSEE
Tennessee State Department of Health and Environment
Vital Records Office
Cordell Hull Building
Nashville, Tennessee 37219-5402
615/741-1763

TEXAS
Texas State Department of Health
Bureau of Vital Statistics
1100 West 49th Street
Austin, Texas 78756-3191
512/458-7111

UTAH
Bureau of Health Statistics
Utah State Department of Health
288 North 1460 West
P.O. Box 16700
Salt Lake City, Utah 84116-0700
801/538-6380

VERMONT
Vermont Department of Health
Public Health Statistics
P.O. Box 70
Burlington, Vermont 05402
802/863-7275

VIRGINIA
Virginia Department of Health
Division of Vital Records
James Madison Building
P.O. Box 1000
Richmond, Virginia 23208-1000
804/786-6221

WASHINGTON
Washington State Department of Social and Health Services
Vital Records
P.O. Box 9709, ET-11
Olympia, Washington 98504
206/753-5936

WEST VIRGINIA
West Virginia State Health Department
Division of Vital Statistics
Charleston, West Virginia 25305
304/348-2931

WISCONSIN
Wisconsin Department of Health and Social Services
Section of Vital Statistics
1 West Wilson Street
P.O. Box 309
Madison, Wisconsin 53701-0309
608/266-0330

WYOMING
Wyoming State Vital Records Services
Hathaway Building
Cheyenne, Wyoming 82002
307/777-7591

APPENDIX C

FORMS FOR TEMPORARY "GUARDIANSHIP" SITUATIONS

CHAPTER	FORM NAME
2	Guardianship Authorization Form

GUARDIANSHIP AUTHORIZATION

MINOR

Name: _____

Birthdate: _____ Age: _____ Year in School: _____

MOTHER

Name: _____

Street Address: _____

City: _____ State _____ Zip Code: _____

Home Phone: _____ Work Phone: _____

FATHER

Name: _____

Street Address: _____

City: _____ State _____ Zip Code: _____

Home Phone: _____ Work Phone: _____

PROPOSED GUARDIAN

Name: _____

Street Address: _____

City: _____ State _____ Zip Code: _____

Home Phone: _____ Work Phone: _____

Relationship to Minor: _____

In case of emergency, if proposed guardian cannot be reached, please contact: _____

_____ Phone: _____

Authorization & Consent of Parent(s)

1. I affirm that the minor indicated above is my child and that I have legal custody of her/him. I give my full authorization and consent for my child to live with the proposed guardian, or for the proposed guardian to set a place of residence for my child.

2. I give the proposed guardian permission to act in my place and make decisions pertaining to my child's educational and religious activities including but not limited to enrollment, permission to participate in activities and consent for medical treatment at school.

3. I give the proposed guardian permission to authorize medical and dental care for my child, including but not limited to medical examinations, X-rays, tests, anesthetic, surgical operations, hospital care or other treatments that in the proposed guardian's sole opinion are needed or useful for my child. Such medical treatment shall only be provided upon the advice of and supervision by a physician, surgeon or dentist or other medical practitioner licensed to practice in the United States.

4. I give the proposed guardian permission to apply for benefits on my child's behalf including but not limited to Social Security, public assistance, health insurance, and Veterans' Administration benefits.

5. I give the proposed guardian permission to apply and obtain for my child any or all of the following: Social Security number, Social Security card, and U.S. passport.

6. This authorization shall cover the period from _____, 19____ to _____, 19____.

7. During the period when the proposed guardian cares for my child, the costs of my child's upkeep, living expenses, medical and dental expenses shall be paid as follows: _____
_____
_____

I declare under penalty of perjury under the laws of the State of California that the foregoing is true and correct.

Mother's Signature: _____ Date: _____, 19____

Father's Signature: _____ Date: _____, 19____

Notarization

State of California
County of _____ } ss.

On this this _____ day of _____, 19____, before me, a notary public of the State of California, personally appeared _____, personally known to me (or proved to me on the basis of satisfactory evidence) to be the person(s) whose name(s) is/are subscribed to this instrument, and acknowledged that she/he/they executed it.

Notary Public: _____ [Seal]

Consent of Proposed Guardian

I solemnly affirm that I will assume full responsibility for the minor who will live with me during the period designated above. I agree to make necessary decisions and to provide consent for the minor as set forth in the above Authorization & Consent by Parent(s). I also agree to the terms of the costs of the minor's upkeep, living expenses, medical and/or dental expenses set forth in the above Authorization & Consent of Parent(s).

I declare under penalty of perjury under the laws of the State of California that the foregoing is true and correct.

Proposed Guardian's Signature : _____ Date: _____, 19____

Notarization

State of California
County of _____ } ss.

On this this _____ day of _____, 19____, before me, a notary public of the State California, personally appeared _____, personally known to m (or proved to me on the basis of satisfactory evidence) to be the person whose name is subscribed to this instrument, and acknowledged that she/he executed it.

Notary Public: _____ [Seal]

APPENDIX D

FORMS FOR OBTAINING A COURT-ORDERED GUARDIANSHIP

CHAPTER	FORM NAME
3	Declaration
3	Additional Page Judicial Council Form
3	Lined Paper (Blank)
3	Request for Dismissal
3	Application for Waiver of Court Fees and Costs
3	Order on Application for Waiver of Court Fees and Costs
4	Guardianship Notification Worksheet
4	Petition Attachment 14: Due Diligence Declaration
4	Consent of Proposed Guardian, Nomination and Waiver of Notice
5	Petition for Appointment of Guardian of Minor
5	Petition Attachment 1c: Information on Additional Minors
5	Declaration Under Uniform Child Custody Jurisdiction Act
5	Notice of Hearing
5	Order Dispensing Notice
5	Order Appointing Guardian of Minor
5	Letters of Guardianship
6	Notice & Acknowledgment of Receipt
6	Proof of Service for Personal Service or by Notice and Acknowledgment of Receipt
6	Proof of Service by Mail
7	Petition for Appointment of Temporary Guardian
7	Order Appointing Temporary Guardian
7	Letters of Temporary Guardianship
7	Ex Parte Motion, Declaration and Order Extending Temporary Guardianship
9	Proof of Service by Mail of Order Appointing Guardian
11	Notification to Court of Address of Ward/Guardian
11	Petition for Transfer of Guardianship Proceeding
11	Order for Transfer of Guardianship Proceeding
12	Petition for Termination of Guardianship
12	Order for Termination of Guardianship

Name, Address and Telephone Number of Attorney(s)	Space Below for Use of Court Clerk Only

Attorney(s) for ....

.... COURT OF CALIFORNIA, COUNTY OF ....
(SUPERIOR, MUNICIPAL, or JUSTICE)

.... (Name of Municipal or Justice Court District or of branch court, if any)

GUARDIANSHIP OF (Name):

Minor

(Abbreviated Title)

CASE NUMBER

REQUEST FOR DISMISSAL
TYPE OF ACTION

☐ Personal Injury Property Damage and Wrongful Death:
    ☐ Motor Vehicle   ☐ Other
☐ Domestic Relations   ☐ Eminent Domain
☐ Other: (Specify) ....

TO THE CLERK: Please dismiss this action as follows: (Check applicable boxes.)

1. ☐ With prejudice   ☐ Without prejudice
2. ☐ Entire action   ☐ Complaint only   ☐ Petition only   ☐ Cross-complaint only
   ☐ Other: (Specify)*

Dated: ....

*If dismissal requested is of specified parties only, of specified causes of action only or of specified cross-complaints only, so state and identify the parties, causes of action or cross-complaints to be dismissed.

Attorney(s) for ....

....
(Type or print attorney(s) name(s))

TO THE CLERK: Consent to the above dismissal is hereby given.**

Dated: ....

**When a cross-complaint (or Response (Marriage) seeking affirmative relief) is on file, the attorney(s) for the cross-complainant (respondent) must sign this consent when required by CCP 581(1), (2) or (5).

Attorney(s) for ....

....
(Type or print attorney(s) name(s))

(To be completed by clerk)
☐ Dismissal entered as requested on ....
☐ Dismissal entered on .... as to only ....
☐ Dismissal not entered as requested for the following reason(s), and attorney(s) notified on ....

...., Clerk

Dated .... By ...., Deputy

Form Adopted by Rule 982 of
The Judicial Council of California
Revised Effective July 1, 1972

REQUEST FOR DISMISSAL

CCP 581, etc.;
Cal. Rules of Court,
Rule 1233

— **THIS FORM MUST BE KEPT CONFIDENTIAL** —

ATTORNEY OR PARTY WITHOUT ATTORNEY *(Name and Address)*:	TELEPHONE NO.:	FOR COURT USE ONLY
ATTORNEY FOR *(Name)*:		
NAME OF COURT:		
STREET ADDRESS:		
MAILING ADDRESS:		
CITY AND ZIP CODE:		
BRANCH NAME:		

GUARDIANSHIP OF (Name):

Minor

APPLICATION FOR WAIVER OF COURT FEES AND COSTS

CASE NUMBER:

I request a court order so that I do not have to pay court fees and costs.

1. My address and date of birth are *(specify)*:

2. ☐ I am receiving financial assistance under one or more of the following programs:
   a. ☐ **SSI and SSP:** The Supplemental Security Income and State Supplemental Payments Programs
   b. ☐ **AFDC:** The Aid to Families with Dependent Children Program
   c. ☐ **Food Stamps:** The Food Stamps Program
   d. ☐ **County Relief, General Relief (G.R.) or General Assistance (G.A.)**

[If you checked box 2 above, sign at the bottom of this side and DO NOT fill out the rest of the form.]

3. ☐ My gross monthly income is less than the amount shown on the Information Sheet on Waiver of Court Fees and Costs available from the clerk's office.

[If you checked box 3 above, skip 4, complete 5 and 6 on the back of this form, and sign at the bottom of this side.]

4. ☐ My income is not enough to pay for the common necessaries of life for me and the people in my family I support and also pay court fees and costs. *[If you checked this box you must complete the back of this form.]*

WARNING: You must immediately tell the court if you become able to pay court fees or costs during this action. For the next three (3) years you may be ordered to appear in court and answer questions about your ability to pay court fees or costs.

I declare under penalty of perjury under the laws of the State of California that the foregoing is true and correct.

Date:

_____ _____
(TYPE OR PRINT NAME)   (SIGNATURE)

Form Adopted by the Judicial Council of California
982(a)(17) [Rev. January 1, 1985]

APPLICATION FOR WAIVER OF COURT FEES AND COSTS
(In Forma Pauperis)

Gov. Code, § 68511.3

2(a)(17) [Rev. January 1, 1985]

APPLICATION FOR WAIVER OF COURT FEES AND COSTS
(In Forma Pauperis)

Page two

GUARDIANSHIP OF (Name):	CASE NUMBER
Minor	

FINANCIAL INFORMATION

5. ☐ My pay changes considerably from month to month. (If you check this box, each of the amounts reported in 6 should be your average for the past 12 months.)

6. My monthly income:
   a. My gross monthly pay is: $ _____
   b. My payroll deductions are (specify purpose and amount):
      (1) _____ $ _____
      (2) _____ $ _____
      (3) _____ $ _____
      (4) _____ $ _____
   c. My TOTAL payroll deduction amount is: $ _____
   d. My monthly take-home pay is (a. minus b.): $ _____
   e. Other money I get each month is (specify source and amount):
      (1) _____ $ _____
      (2) _____ $ _____
   The TOTAL amount of other money is: $ _____
   f. MY TOTAL MONTHLY INCOME IS (c. plus d.): $ _____
   g. The number of people in my family, including me, supported by this money is: _____

7. a. ☐ I am not able to pay any of the court fees and costs.
   b. ☐ I am able to pay only the following court fees and costs (specify):

8. My monthly expenses are:
   a. Rent or house payment & maintenance $ _____
   b. Food and household supplies $ _____
   c. Utilities and telephone $ _____
   d. Clothing $ _____
   e. Laundry and cleaning $ _____
   f. Medical and dental payments $ _____
   g. Insurance (life, health, accident, etc.) $ _____
   h. School, child care $ _____
   i. Child, spousal support (prior marriage) $ _____
   j. Transportation and auto expenses (insurance, gas, repair) $ _____
   k. Installment payments (specify purpose and amount):
      (1) _____ $ _____
      (2) _____ $ _____
      (3) _____ $ _____
   The TOTAL amount of monthly installment payments is: $ _____
   l. Amounts deducted due to wage assignments and earnings withholding orders $ _____
   m. Other expenses (specify)
      (1) _____ $ _____
      (2) _____ $ _____
      (3) _____ $ _____
      (4) _____ $ _____
      (5) _____ $ _____
      (6) _____ $ _____
   The TOTAL amount of other monthly expenses is: $ _____
   n. MY TOTAL MONTHLY EXPENSES ARE (add a. through m.): $ _____

9. I own the following property:
   a. Cash $ _____
   b. Checking, savings and credit union accounts (list banks):
      (1) _____ $ _____
      (2) _____ $ _____
      (3) _____ $ _____
   c. Cars, other vehicles and boat equity (list make, year of each):
      (1) _____ $ _____
      (2) _____ $ _____
      (3) _____ $ _____
   d. Real estate equity $ _____
   e. Other personal property — jewelry, furniture, furs, stocks, bonds, etc. (list separately):

10. Other facts which support this application are (describe unusual medical needs, expenses for recent family emergencies, or other unusual expenses to help the judge understand your budget). If more space is needed, attach page labeled attachment 10.

$ _____

WARNING: You must immediately tell the court if you become able to pay court fees or costs during this action. For the next three (3) years you may be ordered to appear in court and answer questions about your ability to pay court fees or costs.

ATTORNEY OR PARTY WITHOUT ATTORNEY (Name and Address)	TELEPHONE NO.	FOR COURT USE ONLY
ATTORNEY FOR (Name)		
NAME OF COURT, JUDICIAL DISTRICT OR BRANCH COURT, IF ANY:		

GUARDIANSHIP OF (Name):

Minor

ORDER ON APPLICATION FOR WAIVER OF COURT FEES AND COSTS

CASE NUMBER:

1. The application was filed
   a. on (date):
   b. by (name):
2. ☐ **IT IS ORDERED THAT the application is granted and the applicant is permitted to proceed in this action as follows:**
   a. ☐ without payment of any court fees or costs listed in rule 985(i), California Rules of Court.
   b. ☐ without payment of any court fees or costs listed in rule 985(i), California Rules of Court, except the following:

   c. ☐ without payment of the following court fees or costs (specify):

   d. The reasons for denial of any requested waiver are (specify):

   e. ☐ The clerk of the court is directed to mail a copy of this order to the applicant's attorney, if any, or to the applicant if unrepresented.
   f. ☐ All unpaid fees and costs shall be deemed to be taxable costs if applicant is entitled to costs and shall be a lien on any judgment recovered by the applicant and shall be paid to the clerk upon such recovery.
3. ☐ **IT IS ORDERED THAT the application is denied for the following reasons** (specify):

   a. **The applicant must pay any fees and costs due in this action within ten days from the date of service of this order or any paper filed by the applicant with the clerk will be of no effect.**
   b. The clerk of the court is directed to mail a copy of this order to all parties who have appeared in this action.
4. ☐ **IT IS ORDERED THAT a hearing be held.**
   a. The substantial evidentiary conflict to be resolved by the hearing is (specify):

   b. Applicant should be present at the hearing to be held:

hearing date:	time:	in ☐ Dept.:	☐ Div.:	☐ Rm.:
address of court:				

   c. The clerk of the court is directed to mail a copy of this order to the applicant only.

Dated: _____

(Signature of Judge)

(Clerk's certification on page 2)

Form Adopted by Rule 982
Judicial Council of California
Revised effective July 1, 1981

**ORDER ON APPLICATION FOR WAIVER OF COURT FEES AND COSTS
(IN FORMA PAUPERIS)**

Govt Code
§ 68511.3

GUARDIANSHIP OF (Name):	CASE NUMBER:
Minor	

ORDER ON APPLICATION FOR WAIVER OF COURT FEES AND COSTS

CLERK'S CERTIFICATE OF MAILING

I certify that I am not a party to this cause and that a copy of the foregoing was mailed first class, postage prepaid, in a sealed envelope addressed as shown below, and that the mailing and execution of this certificate occurred at (place): ...., California,

on (date): .... Clerk, by .... (Deputy)

CLERK'S CERTIFICATION

I certify that the foregoing is a true copy of the original on file in my office.

Dated: .... Clerk, by .... (Deputy)

(SEAL)

GUARDIANSHIP NOTIFICATION WORKSHEET

PART I. RELATIVES

(1) NAMES AND ADDRESSES OF MINOR'S RELATIVES AND OTHER PEOPLE ENTITLED TO NOTICE	(2) NEED TO LOCATE?	(3) DATE LOCATED	(4) WILL SIGN WAIVER OF NOTICE & CONSENT?	(5) NEED TO HAVE SERVED?	(6) SERVICE TYPE, IF NEED TO HAVE SERVED	(7) DATE SERVED OR ORDER DISPENSING NOTICE	(8) DATE FILED PROOF OF SERVICE
Minor			Cannot sign since under 18	Only if 12 or over, or if minor has a child	Personal (Chapter 6, Section F)		
Minor's mother					Personal or Notice and Acknowledgment of Receipt (Chapter 6, Section F)		
Minor's father					Personal or Notice and Acknowledgment of Receipt (Chapter 6, Section F)		
Minor's maternal grandparents (mother's parents)					Mail (Chapter 6, Section G)		
Minor's paternal grandparents (father's parents)					Mail (Chapter 6, Section G)		
Minor's spouse—can only petition for guardianship of the estate			Can sign only if 18 or over		Mail, and also serve parents, if under 18 (Chapter 6, Section G)		

GUARDIANSHIP NOTIFICATION WORKSHEET

PART I. RELATIVES (continued)

(1) NAMES AND ADDRESSES OF MINOR'S RELATIVES AND OTHER PEOPLE ENTITLED TO NOTICE	(2) NEED TO LOCATE?	(3) DATE LOCATED	(4) WILL SIGN WAIVER OF NOTICE & CONSENT?	(5) NEED TO HAVE SERVED?	(6) SERVICE TYPE, IF NEED TO HAVE SERVED	(7) DATE SERVED OR ORDER DISPENSING NOTICE	(8) DATE FILED PROOF OF SERVICE
Minor's sisters and brothers (include their ages; if parents not listed elsewhere on worksheet, list their names and addresses)			Can sign only if 18 or over	Only if over 12 (and serve parents if under 18)	Mail, if over 12. Serve parents, if under 18 (Chapter 6, Section G)		
Minor's children (if child's other parent not listed elsewhere on worksheet, list name and address)			Cannot sign since under 18		Not required, but must serve both of child's parents		
Anyone presently having legal custody of minor (not including you)					Personal or Notice and Acknowledgment of Receipt (Chapter 6, Section F)		
Anyone nominated minor's legal guardian (not including you)					Personal or Notice and Acknowledgment of Receipt (Chapter 6, Section F)		
Anyone who has physical custody of minor (not including you)					Mail (Chapter 6, Section G)		

PART II. AGENCIES

NAME AND ADDRESS OF AGENCIES ENTITLED TO NOTICE (SEE CHAPTER 6, SECTION E2)	NEED TO HAVE SERVED?	SERVICE TYPE, IF NEED TO HAVE SERVED	DATE SERVED	DATE FILED PROOF OF SERVICE
Local Social Service Agency		Mail (Chapter 6, Section G)		
Court Investigator		Mail (Chapter 6, Section G)		
State Director of Social Services		Mail (Chapter 6, Section G)		
Director of Mental Health		Mail (Chapter 6, Section G)		
Director of Developmental Services		Mail (Chapter 6, Section G)		
Veterans Administration		Mail (Chapter 6, Section G)		

GUARDIANSHIP OF (Name):	Case Number:

ATTACHMENT 14
to Petition for Appointment of Guardian of Minor

I _____, declare that I am _____

in this guardianship case, that I have made the following attempts to locate _____,

who is related to the minor in this action as _____. To date my efforts have

been unsuccessful.

1. ☐ I checked in telephone directories for listings. The details of my attempts are:

2. ☐ I checked with directory assistance. The details of my attempts are:

3. ☐ I checked with friends and relatives. The details of my attempts are:

4. ☐ I checked with former employers. The details of my attempts are:

BACK

ATTACHMENT 14 TO PETITION FOR
APPOINTMENT OF GUARDIAN OF MINOR

NP

GUARDIANSHIP OF (Name):	Case Number:

5. ☐ I checked the last known residence address. The details of my attempts are:

6. ☐ I checked with voter registration records. The details of my attempts are:

7. ☐ I checked with the motor vehicles department. The details of my attempts are:

8. ☐ Other (specify):

Date:

.... _____
(TYPE OR PRINT NAME) (SIGNATURE)

I declare under penalty of perjury under the laws of the state of California that the foregoing is true and correct.

A

Abbreviations, for legal codes, 1/2, 13/6
Abuse, and obtaining guardian, 1/13
Accountings, of minor's estate, 10/8, 12/2
Adoption, 1/12-13, 5/9
Adult, guardianship of, 1/13
Agencies, and service of papers, 6/9-11
Aid to Families with Dependent Children, and guardianship, 2/10, 5/9; and temporary guardianship, 7/2
Alameda Superior Court, and agencies entitled to notice, 6/6-7
Application for Waiver of Court Fees and Costs, 3/12, 3/13-16, 6/3
Appraisal of property, 10/6-8
Assets, transfer of, 10/6
Attachments, to forms, 3/6
Attachments to Petition for Appointment of Guardian of Minor, 5/14
Attorneys. —See— Lawyers

B

Blocked accounts, 10/3; establishing, 10/6
Bluebacks, 3/7
Boarding Home and Institution (BHI), and guardianship, 2/10
Bond, 9/4, 10/2-4, 10/11-12; definition, 10/2; obtaining, 10/5
Branch court, 3/2

C

Canada, travel to, 2/14
Case number, 3/8
Child abuse, and obtaining guardian, 1/13
Co-parents, 1/11
Compensation, as guardian of minor's estate, 10/8, 10/12, 11/11-12
Conflict of interest, 10/11
Consent of Proposed Guardian, 4/12
Consent of [Proposed] Guardian, Nomination, and Waiver of Notice, 4/12-15, 4/16-17, 6/3
Conservatorship, 1/13
Continuance: of hearing, 9/6; of hearing date, 6/5
Contracts, and minor, 10/12, 11/3
Copying documents/forms, 3/7, 6/1-2, 6/3
County bar associations, 13/1
County clerk, 3/3
County seat, 3/2
Court approval, of financial transactions, 10/12
Court calendar, 9/3
Court fees and costs, 3/12-18; waiving, 3/12-18, 6/2, 6/3
Court investigator.—See— Guardianship investigation
Court procedure, stopping, 3/10-11

Custody, and Guardianship Authorization form, 2/3
Custody problems: and guardianship, 5/9, 9/6; and public assistance, 2/11

D

Declaration for Filing and Assignment, 5/30, 6/3
Declaration Under Penalty of Perjury, 3/6
Declaration Under Uniform Child Custody Jurisdiction Act, 5/1, 5/16-20, 6/3n
Dental care, and guardianship, 2/9
Department of Motor Vehicles, 4/7
Deposits in lieu of bond, 10/3, 10/6
Director of Developmental Services, and service of papers, 6/10
Director of Mental Health, and service of papers, 6/10
Director of Social Services, and service of papers, 6/10
Divorce, and guardianship, 5/9
Documents. —See— names of specific documents
Driver License Registration Information Request, 4/7
Driver's license, of minor, 11/3
Due Diligence Declaration, 4/8-11

E

Emancipated minor, 1/3n
Emergencies, and guardianship, 2/9
Enrollment policies, of schools, 2/8
Estate planning, 1/7
Estate transfer fees, 11/11
Ex parte, definition, 7/3
Ex Parte Motion, Declaration and Order Extending Temporary Guardianship, 7/16-17

F

Fee waiver documents, 6/3
Felony, and guardianship, 1/10
Filing fees, 3/12-18
Filing system, 3/2
First Accounting, 10/8
Forms. —See— names of specific forms
Foster Care, and guardianship, 2/10
Foster parents, 1/11-12
Fresno Superior Court, and Guardianship Questionnaire, 6/6

G

Group legal practices, 13/3
Guardian: compensation, 10/8, 10/12, 11/11-12; consent, 4/12; decision to be, 1/8-10; expenses, 11/11-12; nomination, 4/12-13, 4/16-17; reimbursement, 10/12, 11/12; removal, 12/8-9; resignation, 1/14, 3/10n, 12/8; responsibilities, 1/8-10,

10/9-12, 11/1-3; responsibilities to court, 11/3-5; selection, 1/9-10, 1/14; suspension, 12/8-9

Guardianship: contested, 3/1n, 4/1n, 11/12, 13/3; definition, 1/1, 1/3; length of time to obtain, 2/2; needed, 3/1-2; of own child's estate, 1/7-8, 10/9; overview, 1/1-14; resigning, 1/14, 3/10n, 12/8; terminating, 1/8n, 12/2-8; transferring to another California court, 11/5-11; types, 1/3-6; when needed, 1/5, 1/6-8

Guardianship Authorization form, 2/2, 2/3-7; notarization, 2/6; sample, 2/4-5; and single parents, 2/3; when to use, 2/3

Guardianship documents/forms, 3/1-18; amending, 3/9-10; completing, 3/5-7; copies needed, 3/7, 6/1-2, 6/3; filing, 3/2, 3/7-11, 6/1-6; mailing, 3/8; for temporary guardianship, 7/4-15; using, 3/3-18

Guardianship, formal, reasons to avoid, 2/2

Guardianship, informal, 2/1-15

Guardianship investigation, 3/3, 6/4, 8/1-4, 9/4; fees, 3/12, 8/4, 9/7; and investigator's report, 8/3-4; and service of papers, 6/10

Guardianship Notification Worksheet, 4/2-3, 4/4-5, 4/17, 6/8-9, 6/21-24

Guardianship of a minor's estate, 1/3, 1/4, 1/5, 1/6-7, 1/14; 10/1-12; and investigation, 8/2; special procedures, 9/8; termination, 12/2

Guardianship of a minor's person, 1/3-4, 1/5, 1/6; alternatives, 2/1-15; and investigation, 8/2; termination, 12/2-8

Guardianship proceedings, stopping, 1/14

Guardianship, temporary, 1/14, 4/1n, 5/32, 6/3, 6/4n, 9/7; as recommended by investigator, 8/4; documents and forms, 7/4-15; extending, 7/15-17; hearing, 7/15; length of, 7/15; length of time to obtain, 2/2n; of a minor's person, 7/1-17

H

Handwritten forms, 3/3
Health insurance, and guardianship, 2/9-10
Hearing, 9/1-10; attending, 9/3-7; continuance, 9/6; length, 9/4; preparation, 9/1-3
Hearing date, 4/1n, 6/4-5
Home interviews, by investigator, 8/1, 8/3

I

Income, and waiving court fees and costs, 3/12
Inheritance tax referee, 10/7-8
Insurance, and guardianship, 2/9-10, 2/14, 10/11
Inventory and Appraisal form, 10/8
Investigation. —See— Guardianship investigation

J

Joint petitioners, 5/2n
Judicial Council forms, 3/4, 13/7
Juvenile Court actions, and guardianship, 5/9, 12/1n

L

Law libraries, 13/6
Lawsuits against guardian, 1/14
Lawyers, 13/1-5
Legal Aid offices, 13/1
Legal assistance, 1/10-11, 13/1-5
Legal citations, 1/2, 13/5-6
Legal clinics, 13/3-4
Legal fees, 13/4-5
Legal insurance, 13/4
Legal research, 13/5-7
Legal Services for Children, Inc., 13/2
Letter, authorizing travel outside the U.S., 2/14, 2/15
Letters of Guardianship, 9/7-10, 10/6, 11/1; cost, 9/4
Letters of Guardianship (proposed), 3/9, 5/2, 5/30, 5/31, 6/2, 6/3
Letters of Temporary Guardianship, 7/2, 7/15, 7/16; (proposed), 6/2, 6/3, 7/12-14
Liabilities, for minor's acts, 11/2-3
Local court forms, 3/4, 5/30, 5/32, 6/6-7. —See also— names of specific courts
Local court rules, 3/7, 6/5. —See also— names of specific courts
Los Angeles County Court rules, 3/7

M

Marshals, and service of papers, 6/8
Master calendar department, 9/4
Medi-Cal, and guardianship, 2/10-11
Medical care, and guardianship, 2/9
Medical emergencies, and guardianship, 2/9
Medical treatment, for minor, 11/2
Mexico, travel to, 2/14
Military service personnel records, 4/8
Minor, 12 or older, and special procedures, 9/8
Minor, preparing for hearing, 9/2
Minor, and service with notice of guardianship, 6/9, 6/11, 9/8-10
Minor's estate, and guardian. —See— Guardianship of a minor's estate
Money, definition, 10/8n
Moving, and guardianship, 1/3

N

Neglect, and obtaining guardian, 1/13
Nomination of Guardian, 4/12-13, 4/16-17, 10/2n
Non-U.S. citizens, and travel outside the U.S., 2/13
Notary public, 2/6
Notice and Acknowledgement of Receipt, 6/12-14
Notice of Hearing, 5/1, 5/21, 6/3, 6/4, 6/5, 11/10; back of form, 6/17, 6/19-20; filing, 6/20-21
Notice of Hearing, for temporary guardianship, 6/3, 7/14, 7/15

Notice of Hearing, for termination of guardianship, 12/5
Notice of Waiver of Court Fees and Costs, 6/2
Notification to Court of Address of Guardian/Ward, 5/30, 11/3-5
Notification to Court of Address on Guardianship, 6/3
Notification of minor's parents/relatives, 1/13, 4/1-17

O

Order Appointing Guardian, 9/5, 9/7; judge's refusal to sign, 9/6-7
Order Appointing Guardian of Minor (proposed), 3/8, 6/3, 5/1, 5/25-29, 9/2n
Order Appointing Temporary Guardian, 7/2; (proposed), 7/9-12
Order Dispensing Notice (proposed), 5/1, 5/21-24, 6/3
Order for Appointment of Temporary Guardian (proposed), 6/3
Order for Termination of Guardianship (proposed), 12/5, 12/6
Order for Transfer of Guardianship Proceeding (proposed), 11/8-9, 11/11
Order on Application for Waiver of Court Fees and Costs, 3/12, 3/16-18, 6/3
Orders (proposed), 3/8. —See also— names of specific orders

P

Papers, service of, 6/7-24, 7/15. —See also— Service of process
Paralegals, 13/2
Parents of minor, and discussing guardianship, 4/16. —See also— Relatives of minor
Passports, 2/13
Periodic accountings, 10/8
Personal service of papers, 6/11-16
Personal sureties, 10/2, 10/3, 10/5-6
Petition for Appointment of Guardian of Minor, 5/1, 5/2-16, 6/3, 10/2-5; amending, 6/5-6; attachments, 5/14
Petition for Appointment of Temporary Guardian, 6/3, 7/2, 7/4-9, 7/15
Petition for Termination of Guardianship, 12/2-4
Petition for Transfer of Guardianship Proceeding, 11/6-8
Petitioners, number of, 5/2n
Preemptory Challenge, 9/6n
Probate commissioner, 6/4n
Probate courts, 3/2
Probate Division of Superior Court, 3/2
Probate Policy Manual, 3/2, 13/7
Probate referee, 10/7-8
Process servers, 6/7-8, 6/11-12
Process serving, 6/7-24, 7/15
Proof of Service by Mail, 6/16-17, 6/18
Proof of Service by Mail of Order Appointing Guardian of Minor, 9/8-10
Proof of Service for Personal Service or By Notice and Acknowledgment of Receipt, 6/14-16
Proofs of service, filing, 6/20-21
Property, definition, 3/2n
(Proposed) orders, documents, etc. —See— main part of name

Public assistance, and guardianship, 2/10, 5/9, 11/2; and temporary guardianship, 7/2
Public Guardian, 12/1n

Q

Questionnaires, as part of investigation, 8/2

R

Reimbursement, as guardian of minor's estate, 10/12, 11/11-12
Relatives of minor: discussing guardianship with, 4/15-16; locating, 4/6-8; missing, 4/1-2, 4/3, 4/6-8; notifying, 1/13, 4/1-17; and service of papers, 6/9
Removal of guardian, 12/8-9
Representative payee, 2/13
Request for Dismissal form, 3/10-11
Residence of minor, 11/2
Resigning as guardian, 1/14, 3/10n, 12/8

S

Sacramento Superior Court, and civil litigation, 5/32, 6/3
San Mateo Superior Court, and Guardianship Affidavit, 5/32, 6/3
Santa Clara Superior Court, and Declaration in Support of Petition, 5/32, 5/35-36, 6/3
Schools, and guardianship, 2/8
Section 8, and guardianship, 2/11
Service of process, 6/7-24, 7/15 ; definition, 6/7; by mail, 6/16-20, 9/8-10; personal, 6/11-16
Sheriffs, and service of papers, 6/8
Signatures of parents/relatives on forms, 4/16-17
Small Claims Court, 13/3
Social Security, and guardianship, 2/11-13
Social service agencies: entitled to notice, 6/6-7; and investigation, 8/2; and service of papers, 6/9-10
State directors of Developmental/Mental Health/Social Services, and service of papers, 6/10
Stepparents, 1/11
Subsidized housing, and guardianship, 2/11
Supplemental documents, to guardianship forms, 5/2, 5/30, 5/32, 6/3
Support, parents' duty, 10/9
Surety bond, 10/2, 10/5

T

Tax returns, 10/11
Temporary guardianship. —See— Guardianship, temporary
Transfer fees, 11/11
Transfer of assets, 10/6

Traveling with minor outside U.S., 2/13-14, 2/15
Type size, when filling out forms, 3/3

U

Uniform Transfers to Minors Act (UTMA), 1/4n

V

Veterans Administration, and service of papers, 6/10-11
Veterans' Administration benefits, and guardianship, 2/13, 5/9
Videotape of guardians's duties, 9/4
Visitation disputes, 9/6, 11/3
Voter registration records, 4/7

W

Waiver of Notice and Consent, 4/13, 4/15, 4/16-17
Ward, definition, 9/5n
Welfare, and guardianship, 2/10, 5/9
Will, 1/13, 1/14

ABOUT THE AUTHORS

LISA S. GOLDOFTAS is a legal assistant with over a dozen years of law office experience in Ohio and California. She holds a B.A. from the University of Michigan and an M.A. in English from San Francisco State University. She is the co-author of *Collect Your Court Judgment* and *The Conservatorship Book*, both published by Nolo Press. Lisa has never looked back on her decision to go trekking in Nepal instead of going to law school.

DAVID W. BROWN practices law in Monterey, California. He is a graduate of Stanford University (chemistry) and the University of Santa Clara College of Law. David teaches law at the Monterey College of Law and is the author of *Fight Your Ticket, The Landlord's Law Book, Vol. II, Evictions,* and co-author of *The Landlord's Law Book, Vol. I, Rights and Responsibilities* and *How to Change Your Name*, published by Nolo Press.

ABOUT NOLO PRESS

The leading publisher of self-help law books and software since 1971

Nolo Press was founded in 1971 to show people how to do their own routine legal tasks and avoid costly lawyer fees. Bar associations thundered against self-help law, claiming that people needed lawyers for even simple procedures.

But Nolo persisted, sure that informed citizens armed with top-quality self-help materials, didn't have to depend on lawyers. Over the years, more than three million customers have proven us right. Today, Nolo publishes over 70 self-help law books and software packages, and is more committed than ever to making the law accessible.

CATALOG

SELF-HELP LAW BOOKS & SOFTWARE

ESTATE PLANNING & PROBATE

Plan Your Estate With a Living Trust
Attorney Denis Clifford
National 2nd Edition
This book covers every significant aspect of estate planning and gives detailed specific, instructions for preparing a living trust, a document that lets your family avoid expensive and lengthy probate court proceedings after your death. *Plan Your Estate* includes all the tear-out forms and step-by-step instructions to let you prepare an estate plan designed for your special needs.
$19.95/NEST

Nolo's Simple Will Book
Attorney Denis Clifford
National 2nd Edition
It's easy to write a legally valid will using this book. The instructions and forms enable people to draft a will for all needs, including naming a personal guardian for minor children, leaving property to minor children or young adults and updating a will when necessary. Good in all states except Louisiana.
$17.95/SWIL

Who Will Handle Your Finances If You Can't?
Attorneys Denis Clifford and Mary Randolph
National 1st Edition
If illness or old age makes it impossible for you to handle your own day-to-day financial affairs, someone must step in to take care of matters. Usually, a family member must go to court and ask a judge to appoint a conservator—a painful and intrusive process.
But by using this book to create a durable power of attorney for finances you can avoid court involvement altogether. In a durable power of attorney you appoint a trusted person to take care of your finances if it becomes necessary. This book contains tear-out durable power of attorney forms and all the instructions necessary.
$19.95 FINA

The Conservatorship Book
Lisa Goldoftas & Attorney Carolyn Farren
California 1st Edition
When someone becomes incapacitated due to illness or age, a conservator may need to take charge of their medical and financial affairs. *The Conservatorship Book* comes with complete instructions and all the forms necessary to file conservatorship documents, appear in court, be appointed conservator and end a conservatorship.
$24.95/CNSV

How to Probate an Estate
Julia Nissley
California 7th Edition
If you find yourself responsible for winding up the legal and financial affairs of a deceased family member or friend, you can often save costly attorneys' fees by handling the probate process yourself. This book also explains the simple procedures you can use to transfer assets that don't require probate, including property held in joint tenancy or living trusts or as community property.
$34.95/PAE

software

WillMaker
Nolo Press
Version 4.0
This easy-to-use software program lets you prepare and update a legal will—safely, privately and without the expense of a lawyer. Leading you step-by-step in a question-and-answer format, *WillMaker* builds a will around your answers, taking into account your state of residence. *WillMaker* comes with a 200-page legal manual which provides the legal background necessary to make sound choices. Good in all states except Louisiana.
**IBM PC
(3-1/2 & 5-1/4 disks included) $69.95/WI4
MACINTOSH $69.95/WM4**

Nolo's Personal RecordKeeper
(formerly For the Record)

Carol Pladsen & Attorney Ralph Warner
Version 3.0
Nolo's Personal RecordKeeper lets you record the location of personal, financial and legal information in over 200 categories and subcategories. It also allows you to create lists of insured property, compute net worth, consolidate emergency information into one place and export to *Quicken®* home inventory and net worth reports. Includes a 320-page manual filled with practical and legal advice.
**IBM PC
(3-1/2 & 5-1/4 disks included) $49.95/FRI3
MACINTOSH $49.95/FRM3**

Nolo's Living Trust
Attorney Mary Randolph
Version 1.0
A will is an indispensable part of any estate plan, but many people need a living trust as well. By putting certain assets into a trust, you save your heirs the headache, time and expense of probate. *Nolo's Living Trust* lets you set up an individual or shared marital trust, make your trust document legal, transfer your property to the trust, and change or revoke the trust at any time. The 380-page manual guides you through the process step-by-step, and over 100 legal help screens and an on-line glossary explain key legal terms and concepts. Good in all states except Louisiana.
MACINTOSH $79.95/LTM1

GOING TO COURT

Everybody's Guide to Municipal Court
Judge Roderic Duncan
California 1st Edition
Everybody's Guide to Municipal Court explains how to prepare and defend the most common types of contract and personal injury law suits in California Municipal Court. Written by a California judge, the book provides step-by-step instructions for preparing and filing all necessary forms, gathering evidence and appearing in court.
$29.95/MUNI

Everybody's Guide to Small Claims Court
Attorney Ralph Warner
National 5th Edition
California 10th Edition
These books will help you decide if you should sue in Small Claims Court, show you how to file and serve papers, tell you what to bring to court and how to collect a judgment.
National $15.95/NSCC
California $15.95/CSCC

Fight Your Ticket
Attorney David Brown
California 5th Edition
This book shows you how to fight an unfair traffic ticket—when you're stopped, at arraignment, at trial and on appeal.
$17.95/FYT

Collect Your Court Judgment
Gini Graham Scott, Attorney Stephen Elias & Lisa Goldoftas
California 2nd Edition
This book contains step-by-step instructions and all the forms you need to collect a court judgment from the debtor's bank accounts, wages, business receipts, real estate or other assets.
$19.95/JUDG

How to Change Your Name
Attorneys David Loeb & David Brown
California 5th Edition
This book explains how to change your name legally and provides all the necessary court forms with detailed instructions on how to fill them out.
$19.95/NAME

The Criminal Records Book
Attorney Warren Siegel
California 3rd Edition
This book shows you step-by-step how to seal criminal records, dismiss convictions, destroy marijuana records and reduce felony convictions.
$19.95/CRIM

LEGAL REFORM

Legal Breakdown: 40 Ways to Fix Our Legal System
Nolo Press Editors and Staff
National 1st Edition
Legal Breakdown presents 40 common-sense proposals to make our legal system fairer, faster, cheaper and more accessible. It advocates abolishing probate, taking divorce out of court, treating jurors better and a host of other fundamental changes.
$8.95/LEG

BUSINESS/WORKPLACE

The Legal Guide for Starting & Running a Small Business
Attorney Fred S. Steingold
National 1st Edition
This book is an essential resource for every small business owner, whether you are just starting out or are already established. Find out everything you need to know about how to form a sole proprietorship, partnership or corporation, negotiate a favorable lease, hire and fire employees, write contracts and resolve disputes.
$19.95 / RUNS

Sexual Harassment on the Job
Attorneys William Petrocelli & Barbara Kate Repa
National 1st Edition
This is the first comprehensive book dealing with sexual harassment in the workplace. It describes what harassment is, what the laws are that make it illegal and how to put a stop to it. This guide is invaluable both for employees experiencing harassment and for employers interested in creating a policy against sexual harassment and a procedure for handling complaints.
$14.95/HARS

Your Rights in the Workplace
Dan Lacey
National 1st Edition
Your Rights in the Workplace, the first comprehensive guide to workplace rights —from hiring to firing—explains the latest sweeping changes in laws passed to protect workers. Learning about these legal protections can help all workers be sure they're paid fairly and on time, get all employment benefits, and know how to take action if fired or laid off illegally.
$15.95/YRW

How to Write a Business Plan
Mike McKeever
National 4th Edition
If you're thinking of starting a business or raising money to expand an existing one, this book will show you how to write the business plan and loan package necessary to finance your business and make it work.
$19.95/SBS

Marketing Without Advertising
Michael Phillips & Salli Rasberry
National 1st Edition
This book outlines practical steps for building and expanding a small business without spending a lot of money on advertising.
$14.00/MWAD

The Partnership Book
Attorneys Denis Clifford & Ralph Warner
National 4th Edition
This book shows you step-by-step how to write a solid partnership agreement that meets your needs. It covers initial contributions to the business, wages, profit-sharing, buy-outs, death or retirement of a partner and disputes.
$24.95/PART

How to Form A Nonprofit Corporation
Attorney Anthony Mancuso
National 1st Edition
This book explains the legal formalities involved and provides detailed information on the differences in the law among 50 states. It also contains forms for the Articles, Bylaws and Minutes you need, along with complete instructions for obtaining federal 501 (c) (3) tax exemptions and qualifying for public charity status.
$24.95/NNP

The California Nonprofit Corporation Handbook
Attorney Anthony Mancuso
California 6th Edition
This book shows you step-by-step how to form and operate a nonprofit corporation in California. It includes the latest corporate and tax law changes, and the forms for the Articles, Bylaws and Minutes.
$29.95/NON

How to Form Your Own Corporation
Attorney Anthony Mancuso
California 7th Edition
New York 2nd Edition
Texas 4th Edition
Florida 3rd Edition
These books contain the forms, instructions and tax information you need to incorporate a small business yourself and save hundreds of dollars in lawyers' fees.
California $29.95/CCOR
New York $24.95/NYCO
Texas $29.95/TCOR
Florida $24.95/FLCO

The California Professional Corporation Handbook
Attorney Anthony Mancuso
California 4th Edition
Health care professionals, lawyers, accountants and members of certain other professions must fulfill special requirements when forming a corporation in California. This book contains up-to-date tax information plus all the forms and instructions necessary to form a California professional corporation.
$34.95/PROF

The Independent Paralegal's Handbook
Attorney Ralph Warner
National 2nd Edition
The Independent Paralegal's Handbook provides legal and business guidelines for those who want to take routine legal work out of the law office and offer it for a reasonable fee in an independent business.
$19.95/ PARA

Getting Started as an Independent Paralegal
(Two Audio Tapes)
Attorney Ralph Warner
National 2nd Edition
If you are interested in going into business as an Independent Paralegal—helping consumers prepare their own legal paperwork in uncontested proceedings such as bankruptcy, divorce, small business incorporation, landlord-tenant actions and probate—you'll want these tapes. Approximately two hours in length, the tapes will tell you everything you need to know about what legal tasks to handle, how much to charge and how to run a profitable business.
$44.95/GSIP

software

Nolo's Partnership Maker
Attorney Tony Mancuso & Michael Radtke
Version 1.0
Nolo's Partnership Maker prepares a legal partnership agreement for doing business in any state. The program can be used by anyone who plans to pool energy, efforts, money or property with others to run a business, share property, produce a profit or undertake any other type of mutual endeavor. You can select and assemble the standard partnership clauses provided or create your own customized agreement. And the agreement can be updated at any time. Includes on-line legal help screens, glossary and tutorial, and a manual that takes you through the process step-by-step.
**IBM PC
(3-1/2 & 5-1/4 disks included) $129.00/PAGI1**

California Incorporator
Attorney Anthony Mancuso
Version 1.0 *(good only in CA)*
Answer the questions on the screen and this software program will print out the 35-40 pages of documents you need to make your California corporation legal. Comes with a 200-page manual which explains the incorporation process.
**IBM PC
(3-1/2 & 5-1/4 disks included) $129.00/INCI**

books with disk

The California Nonprofit Corporation Handbook
(computer edition)
Attorney Anthony Mancuso
Version 1.0 *(good only in CA)*
This book/software package shows you step-by-step how to form and operate a nonprofit corporation in California. Included on disk are the forms for the Articles, Bylaws and Minutes.
**IBM PC 5-1/4 $69.95/ NPI
IBM PC 3-1/2 $69.95/ NP3I
MACINTOSH $69.95/ NPM**

How to Form Your Own New York Corporation & How to Form Your Own Texas Corporation
(computer editions)
Attorney Anthony Mancuso
These book/software packages contain the instructions and tax information and forms you need to incorporate a small business and save hundreds of dollars in lawyers' fees. All organizational forms are on disk. Both come with a 250-page manual.
**New York 1st Edition
IBM PC 5-1/4 $69.95/ NYCI
IBM PC 3-1/2 $69.95/ NYC3I
MACINTOSH $69.95/ NYCM**

**Texas 1st Edition
IBM PC 5-1/4 $69.95/ TCI
IBM PC 3-1/2 $69.95/ TC3I
MACINTOSH $69.95/ TCM**

THE NEIGHBORHOOD

Neighbor Law: Fences, Trees, Boundaries & Noise
Attorney Cora Jordan
National 1st Edition
Neighbor Law answers common questions about the subjects that most often trigger disputes between neighbors: fences, trees, boundaries and noise. It explains how to find the law and resolve disputes without a nasty lawsuit.
$14.95/NEI

Dog Law
Attorney Mary Randolph
National 1st Edition
Dog Law is a practical guide to the laws that affect dog owners and their neighbors. You'll find answers to common questions on such topics as biting, barking, veterinarians and more.
$12.95/DOG

MONEY MATTERS

Stand Up to the IRS
Attorney Fred Daily
National 1st Edition
Stand Up to the IRS gives detailed stategies on surviving an audit with the minimum amount of damage, appealing an audit decision, going to Tax Court and dealing with IRS collectors. It also discusses filing tax returns when you haven't done so in a while, tax crimes, concerns of small business people and getting help from the IRS ombudsman. This book also includes confidential forms, unavailable to taxpayers, used by the IRS during audits and collection interviews.
$19.95 / SIRS

Money Troubles: Legal Strategies to Cope With Your Debts
Attorney Robin Leonard
National 1st Edition
Are you behind on your credit card bills or loan payments? If you are, then *Money Troubles* is exactly what you need. It covers everything from knowing what your rights are, and asserting them, to helping you evaluate your individual situation. This practical, straightforward book is for anyone who needs help understanding and dealing with the complex and often scary topic of debts.
$16.95/MT

How to File for Bankruptcy
Attorneys Stephen Elias, Albin Renauer & Robin Leonard
National 4th Edition
Trying to decide whether or not filing for bankruptcy makes sense? *How to File for Bankruptcy* contains an overview of the process and all the forms plus step-by-step instructions on the procedures to follow.
$25.95/HFB

Simple Contracts for Personal Use
Attorney Stephen Elias & Marcia Stewart
National 2nd Edition
This book contains clearly written legal form contracts to buy and sell property, borrow and lend money, store and lend personal property, release others from personal liability, or pay a contractor to do home repairs. Includes agreements to arrange childcare and other household help.
$16.95/CONT

FAMILY MATTERS

Divorce & Money
Violet Woodhouse & Victoria Felton-Collins with M.C. Blakeman
National 1st Edition
Divorce & Money explains how to evaluate such major assets as family homes and businesses, investments, pensions, and how to arrive at a division of property that is fair to both sides. Throughout, the book emphasizes the difference between legal reality—how the court evaluates assets, and financial reality—what the assets are really worth.
$19.95/DIMO

The Living Together Kit
Attorneys Toni Ihara & Ralph Warner
National 6th Edition
The Living Together Kit is a detailed guide designed to help the increasing number of unmarried couples living together understand the laws that affect them. Sample agreements and instructions are included.
$17.95/LTK

The Guardianship Book
Lisa Goldoftas & Attorney David Brown
California 1st Edition
The Guardianship Book provides step-by-step instructions and the forms needed to obtain a legal guardianship without a lawyer.
$19.95/GB

A Legal Guide for Lesbian and Gay Couples
Attorneys Hayden Curry & Denis Clifford
National 7th Edition
Laws designed to regulate and protect unmarried couples don't apply to lesbian and gay couples. This book shows you step-by-step how to write a living-together contract, plan for medical emergencies, and plan your estates. Includes forms, sample agreements and lists of both national lesbian and gay legal organizations and AIDS organizations.
$17.95/LG

How to Do Your Own Divorce
Attorney Charles Sherman
(Texas Ed. by Sherman & Simons)
California 17th Edition & Texas 4th Edition
These books contain all the forms and instructions you need to do your own uncontested divorce without a lawyer.
California $18.95/CDIV
Texas $17.95/TDIV

Practical Divorce Solutions
Attorney Charles Sherman
California 2nd Edition
This book is a valuable guide to the emotional aspects of divorce as well as an overview of the legal and financial decisions that must be made.
$12.95/PDS

California Marriage & Divorce Law
Attorneys Ralph Warner, Toni Ihara & Stephen Elias
California 11th Edition
This book explains community property, pre-nuptial contracts, foreign marriages, buying a house, getting a divorce, dividing property, and more.
$19.95/MARR

How to Adopt Your Stepchild in California
Frank Zagone & Attorney Mary Randolph
California 3rd Edition
There are many emotional, financial and legal reasons to adopt a stepchild, but among the most pressing legal reasons is the need to avoid confusion over inheritance or guardianship. This book provides sample forms and step-by-step instructions for completing a simple uncontested adoption by a stepparent.
$19.95/ADOP

JUST FOR FUN

29 Reasons Not to Go to Law School
Attorneys Ralph Warner & Toni Ihara
National 3rd Edition
Filled with humor and piercing observations, this book can save you three years, $70,000 and your sanity.
$9.95/29R

Devil's Advocates: The Unnatural History of Lawyers
by Andrew & Jonathan Roth
National 1st Edition
This book is a painless and hilarious education, tracing the legal profession. Careful attention is given to the world's worst lawyers, most preposterous cases and most ludicrous courtroom strategies.
$12.95/DA

Poetic Justice: The Funniest, Meanest Things Ever Said About Lawyers
Edited by Jonathan & Andrew Roth
National 1st Edition
A great gift for anyone in the legal profession who has managed to maintain a sense of humor.
$8.95/PJ

PATENT, COPYRIGHT & TRADEMARK

Trademark: How to Name Your Business & Product
Attorneys Kate McGrath and Stephen Elias, With Trademark Attorney Sarah Shena
National 1st Edition
This is by far the best comprehensive do-it-yourself trademark book designed for small businesses. It explains step-by-step how to protect names used to market services and products, and shows how to: choose a name or logo that others can't copy, conduct a trademark search, register a trademark with the U.S. Patent and Trademark Office and protect and maintain the trademark.
$29.95 / TRD

Patent It Yourself
Attorney David Pressman
National 3rd Edition
From the patent search to the actual application, this book covers everything including the use and licensing of patents, successful marketing and how to deal with infringement.
$34.95/PAT

The Inventor's Notebook
Fred Grissom & Attorney David Pressman
National 1st Edition
This book helps you document the process of successful independent inventing by providing forms, instructions, references to relevant areas of patent law, a bibliography of legal and non-legal aids and more.
$19.95/INOT

The Copyright Handbook
Attorney Stephen Fishman
National 1st Edition
Writers, editors, publishers, scholars, educators, librarians and others who work with words all need to know about copyright laws. This book provides forms and step-by-step instructions for protecting all types of written expression under U.S. and international copyright law. It contains detailed reference chapters on such major copyright-related topics as copyright infringement, fair use, works for hire and transfers of copyright ownership.
$24.95/COHA

How to Copyright Software
Attorney M.J. Salone
National 3rd Edition
This book tells you how to register your copyright for maximum protection and discusses who owns a copyright on software developed by more than one person.
$39.95/COPY

LANDLORDS & TENANTS

The Landlord's Law Book, Vol. 1: Rights & Responsibilities
Attorneys David Brown & Ralph Warner
California 3rd Edition
This book contains information on deposits, leases and rental agreements, inspections (tenants' privacy rights), habitability (rent withholding), ending a tenancy, liability and rent control.
$29.95/LBRT

The Landlord's Law Book, Vol. 2: Evictions
Attorney David Brown
California 4th Edition
Updated for 1992, this book will show you step-by-step how to go to court and get an eviction for a tenant who won't pay rent—and won't leave. Contains all the tear-out forms and necessary instructions.
$32.95/LBEV

Tenants' Rights
Attorneys Myron Moskovitz & Ralph Warner
California 11th Edition
This book explains how to handle your relationship with your landlord and understand your legal rights when you find yourself in disagreement. A special section on rent control cities is included.
$15.95/CTEN

HOMEOWNERS

How to Buy a House in California
Attorney Ralph Warner, Ira Serkes & George Devine
California 2nd Edition
This book shows you how to find a house, work with a real estate agent, make an offer and negotiate intelligently. Includes information on all types of mortgages as well as private financing options.
$19.95/BHCA

For Sale By Owner
George Devine
California 2nd Edition
For Sale By Owner provides essential information about pricing your house, marketing it, writing a contract and going through escrow.
$24.95/FSBO

Homestead Your House
Attorneys Ralph Warner, Charles Sherman & Toni Ihara
California 8th Edition
This book shows you how to file a Declaration of Homestead and includes complete instructions and tear-out forms.
$9.95/HOME

The Deeds Book
Attorney Mary Randolph
California 2nd Edition
If you own real estate, you'll need to sign a new deed when you transfer the property or put it in trust as part of your estate planning. This book shows you how to find the right kind of deed, complete the tear-out forms and record them in the county recorder's public records.
$15.95/DEED

OLDER AMERICANS

Elder Care: Choosing & Financing Long-Term Care
Attorney Joseph Matthews
National 1st Edition
This book will guide you in choosing and paying for long-term care, alerting you to practical concerns and explaining laws that may affect your decisions.
$16.95/ELD

Social Security, Medicare & Pensions
Attorney Joseph Matthews with Dorothy Matthews Berman
National 5th Edition
This book contains invaluable guidance through the current maze of rights and benefits for those 55 and over, including Medicare, Medicaid and Social Security retirement and disability benefits and age discrimination protections.
$15.95/SOA

REFERENCE

Legal Research: How to Find and Understand the Law
Attorneys Stephen Elias & Susan Levinkind
National 3rd Edition
A valuable tool on its own or as a companion to just about every other Nolo book. This book gives easy-to-use, step-by-step instructions on how to find legal information.
$16.95/LRES

Family Law Dictionary
Attorneys Robin Leonard & Stephen Elias
National 2nd Edition
Finally, a legal dictionary that's written in plain English, not "legalese"! *The Family Law Dictionary* is designed to help the nonlawyer who has a question or problem involving family law—marriage, divorce, adoption or living together.
$13.95/FLD

Legal Research Made Easy: A Roadmap Through the Law Library Maze
2-1/2 hr. videotape and 40-page manual
Nolo Press/Legal Star Communications
National 1st Edition
If you're a law student, paralegal or librarian—or just want to look up the law for yourself—this video is for you. University of California law professor Bob Berring explains how to use all the basic legal research tools in your local law library with an easy-to-follow six-step research plan and a sense of humor.
$89.95/LRME

CONSUMER/REFERENCE

How to Win Your Personal Injury Claim
Attorney Joseph Matthews
National 1st Edition
If you face an insurance company without the information in this book, you may receive a settlement that is only a fraction of what you deserve. If you hire a lawyer, the lawyer will take up to 50% of the settlement in fees and costs. However, settling an injury claim on your own can be simple. You don't need any special training to obtain a full and fair settlement, just some basic information about how the claims process works. This book will show you how to:
- protect your rights after an accident
- understand what your claim is worth
- prepare a claim for compensation
- negotiate a fair settlement.

$24.95/PICL

Nolo's Pocket Guide to California Law
Attorney Lisa Guerin and Nolo Press Editors
California 1st Edition
The only plain English guide to the laws that affect you everyday. Get quick, clear answers to questions about child support, custody, consumer rights, employee rights, government benefits, divorce, bankruptcy, adoption, wills and much more.
$10.95/CLAW

Barbara Kaufman's Consumer Action Guide
Barbara Kaufman
California 1st Edition
This practical handbook is filled with information on hundreds of consumer topics. Barbara Kaufman, the Bay Area's award-winning consumer reporter and producer of KCBS Radio's *Call for Action*, gives consumers access to their legal rights, providing addresses and phone numbers of where to complain when things go wrong, and providing resources if more help is necessary.
$14.95/CAG

VISIT OUR STORE

If you live in the Bay Area, be sure to visit the Nolo Press Bookstore on the corner of 9th & Parker Streets in west Berkeley. You'll find our complete line of books and software—new and "damaged"—all at a discount. We also have t-shirts, posters and a selection of business and legal self-help books from other publishers.

Monday to Friday	10 A.M. to 5 P.M.
Thursdays	10 A.M. to 6 P.M.
Saturdays	10 A.M. to 4:30 P.M.
Sundays	11 A.M. to 4 P.M.

NOLO PRESS / 950 PARKER STREET / BERKELEY CA 94710

ORDER FORM

Name

Address (UPS to street address, Priority Mail to P.O. boxes)

Catalog Code	Quantity	Item	Unit price	Total
		Subtotal		
		Sales tax (California residents only)		
		Shipping & handling		
		2nd day UPS		
		TOTAL		
		PRICES SUBJECT TO CHANGE		

SALES TAX
California residents add your local tax

SHIPPING & HANDLING
$4.00   1 item
$5.00   2-3 items
+$.50   each additional item
Allow 2-3 weeks for delivery

IN A HURRY?
UPS 2nd day delivery is available:
Add $5.00 (contiguous states) or
$8.00 (Alaska & Hawaii) to your regular shipping and handling charges

FOR FASTER SERVICE, USE YOUR CREDIT CARD AND OUR TOLL-FREE NUMBERS:
Monday-Friday, 8 a.m. to 5 p.m. Pacific Time
Order line   1 (800) 992-6656
General Information   1 (510) 549-1976
Fax us your order   1 (800) 645-0895

METHOD OF PAYMENT
☐ Check enclosed
☐ VISA ☐ Mastercard ☐ Discover Card ☐ American Express

Account #   Expiration Date

Signature Authorizing

Phone   GB

NOLO PRESS / 950 PARKER STREET / BERKELEY CA 94710

FREE NOLO NEWS SUBSCRIPTION

When you register, we'll send you our quarterly newspaper, the *Nolo News,* free for two years. (U.S. addresses only.) Here's what you'll get in every issue:

INFORMATIVE ARTICLES

Written by Nolo editors, articles provide practical legal information on issues you encounter in everyday life: family law, wills, debts, consumer rights, and much more.

UPDATE SERVICE

The *Nolo News* keeps you informed of legal changes that affect any Nolo book and software program.

BOOK AND SOFTWARE REVIEWS

We're always looking for good legal and consumer books and software from other publishers. When we find them, we review them and offer them in our mail order catalog.

ANSWERS TO YOUR LEGAL QUESTIONS

Our readers are always challenging us with good questions on a variety of legal issues. So in each issue, "Auntie Nolo" gives sage advice and sound information.

COMPLETE NOLO PRESS CATALOG

The *Nolo News* contains an up-to-the-minute catalog of all Nolo books and software, which you can order using our toll-free "800" order line. And you can see at a glance if you're using an out-of-date version of a Nolo product.

LAWYER JOKES

Nolo's famous lawyer joke column continually gets the goat of the legal establishment. If we print a joke you send in, you'll get a $20 Nolo gift certificate.

We promise *never* to give your name and address to any other organization.

THE GUARDIANSHIP BOOK   Registration Card

We'd like to know what you think! Please take a moment to fill out and return this postage paid card for a free two-year subscription to the *Nolo News.* If you already receive the *Nolo News,* we'll extend your subscription.

Name _____ Ph.(_____) _____

Address _____

City _____ State _____ Zip _____

Where did you hear about this book? _____

For what purpose did you use this book? _____

Did you consult a lawyer?		Yes	No		Not Applicable		
Was it easy for you to use this book?	(very easy)	5	4	3	2	1	(very difficult)
Did you find this book helpful?	(very)	5	4	3	2	1	(not at all)

Comments _____
_____
_____
_____
_____

THANK YOU   GB 1.2

[Nolo books are]…"written in plain language, free of legal mumbo jumbo, and spiced with witty personal observations."

—**ASSOCIATED PRESS**

"Well-produced and slickly written, the [Nolo] books are designed to take the mystery out of seemingly involved procedures, carefully avoiding legalese and leading the reader step-by-step through such everyday legal problems as filling out forms, making up contracts, and even how to behave in court."

—**SAN FRANCISCO EXAMINER**

"…Nolo publications…guide people simply through the how, when, where and why of law."

—**WASHINGTON POST**

"Increasingly, people who are not lawyers are performing tasks usually regarded as legal work… And consumers, using books like Nolo's, do routine legal work themselves."

—**NEW YORK TIMES**

"…All of [Nolo's] books are easy-to-understand, are updated regularly, provide pull-out forms…and are often quite moving in their sense of compassion for the struggles of the lay reader."

—**SAN FRANCISCO CHRONICLE**

BUSINESS REPLY MAIL
FIRST-CLASS MAIL PERMIT NO 3283 BERKELEY CA

POSTAGE WILL BE PAID BY ADDRESSEE

NOLO PRESS
950 Parker Street
Berkeley CA 94710-9867